MW00736395

A

COMMENTARY

ON

ECCLESIASTES.

BY

MOSES STUART,

LATE PROFESSOR OF SACRED LITERATURE IN THE THEOLOGICAL SEMINARY AT ANDOVER.

Edited and Revised

BY

R. D. C. ROBBINS,

PROFESSOR IN MIDDLEBURY COLLEGE.

Wipf & Stock
PUBLISHERS
Eugene, Oregon

Wipf and Stock Publishers
199 W 8th Ave, Suite 3
Eugene, OR 97401

A Commentary on Ecclesiastes
By Stuart, Moses
ISBN: 1-59752-220-1
Publication date 5/25/2005
Previously published by Warren F. Draper, 1864

PREFACE.

THE Book of Ecclesiastes presents many apparent problems which have long been the subject of wonder and dispute among the Jewish Rabbies as well as in the Christian Church. Had not the evidence been strong and decisive of its rightful place in the Canon of the Hebrew sacred writings, it would undoubtedly have been rejected long ago by many, as not being a book of divine authority. Not a few passages seem to speak, at first view, the language of skepticism, *i. e.*, of unbelief or doubt as to a future state, and also of devotedness to sensual enjoyment. It was on this ground that some of the Jewish Rabbies, at the time when the Talmud was written, made an effort, as it would seem, to eject it from the sacred Canon, as we are told in the Talmud, Tract. Shabb. fol. 30, col. 2. Some of the Christian Fathers have intimated the like feelings as existing among some Christians in their times; and since the revival of criticism in its late, and specially in its most recent form, the book has been treated as indeed a clever performance of the kind, but after all as the work of a *skeptical Epicurean.* Even De Wette, with his sober aspect and seeming impartiality, does not hesitate to bestow such an epithet on the author of the book. No wonder that he has had many imitators or followers in Germany.

The evidence that Ecclesiastes was a portion of the sacred Canon sanctioned by Christ and his apostles, is plain, and as certain as anything so remotely historical can be made out to be. This is shown in its proper place, in the Introduction to the Commentary. This admitted, it follows that a serious obligation devolves on us to read the book, and at least to do what we can to understand it. Thousands of sermons have been preached on portions of the book, and a multitude of Commentaries have been written, most of which are merely ethical and hortatory. There is indeed no want of material in the book for a basis to such sermons and homiletic commentary. Much of it is so plain and so forcible, in respect to the pursuits and the destiny of man, as to be both intelligible and un-mistakable. To preach and exhort, in accordance with such portions of the book, is commendable, and may, if well done, be very profitable. But what is to be done with such passages as 2 : 24 ; 3 : 18—21 ; 6 : 12 ; 7 : 15—

17 ; 25—28 ; 8 : 15 ; 9 : 2—10 ? The preacher, for the most part, avoids them in the pulpit; and the commentators (at least most commentators) set themselves seriously to work, in order to soften, to file away, and to change the hue or alter the shape of these obnoxious passages, so that they may be judged to teach neither skepticism nor Epicureanism. The goodness of the intention, in all this, I should cheerfully concede. In itself, the motive may be praiseworthy. But after all, real prudence, a straightforward course, the sound and well-established laws of exegesis to which critical honesty should inflexibly adhere — all this, I am unable to find in such a course. I cannot bring myself to believe that the true interests of religion demand of us to deal unfairly and forcibly with any portion of the Scriptures, in order to make it conform to our views of propriety. If we may do this honestly on any one occasion, we may of course do it on every and all occasions, whenever we may deem it expedient either for the sake of morals and piety or of doctrine. I know of no boundary line, in such a case, but a man's own persuasion or fancy. Once break away from sober grammatico-historical exegesis, and all is afloat without compass or rudder. It is not our business to force a meaning upon Scripture, against which it reluctates; it belongs to us *to deduce one from Scripture*, if we are

able, by the use of fair and honest principles of interpretation.

This rule I have endeavored to comply with, in the following little work now presented to the public. With what success, must be referred to competent judges. I can only say, that in honestly endeavoring to follow it, I have found no serious occasion for stumbling or offence at the book. Here, as in every work of this nature, the *animus auctoris* must be sought after, and if possible discovered. That is, or should be, our guide. If the writer did not design to give us a mere preceptive and ethical treatise, but to *philosophize* on the vanity of human life, and to consider the many objections against a wise and holy Providence, which arise from the miseries of men, and the unequal distribution of prosperity and adversity among them — if such was his design, how can it be strange that he has brought to view many of these objections, in order that the reader may see them, and see the manner in which they are answered? The objections should, in such a case, be taken for what they are, viz., for objections or doubts that naturally arise in a mind on which gospel light has not shined; and the answers to them are to be thoroughly investigated. Paul has pursued a similar course in some of his epistles; and this, not unfrequently, without giving any express intimation that he is going to introduce an objector. He leaves it to the intelligent reader to discover what belongs to his opponent, and what to himself. Why should we concede such a liberty to him, and not to the author of Ecclesiastes? This conceded, the exegesis of the book (a few passages only excepted) becomes comparatively easy and plain. The objections remain objections, and are considered and treated as such; and the answers to them show us the real mind of the writer. With all the alleged and seeming skepticism of the book, it becomes clear as the sun that the writer, after revolving all the difficulties in his mind, comes out from them with a lofty tone of morality, with an unshaken confidence in future judgment and retribution, and with high, adoring, submissive confidence in God, and in his wisdom, goodness, and power. FEAR GOD, AND KEEP HIS COMMANDMENTS, is the final, the grand result of all.

The book has very generally been regarded and treated as little more than a succession of unconnected apothegms, having little or no connection with each other, or dependence on each other. I hope to show the reader that it is one *continuous whole*, having one grand and fundamental theme running through the whole, and spreading its fibres, like a kind of fine and impalpable network,

over every minute portion of it. It has a beginning, a
middle, and an end; a main proposition to be illustrated,
and confirmed; and finally, some very important practical deductions are made from the matter of the book,
in the way of command and exhortation. But the logic
of Aristotle, of the Schoolmen, and of modern times, it
ignores. The Hebrews never wrote in a manner fettered
by this. They reasoned; they drew deductions; they
proved; but they did neither in the way of the Grecian,
or English, or German schools. Paul was a master-rea-
soner; but to *school logic* he seems an utter stranger. No
one should expect this in Coheleth. At all events, he
will not find it. But still the book philosophizes, and
proves, and disproves, and makes deductions, and strenuously urges morality and piety.

I have done what I could to develop the *plan* of the
book, and the execution of this plan by the writer, *more
suo.* This has cost me more laborious study than all the
philological remarks. Others must judge whether my
labor has been bestowed in vain.

The Hebrew student — the aspirant to sacred knowledge — has been in my eye throughout. I have endeavored to leave not a single grammatical difficulty, either
as to the *forms of words* or the *syntax*, untouched. In
every case of difficulty, or where such student might be

in doubt as to the principles admitted, I have referred him to the Grammar and the Lexicon, with indications of the places where he will find illustration or confirmation of that concerning which he doubts. I would hope that the book, now made easily accessible to learners, unless I very much misjudge, may hereafter constitute a part of the course of Hebrew study. It is well deserving of it. The idiom is so unlike most other Hebrew, in certain re-spects, that a knowledge of it must give any one a much freer scope in the language. The Hebrew in itself is rather easy than otherwise ; for great simplicity, generally, reigns in the structure of sentences. Seldom need the student be left in doubt as to a satisfactory meaning, when all investigation is conducted on principles purely philological. Any other method of conducting it, is in the main useless.

In the earlier part of my professional labors here, I undertook to lecture on Ecclesiastes. But at that time I could not satisfy myself, for I could not then obtain either competent or satisfactory aid. I therefore soon aban-doned the attempt, telling my pupils, as my reason for so doing, that I could not lecture on a book which I felt that I did not understand. Lately, I have resumed and repeated the study of it, after more widely extended and protracted discipline in Hebrew. Difficulties have now

2

seemed to vanish apace. I no longer continue to doubt, except as to some individual expressions; and even in regard to these, I have at last succeeded in satisfying myself. When we attain to such a state of feeling, it naturally inspires a hope that we may do something to help or to satisfy others. I would fain hope that not a few of the apparent enigmas of the book will be made to disappear, or else meet with a solution, in the following pages. Many a mind has been, and is still, perplexed with these. If I can afford any aid to anxious and candid seekers after the meaning of the author, I shall regard it as a high reward.

M. STUART.

ANDOVER THEOLOGICAL SEMINARY, 1851.

CONTENTS.

INTRODUCTION.

COMMENTARY.

EXCURSUS:

INTRODUCTION.

§ 1. *General Nature of the Book.*

In many respects the book of *Ecclesiastes* has no parallel in the Hebrew Scriptures. It alone, of all the sacred writings, undertakes to *philosophize*. But this word, as applied to Ecclesiastes, must not be understood in the Grecian or Roman sense, nor even in that of modern European nations. *Ontological* speculations are utterly foreign to Coheleth. That he was in some degree versed in them, might not be improbable, provided we should concede to him the latest period in which the writings of the Old Testament were composed. Grecian philosophy made a conspicuous figure after the time of Socrates and Plato, so that all the nations around the Mediterranean, who had any acquaintance with the Greek language, would be likely, through the medium of their learned men, to have some knowledge of it, or at least some information in respect to it. A mind so strongly bent on inquiry as that of the author of the book before us, could hardly have failed to know something of it, in case he lived as late as the time of Malachi, when Plato was winning renown among all who visited Attica, and especially among all who frequented the groves of Academus. It is quite certain that the *Jews* of Alexandria, at a subsequent period, busied themselves much with the works of Plato, for Philo Judaeus was so engrossed by the later Platonism, that it has been said of him, as exhibited in his works, that "it is difficult to tell whether Philo *platonizes*, or Plato *philonizes*." From *Egyptian* Jews, or

2*

other Jews living in Grecian cities, some knowledge of Grecian philosophy might, and probably would, have been attained by Coheleth, had he lived at a period sufficiently late. But of any such knowledge there is not the least trace in the book before us. In my own apprehension, this fact seems to favor two positions in regard to the book : (1) That the author was not an *Egyptian* Jew of a very late period, for in this case some reference would appear in his work to the learning of the age (*i. e.*, the age of the first two Ptolemies, 323—246 B. C.), and also to the country. (2) That he lived at a period before the Jews in Palestine became acquainted, in any good measure, with the Greek language or philosophy, *i. e.*, before the periods when the chieftains of Alexander's divided empire established themselves in all the countries around the eastern shores of the Mediterranean.   These considerations make against the position, that Ecclesiastes was composed long after the time of Malachi, and more still against the supposition that it was written after the Persian rule in Palestine had ceased.

But, however all this may be, the fact is certain, that Coheleth exhibits no acquaintance with Grecian philosophy. He is, through and through, a *Palestine-Hebrew*, and most probably an inhabitant either of Jerusalem, or of its near neighborhood.   The manner in which he speaks of frequenting religious worship (4: 17—5 : 1 seq.), shows that he speaks of it in a way which would be familiar to those who frequented the temple-service.

We have, then, a work before us, not of ontological and metaphysical speculation, but a work of *practical philosophy.* All the reasonings are built on the results of experience ; and all the precepts which accompany them, are such as have regard, not to mere *abstract* truth, but to wary, considerate, and sober demeanor. The book begins and ends with one and the same theme ; and this theme itself is the result of observation and experience.

The general truth, however, which constitutes this theme, is easily divisible into many particulars, and these require illustration and confirmation. It was the effort to accomplish this object, which gave rise to the apparently variegated and subordinate parts of the work. The general subject is turned round and round; and as often as a new aspect presents itself, the writer stops to describe, to make comments, to show what objections can be made to such a view, and what can be said to confirm and establish it. Nor is it the general theme only which is thus turned round in order to get a view of its different aspects, but the minor particulars, in their turn, are often dealt with in the same way; so that the mere cursory reader is apt to cherish the apprehension, that Coheleth is full of repetitions. A more thorough examination, however, by the aid of competent critical and philological knowledge, will show him, that what he regards as mere repetitions of the same thing, is nothing more nor less than the presentation of the same subject in different attitudes and in different relations. Whatever there is, which strictly speaking is really repeated, is some *general result*, some *ultimate truth* — as it were the focus, toward which all the seemingly divergent rays, when traced back, will be found to converge. It needs much and attentive study to attain to a full perception of this; but with this study, nothing is more certain than that this book, apparently a book of *miscellanies*, assumes the form of a *general unity;* and while all its subordinate parts are interwoven by fine threads, that escape the notice of the more cursory observer, these are the very things which attract and highly excite the attention of inquiring and discerning minds. But of this, more will be said in the sequel.

As a specimen of ancient philosophy, the oldest and the only one among the ancient Hebrews which has come down to us, Ecclesiastes would seem to deserve the notice and attention of modern philosophers, and specially of those who undertake to write the *history* of ancient philosophy. Have the Hebrews, — the only nation on earth, before the Christian era, who had enlightened views of God and of duty, — have they no claim to be heard on the subject of *practical moral philosophy*? If the book of Coheleth were a Chinese production, or Mantchou-Tartar, or Japanese, the literati of Germany and France, if not of England, would break through all the barriers thrown in their way by remoteness of time and strangeness of language, and with glowing zeal bring before the world the important results of their protracted and laborious examination of it. Every year now bears witness to some feat of this kind, which attracts notice and confers celebrity. But Coheleth — alas! who are the *philosophers* that are investigating his work? Neology has indeed furnished some philologists, who have bestowed on this work, quite recently, much and attentive study, and some of it to quite an important purpose. But even here, the chief attraction seems to be the alleged *scepticism* of the writer. These facts indicate, that there is something very attractive to them, in the hope of finding the ancient Hebrews to have been destitute of any belief in a future state. And as not a few things are said in Ecclesiastes, which appear at first view to support such an allegation in respect to Hebrew opinion, the book has lately become a subject, not unfrequently, of discussion and interpretation. But beyond this class of persons, the matter of critical interpretation sleeps in the same quiet nook, where it laid itself down more than a thousand years ago.

After all, however, it is a just subject of reproof to the *historians of philosophy*, that a specimen of it from a writer of the most truly enlightened and religious nation of all antiquity, should have attracted no more of their attention and regard. But it is easier to follow in the footsteps of the thousands, who have written upon Plato, Aristotle, and Plotinus, than it is to become a sufficient master of the Hebrew to make a radical investigation of the book before us. It is quite plain that the attractions of speculative, metaphysical, and ontological philosophy are far greater, in the view of most philosophical inquirers, than anything which a practical and ethical philosophy can present.

The sayings of the earliest Greek sages, in respect to the nature of things or of men, rouse up more curiosity and excite more interest than any philosopher's sayings among the Hebrews, because the Greek nation elevated the literary standard of the world, while the Hebrews remained without any schools of philosophy, or any considerable cultivation of the arts and sciences. It is to be hoped, that after the *literary* race shall come to a pause, for want of farther ground to move upon, that the *moral* and *practical* philosophy of the Hebrews will begin to attract more attention.

§ 2. *Special Design and Method of the Book.*

I couple these together, because it is difficult, if not impossible, to separate them without incurring the danger of frequent repetition.

The general *nature* of the book, as being of the *ethico-philosophical* cast, has already been described. We come, next in order, to the theme, or themes, which are discussed.

The great and appropriate theme of the whole book, is THE VANITY AND NOTHINGNESS OF ALL EARTHLY EFFORTS, PURSUITS, AND OBJECTS. The book commences with this, and employs an intensity of expression in stating it, that can hardly be exceeded: *Vanity of vanities — vanity of vanities, all is vanity.* The repetition of the word *vanity* in the plur. Gen. that follows in the first case, then the repetition of the whole of the same phrase, and lastly the universality or extent of the proposition (*all* is vanity), conspire to render the expression of the main theme the most intense of which language is capable. Thus commences the book before us; and after passing in review a multitude of particular things which belong to this general category, the discussional part of the book ends with the same declaration: VANITY OF VANITIES; ALL IS VANITY! 12:8.

All the intermediate portions of the book bear a more or less intimate connection with this main theme. Not less than some twenty-three times is the general proposition repeated, in the same or in equivalent words, at the close of different illustrations and discussions.[1] Like a net of fine threads, this great theme of *vanity* pervades or spreads over the whole work. A minute and close examination will enable any one to see, that the main *thread of discourse* is never lost sight of, however the writer may seem to make temporary excursions. He always returns, as true as the needle to the pole, to the same stand-point from which he started. His "right hand would as soon forget its cunning," as he forsake, or even lose sight of, the main object that he has in view. It is only a few years since this trait of the book before us was discovered and fully announced. But it can hardly hereafter be forgotten.

But when thus much is said for the *unity* of the book, it must not be too rigidly interpreted. It is true, that there are *subordinate themes* in the book, which do not very directly, but only more remotely, contribute to the confirmation of the main theme. The author of the book before us is far enough from being a dull proser. Life and animation reign throughout. He has, indeed, nothing of the technical and formal method of the schoolmen and mere logicians; for his book is anything rather than an enumeration of particulars in regular logical sequency. He comes upon us unexpectedly at times, with a theme apparently incongruous and irrelative, and we feel for the moment that we are thrown off from our track. But he soon shows us that he is only temporarily diverging from the main line, thus giving a striking variety in his particulars, and avoiding the dulness of a slow and uniform movement. He casts a look at everything, in passing; and sometimes he stops a moment, in order to take observation of a new occurrence or a new object, and then resumes his course.

[1] E. g. 1 : 14, 17. 2 : 1, 11, 15, 17, 19, 21, 23, 26. 3 : 19. 4 : 4, 8, 16. 5 : 9. 6 : 2, 9, 11. 7 : 6. 8 : 10, 14. 11 : 8, 10.

Hence it comes, that the reader who does not thoroughly investigate and understand his plan, may be disposed to complain of his apparently discursive and miscellaneous method of composition; but a closer examination will bring him to see that the author has not forgotten what he set out to do, nor turned aside from it, except in cases where additional interest could be given to the whole by special notice of some particular and interesting objects which lie near to the way where he is passing.

The number of things which he specifically presents to our view as *vanities*, is not indeed very great. But he evidently designs that those which he presents should be regarded as specimens of all the rest, which are of a kindred nature and are not mentioned. This is apparent from the declaration at the beginning and end of the book, viz., that *all* is vanity. But those objects which are presented, are seldom dismissed without showing them in their various aspects and relations. For example; *avarice*, or the greedy pursuit of gain, is *repeatedly* brought to view. First, we have it illustrated in the experiments which Coheleth made in his kingly state, in order to find some stable and enduring good, 2 : 7, 8. The heaping up of treasures in its highest extent he found to be *vanity*. It would not — it could not — confer the happiness desired. Then, again, we are presented with some of the positive evils which attend greediness for gain, 2 : 18—23. After much toil and vexation, a man must leave all which he has acquired to some one who never contributed in the least to acquire it. He next brings to view severe and dexterous toil for riches, which attracts the envy of others around the successful man, 4 : 4. He then presents a solitary man, without child or brother, laboring ceaselessly to acquire that which he can bestow on no one whom he cares for, or who cares for him, 4 : 8. The evils of such a state of seclusion and lonely toil, he illustrates by several proverbial apothegms, 4 : 9—12. After this, he presents a case, in which there is excessive toil to provide for *children*, and yet all is lost by casualty, or misfortune, or mismanagement, 5 : 13—17. Another view of the subject is, the case where riches fall into the hands of *strangers*, instead of being inherited by children, 6 : 2. It is easy, with a little attention, to see that each of these developments is attended with its own peculiarities and grievances, while all, when traced back, are found to be united in one central point, viz. the utter insufficiency of riches to procure solid and lasting happiness.

Several subjects are dealt with in like manner, and although they are repeatedly brought before us, yet they are placed each time in a different attitude and in new relations ; and it soon becomes evident that they are insisted on so frequently, not because the author is in want of something to say, but because of their relative importance to his main object.

But one source of evil to man seems to bear upon his mind with more galling, if not heavier, weight than any other, viz., *civil oppression.* If there be any one thing which urges him, beyond all the rest, to be dissatisfied with, or to doubt, the doctrine that wickedness speedily brings punishment, it is the permission and toleration of oppressive and wicked rulers. The first glance he takes of the subject, is directed toward the *bench of justice,* or at least toward the place where justice is looked for, and with right expected. There he finds wickedness to be seated, and iniquity to take the place of righteousness, 3 : 16. His first emotion, called forth by pious feelings, bids him to hope that God will bring oppressors to judgment, 3 : 17. But still farther contemplation of the spectacle makes him almost to despair of the destinies of man, and to feel that Heaven designs men to know that they are little if any better than the beasts, 3 : 18—21. In the midst of this, however, he essays to comfort himself with the thought, that man, although perishable, can after all have some enjoyment at least in the fruit of his labors. But then a renewed look at the effects of oppression, at " the tears of the oppressed who had no comforter," and the consideration that " on the side of the oppressors was power," bring him again to a state of despair, even so as to count death more desirable than life, and to wish that he had never been born, 4 : 1—3. Grievous indeed must have been the oppression under which he groaned, when it forced from him such outbursts of feeling as these. After descanting on the vanity of a greedy desire for riches — and with this the oppression of rulers in their exactions naturally connects itself — his mind again recurs to the ruler of his land, of whom he speaks in terms of great severity: "Better is a poor and a wise child, than an old and foolish king, who will no more be admonished," 4 : 13. He next brings the subject of religious duties into view, and seems to return from the consideration of these, with his excitement somewhat abated, and in a state of more calm reflection. He says, that if one "sees the oppression of the poor and violent perverting of judgment and justice," he must repress his wonder by the reflection, that there is One higher than the highest earthly magistrate, who will take cognizance of the matter, 5 : 8. In ch. 7 : 7, he touches again on the subject, and seems to set forth more fully the bitter consequences of oppression, by declaring that "it renders those madmen who practise it, and that bribes destroy their understanding." But here a caution is introduced against being hastily provoked by oppression, and against comparing the present oppressive times with former and better days, from which no good can come, 7 : 8—10. Again he sees "the just perishing by his righteousness, and the wicked prolonging his days by wickedness," 7 : 15. That is, the one falls a victim to the anger or the avarice of the ruler, and the other buys himself off from the retributions of justice when it threatens to overtake him. Yet even here, he prudently cautions against believing every report that is whispered about respecting rulers, 7 : 21, 22. He well knew that such matters are wont to be exaggerated. But caution of this nature, as he thinks, may be carried too far. To illustrate this, he introduces one counselling to yield universal and implicit obedience to the ruler, and this as the only means of safety, because the power is in his hands and he can punish at pleasure, 8 : 2—4. But to this he answers, that such undistinguishing obedience, rendered through selfish fear of consequences, must lead one to do that which is evil; and that it is better to call to mind that there is a time when all the actions of men will be judged, and both the wicked ruler, and his obedient subject, who was willing to do wrong at his bidding, will be tried and rewarded, because that none can escape the dread season of reckoning, 8 : 5—8. He sees, indeed, that one rules over another to his great injury ; but in looking farther on, he sees the wicked carried out from the city to the tomb, and anticipates that the memory of him will soon perish, 8 : 9, 10. The passionate and overbearing demeanor of rulers is next alluded to (10 : 4), and caution given against manifesting offence at it in their presence. That arbitrary power, which sets folly on the seat of dignity, which puts servants upon horses and makes princes to walk on foot as their waiters, is next brought under view, 10 : 5—7. By various proverbial sayings, he illustrates the importance of a wise and discreet demeanor, on occasions when such things are presented to view ; specially does he recommend discretion in regard to what one *says* on such occasions, for his words, if they be severe, may be fatal in their consequences, 10 : 12—14. Still, his own heart is deeply grieved at the evil; and be breaks out into the pathetic exclamation : " Woe to thee, O land, when thy king is a child, and thy princes feast in the morning!" 10 : 16, *i. e.*, when thy king is incapable of governing with discretion, and thy princes are luxurious and profligate. It would seem that the *old and foolish king*, mentioned in 4 : 13, as then reigning had now deceased, and had been succeeded by a mere *child.* Matters, as it appears, had grown no better — the king was now an imbecile, the nobles profligate. In fact, the whole of Chapter X. is occupied with the subject of bad and incompetent rulers, who are represented (vs. 18, 19) as slothful, and as being gluttons and drunkards. This is the last expression of his views and feelings in regard to this "sore evil;" and here, although his heart is beating high with scorn and indignation, he still protests against " cursing the king," even in the most retired and secret places; for, in some way unexpected, that king may come to the knowledge of the curses uttered, and this will bring additional evil upon the malcontent.

This now, with the preceding case of *avarice*, may serve fully to illustrate my remarks on the alleged discursive method of Coheleth, and the repetitions which are charged upon him. Here, half a score of times and more, the subject of *civil oppression* and *wicked rulers* is brought to view. Yet, no two of these representations are alike. Each time something is added to the strength of the impression already made by the writer. This, then, can hardly be deemed mere *repetition*. On the contrary, since the subject is not presented as a *whole* at any one time and place, it behooved the writer, since he laid the matter so much to heart, *gradually* to fill out the entire picture.

The examples now produced will illustrate the *method* of Coheleth sufficiently for our present purpose. We may deduce from them conclusions, in regard to the manner in which some other topics, particularly that of *wisdom*, are treated in this book. In one sense, the composition is *fragmentary, i. e.*, different portions or attitudes of a subject are introduced here and there with various interruptions, and never continuously so as to exhaust the subject in any one passage. In another sense, it is far from being fragmentary. It is no *compound* of scraps, one here and another there, just as the writer might happen to light upon them, or to devise them. It is far remote from being a mere *Collectaneum*, like Robert Southey's memorandum-book, or like the great mass of scrap-books. The seeming fragments are, after all, only portions or particulars of one great whole, and more or less remotely stand related to it, or have a bearing upon it. Those who have not thoroughly examined the book will be slow, perhaps, to believe this. Before they get through the Commentary that follows, however, I would fain hope that they will be ready to admit it.

No impression is more common, than that Coheleth is like to the book of Proverbs, in its *manner and method;* and yet this is far, very far, from the truth. Even De Wette says, that "this book attaches itself, in every respect, to the *gnomological and didactic poetry* of the Hebrews," Einl. § 282. Instead of saying (with him) *in every respect,* I should be nearer the truth if I said : *In no respect.* This, indeed, would be going too far ; but let us examine and see how much is, or is not, true. As to *poetry,* if *parallelism* be a necessary ingredient of this, then there is little or none of it here. In a few solitary cases, where *apothegms* are quoted, and applied to the subject in hand, we find the usual form of Hebrew proverbs, i. e., *parallelism.* But they belong, not to the writer of the book, but to the maxims which he quotes. In one description, viz., that of old age, in chap. xii., the writer does indeed border very closely on Hebrew poetry ; or rather, it is altogether poetry in the spirit of the composition, and it is nearly so in the form of the sentences. But this comprises only seven verses, 12 : 1—7. Elsewhere there is, now and then, a kind of *couplet,* in which contrast is presented, or some special analogy ; and this of course assumes nearly the form of poetry in respect to parallelism. But so it would do, in a writing merely prosaic. With these exceptions, all is *prose,* mere prose, without any attempt to soar on the wings of the Muse.

That the book is *didactic,* I freely admit. But this does not necessarily make it poetic. Some of the later prophets are didactic ; the evangelists are didactic ; Paul is didactic ; but none of these writers are *poets.*

There is some foundation for asserting that the book has a *gnomological cast;* and yet very much less than De Wette seems to suppose. *Gnomes* are *sententiae, proverbs, maxims, apothegms,* i. e., short and pithy sayings. The book of Proverbs, for example, is made up of these, from chap. x. on to the end of the book. The distinguishing trait of them all is, that they are *isolated,* and are without any unity or bond of alliance, excepting that all are of a proverbial nature. Rarely can more than two verses be found, where the same subject is continued; generally it is dispatched in one verse, which for the most part consists of parallelism, and therefore takes the form of poetry. How different is the case in Coheleth! Here an under-current never fails. The whole is pervaded by that solemn and monitory truth : ALL IS VANITY. Discursive, in a measure, are some of the remarks that are made; yet seldom do they go beyond quite narrow bounds. But what all-pervading *unity* is there in the book of Proverbs? Certainly none. Nearly every verse is unlike its nearest neighbor. There are, indeed, *apothegms* in Coheleth. But they are pearls strung upon one and the same string. When they assume a poetic form (parallelism), they are evidently *quotations* and not matters of the writer's own device.

In illustration of what has just been said, I would refer to chap. 10 : 8—11. Here are four verses in succession, which at first view seem to be not only independent of each other, but also of the context. They run thus :

(8) He who diggeth a ditch may fall into it; he who breaketh down a wall, a serpent may bite him. (9) He who plucketh up stones may be annoyed by them; he who cleaveth wood will be endangered thereby. (10) If one has dulled the iron, and there is no edge, he swings it so that he may increase the force; an advantage is the dexterous use of wisdom. (11) If the serpent bite without enchantment, then is there no advantage to him that hath a tongue.

In the context it is said that a little folly is ruinous to wisdom ; that wisdom or sagacity will be dexterous in the application of proper means to guard against evil. It adduces as a signal example of folly, the conduct of kings who put high personages in low places, and low personages in high places. All this and the like, as the writer means to intimate, wisdom would teach a considerate man to void. Still farther to illustrate the principle in question, he quotes the various apothegms above exhibited, in

3*

which it is shown that, even in the most common affairs of life, the want of wise precaution will occasion mischief. They all differ, indeed, specifically from each other, but all have a unity of object in view. This object is developed in the final clause of v. 10, which declares, that *"the dexterous use of wisdom is an advantage."* This is doubtless intended as a key to the whole of the seemingly unconnected passage which sounds as if one were reading merely in a book of proverbs. Yet even v. 11, at the close of the apothegms, is clearly of the same tenor as the rest. The meaning plainly is, that he who has a tongue that can enchant, should be wise enough to employ it to purpose, at a time when he is in danger from serpents ; otherwise his tongue of enchantment is of no use to him, because he lacks wisdom to know when to use it. After all this, the author goes on to show how often and how easily the words of a fool injure him, for want of discretion or wisdom.

In all this, now, the most prominent of all the apothegmatic passages in Coheleth, there is not a single instance in which the proverb is quoted for its own sake, but merely to illustrate the sentiment of the writer, that, even in the most common concerns and transactions of life, discretion and foresight are needed, in order to avoid·danger, and to make undertakings successful.

Let us now adduce another example, that will show the manner in which a *single* apothegm is quoted, merely for the purpose of illustrating a sentiment of the text. In 7 : 1, we find the declaration : "A good name is better than precious ointment." But why say this? The writer had been saying nothing about the desirableness or importance of a *good name*. The sentiment in itself seems wholly foreign to his purpose. It is so, in fact, as it regards what he has already said, but not so in regard to what he is going to say ; for he immediately subjoins to the declaration : " The day of death [is better] than the day of one's birth." The two parts of the verse are members of a comparison. What is meant, is simply this : " The day of one's death is as much better than that of his birth, as a good name is better than precious ointment." Yet between the members of this comparison, there is no *particle* of similitude inserted (e. g. כְּ *as*, or מִן *better than*). But here is a fair specimen of the peculiar idiom of the Hebrew. In scores of cases, perhaps even in the greater number, where *comparison* is made, there is no other particle employed but וְ, which, in such cases, should be rendered *and so*. Our translators seem to have been in a great measure unacquainted with this peculiar idiom of the language; and consequently, they have often given an appearance of incongruity to expressions in English, where mere *comparison* is aimed at in the Hebrew. Almost everywhere, in the book of Proverbs, have they seemed to overlook this distinctive idiom, in regard to the particle in question. The Hebrews said: " Such a thing is so or so; *and* such another thing is so or so," when the meaning is simply : "*As* such a thing is, *so* is such another thing." How many apparent difficulties of the sacred text would be easily solved, by a correct view of this principle, the attentive and critical reader may easily discern. In the case above, it is no part of the writer's object to teach us simply that fame is better than perfumed oil; for although it be true, yet by itself it is not apposite here, and in itself it would hardly need inspiration to teach it, nor would it add much to the didactics of the book. But this common and well-known proverb is cited for the purpose of illustrating a much graver sentiment, to which all readers would not so readily accede. When this purpose is answered, the design of quoting the proverb is fully accomplished.

Again; in chap. 10 : 1, we have a declaration, that seems more remote still from the context, and which almost startles one, at first, by its apparent incongruity. It runs thus : "Dead flies make the ointment of the apothecary to stink; to ferment, — a little folly is more weighty than wisdom, and also than what is costly." Plainly, the first clause is not cited for the sake of disclosing the physical fact or truth in question ; for this was of small moment, and wholly foreign to the writer's object. But this acknowledged physical truth is adduced because it affords a striking ground of comparison. The plain sentiment of the whole is : "*As* dead flies — those little insignificant animals — will corrupt and destroy the most precious ointment, *so* a little of folly will mar all the plans of wisdom, and prevent any advantage from them." The sequel brings to view many cases, where the want of wisdom, or rather a little of positive folly, ruins undertakings of many different kinds.

The examples produced are sufficient for our present purpose. They are a fair specimen of all the proverbs contained in Coheleth. How then can we concede to De Wette, that, on the ground of such apothegms — which after all are not very numerous — this book — Ecclesiastes — must *in every respect* be classed with the *gnomological* writings of the Hebrews ? When Solomon writes *proverbs*, or selects them, he does so for their own sake, *i. e.*, because of the instruction which they are designed to convey of and in themselves. But this Coheleth never does. The primary meaning of them is not what he designs to inculcate ; but, taking this as a conceded truth, he builds on it a comparison or illustration.

Had De Wette said merely, that the style of Coheleth in many respects resembles that of the gnomological books of the Hebrews, he would have said what is evident on the very first opening of the book. Everywhere this presents itself. For example :

(Chap. 7 : 4.) The heart of the wise is in the house of mourning, but the heart of the fool is in the house of mirth. (5) It is better to hear the rebuke of the wise, than for a man to hear the song of fools. (7) Surely oppression maketh mad a wise man, and a gift destroyeth the heart. (8) Better is the end of a thing, than the beginning thereof; the patient in spirit is better than the proud in spirit. (9) Be not hasty in thy spirit to be angry, for anger resteth in the bosom of fools.

(Chap. 10 : 13). The beginning of the words of his [the fool's] mouth is folly, and the ending of his mouth is grievous madness. (14) The fool multiplieth words, when no man can know what shall be ; for what shall be after him, who can tell ? (Chap. 11 : 1.) Cast thy bread upon the waters, for after many days thou shalt find it. (2) Make a portion into seven, and even into eight, for thou knowest not evil which shall be on earth. (4) He who watcheth the wind will not sow, and he who observeth the clouds will not reap. (7) Truly the light is sweet, and a pleasant thing it is for the eyes to behold the light of the sun. (9) Rejoice, O young man, in thy youth, and let thine heart cheer thee in the days of thine early life ; and walk thou in the way of thy desire, and by the sight of thine eyes. (10) Put away vexation from thy heart, and remove evil from thy flesh.

These are striking specimens of the sententious. But these might be increased by many more, from almost all parts of the book. Their first appearance is that of mere *gnomes*. A closer examination, however, shows that beneath them all there is an under-current. Unlike the Book of Proverbs, they all refer to some position which is designed to be illustrated or confirmed.

It should be remembered, in a *critique* on the style of Coheleth or his method of writing, that the book is not one of *narration* or *history*. The only part which approaches narration is a portion of chap. ii., which relates Coheleth's experience. But even here, the style approaches the sententious. The rest is *philosophizing*. Not a treatise on moral philosophy ; not a digest of practical and ethical science, orderly and consecutively laid down ; nor yet, on the other hand, a mere mass of *miscellany*. There is a *plan* — an evident plan or design — running through the whole. But one must not look for a chapter of Dr. Paley's moral philosophy here, or of Reinhardt's science of ethics. The Aristotelian logic was not in fashion among the Hebrews, and probably would not have been, had our author lived five hundred years earlier than he did. Successive syllogisms, in logical succession and continuity, are not to be found in the Hebrew writings.

Even the discourses of Christ himself do not exhibit them ; and
Paul, the greatest logician of all the sacred writers, even in the
epistles to the Romans, Galatians, and Hebrews, has nothing that
even approaches the *school-logic*. Nothing can be more diverse
from such methods of argument as Paley, Locke, Bentley, and
Whewell employ, than the whole mass of the Hebrew writings,
earlier and later. The Hebrews address the understanding and the
heart directly with the declarations of truth, and never rely on
any syllogistic concatenations of reasoning. And what all others
do, Coheleth does. He brings one matter and another before
us ; says something important and to be remembered concerning
it ; and then passes on to other kindred subjects. When occasion
prompts, he calls up again the same subject, and says something else about it, equally to be remembered. And it is thus
that Coheleth moralizes and philosophizes, through his whole
book.

It is evident from the nature of the book — a book of practical ethical philosophy — that there must be, in some respects, a
diction peculiar to itself ; I mean, that language adapted to *philosophy* must be employed. Hence many words in the book, which
are not elsewhere found in the Hebrew. To this account, I can
hardly doubt, not a few of the words may be put, which are
classed by Knobel and others among the later or the latest Hebrew. We shall see, on another occasion, that there are serious
difficulties in the way of a part of this classification, inasmuch as
the Phenician monuments exhibit many such words, which must
of course have belonged to the *older* Hebrew.

I have stated, at the beginning of this section, the great and
leading design of the book before us. *The vanity and utter insufficiency of all earthly pursuits and objects to confer solid and
lasting happiness*, is the theme with which the book begins and
ends ; and which, as we have seen, spreads as a network over all
its intermediate and subordinate parts. But there are other objects also in view, besides the illustration and confirmation of this

great proposition. The writer not only presents us with the pictures of many of the trials and disappointments of life, but also *instructs his readers how to demean themselves when these occur.* Doubtless this is second only to the main object of the work. It would have been of little avail to convince men in what a vain and perishing world they live — for their own experience and observation would teach them this ; — he felt it incumbent on him to tell them also what they should do, when placed in this danger or that, in this trial and state of suffering or in that, amid these disappointments and those. Salutary in a high degree are many of his precepts. They are instinct with life, and clothed with energy of language ; and springing, as they usually do, from the occasion of the moment, are destitute of all the formality, the stiffness, and the tameness of a string of ordinary moral and practical precepts.

That the writer was a nice observer of human life and actions, as well as of the nature and course of things, no one will deny. That he had moral and practical ends in view, subservient to sober, cautious, and prudent demeanor ; that he was penetrated with the deepest reverence for God, and inculcates the most unqualified confidence in him and submission to him, lies in open day and on the very face of his work. That he was no Epicurean, no Fatalist (in the heathen sense), and on the great points of morality and of religion no sceptic, will appear quite clear, as it seems to me, to every attentive and candid reader. To the numerous charges preferred against him in these respects, the result of hasty one-sided views of his book, the Commentary will, as I hope and trust, be a sufficient refutation.

That a great variety of precept — moral, prudential, and religious — should be the result of his plan, is evident. Instead of embodying in one series the directions which he gives, as results of his various investigations and reflection, — which is what most writers of our day would do, — he everywhere intermingles his advice or commands with the occasions that prompted them.

Whether *logical* or not, it will be conceded by every discerning reader, that the author has taken the *best* method to produce the strongest and most lasting impression on the mind. Many a maxim will be remembered from the spirited manner in which it is announced, and many a reader will be kept wide awake with his vivacity and energy, who would nod over formally correct, but dull and tame pages.

Many and discrepant opinions have been brought forward, respecting the nature and design of Coheleth. Most of the later German writers charge him with *scepticism* and with *unbelief* in a future state of existence. Even Umbreit, from whom we should expect something different, has written a volume, which is entitled *Coheleth Scepticus de summo bono*. But De Wette has far outstripped him. He says: "The doctrine of *retribution*, which constitutes the religious element of the book, has many strong doubts to contend with, and these his own experience of misfortunes helped to supply. . . . . The more unhappy the times were, and the more they led to despair, the more also that belief and animation grew cold, the stronger did those doubts become; so that they finally shaped themselves into the ordinary system of *Epicureanism* joined with *Fatalism*. This the author of the book professes," § 282. That Coheleth has often raised and expressed doubts respecting retribution and a future state, I readily concede. It is impossible to read with candor such passages as 3 : 18—21. 9 : 2—6, and even 6 : 2—8. 9 : 11, 12, without feeling that they are effusions of a mind disturbed by difficulties and doubts, if they are considered separately and as standing alone. But why did not De Wette consider more thoroughly the whole plan and design of the book, before he had made up his opinion from such passages as these, and took it for granted that Coheleth has expressed in them his own settled and ultimate conclusions? What if one should go into Paul's epistles, and extract from them all the passages which he designed should be put to the *objector's* account, and insist that these are opinions of Paul?

Would the apostle agree to be treated thus? Certainly not.
He would say, that he had not, indeed, formally and always mentioned the objector by name, as often as he has introduced him,
because he trusted to the good sense of the reader and the tenor
of the context,' as sufficient to make it manifest when he speaks
himself, and when he makes another to speak. What if the
Psalmist's words, in Ps. 73 : 3—14, should be put to his account,
as expressing his own settled opinion? Then what is to become
of the remainder of the Psalm, where he declares that he was
foolish and brutish in speaking as he had done? Then, in the
Book of Job, are the speeches of his *opponents*, who, as God
himself declares (Job 42 : 7), "did not speak the thing that was
right concerning him," to be taken as a guide to our faith and
our practice? The absurdity of such a course is manifest, by
the mere statement of the case. Why, then, may not the same
justice be done to Coheleth as to others? Undoubtedly, there
are some things said in his book which he does not design should
be taken as the exponents of his own settled opinion. He raises
doubts sometimes for the very purpose of answering them. He
sometimes exhibits erroneous maxims and precepts, and then
corrects them. The most natural account of the plan of the
book seems to be this, viz., that *the writer has given a picture of
the struggle and contest through which his own mind had passed,
when he set out on the road of philosophical inquiry.* Just such
is the account given by the Psalmist of his own mind, when he
saw the wicked flourishing and the just perishing. Before the
prying and inquisitive mind of Coheleth, a multitude of difficulties started up, when he came to inquire into the condition and
course of things as ordinarily developed.

It should be called to mind here, that the great moral stum-
bling-block of the ancient world was, the reconciliation of the
doctrine of *retribution* with the phenomena that are constantly
presenting themselves to our view. The wicked prosper; the
righteous are miserable, or perish. All share one common destiny,

4

since all are appointed unto death. The *moral* sense of men had a strong perception of the necessity of a retribution both just and adequate. Experience contradicted this, as to the present world. To those who had not a strong and lively faith in a *future* state and retribution, these two things appeared contradictory and very perplexing. This is the grand problem which constitutes the basis of the whole Book of Job. His opponents assert complete retribution in the present world. Job denies it. The dispute gives occasion to all the lofty and soul-stirring sentiments of this great moral epic. The matter in dispute is placed in every position, examined on every side, and everything right and wrong is said about it by the disputants. And after all, the *nodus* is not untied, but cut. God's dealings are an acknowledged mystery. He does not give his reasons to man, why he has so ordered things ; but he insists on it, that his wisdom, and knowledge, and justice, and merey, and sovereignty shall be fully acknowledged. The issue of the whole dispute is, that duty requires us to take and occupy this ground of acknowledgment. To the future world, where all things will be adjusted, no direct appeal is made. The *solvent,* which of all others a Christian would now expect to be applied, and which is sufficient and satisfactory, viz., that of *adequate future retribution,* is never employed in the Book of Job. What more than this, if as much, can be said of Coheleth? It has many more recognitions, more or less direct, of a future existence and reward than the Book of Job.

Let us consider more particularly, for a moment, some of the features of the plan, not as yet fully developed. The writer lived, as is plain from the tenor of his work, at a time when the same subject which is the *nodus* of the Book of Job, was exciting the anxious minds of many. The interest which they took in the theme of retribution, was greatly augmented by the grinding oppression and aggravated injustice of rulers and magistrates. Life was embittered (see 4 : 1—3), and multitudes were ex-

claiming: " O Lord, how long?" His own mind had passed
through all the stages of inquiry and perplexity, before it
came to settled and permanent conclusions in regard to some of
the topics of inquiry. It is evident, in the progress of his work,
that his mind is becoming more settled and peaceful. He comes
at last to a final conclusion, the crowning reward of all his inquiries, which is, that " we should fear God, and keep his commandments, because this is the duty of every man." He comes
too, after all his struggles and distresses in relation to the doctrine
of *retribution*, to a full and definite conclusion, viz., that " God
will bring to judgment every work, with every secret thing,
whether it be good, or whether it be evil," 12 : 13, 14. Well did
he know that other inquiring minds would have the same battles
to fight which he had fought ; and in his book, he has laid before
the reader all the struggles through which he passed himself, and
the obstacles which he had to overcome. What he had felt,
others might feel. But many others, perhaps, would, if left
without special aid, be less successful as to their result than he
had been. He wished to show his sympathy for them, and to
proffer them all the aid in his power. He accordingly brings
before them the doubts which were suggested by observation and
reflection, or in some cases, perhaps, were presented to him by
others. Many interpreters of the book have taken the passages
that exhibit these doubts, for the expressions of the author's own
deliberate opinion. But such doubts should be put in the same
category with the sentiments of Paul's objectors. It matters not
that they had passed through the author's own mind, for they had
greatly perplexed and disturbed him. The passing through his
mind does not stamp them with the authority of opinions settled,
deliberate, and final. It only shows what embarrassments the
writer had to remove, what perplexities to contend with. The
question is not, whether this or that thought once occupied his
mind, which he has recorded in writing, but whether this or that

thought was *adopted* by him, and made up a part of his settled and ultimate opinion.

If the book be carefully read, with such considerations in view as have now been suggested, I venture to say it will appear in a new and much less exceptionable light to many readers. Indeed, there will be only one serious difficulty remaining; which is, that we can hardly help wondering, that one who believed in future retribution and happiness, should not appeal to it oftener and more plainly than he does. But on looking farther, we find this equally applicable to nearly every part of the Old Testament. Moses does not enforce his laws by considerations drawn from the future world, nor by such penalties or promises as the New Testament holds up before Christians. Nor do the Psalms, Proverbs, Job, or the Prophets, speak more plainly on the point of a future world, than Coheleth has done. Why should we demand that he should so far outstrip all his contemporaries and predecessors, as to make his book a *gospel-treatise*, instead of an Old Testament production?

Let no one suggest that the view just taken of Coheleth's object, is one got up merely for the sake of parrying or avoiding difficulties. I can truly say, that it did not present itself to my mind in this way. It came from the often-repeated study of the book, and efforts to trace the writer's plan and object. In order to come to a result like that stated above, several things were to be considered. First, that no writer of such powers as the author of this book, would knowingly and palpably contradict himself, and this too within limits so narrow, that in a few minutes he could overlook everything that he had written. Secondly, that in a book of evident and professed disquisition and inquiry, it is to be expected that *objections* will be considered and answered, as well as thetical propositions made out, and moral and prudential precepts given. Thirdly, that the *final* conclusions in such a disquisitive work, are naturally to be taken as the index of the writer's ultimate and established opinion. Now, taking

these obvious principles into view, and conceding to them their
due weight, I venture to say that one would come, as a matter
of course, to adopt the views which have been stated above. By
far the greater part, indeed almost the entirety, of the book is on
the side of sound morals, and insists upon watchful demeanor,
sobriety, humility, trust in God, submission to his will, and a
radical weanedness from the vanities of the world. Intermixed
with these grave subjects are many prudential maxims, in respect
to industry, thrift, envy and slander of the great, and other
objects both social and industrial. But the parts which have
given occasion to the accusations of De Wette, and others, are
actually of little extent, and are also sparse. To characterize
the whole book from these, and to take these as the true exponents of the writer's opinions, is far from either justice or
candor.

Indeed, the last thing that one should think of in respect to
Coheleth, is to charge him with *Epicureanism.* In the narration
of that series of experiments which he had made, as exhibited in
chap. ii., he tells us at the beginning and at the close, that his
wisdom remained with him through the whole. He did not
wallow in pleasure, nor indulge in any excess. He made sober
experiments in the way of inquiry. In the somewhat numerous
passages, where, after having described some vanity of human
pursuit, he exhorts " to eat, and to drink, and to enjoy the good
of one's labor," there is not one which savors of encouragement
to drunkenness, or gluttony, or revelling. In 10 : 17, 18, he has
most clearly shown his condemning opinion of these excesses.
When he exhorts the young to make the best of life, and cheerfully to enjoy it, he throws in the salutary and soul-stirring caution, " But know thou, that for all these things God will bring
thee to judgment," 11 : 9. In other words, " Do all this, with the
constant recognition and remembrance of the truth, that you are
to give an account to God, for the manner in which you demean
yourself amid all your enjoyments."

Again and again does he remind those, whom he addresses and exhorts to enjoy the fruits of their labor, that all which they enjoy is the gift of God, 2 : 24, 26. 5 : 18. 3 : 13. 9 : 7—9. In other words, "Enjoy the gifts of God, the fruits of toil ; but remember the hand from whence they come, and be grateful to the Giver of all good." Coheleth, with all his trials and sorrows, is indeed no *ascetic*, no Franciscan *monk*. He exhorts not to go bowed down all one's days, covered with sackcloth, assuming a gloomy countenance, and mortifying the body. Men's garments should be white, *i. e.*, of a cheerful cast, and they should see that their heads lack not spikenard (used on occasions of joy) ; yea, and that they should live joyfully with the wife of their youth, 9 : 7—9. But in all this there is, or need be found, only a cheerful and thankful acceptance of the gifts of God. To charge this with *Epicureanism*, is doing the writer a manifest injustice.

Then as to the charge of *scepticism* made by De Wette, — if the book is read in the light where it ought to be placed, there is no solid ground for making such a charge. That which objectors say, or else that which doubts presenting themselves to the mind of the inquisitive writer would say, is regarded by De Wette as the expression of the writer's settled opinions. If Coheleth be a *sceptic*, he is not one, at all events, in respect to God, or his wisdom, or goodness, or sovereignty, or hatred of sin, or love of righteousness. Let us follow him through a few of these particulars.

All which man enjoys as the fruit of his toil, is to be regarded as the gift of God, 2 : 24. God has made everything יָפֶה, *i. e.*, *fit*, *proper*, *comely*, in its time, and made man intelligent, so that he may discern this, 3 : 11. To this he has added the power, and bestowed the means, of enjoying the reward of toil, 3 : 13. God is sovereign in the disposal of all things and all events ; and he preserves this attitude of a sovereign, in order that men may yield him that reverential homage which is his due, 3 : 14. When men, to their great grief, behold oppression and wickedness, they should call to mind, that " God will judge the right-eous and the wicked, since there is a time [of judgment] for every undertaking and every work," 3 : 17. It is an *objection* which suggests, in the sequel, that the object of the divine Being, in permitting so much oppression and wickedness, is to let men see that they are no better than the brutes, and that all must perish in the same way as they do, without any distinction, 3 : 18 —21. God is to be worshipped with the deepest reverence, and in spirit and in truth, instead of trusting in sacrifices and offerings, 4 : 17 (5 : 1. Eng.). Vows unto God are allowable, but not rash and foolish ones, and above all not deceitful ones, 5 : 1—4 (5 : 2—5). God will summarily punish false vows, 5 : 5 (5 : 6). In all that has respect to religion, God is to be regarded with reverential fear, 5 : 6 (5 : 7).

When oppressive rulers do violence and wrong, we must call to mind that there is ONE MOST HIGH over them all, 5 : 7 (5 : 8). God gives men the fruits of their labor, and the power of enjoying them ; and all these things are to be regarded as his gift, 5 : 17, 18 (5 : 18, 19). 6 : 2. God has fixed the order, and measure, and manner of all things and all events ; he has con-trasted prosperity with adversity, and made them to alternate in such a way, that man cannot with confidence foretell the future, 7 : 13, 14. Whoever pleases God shall be delivered from the fatal snares of seductive women, 7 : 26. Men must not charge their sins upon God ; for he made man upright, and it is man who has sought out many evil inventions, 7 : 29. " It shall be well with them that fear God, and ill with those who do not fear him," 8 : 12, 13. The work of God is inscrutable, 8 : 17. The righteous and their works are in the hand of God. All is at his disposal, so that many things take place, the ground and reason of which lie not within our reach of understanding, 9 : 1. When prosperity comes, enjoy it, and regard it as divine favor, 9 : 7. God's ways are unsearchable, 11 : 5. God, our Creator, is to be remembered even in our youth, 12 : 1. The spirit returns to

God who gave it, 12 : 7. The grand conclusion of the whole
book is, that we should " fear God, and keep his commandments ;
because God will bring everything, whether good or evil, into
judgment," 12 : 13, 14.

Such are the writer's views of God, of his providence, and of
his relations to men. In all this, where is there a trace of *scepticism ?* Nay, we may go much farther : Where is there more
unqualified reverence, submission, confidence, and obedience required, than in this book ? A submission the more to be commended and admired, because of the deep political and civil
gloom spread all around the writer. Indeed, his reverence for
God must have been of the highest kind ; for how else could it
sustain him, and encourage him to look up with such unqualified submission ? Holy Job broke forth into cursing the day of
his birth, and allegations of partiality in the dealings of divine
Providence. Coheleth, too, was led, for a time, to loathe life,
because of severe oppression ; but he does not take the position
of Job, nor does he complain of either partiality or injustice on
the part of his Maker. And all this filial submission is greatly
magnified, when we call to mind how faint his views of the
future were, in comparison with those which the gospel has presented to us. Such submission and reverence, under such
circumstances, are enough to make us heartily ashamed of
ourselves, when we murmur and are disquieted in a condition
such as ours.

In respect to the *Fatalism* which is charged against the book,
the preceding views of God and of his doings are a sufficient
answer. The order of nature, of events, of trial and suffering,
and of enjoyment, too, is indeed fixed by an overruling Providence. Man cannot change it. But what more of fatalism is
there in all this, than there is in Rom. 8 : 9, and in many
other parts of the Bible ? What more, than in nearly all the
Reformed Creeds of Christendom ? That God has *foreordained*
all things, is the common doctrine of all. But still, it is man

"who seeks out many inventions." The sinner can plead no *fatality*, in extenuation of his guilt. God has foreordained that he should act *freely*.

Wherein, then, consists the *scepticism* in question ? " In the fact," De Wette would doubtless reply, " that Coheleth believed nothing of a *future state* and a future *retribution*." He does not venture to say that there is nothing of it ; for 3 : 21 shows that the question, *whether the spirit goeth upward*, was within the reach of his inquiry, and of course that he knew something of this subject. Then what is the proof of the *unbelief* in question ? The very same proof as in the case of *Epicureanism ; i. e.*, it is drawn from the former doubts of the writer's own mind, or else from allegations of *objectors*. But are there not declarations enough to show that the mind of Coheleth had a different persuasion from that which these doubts indicate ? This question is easy to answer, and of much importance.

Let the reader, then, turn to 3 : 17. After stating that he had seen the tribunals of justice filled with oppression and wickedness, the writer says that " God will judge the righteous and the wicked," and that he has appointed a *time* in which all will come under the judicial cognizance of his tribunal. Again ; there is ONE higher than the highest earthly ruler (5 : 8), namely, One who will punish oppressors — for of course this is the intimation ; — there is One who will vindicate the oppressed, that have no comforter here, 4 : 1. The young may indeed rejoice in their blessings ; but they are always to keep in view the judgment to come, 11 : 9. " God will bring to judgment every work, with every secret thing, whether it be good, or whether it be evil," 12 : 14. Even Knobel acknowledges that this last passage indicates, beyond all doubt, a future retribution. But since he agrees with De Wette as to the *skepticism* of the book, he is driven to maintain that this passage was added by a later and a foreign hand.

Thus much for passages bearing directly on the idea of a judgment to come. Intimately and necessarily connected with these, are all those passages which speak of a *just retribution.* God is to be *feared,* 3 : 14. Sin makes him *angry,* 5 : 6. Why feared? And what will his anger do? Those that fear God, shall experience deliverance, 7 : 18. Wickedness shall not deliver those who are given to it, 8 : 8. " It shall be well with them who fear God," 8 : 12. " It shall *not* be well with those who do not fear him," 8 : 13. " Remember thy Creator," 12 : 1 ; — with the implication of reward, in case of obedience. " Fear God, and keep his commandments," 12 : 13 ; — with the same implication.

Thus the doctrine of a *retribution* for good and evil, and of a *time* when every action will be scanned and judged, lies scattered through the whole book of Coheleth. It is impossible reasonably to doubt the state of his mind in regard to these things. But in order to cast farther light on his meaning, it is necessary to take into view other things which he has said in relation to this subject. He has, in different ways, fully developed the sentiment, that *retribution is not made in the present life.* All experience the same evils ; all die alike ; all are subject to the same disappointments ; the lot which the righteous deserves often falls to the wicked, and so *vice versâ ;* the righteous perish not only *in* their righteousness, but *because of* it ; and so the wicked prosper *by reason of* their wickedness. Time and chance happen to all alike ; there is one event or destiny to the righteous and to the wicked, to the clean and to the unclean. (See 2 : 14, 15. 3 : 18—21. 4 : 1—3. 6 : 8. 7 : 15. 8 : 14. 9 : 1, 2, 11.) Now, although some of this is the language of objection, yet the *facts* stated are such as cannot be denied. The force of the objection arises from deductions made out of the facts, and does not consist in the facts themselves.

We assume it, then, as a plain doctrine in Coheleth, that — since such facts cannot be denied — *retribution, adequate and final, does not take place in the present world.* Indeed, the testimony of all ages unites in the confirmation of this position. We are brought, then, by all this, into a predicament where we are fully and entirely at liberty, and indeed are entitled, to make out the following syllogism :

(1) Retribution, adequate and just, of good and evil, will certainly be made. (2) It is not made in the present world. Therefore, (3) It must be made in a future world.

If there be any way of properly shunning or avoiding this conclusion, it is unknown to me. That this process of reasoning is built upon the book itself, is quite plain and certain, from what has been produced. It would seem that no intelligent and considerate man ought to estimate the understanding of Coheleth at so low a rate, as to suppose him designedly to have presented a medley of palpable contradictions in his book, which, if really admitted, would utterly destroy respect for himself as a writer, and mar all the credit of his work. On the contrary, one feels, in reading the book intelligently and carefully, the grasp of a powerful mind and of an acute observer of men and things.. What credit could he expect *Epicurean skepticism* would gain for a book, among such a people as the Hebrews? What is there in the Old Testament which is congenial with this? Nothing — nothing at all. How, then, can De Wette's views be made probable? — views in direct opposition to all that is Hebrew? And how is it possible to attribute the numerous passages of the book before us (which take high ground on the subject of retribution, and of God's hatred of sin and love of holiness and spiritual obedience) to a devotee of pleasure and a skeptic? This question calls for an answer; and an answer I have endeavored to give, in the preceding remarks; an answer, however, directly the reverse of De Wette's. And I may appeal to every intelligent reader and candid critic, whether my answer is not fairly sustained by the book itself? If so, then the principles of exegesis, applicable to the book, must be conceded to be such as I have advocated above.

The attentive reader must have observed, that I have as yet

made no appeal to the *inspiration* of the book, in order to sustain its claims to our regard. I have purposely avoided this, because those with whom I have been arguing, do not admit the claim or the reality of inspiration. But after passing through this contest on merely ethical and critical grounds, I now come to say, that the Book of Ecclesiastes has, in common with the other Old Testament books, a claim to the place which it holds -as one of the *inspired writings*. The author does not, indeed, assert himself to be inspired ; but neither do many other writers in the Old Testament assert this of themselves. There the book is, in the midst of the Hebrew Scriptures ; and there it has been, at least ever since the period when the Hebrew canon was closed. There at all events it was, when our Saviour and the apostles declared the Jewish Scriptures to be of *divine origin and authority*. I need not trace the history of its canonical reception and place here ; and more especially may I omit to do this, inasmuch as I have already, in my little volume on the Canon of the Old Testament Scriptures, canvassed the whole subject. Enough for us that the Jews of our Saviour's time held fast to this book, and that this usage was sanctioned by Christ and his apostles.

But there is another point of view in which this subject should now be placed. Would Christ and the apostles have sanctioned a work which taught *Epicurean skepticism?* It would seem as if this question needed no answer, except that which the very asking of it suggests. Where is there any parallel to such a proceeding, in the history of the sacred Canon? It is not supposable that they took such a view of the book as De Wette's.

" But the New Testament," it is said, " never quotes or refers to Ecclesiastes." True ; but where does it quote Ruth, Esther, Lamentations, Obadiah, and some other books ? The reason is plain and simple, viz., that no occasion required quotation. The *argumentum a silentio* is a very weak and unsatisfactory argument, in all cases of such a nature.

We seem, then, to be bound to concede, that the book was regarded by Christ and the apostles in a manner very different from that of De Wette, Knobel, Hitzig, Heiligstedt, and many others. And if so, then the former found in it, most surely, no *Epicurean skepticism*. No laws of fair exegesis oblige us to find it. We can dispose of the seemingly obnoxious sentiments, in some parts of it, in the same way as we do of the like sentiments in the Book of Job, where the objectors appear *in propria persona;* and just as we do in Paul's epistles, where they appear without being named, as they do in the book before us. We dispose of them in the same way as we do of what the Scribes and Pharisees say, as reported in the gospels. What they utter is not authoritative either in doctrine or practice ; nor were they at all inspired. But an *inspired writer* has told us what they said and did, and we give full credit to his narration. Just so in the case before us. The writer — I believe him to be an *inspired* writer — has told us what doubts and difficulties once passed through his own mind, or were suggested to him by others ; and we set them down merely for what he intended them to be considered. I say that he intended them to be regarded as mere *objections*, because I cannot force myself to believe him to be so weak a man as to contradict himself so egregiously as De Wette makes him to do, or rather would make him to do, if he had brought both sides of the question into view. But he has taken care to shun the doing of this, and has made out Coheleth's settled opinions merely from his doubts and difficulties. This does not seem to be holding the balance with the equable hand of justice.

I feel compelled to say of De Wette's introduction to his book (in his Einleitung), that it is one of the most hasty and incondite of his productions ; and nothing can be more evident to one who has thoroughly studied the book, than that he bestowed very little more than a hasty and superficial glance at the

5

whole matter.   The section containing the introduction was probably the work of a single session in his study.

In the investigation of the question respecting the design of ·Coheleth, we have come at least to a *negative* conclusion, in addition to the preceding positive ones, viz., that *it was not the author's design to teach either Epicureanism or Fatalism.*

But have we yet brought to view all the topics about which the book descants?   We have exhibited the main topic, and the one which stands next to this, namely, *lessons* or *precepts of practical wisdom.*   We have also touched on that of *avarice*, and that of *civil oppression and misrule.*   A few more topics must be briefly suggested, before we can complete our view of the author's whole design.

No individual and special topic is so often discussed, in the book before us, as that of *wisdom.*   For the most part, this word has a meaning here, different from that which it more usually has in Proverbs, Psalms, and other Old Testament books.   In general, it is equivalent here to *sagacity, prudential dexterity, shrewdness, cunning* in the better sense of the word.   Sometimes it designates that prudential foresight which leads one to fear and obey God; for there is sometimes developed in the book a *religious* and *ethical wisdom;* but in most cases the word is applied to *practical sagacious management* of affairs, or *wise demeanor;* or if not to these, then to *sagacity* in the investigation of various matters, and ability to make distinctions between things that differ.

In the commencing part of the book, after giving us a striking picture of the vanity of all things and their ceaseless round of uniformity, the author proposes, as one great object before him, to "investigate *by wisdom* respecting everything that is done under the sun," 1 : 13.   He tells us that "he acquired *wisdom* above all who were before him in Jerusalem;" and that in order more fully to understand wisdom, he contrasted it with folly and madness, 1 : 16, 17.   Yet, such an ardent pursuit of it brought with it much vexation and sorrow, 1 : 18. In the experiments he made by resorting to all the different means or sources of pleasure, he cautiously took wisdom, *i. e.*, prudential foresight, along with him, so that he might make experiments in the best manner; see 2 : 1—11, and especially vs. 3, 9. In examining the wisdom possessed by him, in order to find its excellence or principal advantage, he found that such as possessed it could often see where others were more or less blind, 2 : 13, 14. Yet wisdom could not guard him against many ills of life, which come equally on the wise and the foolish. In this respect, therefore, he found it to be *vanity*. Nor could wisdom secure his future fame ; for all die and are *forgotten*. Here again it showed itself to be vanity, even an empty pursuit, 2 : 14—17. Wisdom, as employed in the acquisition of wealth, is defeated in its ends ; for the effort and trouble are great, and all that is amassed soon goes into other hands, it may be into those of a fool, 2 : 18—23. But however wisdom may contribute to one's enjoyment, by enabling him to make a dexterous use of things, it must be acknowledged rather as the gift of God, than as anything of which we can boast, 2 : 24—26. Wisdom enables even a child to act more successfully than the aged who are foolish, 4 : 13. But in regard to many evils that come upon us, the wise man has no advantage over the fool, 6 : 8. Rebuke from the wise is salutary. 7 : 5. If a man that is wise, betakes himself to oppression, it will soon make him like to a madman, 7 : 7. Wisdom is of some avail, as well as wealth ; for it often protects men from threatened evils, even where money would not do this, 7 : 11, 12. It is better than the forces and weapons of war, 7 : 19. In seeking for examples of it, in order to pry into its true nature, he has very rarely been able to find them, 7 : 25—28. In fact, the thing is too recondite and deep to be fully attained, as to its real nature, 7 : 23—25. Wisdom will exhilarate the man who can apply it to the solution of difficult things, 8 : 1. Wisdom will teach discreet behavior in presence of rulers, 8 : 5.

Wisdom, as to all matters that are transacted, is difficult of attainment, and no one can thoroughly explore it, 8 : 16, 17. Wisdom belongs to the present life, 9 : 10 ; will not always be successful, 9 : 11 ; yet sometimes it achieves important things in the defence of those who are attacked, 9 : 13—15. It is better than weapons of war, 9 : 18. It is spoiled by a little folly, 10 : 1. It is needed and is useful in almost all of even the common concerns of life, 10 : 2—15. The preacher, as a wise man (a *Hākām*), taught the people knowledge, 12 : 9. The words of the wise are a powerful stimulus to the minds of men, who are inclined to be inefficient or to do but little, 12 : 11.

Wisdom, then, is placed in a great variety of attitudes, some of which seem, at first view, to be incongruous with others. First, he sought wisdom with much eagerness, and made himself more wise than any before him at Jerusalem. Then he found wisdom to be of no avail in many cases, and that the pursuit of it was vanity. At another time we find him saying, that when he sought after it, he found it was too deep and remote to be explored, 7 : 23, 24. At one time, like every other thing that man pursues, it is vanity ; at another, it answers important purposes in commanding success, and in defending from dangers that threaten. At one time, we feel almost as if he were speaking ironically concerning it, when he speaks of it as merely enabling one to see what the fool does not see. But when all parts of the picture are carefully compared, it will be found that wisdom is often spoken of *relatively, i. e.,* as related to certain things over which we have no control. In such a case, he calls it *vanity.* Whatever may be its value in other respects, it cannot keep off many of the ills of life, nor prevent our exposedness to many losses and trials, nor enable us to escape from death. It can avail us only in prudential matters, where caution and sagacity are useful and necessary to guard against danger, or to win success. Here, indeed, there is something valuable in it, and worthy of being possessed. But when *speculatively* investigated (7 : 23 seq.), it soon presents difficulties that we cannot overcome, and we are forced to abandon the pursuit. But when *practically* exercised, it is that which is needed in all the concerns of life, in a greater or less degree, if they are capable of being managed, and require to be managed, so as to meet our wishes.

The author seems to hold on to this *mental* quality, with much more tenacity than he does to any of the ordinary pursuits of business or pleasure among men. The reputation of Solomon for *wisdom*, seems to have thrown a charm around the acquisition of it. Yet after all, conceding the aid which it gives, and its preëminence above folly, it is not that high and enduring good after which he is seeking. Some credit, indeed, is due to it, for in many ways it is useful; but it lacks the power of making us superior to the common and unavoidable evils of life.

In this view of the subject, we find at once a justification of the definition of *wisdom*, as employed in this book, which I have given above. It is not wisdom in the high sense which the word often bears in the book of Proverbs. *The fear of God* is there regarded as *the beginning of wisdom.* *Obedience to his commands* as the *consummation of it.* It is almost the equivalent of *piety ;* while *folly* is another name for *wickedness.* Not so in the book before us. Wisdom and folly are indeed abundantly brought into contrast; but here they are equivalent to sagacity and to the lack of it; here they are prudent caution and foresight, or the want of it; and here they are dexterity of management, or the want of it. In a word, they are *practical wisdom* or *the want of it,* as developed in all the circumstances and engagements of life.

This, it is evident, is altogether adapted to one of the leading purposes of the book, viz., that of giving prudential maxims or rules of life, so that we may avoid as many evils as possible, and acquire and enjoy as much good. While the author gives us such a vivid picture of the vanity of the present world, he endeavors to guide us in such a way, as that we may suffer the least that is possible in consequence of this vanity. Wisdom is so important to the attainment of this end, that it cannot be dispensed with; but the man who pursues it with the expectation that, in itself, it is adequate to procure for him stable and certain good, will always be disappointed. But of wisdom in the sense of *religion* or *piety*, this cannot be truly said ; for the contrary is true. It is manifest, then, that this is not the kind of wisdom which is so often discussed by Coheleth.

On the whole, that a philosopher (for such Coheleth professes himself to be, *i. e.*, a חָכָם), should concern himself with the examination and discussion of *wisdom*, is altogether congruous with the nature of his book, and is what we might naturally expect. But how different are his views from those of Plato and even of Socrates. Speculative discriminations, and the power of making them acutely, are the σοφία of the Greeks ; while with the Hebrews, either religion, or practical sagacity and prudence in the affairs of life, constitute the essence of wisdom. Of metaphysical reasoning and subtilties they had little or no conception, or at any rate, they felt little or no interest in them.

As I have already intimated, there is not the least trace of any acquaintance, on the part of Coheleth, with the *Greek philosophy*, in any portion of his book. But still, the fame of Grecian philosophy might have been one of the moving causes of writing the book. The heathen was disposed to say to the Jew : "What ground for claiming preëminence have you ? The knowledge of σοφία does not exist among you ? " Coheleth has written a book which furnishes an answer to this taunting allegation, although perhaps it was not designed to do so. " Here is our philosophy," a Jew might reply, who held this book in his hand. And there indeed it was ; and in a religious, moral, and practical point of view, it was worth more than all the philosophy of Greece.

Before we quit the present subject, it will be well to notice the singular theory of Ewald, Hitzig, and some others, in regard to *wisdom* in this book. It is this, viz., that *Coheleth* is but another name for *wisdom;* and inasmuch as Solomon was regarded by some of the later Hebrews as *wisdom incarnate* (Wisd. 9 : 7, 8. 7 : 1 seq.), so it is *incarnate Wisdom* in the person of Solomon, who speaks throughout this book ; (Hitz. Comm. on 1 : 1). But how such a theory as this could be soberly advanced and defended, I cannot well imagine. (1) In the Book of Proverbs, chap. viii. ix., in Sirach chap. xxiv., where *wisdom* is personified, we have the most express intimations of it ; which is as much as to say, that without these intimations the reader would be in danger of mistaking the writer. Nothing of this kind, however, is seen in Coheleth. He appears, speaks, acts, everywhere as a simple personage, and not as a mysterious symbol. If such were not the case, we might reasonably expect to be advertised of it. (2) Whenever wisdom is elsewhere *personified, i. e.*, introduced as a person, she is not personified in another individual, but only in and by herself. In other words, she is introduced as personified Wisdom, and not as Solomon. (3) Things are attributed to wisdom here, which, if we suppose abstract and absolute wisdom to be meant by the word, are utterly incompatible with its nature. For example, wisdom is introduced (*i. e.*, provided Coheleth is its representative or incarnation) as making strenuous efforts to acquire itself, and does actually acquire itself with success ; 1 : 16, 17. 2 : 12. Wisdom remained with itself, 2 : 9 ; and yet wisdom was far away from wisdom, and too deep and remote to be understood, 7 : 23, 24. In wisdom is much vexation, 1 : 18. Wisdom is altogether vanity, 2 : 15, 16. Wisdom exerts itself most strenuously to find out itself, but is unable to do it, 8 : 16, 17.

How is it possible now, I ask, to predicate all these things of *wisdom absolute*, as dwelling in Coheleth? The bare inspection of them supersedes all argument in the case. It is clear as the sun, that Coheleth is a *person* seeking to obtain wisdom, that he obtains it imperfectly, and finds it on many occasions useful, while in many others it is quite powerless. Could *abstract wisdom* say of herself, that she was vanity, and unknown to herself, and unknowable ? And although this theory can boast of patrons with such names as Geier, Le Clerc, Rambach, Carpzov, Köster, and others of past days, and of Ewald and Hitzig, now living, it must be regarded still (at least it seems so me) as coming from the land of dreams ; and these appear to be rather disturbed ones.

Another topic, which comes under frequent discussion, viz., that of *riches, and efforts to amass them,* has been somewhat fully exhibited, near the beginning of the present section. I merely avert to it here. It would seem, from the vivid pictures of *avarice,* or of amassing great wealth, that it was probably a frequent vice in the time of Coheleth, and that he regarded it with that strong disapprobation which is everywhere expressed in his book. It is not the mere matter of possessing or acquiring, which he disapproves, but the *setting one's heart on wealth,* and the expectation that any solid happiness can be secured by it.

Other topics are also included in the book. But they are merely touched upon, as it were incidentally, and do not appear to have belonged to the main parts of his design. For example, the folly of *ambition* is represented in strong colors, in 4 : 13—16. One cannot help thinking of "the old and foolish king," as being Solomon, in his old age, when led away by his heathen wives. The young man who comes into his place, seems to be Jeroboam, who led away ten parts of the Hebrew nation. His unhappy doom is briefly but forcibly related. But we miss, in this book, many of the topics which we might naturally expect would be touched on, as they concern the means in vain resorted to for the sake of securing enjoyment. Whoredom and concubinage are scarcely brought to view. Many vices that were common, such as defrauding, stealing, idleness, prodigality, and the like, so often treated of in the Book of Proverbs, are scarcely, or not at all, glanced at here. It was not within the scope of the author's design, to bring all vices into view. As a remarkable circumstance of this nature, may be mentioned the entire omission of any reference to, or mention of, *idolatry*. One is ready to ask : When could this book have been written ? Under *good* kings, none or little of the oppression and perversion of justice, so often complained of, would exist; the *bad* kings were, nearly or quite all of them, *idolaters*. Yet oppression is a topic rife in the book ; but not one complaint is there of idolatry, and nothing is said of the heathen. May not this circumstance have some important bearing on the *time when* the book was written ?

From all that has been said, we may safely deduce the conclusion, that it was not the design of the author to compose a complete *Code of Morals*. His great theme is the *vanity of all earthly objects and pursuits ;* and whatever will best illustrate and confirm this, we may expect to find in his work. Lesser things are omitted, and only the more important, which will leave a deep impression, brought to view. Having gone through with these, his work is complete, for he has done all which he intended to do.

Having stated at great length the general object or design of the book, and also the leading particulars which it comprises, and everywhere appealed to the book itself in the way of verification, I deem it unnecessary to canvass at any length the many and different theories in relation to this subject. I shall merely glance at some of them. (1) Some, *e. g.*, Desvoeux, Stäudlin, and Rohde, make the author's object exclusively a *religious* one. But the small portion of the book, which bears directly on this subject, will hardly sustain this view. (2) Others, *e. g.*, Luther, Bauer, Gaab, Bertholdt, Haenlein, Jahn, and Schmidt, make it a *practical essay*, designed, as some of them assert, to teach us how to live joyfully and quietly amidst the sorrows and troubles of life ; others, to show us how to avoid suffering ; others, how to bear with sorrow and joy, good fortune and misfortune; others, to stop the mouths of complaining and murmuring men; others, to direct all our efforts, and keep them within due bounds. All of these theories have some foundation in particulars here and there of the book, but only in particulars. The general tenor of the book does not correspond with any of them. (3) Others admit a *theoretical* design. Herder, Eichhorn, De Wette, and Friedlander, state simply, that the author designed to show the vanity of human affairs. So far as this goes, since it has a generic aspect, it is correct; but it does not of itself cover the whole ground, as we have seen above. (4) Paulus, Umbreit, and Köster, maintain that the subject is the inquiry: What is man's highest good in his present state? But this gives the book too much the aspect of theoretical Greek philosophizing. (5) Döderlein, Van der Palm, and Rosenmüller, state the object to be both *theoretical* and *practical*, viz., to show the nothingness of human life and human things, and to give practical rules which grow out of this. Rosenmüller adds, that the author designs to show how a man may enjoy present good, and live virtuously and piously so as to please God. This comes near to the true mark. Knobel has done best of all: " *The design is, to show the nothingness of human life and efforts, and to impart such practical instruction relative to the conduct of men, as their present condition demands.*" Comm. s. 39.

It is hardly worth mentioning, that Kaiser, a man of some note for learning and acuteness in Germany, has found in Coheleth an *allegorico-historical poem*, exhibiting the lives of the Jewish kings from Solomon down to Zedekiah. In constructing this fancy-work he has shown much acuteness, exhibited vast reading and extensive learning, and manifested a shrewdness at combination which is uncommon. So far as I know, he has never made a single convert to his opinion. Few minds out of Germany are gifted with such powers of discovery, as are developed here in his schemes. They may well rest contented, however, with their lack of such a rare gift as this writer seemed to himself to possess.

It is a striking fact, that most interpreters of Coheleth have found in it *no plan* at all. It is made up, in their view, of various apothegms, proverbs, maxims, etc., thrown together without regard to order or method, and is a real *thesaurus of miscellanies*. Nachtigal maintains that it is a collection of *rival songs*, gathered from various Schools of the Prophets. This deserves the next place to the plan of Kaiser. What has been adduced above in order to show the nature of the plan, renders any discussion here of Nachtigal's view unnecessary. Umbreit, Van der Palm, Spohn, and Paulus, find this work filled with transpositions of order, and dislocations. Whoever reads the book, however, with attention, when placed in the light that has of late been cast upon it, will need no other refutation of such a theory.

Others, *e. g.*, Michaelis, Rosenmüller, Van der Palm, and Paulus, divide the book into two parts (to which, however, they assign diverse limits), in the one of which the vanity of things is established, and in the other precepts are given how to demean one's self, and how to secure any good. Köster makes four divisions. (1) "Disclosure of the absolute good. (2) Of the relative good. (3) The fool and the wise are contrasted, and true wisdom pointed out. (4) This wisdom is considered in its relation to the various conditions of life." But it would be very difficult to draw palpable lines of separation between these parts, or to show that they do not intermingle with each other. Herder, Eichhorn, Friedlander, and Döderlein, acknowledge a general *unity* of the book, and a somewhat regular progress in its contents. But as to any preconcerted plan of arrangement in respect to particulars, they think that nothing certain can be made out. The contents have throughout a general relation, but the particulars are too miscellaneous, as they think, to be separated and arranged in any specific order.

In a work such as that before us, and after the representations

given above of what has been actually done by the author, no
one will expect that the critic can make out a regular and formal
disposition of the whole, after the manner which modern logic
and rhetoric would demand. As has already been said (p. 33),
the Hebrews were strangers to the training of schools of art, and
their writings never exhibit any special regard to it. But still,
there is " a beginning, a middle, and an end," in Coheleth, independent of the mere *local* position of its contents. His first
object is, *to show the vanity of human efforts and of all earthly
things in which men seek satisfaction.* This part comprises the
first four chapters. He begins with the unchangeable order of
things in the natural world. Over this, man can acquire no influence, and have no control (1 : 4—11). He then proceeds, in
various ways, to illustrate and establish the position, that all
human efforts to obtain abiding good in the present world are
vain and fruitless. The acquisition of wisdom, or riches or honors, and also indulgence in sensual pleasure, fails of its end. The
most to which one can attain, is to enjoy the fruits of his toil in
the sober gratification of natural appetites. Providence has so
arranged the vicissitudes of things, that they all have their regular course ; and all that we can do is merely to submit to this,
having no power to change or arrest it. After all the strivings
of men, all go down to the grave, and perish in common with
other living creatures around them. In fact, so multiplied are
the sorrows of life, resulting from man's weakness, and springing from oppression, and from vain strife for wealth and defeated
projects of ambition, that it is better to die than to live (1 : 12
—4 : 16).

Thus far the *theory* of the book. In all this, there is only
some three or four hints of a *practical* nature, such as 2 : 24.
3 : 12, 13. 4 : 6, 9. These seem to proceed from spontaneous
bursts of feeling, which are occasioned by reflection on the subject-matter before him. But the general theory being thus
established, he now comes to the part where he mingles precept

and practical instruction with the representation of facts and occurrences. In 4 : 17 of the Hebrew (it should be 5 : 1, as in our English translation), he first begins to speak *imperatively* or in the way of exhortation. His very first topic, now, is that of *religion*. Frequenting the place of worship, prayer, offerings, and vows, are here brought to view, and instructions are given. Thence he proceeds to descant on a variety of topics, with which the happiness and comfort of men are deeply concerned. Several of these topics, *e. g.*, riches, wisdom, the oppression of rulers, etc., are introduced again and again, as occasion prompts, and in order to present them in all their important aspects. In the course of this part of his work, divers objections are presented; some of which are answered forthwith, and some after intervening matter has been thrown in, which pressed upon his mind. To trace the course of thought through this part of his work requires not a little of study and effort. Most commentators have, indeed, abandoned all effort to trace any connection here, or to find any general thread of discourse — any generic unity in the whole. But the intelligent and diligent reader may still find reward here for his toil.

When we come to chap. ix., the whole discourse takes a different turn. We have thenceforth no more of the desponding declarations: *All this have I seen ; all this have I tried ;* no more of the cheerless conclusion: *All this is vanity.* The doubts and queries are dismissed, and chap. ix., stands on new ground. The ultimate conclusions to which Coheleth has come, after examining into the whole matter before him, are now brought before us. God is supreme, and all things and all men are in his hands. He has made, and intends to make, no distinction between men, as to their mortality and exposedness to suffering. This, although it is a source of much concern and sorrow, must be borne as having been appointed by him. Rational and cheerful enjoyment, so far as practicable, he permits and even enjoins. Moreover, wisdom may alleviate some evils, and prevent some others; so that

6

although it is not itself the chief good, and cannot of itself secure solid and lasting happiness, it may be of much use, even in the common affairs of life. In the midst of exposure to oppression and misfortune, it may help to direct our conduct, so far as to avoid as much evil, and secure as much good, as is possible. A diligent observance of active duty, and a thankful enjoyment of what can be enjoyed, are the sum of what we can do to mitigate the sorrows and trials of life. Through all and in all with which we are concerned, and at all seasons of life, God is to be remembered, and also his judicial power to be recognized. Then comes, as a very apposite conclusion to the whole, a description of *old age*, and its preparation for, and approach to the tomb. Here the writer rises above himself, and breaks out into a strain almost purely poetical. In his own mind, he looks back on all the various struggles and suffering of life which had preceded; and now he goes on to show here, that the end of life must be after the like tenor with the preceding part of it. It ends in weakness, rendered more grievous by infirmity and sorrow. The dust returns to dust. And as he has before declared, that there is an appointed time for retributive justice to be executed, so the soul returns to the God who gave it, in order that this may be accomplished.

Thus ends, very appropriately, the book before us. Its end is consonant with its beginning. The final and solemn declaration over the grave of departed man is : VANITY OF VANITIES ! ALL IS VANITY ! All that is added by the writer, is merely a brief account of himself, and of his object in writing the book ; which is, that we should FEAR GOD, AND KEEP HIS COMMANDMENTS, BECAUSE HE WILL BRING EVERY WORK AND EVERY SECRET THING INTO JUDGMENT BEFORE HIM.

After having taken such an extended view of the method and design of Ecclesiastes, I venture to say, that those who regard the book as without plan, and without any unity of design, can hardly have read it with becoming attention. *Plan there is not,* in the modern logical and rhetorical sense of that word, as has already been fully conceded; but as to a *definite design*, and the general features of its execution, there can hardly be any room for doubt. In a word, it is *Hebrew* philosophizing, and not Greek or English philosophizing.

And now a word more on the great question so often asked: "How could the writer, if he believed in *future retribution*, have everywhere avoided bringing it into view? Where else, in such a world as he describes this to be, could any one go for comfort? Where else find a ray of hope? It is spontaneous with us, when we look at the multiplied evils of life, to resort to the future world as a ground of hope and satisfaction. We look to a future tribunal, to satisfy our minds concerning the justice of God, and we feel that his providential dealings are all to be vindicated and reconciled at that tribunal. Why did not Coheleth act in the same way?"

After having so fully discussed this subject above (p. 46 seq.), and also in my Commentary (on 3 : 17), it is needless for me to say much here. But I may remark, that there is something of the *a priori* in this demand on Coheleth. We decide within ourselves rather what *he ought to have written*, than occupy ourselves only with what *he has written*. But passing this, let me in all sincerity and earnestness ask : Is there any more reference, in the copious Book of Job, to a *future state*, than in the brief one of Coheleth? There can be, as I think, but one answer. There is not anything like as much reference of this nature ; and what there is, or what is implied, is far short of Coheleth in explicitness. I am aware that many readers will start at this, and point me, with confidence that I am mistaken, to that famous passage in Job, 19 : 25 seq., beginning with : *I know that my Redeemer liveth, etc.* But, alas! I cannot accede to their exegesis. On the contrary, I think it can be shown beyond the reach of fair philological contradiction, that the passage has no reference to Christ, Christianity, or the final resurrection of the body. It is

simply the declaration of Job, ready to faint under the accusations of his friends (which were that he was suffering because of
some peculiar and heinous guilt); and his declaration that he still
hoped in God, who would yet appear as his *vindicator* (גֹּאֵל).
He trusted that he would, at some future period (אַחֲרוֹן), take his
stand on earth (as he did, see in chap. xxxviii., coming in the
whirlwind), and rescue him, though wasted away to a skeleton-
state (מִבְּשָׂרִי); so that he should still see him, when restored to a
state of renewed strength and health. "*I shall see him*," exclaims
he, "*for myself, with my own eyes behold him; but not a stranger
or enemy*" [shall behold him]. That is, I shall see him on my
side, taking my part; but these my accusers, who act like strangers or enemies to me, shall not see him taking their part. Such
was the fact, see 38:1 seq., and compare 42:7. But if this
alleged resurrection of Job means the *final* resurrection, how
shall we solve the nodus, which is presented by the allegation that
Job will see him, but not his accusers? Were they, then, to have
no part in the resurrection? Other insuperable difficulties might
be urged against this view of the passage; but I am digressing.
Yet not altogether so, for it was incumbent on me to sustain my
allegation relative to the proportional mention of, or reference to,
the *future*, in the two books before us. Indeed, I hesitate not to
say, that no book in the Old Testament has so many references
to the retribution and judgment, at a future period, as that of
Coheleth. For proof of this, I refer to the views given above.

In respect to GOD, there is no part of the Old Testament
which inculcates more thoroughly the fear of him, reverence for
him, his supremacy, and his sovereign right to order all things
and direct all concerns. In what part of the Old Testament is
there more spirituality as to worshipping him inculcated, or the
fear of offending more emphatically enjoined? See 4:17—5:6
(5:1—7), and other passages quoted on page 42 seq., above.
There is, indeed, in the Psalms, more of adoration and praise,
and thanksgiving, and confession, and supplication; and all this

for the obvious reason, that the Psalms are composed for this very purpose, and of course are made up of such matter. But even in the Psalms, numerous as they are, there are not so many passages concerning future retribution, as in this book; nor is the character of God set forth, and his claims vindicated, with a stronger hand. But if we go to the Pentateuch, the great work of the Jewish lawgiver, we find scarcely a trace of *futurity*, excepting what rests on mere implication or inference. How came it that Moses did not present to the rebellious and idolatrously inclined Jews of his time, the awful terrors of the world to come? Yet in that solemn chapter on blessings for obedience, — that fearful chapter on curses for disobedience (written at the close of Moses' life, Deut. xxviii.), the *blessings* consist of abundance as to the necessaries and comforts of life, protection from enemies and superiority over them, and increase in numbers with great renown. Even "the first commandment with promise," in the Mosaic law, offers no better promise than protracted length of days in the goodly land. On the other hand, the *curses* are drought, famine, pestilence, and various other diseases, loss of children and of property, slavish subjection to foreign nations, and finally, exile in a foreign land. Why did Moses stop here? Why not hold up before that perverse generation all the terrors of the future world of woe, and all the allurements of the world of peace and joy? Can any one give any other reason for this, than that which has already been suggested above, viz., that under the ancient dispensation there was but the *dawning* of the day which was to come? Life and immortality were to be brought fully to light, only by him who is *the Light of the world*. " No man hath seen God at any time." Neither Moses, nor the prophets, lived under any more light than shines in the *dawn* of revelation. What God had not yet revealed, they could not fully disclose. At all events, they have not fully disclosed any more than some of the first elements of future things; and even their hints respecting these, are few and far between. Readers of our

6*

day find much of a future world in the Old Testament only by
carrying back, to the interpretation of it, what they have learned
in the New Testament. The only proper question is simply :
What did the Old Testament, interpreted without the aid of the
New, fairly disclose to the Jews?

When this question is asked, I venture to assert, without the
fear of being reasonably contradicted, that Coheleth has more
often alluded to future retribution, and more strongly affirmed it,
than any other writer in the Old Testament. Can any one find
such a retribution in the Pent., histories, prophecies, Psalms,
Proverbs, more often, or more plainly than here? I look in vain
for anything like the *frequency* of his allusions to an adequate
retribution, in any part of the Hebrew Scriptures, of the same
length as Coheleth. In the Book of Job, which most of all resembles that of Ecclesiastes, in its *theme ;* the friends of Job warmly
defend the idea of an adequate retribution in the present life.
Sin is speedily followed, as they maintain, by condign punishment. Job as warmly denies this; and God has decided that he
was in the right, 42 : 7. How could such a dispute be so zeal-
ously and perseveringly maintained, in case the subject of retribution had been fully revealed in the Hebrew Scriptures? I
trust the answer to this will not be, that the Book of Job was
written before the other Scriptures. When brought to the tribunal of impartial criticism, this assertion, as nearly all now concede, cannot well stand the test. The composition bears evident
marks of a time nearly synchronous with that of Coheleth. The
same subject is discussed. The same difficulties and objections
are urged. But Coheleth takes a position opposite to that of
Job's friends; and, while conceding the point of imperfect and
merely initiatory retribution in the present world, it still maintains that it is to be confidently expected at a future period. One
is reminded, at every step, as he is surveying the ground of
Coheleth, of the kindred feelings, sentiments, and even diction
in the Book of Job.

Now we do not undertake to eject the Book of Job from the Canon, because we cannot appeal to the speeches of Job's friends as *authority*, in establishing any point of doctrine. I say *cannot appeal*, because, as God himself (42 : 7) has plainly declared that those friends had " said the things concerning him which *were not right*," it follows surely that we cannot now appeal to what is not right, in order to establish a doctrine. Many things, indeed, which Job's friends said, were true; but the truth rests not on their authority. It must be established elsewhere, and by other means. We do not receive it as true because they said it, but because experience or some of the sacred writings have established its truth.

Let all this, so plain and so reasonable, be applied now to Coheleth. The *objections* to the great truths which he declares are no more binding on us than the speeches of Job's friends, or the arguments of objectors, introduced so often by Paul. This, when thoroughly considered and carried out, removes most of the difficulties in Coheleth, and places him in the rank of those who in ancient times taught the doctrine of a future retribution, gave precepts in accordance with this truth, and disclosed sublime and vivid conceptions of the holiness, the power, the sovereignty, the wisdom, and the goodness of God. The question, why he did not more explicitly urge the great spiritual truth to which I have alluded, is one that justice to him requires us to ask respecting all the other sacred writers of the Old Testament. And if we do ask it, the answer is plain. In this state of things, then, we are permitted to repeat again the question, which has been asked before, viz., Why should more be demanded of Coheleth than of any other Old Testament writer ?

In canvassing the question respecting the design of the book, and showing that it was neither to teach *Epicureanism* nor *Skepticism*, I have taken a wider range than I had at first intended. The questions of interest, more or less connected with the leading theme here, demanded discussion somewhere ; and although rigid regard to order might have placed some of them under another category, no special advantage to the discussion of them could be gained by transferring them thither. Liberally interpreted, my category is ample enough to comprise them all.

The general nature of the work; the design of it as manifested by the principal theme, and by the various topics of discussion; the method in which the writer has pursued the attainment of his object, as developed first in the respective parts of the book and then in the modes of representation and discussion; — all these have now been developed with sufficient copiousness. We may proceed, then, to other subjects of interest that yet remain to be discussed.

§ 3.   *Unity of the Book.*

After all that has been said above in developing the design and method of the book, little need be said under the present category.   Its *unity* is manifest from the fact, that the book has a beginning, a middle, and an end, all consentaneous ; as has been fully shown above.   It is manifest from the fact, that the great theme — *all is vanity* — is repeated some twenty-three times in different portions of the book; which shows, beyond any reasonable doubt, that the same writer who proposed the theme, has carried on the discussion of it through the work.   It is granted, that there are some digressions.   Yet, when strictly examined, they are found to be very few.   The *sententious* consists mainly in precept; the *apothegmatic* (which really constitutes but a very minute portion of the work) is introduced not for its own sake, as in the Book of Proverbs, but only for the sake of comparison and illustration.   But wherever sententious precept or apothegm is introduced, they are speedily dismissed, and there is a return to the consideration of some one of the vanities of human plans and efforts, which is presented in a new attitude.   There is not a book in all the Old Testament, unless it be the Book of Daniel, which is more firmly compacted together in its principal framework, nor one which keeps more steadily in view the great object which is designed to be accomplished. All this renders it utterly improbable that the works of different authors are here joined together. We can reasonably expect such an arrangement only from the hand of *one and the same author.*

To him who can read and duly appreciate the *original Hebrew,* nothing can be said that will convince him of a *diversity* of authorship. First of all, the language or diction is so strikingly *sui generis,* that no other book in the Old Testament approaches near to it. There is plainly a peculiarity — a something to be *felt,* however, rather than described — which runs through the book from the beginning to the end. No careful reader, as it seems to me, can possibly doubt of this. The impress of the writer upon the book throughout, is nearly or quite as palpable as is that of Daniel on his work ; and it would be difficult to say more of any book. I cannot hesitate to say, that the writing is as strongly marked throughout, as (for example) the works of Thomas Carlyle of the present day. I do not mean to say that the peculiarity of it is as revolting to simple and refined taste as his ; for this I do not believe, and cannot admit. But the modes of expression in Coheleth, and the diction, and the distinctive kinds of development which he employs, are altogether as different and as segregating from others, as are those of Carlyle. There arises a *feeling,* in every one who reads Coheleth with a power of nice critical discernment, which makes it all but absolutely certain that one and the same hand penned down the whole book. Almost without exception this is now conceded among critics.

Time has been, as has been said, when there were various theories on this subject. Paulus maintained that the book exhibits what passed in a *discussion* of a Literary Society of the writer's day, of which he was a member. The theory of

Nachtigal, that the book consists of *rival poems* derived from different schools of the prophets, which are strung together like Wolf and Heyne's different rhapsodies of various poets, eking out *one Iliad* at last, has been previously mentioned. But first, we know nothing of such *literary* discussions among the prophets. Secondly, the book is not poetry. Lastly, the several parts are *not* put together without order and sequency. Others have maintained the mere *fragmentary* state of the book, — fragments joined together by some unknown hand. Stäudlin maintained that the book first consisted of various rough sketches of Solomon, which were subsequently brought together, filled up, and then some junction-links added. Others have given it out as a mere *mass of aphorisms*, brought together from all quarters, like the Book of Proverbs, and thrown under one category for the sake of mere convenience. In point of extravagance and improbability, Kaiser and Nachtigal may deservedly claim the preëminence; and even such a preëminence is not destitute of attractions for some. The sober inquirer has reason to be thankful that a better day has dawned on philological pursuits.

It would be useless to pursue, at any greater length, the question in respect to the *unity* of the book before us. The general and particular grounds for admitting this have been briefly stated; and we need not urge the proof of a proposition, which no good Hebrew scholar now ventures to call in question.

§ 4. *Diction of the Book.*

Long ago Luther remarked, that "this book has *singularem quandam phrasin, quae a communis linguae usu saepe recedit, et a nostrâ consuetudine valde aliena est.*" This is entirely correct and true, as to diction and peculiarity of phraseology. One reason doubtless is, that the book is of a different tenor from any other in the Old Testament. Where else is there a book of *philosophizing?* And would not this bring with it, of necessity, some new terminology and new words, just as it does with us? As to the younger books of the Old Testament (such as Dan., Ezra, Neh., Esth.), they have themes entirely discrepant from those in Coheleth, but still present many words belonging only to the later Hebrew, and therefore common to them and Coheleth. Many a phrase, however, in the latter, appears nowhere else; and many phrases and words here, which do appear elsewhere, have a sense different from that in other books.

The *formulas of phraseology* first claim our attention. Not a few of these take their rise from the course of thought and inquiry. A large portion of the book is occupied with giving the results of the author's own experience and trials. To designate this, he commences with פָּנִיתִי לִרְאוֹת, *I turned myself to see,* 2 : 11. But oftener still he says simply : רָאִיתִי, *I perceived,* 1 : 14; 3 : 10; 4 : 4; 5 : 12; 6 : 1; 7 : 15; 8 : 9, 10, 18; 9 : 13; 10 : 7. Again, he says : סַבּוֹתִי לָדַעַת, *I turned myself in order to know,* 7 : 25 ; 2 : 20. When he speaks of continued or repeated investigation, he varies the phraseology somewhat; as, שַׁבְתִּי וָאֶרְאֶה, *again I saw,* or, עוֹד רָאִיתִי, *I further considered,* 3 : 16 ; 4 : 1, 7 ; 9 : 11. With a slightly different meaning still, he says : נָתַתִּי אֶת־לִבִּי, *I directed* or *gave my mind,* viz. to the consideration of this or that, 9 : 1.

In order to designate the thoughts produced in his mind by experiment or reflective contemplation, he says : אָמַרְתִּי בְלִבִּי, *I said to myself* or *in my mind,* i. e. I thought, 3 : 17, 18 ; comp. 2 : 1 ; 8 : 14 ; 9 : 16. With the same meaning he employs דִּבַּרְתִּי עִם לִבִּי or בְלִבִּי; 1 : 16 ; 2 : 15. In expressing a definite sentiment, to which he had come by experience, he says : רָאִיתִי, *I saw,* 2 : 13, 24 ; 3 : 22 ; 5 : 17 ; 8 : 17. He also employs יָדַעְתִּי, *I knew,* 1 : 17 ; 2 : 24 ; 3 : 12, 14 ; and sometimes מָצָאתִי, *I found,* 7 : 27, 29 ; comp. 3 : 11 ; 7 : 14 ; 8 : 17.

Next as to the *objects of consideration or examination.* The generic phraseology (used as it were *adjectively*) for designating *sublunary, earthly, human things,* is that they are תַּחַת הַשָּׁמֶשׁ,

under the sun, 1 : 14; 2 : 11, 17, 18, 19, 20, 22; 3 : 16; 4 : 1, 3, 7, 15; 5 : 12, 17; 6 : 1, 12; 8 : 9, 15, 17; 9 : 3, 6, 9, 11, 13; 10 : 5. Sometimes, instead of this, we have תַּחַת הַשָּׁמַיִם, *under heaven,* 1 : 3; 3 : 1. Once more, simply עַל הָאָרֶץ, *on earth,* 8 : 14, 16. *Things* or *objects* themselves are called דָּבָר or דְּבָרִים, i. e. *thing* or *things* in the secondary sense of these words (see Lex.), 1 : 8, 10; 6 : 11; 7 : 8; 8 : 1, 3, 5. The meaning comprises both *actions* and *events.* When *events* are meant, the verb הָיָה is connected with דָּבָר, and then the phrase means *thing that has happened, occurred,* or *taken place,* 1 : 9; 3 : 22; 6 : 12; 8 : 7; 10 : 14; 11 : 2. When *actions* are spoken of, then the verb נַעֲשָׂה, *done, performed,* is employed; 1 : 9, 13, 14; 2 : 17; 4 : 3; 8 : 14, 16; 9 : 3, 6. The active form of the verb עָשָׂה is connected with the *agent who does,* 2 : 3; 3 : 9; 8 : 10. Hence the participial nouns, מַעֲשֶׂה, מַעֲשִׂים, are the predominant designations of *actions* themselves, 1 : 14; 2 : 17, 22; 3 : 17; 4 : 3, 4; 8 : 9, 14; 9 : 7, 10. But sometimes, in order to designate what we appropriately call *business,* the word חֵפֶץ is used, 3 : 1, 17; 5 : 7; 8 : 6. This seems to be of later usage, as employed in this sense. In a like sense is עִנְיָן employed, but it verges on the meaning of *disagreeable* or *unfortunate business,* as in 1 : 13; 2 : 23, 26; 3 : 10; 4 : 8; 5 : 2, 13; 8 : 16. More often occurs the word עָמָל, which properly means *toil, wearisome labor,* 1 : 3; 2 : 10, 11, 18, 20, 21, 22, 24; 3 : 13; 4 : 4, 6, 8; 5 : 14, 17, 18; 6 : 7; 8 : 15; 9 : 9. In like manner, the verb עָמַל and the participial עָמֵל are employed, meaning *to perform toil,* etc.

The *result* of toil and effort is sometimes called שָׂכָר, *reward* or *advantage,* 4 : 9; 9 : 5; at others, חֵלֶק, *portion, part,* as the result of labor, 2 : 10, 21; 3 : 22; 5 : 17, 18; 9 : 9; but finally, more often than any other word, does he employ יִתְרוֹן, *advantage, profit, avail,* 1 : 3; 2 : 11; 3 : 9; 5 : 8, 15; 10 : 10, 11. As to all efforts which fail to yield solid profit, he calls them רְעוּת רוּחַ, רְעִיוֹן רוּחַ, lit. *a windy affair,* i. e. a fruitless business.

The *destiny,* or *appointed lot,* of man he names מִקְרֶה, a deri-

vate of קָרָה, *to happen*, 2 : 14, 15 ; 3 : 19 ; 9 : 2, 3, 11. Sometimes he names it פֶּגַע, *occurrence*, 8 : 14. *Evil destiny* he calls
רָע, רָעָה, *evil, misfortune*, 2 : 21 ; 6 : 1 ; 8 : 6 ; 9 : 3 ; 10 : 5 ; 11 : 2,
10 ; 12 : 1. Sometimes it is רָעָה חוֹלָה, *a grievous evil*, 5 : 12, 15 ;
or חֳלִי רָע, of the same meaning, 6 : 2.

All the efforts and occurrences of life, taken together, he calls
הֶבֶל, when he characterizes them, i. e. *nothingness, vanity ;* and
this he does some twenty-five times in the book ; see on page 21
above. *Enjoyment* or *happiness* he now calls שִׂמְחָה, 2 : 1, 2, 10 ;
7 : 4 ; 8 : 15 ; and then טוֹב or טוֹבָה, 2 : 1, 24 ; 4 : 8 ; 5 : 10, 17 ;
6 : 3, 6 ; 7 : 14. *To enjoy good*, is רָאָה טוֹב, or טוֹבָה, or בְּטוֹב,
2 : 24 ; 3 : 13 ; 5 : 17 ; 2 : 1 ; 6 : 6. Once, עָשָׂה טוֹב, 3 : 12.

The word *wisdom*, חׇכְמָה, is sometimes equivalent to *intelligence, power of insight ;* e. g. 1 : 18 ; 7 : 23, 24 ; 8 : 17 ; in which
case it can hardly be distinguished from דַּעַת. But usually it
denotes *practical wisdom, sagacity, dexterity ;* as in 2 : 21, 26 ;
4 : 13 ; 7 : 19 ; 9 : 15, 16, 18 ; 10 : 1, 10. The *religious* use of it, as
in Psalms and Proverbs, is unfrequent and only indirect here.
The opposite of this is סִכְלוּת, סֶכֶל, i. e. *practical folly*, manifested
in a great variety of ways, and assuming a variety of forms.
For example : the *fool* exposes his folly, 10 : 3 ; knows not how
to demean himself in the relations of life, 6 : 8 ; undertakes
things in a wrong way, 2 : 13, 14 ; 10 : 2, 15 ; gives loose to
paroxysms of indignation, 7 : 9 ; blusters among fools, 9 : 17 ; is
given to prating, 10 : 14 ; utters language injurious to himself,
10 : 12 ; gives up himself to lawless pleasure, 2 : 3 ; 7 : 4, 5, 6 ;
brings himself into straits by idleness, 4 : 5 ; breaks his vows,
5 : 3 ; and the like. When *wisdom* has a relation to *moral* deport-
ment (7 : 16 ; 9 : 1 seq.), it of course resembles the *religious wisdom* (חׇכְמָה) of other books. It is so with the opposite word,
סִכְלוּת, i. e. this has sometimes the sense of *immorality ;* see 7 : 7,
17, 25. An equivalent of חׇכְמָה is חֶשְׁבּוֹן, *consideration, calcu-
lation*, 7 : 25 ; 9 : 10 ; and the opposite of this is הוֹלֵלוּת, 1 : 17 ;
2 : 12 ; 7 : 15 ; 9 : 3 ; 10 : 13. The phrases *to know* or *see wisdom*

7

and *folly*, mean *to understand* and *explain* them in their various
developments, 1 : 17 ; 2 : 12. But the phrase, *the heart sees wisdom*, means that it is itself cognizant of it, or experiences its
power.

 . *The work of God*, Coheleth designates in a variety of ways.
The omnipotent and immutable control of God is called מַעֲשֵׂה
הָאֱלֹהִים, *the work of God*, 7 : 13 ; 8 : 17 ; 11 : 5. When he controls the actions and destinies of men, it is said נָתַן אֱלֹהִים, i. e.
lit. *God gives, puts*, or *places*, 1 : 13 ; 2 : 26 ; 3 : 10 ; 5 : 17, 18 ;
6 : 2 ; 8 : 15 ; 9 : 9. His kindness is מַתַּת, the *gift* of God, 3 : 13 ;
5 : 18 ; comp. 2 : 24.

Many of the above words, and some of the phrases, are elsewhere used, but rarely in such a sense as here. The reader of
Hebrew in the other books, when he meets such phrases here,
feels himself to be treading on new ground. (1) New phraseology and new meanings of words arise from the novel subject
of which the writer is treating, i. e. his *philosophizing* on the
vanity of the world. He was at liberty, like all other writers,
to choose language adapted to his own purpose. We see in it
little indeed of *technicality ;* but still we perceive that we are by
no means reading the common Hebrew of the other books. But
it would be far from candor and fairness to accuse Coheleth of
unacquaintance with good Hebrew usage, because he feels himself constrained to employ terms and phrases not elsewhere to
be found. *Cuique suum.* It is his right to choose language
adapted to the nature of his discussion. But (2) There are
other peculiarities, which spring not of necessity from the nature
of the subject, but belong properly to the peculiar and characteristic style of the author. There is a *prolixity*, or *frequency of
repetition*, in a part of the phraseology, particularly such a part
as marks transitions of any kind. *I said in myself; I turned to
see ; I saw ; I knew ;* and the like, are repeated beyond any
example in the Scriptures ; and repeated where our present
method of writing would readily dispense with them. This is

often done, without any important addition to the general meaning; and is, therefore, indicative of peculiarity. Among these repetitions, however, we must not reckon those cases in which repetition is employed merely in order to make out *intensity* of expression; *e. g.*, 2 : 2, 6; 3 : 16; 4 : 1; 9 : 9, etc.

To this general category, moreover, in an enlarged sense, belong many *pleonasms* of expression, such as the following, viz. אֲנִי before verbs in the first person, in cases where no emphasis is required, as דִּבַּרְתִּי אֲנִי, אָמַרְתִּי אֲנִי, etc. See in 1 : 16; 2 : 1, 11, 12, 13, 14, 15, 18, 20, 24; 3 : 17, 18; 4 : 1, 4, 7; 5 : 17; 7 : 25; 8 : 15; 9 : 16, et al. *Pleonastic* are such expressions as הַיָּם אֵינֶנּוּ מָלֵא, "The sea, *it* is not full," 1 : 7; "To their posterity, *to them* shall be no remembrance," 1 : 11; "Woe to him, *to the one*," 4 : 10; "He shall take hold on him, *on the one*," 4 : 12. The like 3 : 18; 5 : 11, al. These, indeed, are proper Hebraisms; but their *frequency* here is what strikes us. The discrepancy between the *number* of the verb and its subject, in 2 : 7 and 10 : 15, al., is an unusual thing, although certainly not without parallel. In the hortatory and didactic parts of the book, repetitions like the above are unfrequent. Indeed, the conciseness and energy of expression there is like that in Proverbs and Job. See in chaps. vii., x.

Very frequent, unusually so, is the use of a verb and its conjugate noun; *e. g.*, עָמַל עָמָל, 1 : 3; 2 : 11, 18, 19, 20, 22; 5 : 17; 9 : 9. So עָשָׂה מַעֲשֶׂה, 1 : 14; 2 : 17; 3 : 11; 4 : 3; 8 : 9; קָרָה מִקְרֶה, 2 : 14; נָדַר נֶדֶר, 5 : 3; עָנָה עִנְיָן, 1 : 13; 3 : 10. This is genuine Hebraism, but it is unusually frequent here.

Another marked peculiarity here, like that in the Book of Daniel, is *the frequent use of the participle for the verb*, specially to designate present or continued action; as עֹשֶׂה, הֹלֵךְ, אֹהֵב, and the like, 1 : 4, 6, 7; 2 : 14, 19, 21; 3 : 20; 4 : 5; 5 : 7, 9; 6 : 12; 8 : 12, 14, 16; 9 : 5; 10 : 3, 19; 12 : 5, al. Often a *pronoun* is joined with such participles, thus making out a finite verb, as זוֹרֵחַ הוּא, מֹצֵא אֲנִי, etc.; as 1 : 5, 7; 3 : 21; 4 : 8; 7 : 26; 8 : 12;

9 : 10. The *participial* or *verbal adjective* performs the same office; as הוּא כָּמַל, etc., 2 : 18, 22 ; 3 : 9 ; 4 : 2, 8 ; 6 : 2 ; 9 : 9. A *negative* for any of these forms is made by אֵין with a suff. pronoun of the subject, *e. g.*, אֵינְךָ יוֹדֵעַ, *thou knowest not;* 1 : 7 ; 4 : 17 ; 5 : 11 ; 6 : 2 ; 8 : 7, 13, 16 ; 9 : 1, 2, 5, 16 ; 11 : 5, 6.

The use of יֵשׁ to indicate the simple *there is* (like the French *il y a*), is beyond precedent as to *frequency;* *e. g.*, 1 : 10 ; 2 : 13, 21 ; 4 : 8 ; 5 : 12 ; 6 : 1, 11 ; 7 : 15 ; 8 : 6, 14 ; 9 : 4 ; 10 : 5.

The *personal pronouns* are employed here with peculiar frequency in a sense which indicates that they include the verb הָיָה, *to be;* and often beyond example elsewhere as to frequency, they designate merely and simply *the verb of existence* itself; *e. g.*, זֶה חָדָשׁ הוּא, *this is new,* 1 : 10. The real shape of the Heb. is thus : *As to this, it is new;* and so in זֶה מַתַּת אֱלֹהִים הִיא, 5 : 18, et al. But in שֶׁהֶם בְּהֵמָה הֵמָּה, *that they are beasts*, we cannot well apply the same solution, for the last pronoun can be translated only by *are*, 3 : 18. And thus, in the one or the other of these ways, in 1 : 5, 7 ; 2 : 1, 23, 24 ; 3 : 13, 15, 22 ; 4 : 2, 4, 8 ; 5 : 5, 8, 17 ; 6 : 1, 2, 10 ; 7 : 2 ; 9 : 4, 13 ; 10 : 3, al.

The book never employs the common intensive מְאֹד, *very, very much*. Instead of this, it commonly and very frequently employs the Inf. of Hiph. הַרְבֵּה (lit. *multiplicando*), in the *adverbial* sense of *much, very much* (see Heb. Gramm. § 98. 2. *d*), as 1 : 16 ; 2 : 7 ; 5 : 6, 11, 16, 19 ; 6 : 11 ; 7 : 16, 17 ; 9 : 18 ; 11 : 8. In a like sense, the participial יוֹתֵר is employed, 2 : 15 ; 7 : 16. The opposite negative is אֵין מְאוּמָה, *not anything*, 5 : 13 ; 9 : 5.

The pronoun אֲשֶׁר, specially in its abridged form שֶׁ , is employed in a greater variety of ways than anywhere else in the Scriptures; *e. g.*, (1) *That, in order that;* 3 : 14 ; 6 : 10 ; 7 : 14 ; 8 : 12, 14 ; 9 : 1, 5. (2) *Because*, or *for that;* 4 : 3, 9 ; 6 : 12 ; 8 : 11, 12, 13, 15 ; 10 : 15. (3) *Provided that, if;* 8 : 12. (4) *When;* 8 : 16. So with prepositions before the pronoun; as בַּאֲשֶׁר or בְּשֶׁ , *because, on account of that,* 2 : 16 ; 3 : 9 ; 7 : 2 ; 8 : 4. So כַּאֲשֶׁר and כְּשֶׁ , *when;* 4 : 17 ; 5 : 3 ; 9 : 12 ; 10 : 3.

In like manner, מֵאֲשֶׁר and מִשּׁ, *than that, than;* 3 : 22 ; 5 : 4. Like to these are עַד אֲשֶׁר, *until that;* 2 : 3 ; מִבְּלִי אֲשֶׁר, *without which,* etc. This is explicable on the ground that אֲשֶׁר is a note of *relation* generally, and therefore may stand between sentences or clauses which stand related. With all this, the use of ὅτι in Hellenistic Greek may be well compared.

(3) Coheleth contains very much which belongs to the *later Hebrew*. From this are to be distinguished (if indeed we can make the distinction) the *Chaldaisms* of the book, or (to speak more generically) the *Aramaeisms*. The allegations often made in regard to these, and made even by such a critic as Knobel, are somewhat extravagant, and certainly in a measure ungrounded. Herzfeld has, with great acuteness, gone through the list of Knobel, and made much abatement from it. With him let us consider —

I. THE LATER HEBREW ELEMENT. Knobel attaches to this category the following words, which cannot properly be put there; and which, for convenience sake, may be divided into *two classes,* viz. : (*a*) Those which are also found in the old Hebrew, but which, as he says, have in Coheleth a *new sense attached to them;* viz., חֵפֶץ, *thing, affair,* 3 : 1, 17 ; 5 : 17 ; 8 : 6. But this sense is not new. In Prov. 31 : 13 is the same meaning. So מַלְאָךְ, *priest,* 5 : 5 ; but the word is everywhere used in the old Hebrew in a sense which well fits this passage, viz., *the messenger* of God who declares his word, and the meaning, *priest,* is not necessary in Coheleth ; and so too, in respect to this word, in Hag. 1 : 13 ; Mal. 2 : 7 ; 3 : 1. — מִקְרֶה (five times) means *destiny;* but the proper meaning of the word is *occurrence;* and in this sense we find it in Ruth 2 : 3. — עָמַד, *to rise up, to stand forth,* 8 : 3, he says is *new;* but the answer is, that the verb has not that sense here, for it means *to continue to stand, to persevere,* which meaning it has also in Josh. 10 : 13 ; 1 Sam. 20 : 38 ; Ezek. 21 : 35. — Again, כְּאֶחָד, *together,* 11 : 6 ; but we have the same word in the same sense, in Is. 65 : 25, which at all events is not written in the style of the later Hebrew — כָּל־עֻמַּת, *alto-gether as*, 5 : 15; but this is a form of *intensity* merely. The word עֻמַּת itself is, in the like sense as here, an ancient one, Ex. 25 : 27; 28 : 27. — מָכַךְ (יִמַּךְ in 10 : 18) is used in the same sense as the old word מוּךְ, *to rot, to moulder away;* but the exchange of forms in verbs *Ayin Vaf and Ayin doubled* is an old custom, extant in many verbs from the beginning of the written language. Moreover, in Job 24 : 24, is found the Hophal of this form, as is the Kal in Ps. 106 : 43. The *plur.* noun in 10 : 12, *i. e.*, שִׂפְרוֹת, instead of the *dual,* is no novelty, as Knobel alleges; see Ps. 45 : 3.

The numerous nouns in Ecc. which end in וּת–, Knobel sets to the account of the *younger Hebrew*, not venturing to call this *Chaldaism*, because the ancient Heb. has the same forms. The instances are שַׁחֲרוּת, רְעוּת, שִׂכְלוּת, סִכְלוּת, מַלְכוּת, יַלְדוּת, הֹלֵלוּת, שִׁפְלוּת. But abundance of the same forms are in the older Hebrew; *e. g.*, see Gen. 1 : 26; 38 : 14. Ex. 8 : 19; 11 : 2; 14 : 25; 28 : 22. Num. 24 : 7; 32 : 14. Deut. 24 : 1; 29 : 18. Ps. 22 : 20; 110 : 3. Prov. 3 : 8; 4 : 24; 9 : 13; 23 : 29; 27 : 4. Hos. 6 : 11. Amos 1 : 6. Is. 2 : 11; 12 : 5; 21 : 2; 21 : 4. Hab. 3 : 14, al. The only difference is in *frequency;* a thing which belongs to the *style* of the writer, and not to the species of the Hebrew.

As to nouns in וֹן–, and וֹן—, which he puts to the account of the younger Heb., they abound in the older. They are indeed unusually frequent in Ecc.; *e. g.*, עִנְיָן, בִּטָּחוֹן, זִכָּרוֹן, הֶסְרוֹן, יִתְרוֹן, חֶשְׁבּוֹן, כִּשָּׁרוֹן. But the same forms are found in Gen. 24 : 53; 38 : 11. Ex. 25 : 23. Lev. 1 : 2. Hos. 9 : 1. Gen. 3 : 16; 13 : 18; 33 : 2; 35 : 8; 38 : 17; 40 : 5, 17; 41 : 36; 42 : 19. Ex. 12 : 14; 15 : 7; 16 : 23; 21 : 30. Num. 21 : 20; 25 : 4. Deut. 8 : 15; 15 : 4; 28 : 22, 65; 32 : 10. Judg. 3 : 23; 8 : 21. Hos. 9 : 11. Is. 1 : 1; 8 : 1; 9 : 13; 22 : 13; 32 : 14; 25 : 5; 36 : 4; 47 : 9. Prov. 1 : 22; 15 : 11; 26 : 26. Ps. 32 : 4; 92 : 4; besides many proper names of this form, as עַמּוֹן, חֶשְׁבּוֹן,

חֶרְמוֹן, etc. And there are many such forms, besides those which are here produced.

If one will now call to mind how often *abstracts* are required in a treatise of *philosophy* like the present, he will think it nothing strange, and no special proof of later Hebrew, that such nouns are frequent in Coheleth. There are, however, only a few here that are not elsewhere found, viz., כִּשָׁרוֹן, יִתְרוֹן, חֶסְרוֹן, עִנְיָן, שִׁלְטוֹן, רְעוּת, רַעְיוֹן (as an abstract) חֶשְׁבּוֹן. The easy and obvious formation of these for the writer's purpose, renders it difficult for us to establish anything from them in regard to *the age* of such forms. The use of them depended, obviously and merely, on the need of them; for the form is altogether *normal* and *analogous*.

The same principle will apply to the frequent use of תַּחַת הַשֶּׁמֶשׁ and הַשָּׁמַיִם, scarcely found anywhere else. The great question in Ecc. is, the vanity of *earthly things.* An *adjective* from הָאָרֶץ the Heb. has not; and to make the so often necessary sense of *earthly*, the writer had to betake himself to circumlocution. But the Heb. itself, in both expressions, is *old;* and the meaning here is *not new*. The use belongs to the nature of the subject, and to the style of the writer, and is not to be ascribed to the later Hebrew.

The plur. גְּבֹהִים, for *the Most High*, in 5 : 7, is no indication, as is asserted, of later usage. We have קְדֹשִׁים for the *Most Holy*, in Hos. 12 : 1, and the like elsewhere. So חוּץ מִן, *without*, 2 : 25, does not therefore belong to the Rabbinic Hebrew (where it is common), because we find this compound form of the word nowhere else in the Heb. Scriptures. We have חוּץ לְ and מֵחוּץ in the old Heb.; and what hindered the use of חוּץ מִן? The *argumentum a silentio* proves little in such a case. And the like may be said of שַׁחֲרוּת in 11 : 10, which is employed in the Mishna, and put by Knobel to the account of *Rabbinism.* The word is truly poetical, normally formed, and beautifully applied.

Perhaps Coheleth himself first coined it. But it is so exactly

analogous to the multitude of the earlier Heb. words which have
the same form, that nothing can be argued from its use as to the
lateness of the book.

Knobel sets to the account of *later Hebrew* the usage of Ecc.
in rejecting the imperf. with *Vav consecutive* in narration, *e. g.*,
in chap. ii., which gives the history of Coheleth's experience.
So much is true, viz., that only the later Hebrew neglects this
usage; which (by the way) none of the other Semitic dialects
exhibit at all, except that the Arabic, in one case, only has some
approach to it in the shortened Future. But still, there is so
very little of *historical* narrative in the book, that much cannot be
made out of this. The Imperf. with Vav *consecutive* is altogether
appropriate to the *historical*, and not being needed here, it is not
employed. If the book were of a historical nature, then some
argument might be adduced from this peculiarity.

Knobel also insists that שֶׁ, so often used for אֲשֶׁר, is *Talmudic*.
But the *frequency* alone can be appealed to here; for the use of
this form (שֶׁ) is ancient; see Judg. 5 : 7; 6 : 17; 7 : 12; 8 : 26. Job
19 : 29. In Cant. (of uncertain age) it occurs 32 times; and in
the Psalms, 17 times. In the Talmud, it has almost expelled
אֲשֶׁר; but in Coheleth, it is used 68 times, and אֲשֶׁר 89 times.
We have better evidence still of its antiquity. Gesenius, in his
Monumenta Ling. Phoenic. (see Hal. Lit. Zeit. 1837, No. 81),
thus expresses himself: "The Phenician Remains are more kindred to the later than to the earlier Hebrew; *e. g.*, the *relative* is
always שֶׁ instead of אֲשֶׁר; *an important circumstance for the history of the Hebrew language.*" Truly it is so; for the Phenician
Remains can have come only from the *earlier* era of the language. I acknowledge that it is difficult, in reading Coheleth, to
avoid the feeling that we have a kind of *Rabbinic diction* in the
frequency with which we meet שֶׁ; and yet we see that in the
Phenician (a daughter of the *older* Hebrew) we have this
abridged form even to the entire exclusion of the other. In this
predicament we cannot make much out of this argument.

We have then, after having examined Knobel's list of the later Hebrew words, only a few remaining. Of those which will best bear the test, there remain יוֹתֵר in the sense of *more than ;* מַדָּע, 10 : 20, found elsewhere only in Dan. and Chron. ; בְּכֵן, 8 : 10, elsewhere only in Esth. 4 : 16 ; שֶׁל, 8 : 17, compounded of אֲשֶׁר־לְ, but even this is found only in Jonah 1 : 7, 12 ; אִלּוּ, 6 : 6. 4 : 10, a compound prep., like the later ones, elsewhere only in Esth. 7 : 4 ; and אַי, woe ! 4 : 10 ; 10 : 16, frequent in the Talmud only. To these, noticed by Knobel, some more are added by Herzfeld, viz., עָמַד לְ, 2 : 9, *to stand by* or *aid one ;* מְדִינָה, *province,* 2 : 8 ; elsewhere only in Lam., Daniel, Ezek., and Neh. ; כָּשֵׁר, 11 : 6, *to prosper,* instead of the earlier צָלַח, elsewhere only in Esth. 8 : 5. Perhaps the insertion of the pronoun אֲנִי after a verb in the 1st pers., and without any special emphasis, may be put to the *later* usage ; for this is rare in the earlier Hebrew.

As to רָאָה, followed by מִלִּפְנֵי (instead of מִפְּנֵי), in 4 : 10 ; 10 : 16, and put by Herzfeld himself to the later Hebrew, we find it in 1 Sam. 18 : 12 ; מִעֲטִים, 5 : 1, is also found in Ps. 109 : 8 ; נְכָסִים, *treasures,* 5 : 18 ; 6 : 2, is found in Josh. 22 : 8 ; and as to נַחַת in 6 : 5 ; 4 : 6, we have it in Is. 30 : 15. These must, therefore, be excepted from his list.

Taking the amount of what is left, we find only some 10 or 11 cases, which may fairly be brought within the confines of later Hebrew. And some doubt must even hang over these. It cannot for a moment be assumed that the present Hebrew Scriptures contain all the stores of the ancient language. Very many words it must have had which are not here employed, and many also it employed in different senses from those which are now to be found. Where the words are *normally* constructed, and where, following analogy, they might have been easily constructed and readily used in ancient times, although they do not now appear in the Hebrew Scriptures, we can hardly affirm with confidence that this word and that belong only to the later Hebrew. The case of שֶׁ for אֲשֶׁר in the Phenician (which is surely a dialect of the *old* Hebrew), is full of instruction and caution. The most that we can say is, that we find this word and that *only in the later Hebrew books.* Books of the same age have nearly the same idiom ; and from this general principle we may draw some conclusion as to the time when Coheleth was written.

II. THE CHALDEE ELEMENT. To this Knobel attributes זִיו, 12 : 3. But Hebrew derivates of this root are found in Is. 28 : 19 ; Hab. 2 : 7 ; so that the word must be Hebrew. Again, פֶּנַס, 2 : 8, 26 ; 3 : 5, is no Chaldee word ; for we have it in Is. 28 : 20 ; Ps. 33 : 7 ; 147 : 2. — כָּשֵׁר, 11 : 6 ; 10 : 10, is not Chaldee ; neither is כִּשְׁרוֹן ; for we have כְּשָׁרוֹת in Ps. 68 : 7, and כִּישׁוֹר in Prov. 31 : 19 ; שַׁלַּט 2 : 19 ; 5 : 18 ; 6 : 2 ; 8 : 9, is also Heb., as שַׁלִּיט, Gen. 42 : 6 shows. So יִתְרוֹן must be called Heb. ; for we have יוֹתֶרֶת in Est. 29 : 13. — מְדִינָה is of *late* use, but is not Chaldee ; see Lex. Also מִסְכֵּן, 4 : 13 ; 9 : 15, 16, is Heb. ; for we have Heb. forms from the root in Is. 40 : 20 ; Deut. 8 : 9. — נְכָסִים, 5 : 18 ; 6 : 2, is not Chaldee ; for we find it in Josh. 22 : 8. — סוֹף, 3 : 11 ; 7 : 2, is found also in Joel 2 : 20, which shows it to be Hebrew. It is difficult, moreover, to see why Knobel puts פַּרְדֵּס, 2 : 5, among the Chaldaisms ; for it is found in Cant. 2 : 5 ; and, at most, we cannot tell when this *foreign* word came into the Hebrew. It is probably of Sanscrit origin, which employs *paradesha* in a like sense. That רְעוּת רוּחַ and רַעְיוֹן רוּחַ may be Hebrew and not Chaldee, is shown by רְעֶה רוּחַ Hos. 12 : 2. In regard to the *Hebraicity* of תָּקַח and הִתְקִיף, 6 : 10, see Job 14 : 20 ; 15 : 24. For the *form* of the latter, see שַׁלִּיט in Gen. 42 : 6. That בְּכֵן, 8 : 10, is of later usage, is probable ; but there is no particular evidence of its being Chaldee. — מַה־שֶּׁ is as little Chaldee as מִי־אֲשֶׁר in Ex. 32 : 33. That סָכַן, 10 : 9, is Heb., see Job 22 : 22 ; 34 : 9. — עוֹלָם is Chaldee in 3 : 11, only in case we interpret it as meaning *world.* But as this exegesis will not bear, we strike it from the list. See the remarks on 3 : 11, in the Comm. That עָקַר, *uproot,* is not Chaldee, is shown by Zeph. 2 : 4.

As to forms: Knobel makes יְהוּא, 11 : 3; a *Chaldee* form ; but this would be יְחֵוֵא. It is an apoc. form, like יִשְׁתַּחוּ, and stands for יְחוּ with an א *otiant.* And so is א otiant in חוּא, הִיא, etc. With these forms the verb הָיָה stands connected. — הֵבֵל, 1 : 21, is const. of הָבֵל, and no more Chaldee than עֲרֵל which comes from עָרֵל, only it is a more normal const. form. — הָסוּרִים, 4 : 14, Knob. makes it to be Chaldaic, because he supposes it to be = הָאֲסוּרִים ; but this probably is not so (see Comm.) ; and even if it were, it would prove nothimg, for in many Hebrew words א is dropped in the writing. Finally, that עֲדֶנָּה and עֲדֶן, 4 : 2, 3, are Chaldee, is, as Herzfeld says, *an exegetical hieroglyph ;* for no proof is, or can be, adduced.

We come, then, to a small list of what may be called *probable Chaldaisms :* viz., כְּבָד, 1 : 10, al. saepe ; בָּטֵל for *cease,* 12 : 3 ; תָּקַן, 1 : 15 ; 7 : 13 ; 12 : 9, *to make straight ;* גּוּמָּץ, 10 : 8, *pit,* עֲבָד, 9 : 1, for מַעֲשֶׂה ; פִּתְגָּם, 8 : 11 ; זְמָן, 3 : 1, for עֵת ; and last, such Aramaean forms as מֹצָא, 7 : 26 ; רְשָׁעָא, 8 : 1 ; חֹטָא, 8 : 12 ; 9 : 18 ; מַרְפֵּא, 10 : 4 ; יֹצֵא, 10 : 5, are probably conformities to Chaldee in respect to their final vowel. — הוּשׁ, 2 : 25, and בּוּר, 9 : 1, are doubtful, and cannot be shown to be Chaldaic.

I may refer the reader here to what is said, at the close of the list, of *later Hebrew.* It is impossible to prove that more or less of this last class of words were not extant in the older Hebrew, or that they are not normal derivates of the Hebrew. But this last list of probable Chaldaisms is small, amounting to only some eight or ten words at most.

I am much indebted to Herzfeld for his labors on both parts of this list. He has pursued the examination with a diligence, a discrimination, and an accuracy, that are worthy of all commendation.

The general result is, that the book, for so short a one, partakes, after all, somewhat largely of the two elements of *later Hebrew* and *Chaldee,* at least of what we are forced to regard as such. That its style, and diction, and coloring throughout, re-

semble most of all the later books, viz., Ezra, Neh., Esth., and
Daniel, every reader familiar with these books must feel. That
he is moving in an element greatly diverse from that of the earlier Hebrew, becomes a matter of immediate consciousness,
when one reads Coheleth. This is, indeed, no objection to the
book; for the later Hebrew may convey truth as well and as intelligibly as the earlier. We need not call the dialect *Doric* or
Boeotian, much less *Yorkshire* or *Patois*. The laws of grammar
are, for the most part, strictly observed; the forms of the words
are normal; the tenses are not unskilfully used, but the contrary;
and as little anomaly is found, on the whole, as in most of the
later books. In the use of the particles there is great latitude,
specially in respect to וְ, כִּי, בְּ, לְ, and the conjunction אֲשֶׁר, (שֶׁ);
and in this respect the style resembles that of the other late
books. This of itself is an indication of an advanced state of
the language, which must always be changing.

Having been through the preceding investigations, in respect to
the nature, contents, design, form, style, and diction of the book,
we are now prepared to enter upon the next question, in which
many readers will feel a special interest; viz.,

§ 5. *Who was the Author?*

If this question be referred to the decision of past times, then
is it easily answered. One and all of the older writers declare
for *Solomon*. The tradition in the Talmud (Baba Bath. fol. 14,
15), that Hezekiah and his Society wrote (כָּתְבוּ, *wrote out,
copied*) Coheleth and some other books; or the saying of Rabbi
Gedaliah, that Isaiah *wrote* not only his own book, but Coheleth
and some others (Shalshel. Hakkab. fol. 66); make nothing
against the general position, because כָּתַב, as they employ it,
means merely *copied, wrote down*, or *wrote out*.

So far as I know, Grotius was the first, in modern times, who
raised a doubt as to the correctness of general tradition in regard

to the author of Ecclesiastes. In his Comm. he says : " Ego
tamen Salomonis esse non puto, sed scriptum serius sub illius
regis tanquam poenitentia ducti nomine." He then goes on to
adduce, as a reason for this opinion, that the book has many
words which can be found only in Daniel, Ezra, and the Chaldee
Targumists. Hermann Von der Hardt, in an Essay on Ecc.,
endeavored to sustain this view, by the like arguments. Against
him rose up Huet, Calov, Witsius, Carpzov, and Van der Palm.
So, also, most of the older critics, S. Schmidt, Geier, Le Clerc,
Rambach, J. D. Michaelis, L. Ewald, Schelling, etc. On the
other hand, Grotius found many ardent defenders ; such as Eichhorn, Schmidt, Döderlein, Bauer, Augusti, Bertholdt, Umbreit,
De Wette, Rosenmüller, Gesenius, Jahn, Ewald, Hitzig, Heiligstedt, and others. Of late, scarcely an advocate of the old
tradition has appeared. When we have reviewed the ground
occupied by the question, we shall perhaps deem it strange if any
future critic should engage in such an undertaking.

That the book purports, by its title, to be the words of Solomon, is plain. It begins thus : " *The words of Coheleth, the son
of David, king in Jerusalem.*" *King* belongs, here, to Coheleth,
as being in apposition with it, and not to David, which merely
connects with *son.* Now, no one of David's sons was *king in
Jerusalem* excepting *Solomon.* Coheleth, then, was *Solomon ;*
and Coheleth was *king.* So v. 12 : " I, Coheleth, was king over
Israel in Jerusalem." At the close of the book, Coheleth again
speaks of himself and his work. In 12 : 9 he says that he was
a חָכָם, *i. e.*, a *Hakim* or philosopher in the ethical sense, and
that "he sought out and arranged many מְשָׁלִים, which contained words of truth." But no reference is here made to his
kingly condition.

For the meaning of the word *Coheleth*, I must refer the reader
to the Comm. on 1 : 1, where it is sufficiently illustrated. Although fem. in *form*, it is masc. in sense, as the masc. verbs,
everywhere joined with it, sufficiently show. It is like our titles

of *excellency, majesty, grace, highness,* etc., when indicative of
office, honor, or station.   So *Kaliph* in Arabic is כַּלִיפַת, *i. e.,* it is
fem.; and the like is found in almost every language.   *Preacher,*
in the common sense of this English word, Coheleth was not;
for the name imports nothing more than that he addresses assembled men (possibly including the idea that he did it) in
the *hortative* strain; at least, this is very frequent in the book
before us.

Was it the design, then, of the writer of this book to declare
himself to be *King Solomon?*   Or does he introduce Solomon
purposely upon the stage as an agent, and give us what he might
well be supposed to say?   In other words: Is Solomon an *actor*
only in the book, or is he the real *author* of it?

Great difficulties lie in the way of the last assumption.   (1)
*Many things are said by Coheleth, which show that Solomon is
only occasionally, and not constantly, speaking.*   He says in 1 : 12,
that "he *was* king in *Jerusalem.*"   The Praeterite tense here
(הָיִיתִי *I was*) refers, of course, to a *past* time, and it conveys the
idea that, when the passage was written, he was no longer
king.[1]   But Solomon was king until his death, and could therefore never have said, "I *was* king, but am not now."   Then,

---

[1] A frequent secondary use of the Praeter tense of the Hebrew verb is to
"indicate a state of being which, beginning at some former period, still continues to exist at the time of narration."   See Nordheimer's Gram. § 764,
1 a, and references there; Stuart's Roediger, § 124. 3, and Comm. 3 : 15, and
6 : 10 below.   Compare, also, the use of this same form of the verb הָיָה in
Gen. 32 : 11.   Ex. 2 : 22; 18 : 3.   1 Sam. 29 : 8.   Jer. 2 : 31; 20 : 7; 23 : 9;
31 : 9.   Ps. 31 : 12, et. al. saep.   There should seem to be no objection, as far
as the language is concerned, to understanding the author here to mean, "I,
Coheleth, who hold the office of king over Israel in Jerusalem."   It is true
the verb might have been omitted, but is doubtless used for the sake of emphasis.   Without the verb מֶלֶךְ, *king* would have been a mere designation
of character or condition; but with it, emphasis is laid upon the fact that he
was in condition specially favorable for the investigations subsequently
designated. — *Ed.*

again, how passing strange for him, as Solomon, to tell those
whom he was addressing that he was *king in Jerusalem!* Could
he suppose that they needed to be informed of this? But a
writer in times long after Solomon might easily slide into the
expression that Coheleth *had been* king.

In 1 : 16 he says : " I acquired more wisdom than all who were
in Jerusalem before me." Doubtless, being a king, he compares
himself with others of the same rank, *i. e.*, with *kings ;* and how
many of these were in Jerusalem before Solomon? *One only*,
viz., David. Who, then, constitute the *all*? It is only a later
writer who would speak thus; and even such a one could so
speak only by omitting any special reference to the incongruity
seemingly apparent in the declaration as attributed to Solomon.
The sentence looks like that of some writer who lived after there
had been many kings at Jerusalem. Moreover, in the mouth of
Solomon himself, this would wear somewhat of the air of self-
magnifying ; while a later writer, who admired Solomon, would
naturally speak thus of him. In like manner, in 2 : 7, 9, he
speaks of surpassing, in various respects, " all who were in Jerusalem before him." But in the respects there named, only *kings*
could well be brought into comparison with him who was a great
king ; and therefore the same difficulty arises as before.

In 1 : 16; 2 : 9, 15, 19, he speaks of his *own wisdom ;* and in
this he tells us that he far exceeded all others. This was true,
indeed, of Solomon ; but it was hardly the dictate of *modest* wisdom to speak thus of himself. A later writer might well speak
thus of him, although there seems to be some little incongruity
in attributing the words to him.

If 4 : 8 could be shown to have a particular personal meaning,
and that the person in view was the writer of the book himself,
it would bring before us a striking incongruity. The case there
supposed is one where the individual has neither *son* nor *brother.*
Solomon had both. But my apprehension of that text is, that
the case in question is merely one *supposed,* for the sake of illus-

tration. But in 4 : 14 a case is stated, where it is difficult to avoid the conclusion that *Solomon* and *Jeroboam* are meant. In this case, if *Solomon* be the writer, then he speaks of himself as "an old and foolish king," while Jeroboam is "the wise and prosperous young man." This would sound very strangely in the mouth of Solomon.

In 8 : 3, an adviser is introduced, who counsels the prudent course of obeying the king in everything. This would not be strange for a king to say; but when one clause declares that the prudent individual "must not hesitate or delay even in respect to a *wicked command*," it would seem very singular to find Solomon thus characterizing his own commands. Then, again, when the writer gives his own view of this matter of unlimited obedience, in vs. 5, 6, he says, that such indiscriminate and blind obedience will incur the guilt of sin, and bring the inevitable judgment of God upon him who yields it; vs. 7, 8. All this is hardly congruous with *kingly* opinions.

In 5 : 7, the writer speaks of "the oppressing the poor, and robbing him of justice." In 3 : 16, he says that "in the place of judgment and justice was wickedness." In 4 : 1, he describes himself as a witness "of oppressions which were committed, and of the tears of the oppressed who had no comforter." In 7 : 7, he declares that "oppression is making even a wise man mad." In 7 : 10, he alludes to "former days which were better than the present." In the sequel (v. 15), he speaks of "the righteous man as perishing because of his righteousness, and the wicked man as prolonging his days by his wickedness." In 8 : 9, he speaks of "one man ruling over another to his injury." In 10 : 4, he describes rulers as being passionate and excessive in their anger. In 10 : 5—7, he describes the ruler as "setting fools on high, while the wealthy and princes occupy a low place, and act as servants of the fools." In 10 : 16—19, he covertly speaks of rulers as gluttons, drunkards, and sluggards; and even in *blessing* such kings as are of an opposite character, he says the same thing in the way of implication. Can we now, in any way, suppose all these to be the words of *Solomon*, describing himself as a haughty, violent, unjust, tyrannical, oppressor? Was he a glutton, a drunkard, and an idler — he who spake 3000 proverbs, wrote 1005 songs, and many treatises of botany, besides managing wisely all the affairs of his kingdom? 1 K. 4 : 32 seq. Did he permit the land to be full of oppressive magistrates, who caught at bribes, condemned the righteous, and acquitted the wicked? Was not the power in his own hands to remedy all this, and to do judgment and justice? And yet Coheleth says, in 4 : 2, 3, that death is preferable to life, under the then existing oppression. Yea, in his impatience, he even wishes he had never been born. And all this when, if Solomon be concerned in the matter, it was at any moment in his power to put a stop to the evils complained of! How is it possible to suppose that Solomon ascribes all this great wickedness and folly to himself? Let any one read the history of his enlightened and peaceful reign, as given in the books of Kings and Chronicles, and he will see a picture directly the opposite of all this. The matter of *Solomon's authorship*, in respect to such passages, seems quite impossible.

(2) *The general state and condition of things, when this book was written, indicates a period very different from that of Solomon's reign.* We must keep in view here what has already been said above respecting the *civil* condition of the kingdom, and the dreadful oppression, on the one hand, by which the righteous were persecuted and destroyed, and the favoritism, on the other, by which the wicked were exalted. This, of itself, is strong testimony against the *royal* authorship. But, beyond this, there was a general gloom that overspread all ranks and conditions in life. Wherever the writer turns his eyes, he sees little except vexation and disappointment and suffering. So deeply are all these things impressed on him, that even the joyous youth is cautioned by him not to rely for a moment on the endurance of

8*

any good. The writer is, indeed, very far, after all, from being
such a gloomy cynic. He has no malevolent or embittered
feeling. But he sees before him, on all sides, innumerable proofs
of the frailty, the vanity, and uncertainty of human life and
human endeavors; and also the utter impossibility of effecting
any substantial change for the better. He comes fully to the
conclusion, that "the day of one's death is better than the day
of his birth," 7 : 1. Does all this look like being written during
the peaceful, plentiful, joyful reign of Solomon? — such a reign
as the Hebrews never saw before or since ? To my mind this
seems almost impossible. Every writer is influenced by the
things around him, and the circumstances in which he is placed.
So far as we know from Old Testament history, the times here supposed and described belong not to the period of Solomon's reign.
It is true that this king, in his old age, was guilty of back-
sliding, and that he was chastised for it. But as to the state
of his kingdom in general, it seems to have been in a condition
directly opposite, in most respects, to that which has been
described above.

The passage in 4 : 17, speaks in such a way respecting temple-
offerings and services, as hardly accords with the views given in
1 K. 3 : 3 ; 4 : 15 ; 8 : 5, 62—64 ; 10 : 5 ; 11 : 7. I do not say
that Solomon had views in substance contrary to the spirit of
Ecc. 4 : 17, but that the methods of expression there adopted
seem foreign to the condition and circumstances of him who
had built the temple, and made magnificent preparations for
offerings.

The peculiar passage, in 7 : 26—28, respecting the extreme
baseness of women, seems hardly consonant with the views of
him who had 700 wives and 300 concubines, 1 K. 11 : 1—8 ; and
who was devoted, as it would seem, more than any other Jewish
king known to us, to amatory enjoyments. Another and later
writer, who looked attentively at the history of the close of Solomon's life, might well speak of such women as were in Solomon's

harem as he has done. Most of them were probably of heathen origin ; comp. vs. 2—5.

(3) *Another source of doubt as to the authorship of Solomon springs from the style and diction of the book.*

Whoever comes from an attentive, critical reading of the Book of Proverbs, written or compiled by Solomon for the most part, to that of Coheleth, will find himself in a region entirely new. William of Malmesbury is scarcely more diverse from Macaulay, or Chaucer from Pope, than Coheleth is from Proverbs. It ·is impossible to feel that one is in the hands of the same writer. The subjects are exceedingly diverse. In Proverbs, incontinence, falsehood, lying, deceiving, marriage, parents and children, education, neatness, industry, thrift, and the like, are the subjects treated of ; in Coheleth, the vanity of all things, the nothingness of human ends and aims, the oppression of wicked rulers, and the like, are the theme throughout. Of all these, there is scarcely anything in the Book of Proverbs. However, this would not prove much, if it stood alone ; for the same writer might change his theme. But when we come to *the coloring of the style and diction*, it is impossible to make out anything but the widest diversity.

We have seen above how much of the *later Hebrew* and of *Chaldaism* there is in Coheleth. But where are these to be found, in any such measure, in the Book of Proverbs ? Nowhere. Here is the *golden* Hebrew of the golden age. But in the dark and distressing times of Coheleth, the Hebrew idiom, or at least the *diction* and *style*, had greatly changed. A mere English reader can, indeed, see but little of this ; for all the ingredients are melted down together in an *English* crucible. But the very first paragraph in Coheleth tells a Hebrew reader that he has come to a new and different region. This is a thing, however, which can only be *felt* by a reader familiar with the Hebrew, and therefore one of which an adequate description cannot well be given.

When we are gravely told that this change of style is to be
ascribed to *Solomon's* intercourse with foreign women, we may
rather smile than feel compelled to argue.   Would Solomon, in
his old age, be likely to change his mother-tongue ?   Had he
respect enough for his women to become a learner of foreign languages from them ?   Would a mere momentary, casual intercourse
with them, such as his was, produce such an influence on his
idiom ?   And then, who can tell whether the idiom of any of
these women resembled that of Coheleth ?   Last of all, Would
the Spirit of inspiration move Solomon to write in the idiom of
his heathen concubines, who were unlawfully selected ?   See Ex.
34 : 15, 16.   In whatever way we look at this matter, it is
vanity of vanities.

At all events, the *Book of Proverbs* is opposed to ascribing
Coheleth to Solomon.   There brevity, precision, compactness,
and energy of expression, predominate.   But, if we except the
few aphorisms in Coheleth, and the precepts here and there
given, the mode of representation is the reverse of this.   Not
that there is not an energy running through the whole composition of the latter, but that the repetitious phrases are very numerous, and the style here and there expansive or diluted.   What
most of all distinguishes Coheleth from Proverbs is, that the former repeats, beyond all example in the Scriptures, certain
phrases entirely *sui generis,* which never occur at all in the Book
of Proverbs.   Such are *under the sun, under heaven, I turned
to see, I said in my heart,* and the like.   If Solomon wrote Coheleth, how could such favorite expressions, everywhere introduced
in this book, have never appeared at all in Proverbs ?   No efforts
can remove, or even diminish, these palpable discrepancies in regard to style and manner between the two books.   There is
more diversity than exists between Isaiah and Malachi, or
between the narrations in Genesis and those in the Chronicles.
Conciliation of *manner* is indeed out of the question.

Thus far, then, we have made, as it would seem, but little

progress towards discovering the author of the book. If our mode of reasoning and drawing conclusions be valid, we have thus far only come to the decision that *Solomon was not the author*. *Who*, then, was he, and *when* did he live?

According to Hermann Von der Hardt, he was a man by the name of *Jesus*, the third son of the high-priest Jehoiadah, who lived under the reign of Artaxerxes Long., Xerxes II., and Darius Nothus (464—404 B. C.). If we ask for proof of this, none is or can be produced. Proof was not necessary to Von der Hardt, and he deals very little in it. Kaiser makes Zerubbabel, famous in the annals of the exiled and returning Jews, the author; and even Grotius intimates that 'the collection of the miscellanies [?] in the book was made by the scribes, under his order;' — all, again, without any proof.

As the real author has told us, at the close, that he was a חָכָם, (*i. e.*, in modern Arabic, a *Hakim*, or *Ulema*), a μάγος, 12 : 9, who collected and compared, and arranged מְשָׁלִים, and has spoken of himself only by an *official* designation, viz., *Coheleth*, we find nothing in the book that leads to the individual and proper name of the writer. We may give up, then, our pursuit after this, and must try to content ourselves, in this particular case, with the simple verdict of *ignoramus*.

The *times* in which the author lived are the only thing now left by which we may find some traces of him. The nature of these has been amply described above. They were times of kingly government; of great oppression by all classes of the magistracy ; of luxury, extravagance, idleness, and debauchery among the upper classes ; of persecution in respect to the righteous, and of promotion and prosperity in regard to the wicked ; times in which the poor and the just were reduced to despair, so that life became a burden ; times in which a whisper against the tyrants of the land was followed by severe penalties : and, in a word, days of darkness, even of thick and impenetrable gloom, so that to go to the house of mourning was preferable to attendance on a feast,

because of the feeling that the dead had escaped from the miseries of the living. So much lies on the face of the book, and is
interwoven with its very texture. But when was there such
times in Judea? We might be inclined to answer: 'Under Manasseh, who reigned fifty-five years, who became a heathen, and
filled Jerusalem with innocent blood, 2 K. xxi. All the evils
just mentioned doubtless may have existed under him.'—But
still it would be utterly unaccountable that not a word should be
said about idolatry, or concerning martyrdom. Possibly, however,
such a passage as 7 : 15 might occupy the ground of the latter.
But, inasmuch as no reference is made to the interruption of Le-
vitical rites and temple-worship, but, on the contrary, they are
spoken of as being an ordinary thing (4 : 17 seq.), it is difficult
to suppose 'the writer (whose object it is to bring together the
various vanities of human life as then exhibited) could have
passed through his whole work without making any complaint
of such things. The moderated tone in which the author speaks
of *ritual worship,* seems to indicate a period in which the religious Jews had fallen off from the earlier and ardent attachment
to rites and sacrifices. The spirit of the day, when Malachi
wrote his book, will help us to understand this; for, so far had it
gone from high regard to the externals of worship, that the
prophet felt moved to rebuke the Jews for "robbing God of his
offerings," Mal. 3 : 8 seq. Such is the natural effect of a seventy
years' exile, when ritual and temple worship was suspended.
Still, so long as the Mosaic Law was acknowledged as the constitution of the state, something must be done in this way, and it
should be done with decorum; and Malachi finds it to be a matter
of reproof that the returned Jews neglected their duty in this
respect. His design, however, is consistent with such a spirit as
Coheleth shows; for the latter calls neither offerings nor vows, as
such, in question, but cautions against a slight, superficial, merely
external, and hypocritical performance of such duties. He has,
evidently, an enlightened view of the *spirituality* necessary to an

acceptable performance of them. But this, of itself, will not decide for us the question, *When* did he live and write? For some Jews in every age, as we may well suppose, cherished similar sentiments.

But if we go down lower than the time of Manasseh, we find, indeed, tyrannical kings, and a distracted state of the commonwealth ; but still we find these kings, in all probability, in the practice of heathen and idolatrous rites, for it is said of both Jehoiakim and Zedekiah, that " they did evil in the sight of the Lord," which more usually designates the practice of idolatry, as employed in the Book of Kings. After this there was no indigenous king in Judea until the time of the Hasmonean family, or the age of Judas Maccabaeus. If the book was written after the exile, it must have been under the reign of the *Persian* kings, and before the Greek kings of Egypt or of Syria had dominion over Palestine. Oppression under these last-named kings did not take place seriously until about the time when Antiochus Epiphanes came on the stage of action, *i. e.*, 175 B. c. *Oppression* under the Persian kings might have happened, and did sometimes happen ; see Ezra 3 : 5 ; 4 : 1—24. Neh. 6 : 5—19, especially Neh. 9 : 37. After Ezra came to Palestine (about 457 B. c.), the Jews were generally, but not always (see texts just cited), on a good footing with the Persian kings, so far as the sacred history carries us, *i. e.*, down to some 434 B. c. It would, on the whole, seem most probable that between the first return of the Jews from exile (535 B. c.), down to the time of Ezra (about 80 years afterward), is the period most likely to exhibit the phenomena which we have brought to view above. The neighbors of the Jews gave them much trouble, often misrepresented them to the kings of Persia, and occasioned them many grievances. The governors of Judea were probably corrupt men, under those Persian kings who troubled the Jews ; and a state of things such as the book before us brings to view might easily have existed through their management. Persia, moreover, never

worshipped idols. And this may be the reason why Coheleth
never speaks of *idolatry* as the vice of either kings or nobles.

The only difficulty in the case seems to be, that the king
appears to be spoken of as if he were a proper Jewish king,
belonging to the country. But still the lines are not drawn
strictly here. The fact that *the province* (הַמְּדִינָה with the
article) is spoken of in 5 : 7, favors the period of Persian domi-
nation at the time when the book was written; for Judea was
plainly a *province* of the Persian empire. The Jews belonged
to Cyrus, by virtue of his conquest of Babylonia, where they
then lived. They were afterwards treated as a *province* by the
Persian kings, as the books of Ezra and Nehemiah abundantly
testify. The difficulty in carrying out a scheme of proof, lies in
the want of more minute historical documents respecting the
period in question. We have only a short passage in Ezra
which specially refers to this period, and this is occupied mainly
with civil troubles and embarrassments. We can argue, therefore, only from analogy drawn from other periods. And this
will easily serve to convince us that matters may have then been
in the dismal state which Coheleth so vividly describes. The
assertion by some critics, that Ecc. was written at the Macca-
baean period, is altogether destitute of probability. It must
needs have taken its hue from those bitter and bloody times, and
have administered severe rebuke to the blood-thirsty Syrian
tyrant who was desolating the country by his persecution and
his massacres. Besides, it is made quite clear by Josephus
(Cont. Ap. i. 8) that no book was introduced into the Jewish
Canon after the reign of Artaxerxes, the son of Xerxes I. Coheleth, therefore, could not have been written so late.

Several critics speak of the lateness of the period as necessarily connected with the knowledge of Grecian philosophy,
which, as they think, the book evinces. But Knobel himself
confesses (and so Hitzig) that there is not a tint of Greek
philosophy in the whole book ; and nothing can be plainer than

this. We are then under no necessity of placing the composition of the book at a period subsequent to the conquest of Alexander the Great, and the introduction of Greek learning into the East. The book is *through and through of Hebrew spirit*, and is indeed nothing but Hebrew. But it is not the work of a stickler for rites and offerings; for it exhibits enlightened and spiritual views in regard to this subject.

I have given the sum of what can be alleged, both in favor of a later period of writing, and against *the personal authorship* of Solomon. But whoever the writer was, *he unquestionably introduces Solomon into his book*, as speaking many things there suggested. Chap. ii., in particular, comes under this category; and it can hardly be made to apply to any other Jewish king than Solomon. Not unfrequently, however, the writer speaks of kings *as a third person* would speak who was a mere spectator of their demeanor, and not himself the subject of what is said. We have seen how strangely many passages concerning rulers and oppression would sound in the mouth of Solomon himself. It is against all critcal probability, therefore, that Solomon was the author. But the writer has shown us no other metes and bounds to separate what he says himself from what Solomon is represented as saying, excepting what the matter spoken supplies. Nor is it important that he should do this; for it is he who really speaks in both cases, but in one of them he speaks through the medium of a supposed and apparently different person. He gives Solomon's experience; and, in giving it, he figuratively introduces Solomon as himself relating it. This belongs merely to *the form*, and not to the substance of the book. No one can justly take offence at this. Why may not the author do so, as well as Solomon could introduce Wisdom as speaking in her own person? Prov. viii. The apocryphal book, the Wisdom of Solomon, doubtless in imitation of Coheleth's example, introduces Solomon as speaking throughout; see chap. 7 : 1, seq. In other words, wisdom is *personified* in Solomon. And although we can-

9

not, with Ewald and Hitzig, admit such a personification here, (see p. 41, above), yet the general principle, in respect to *manner*, is the same in Coheleth as in the other books just named. In Proverbs, Wisdom itself is personified simply; in the Book of Wisdom, Solomon is her representative and personification; while in Coheleth, Solomon is introduced, not as wisdom, but as relating his own experience in a variety of things, and among these, in his search after wisdom. The writer has chosen to introduce him as saying this and that, because Solomon was specially qualified to say it.

I cannot see, then, any need of introducing, as Augusti does, Solomon's *ghost* as the speaker. On this I have already made remarks in the preceding pages. The Hebrews did not deal in ghosts, much less set them to carry on dialogues with the living. There is no intimation of anything of this nature in the book itself. It is not a part of Hebrew *machinery*.

There are several reasons why the author should introduce Solomon so often as speaker in his book. (1) As the great theme of the book is the *vanity* of all earthly things, even in their best estate, no person could be introduced whose experience in regard to all that could adorn life and render it happy was so signally marked as that of Solomon. If the world could not make him happy, then it could promise happiness to no one else. Chap. ii. gives a vivid description of Solomon's experience, and pronounces the general sentence upon it. (2) No topic is so frequently introduced into the book as that of *wisdom*. Solomon's experience in respect to this was beyond that of any other man. Hence the appropriateness of introducing him to speak concerning it. Whoever will attentively peruse 1 K. 2 : 6 ; 3 : 12, 28 ; 4 : 29—34 ; 11 : 41 ; 10:23, 24, will see the ground of Solomon's high and lasting reputation for *wisdom*. The son of Sirach, 47 : 14—19, has shown how this matter stood in his time ; and Matt. 12 : 42, Luke 11 : 31, advert to the same matter as it stood during the first century of the Christian era.

These considerations are sufficient to vindicate the author of Coheleth for introducing another personage than himself, viz., Solomon. And all that has been said above, as it seems to me, is sufficient to show that the person introduced is merely an *agent in the writer's hands*, and not one who simply acts for himself. But be this as it may, it will alter neither the design nor the general meaning of the book before us. It is not a question *de re ipsa*, but only one *de modo in quo*.

§ 6. *Credit and general History of the Book.*

It cannot seem strange, to any reflecting mind, that a book replete with so many things, which at first view seem to be paradoxical, or skeptical, or in opposition to sound morals, should have excited in some minds suspicions of its orthodoxy and divine authority. If it be read, as most readers in ancient times seem to have read it, as containing nothing but the sentiments of Solomon himself, it is indeed a task more difficult than that which Oedipus had to perform in solving the riddle of the Sphinx, to make out such a solution of some parts of the book as will cause them to speak *orthodoxy*.

The author of the Book of Wisdom seems to have felt the difficulties presented by Ecclesiastes. In 2 : 1—9 he has exhibited what looks like a series of quotations and abridged views of parts of Coheleth; and this series he prefaces by saying: "They say to themselves who speak *not rightly;*" after which follow the apparent citations just referred to. When these are ended he makes a few additions of the like tenor, and then winds up with saying: "Thus they reason, and are deceived; their evil disposition has blinded them, and they know not the mysteries of God, neither do they hope for reward of holiness, nor regard the reward of spotless souls;" Wisd. 1 : 21, 22. But to understand this matter fully, the reader must compare the following passages:

Wisdom, Chap. ii.

(v. 1) comp. *Ecc.* 2 : 23, 3 ; 5 : 17 ; 6 : 12 ; 8 : 8 ; 3 : 22.
  (2) " 9 : 11 ; 3 : 2 ; 9 : 4, 5, 6, comp. 3 : 18—21.
  (3) " 3 : 20 ; 12 : 7.
  (4) " 1 : 11 ; 2 : 16 ; 9 : 5, comp. 4 : 16.
  (5) " 6 : 12 ; 11 : 8 ; 9 : 10 ; 12 : 5 ; 3 : 22.
  (6) " 3 : 12 ; 6 : 9 ; 11 : 9, comp. 3 : 22 ; 5 : 17 ; 9 : 7—
       9 ; 11 : 8.
  (7) " 9 : 8.
  (8) " id.
  (9) " 3 : 22 ; 5 : 17, 18 ; 8 : 15 ; 9 : 9.

At first view, it would seem as if there could not be much doubt whether the book of Coheleth is cited in Wisdom. From what the writer says, immediately before and after the apparent citations, it is plain that he sets himself in array against the sentiments contained in them. But, even supposing them to be actual citations, a question still would arise here, viz., Whether he is opposing *Coheleth*, or the *wrong use* of Coheleth? Perhaps we cannot answer this question with entire certainty. But the high respect which the author of Wisdom shows for the law of the Lord, his precepts, and the religious fear of him, indicates a great regard for religion, and of course for the Scriptures ; and beyond all doubt Coheleth was attached to the Hebrew Scriptures long before his time. That he should array himself against the book itself, then, is very improbable ; and at all events, it is without any parallel in any other Jewish apocryphal writer. The Jewish tone of those days is very far from anything which would look like abating from the high claims of the sacred books. For these reasons, I must believe that the author of Wisdom, if he has quoted Ecc., is describing the mal-practice of those who deduced such doctrines as he mentions from the book in question, instead of reading and interpreting it according to its true design and intention. In speaking thus, the implication is that he understood the *objectionable passages* as coming from an *objector*. Others, supposing them to exhibit Solomon's true views, appealed to them as good authority for skepticism and sensuality; and these he designs to reprove. But as we do not know the degree of light which the writer of the Book of Wisdom had respecting the nature of Coheleth, we cannot decide with entire certainty whether he speaks in opposition to the book or to the abuse of it. The latter is, at all events, by far the most probable supposition in respect to a high-minded and orthodox Jew.

A *minute* inspection, however, and a comparison of the passages referred to above, will, after all, suggest doubts whether the author of Wisdom meant to *quote* Coheleth. There are several turns of expression which seem to come from Ecc., for they spontaneously remind the reader of expressions in that book. But there are others which are quite unlike to Ecc.; and these are sufficiently numerous to raise some doubt. Hitzig rejects the idea; Knobel strives to vindicate it at length, Einl. § 10. What the latter quotes as citations is comprised in 2 : 2—9, as exhibited above. Then follow 11 vs. of his own language; and it is only in vs. 21, 22, that we find a condemning sentence passed. Now, if vs. 1—9 contained what he aimed to oppose and condemn, we should expect the condemning sentence to be produced in v. 10, instead of v. 21. As the text now stands, it looks as if the author regarded the whole of 2 : 1—22 as the expression of his own language, although it hardly admits of a doubt that his expressions were *modified* by the reading of Ecclesiastes. The fact that no other Heb. writer of that day, and long afterwards, ever opposes any part of the O. Test., makes against the views of Knobel, and in favor of the sentiment of Hitzig.

The Talmud seems to intimate that some Jewish teachers were at that time seeking to show that Ecc. was a book which did not spring from divine inspiration. In Tract. Shabb. fol. 30, col. 2, it is said: "The learned ⌐the חֲכָמִים] sought to *lay aside* (לִגְנוֹז

9*

lit. *to hide*) the book Coheleth, because the declarations thereof
contradict each other." In Pesich. Rab. fol. 33, col. 1, in Vay-
yiqra Rabba, fol. 161, col. 2, and in Midr. Kohel. fol. 311, col. 1,
it is said: " The learned sought to lay aside the book Coheleth,
because they found therein words leaning to the side of the here-
tics." In Midr. Kohel. fol. 114, col. 1, a different reason is
given, viz.: " Because all the wisdom of Solomon consists at
last in this: Rejoice, O young man, in thy youth, etc.; which is
at variance with Num. 15 : 39." Jerome relates like things of
the Hebrews of his day. According to him they say: " Among
other writings of Solomon, which have become antiquated, and
the memory of them lost, this book deserves to be obliterated,
because it asserts that all the creatures of God are vain, and regards them as nothing, and it gives the preference to eating and
drinking, and other transitory pleasures," Comm. in Ecc. 2 : 13.
He himself pronounces the book to be one of authority, and
worthy to be numbered with the divine books, because it ends
with the conclusion that " We should fear God, and keep his
commandments," ib. In Midr. Kohel. and Tract. Shabb., as
above cited, the writers subjoin to what is there quoted: " And
why did they not lay it aside? Because at the beginning are
words of the law, and at the end are words of the law." Not a
bad reason, so far as it goes; but it cannot go far, for a book
might have *words of the Law* at the beginning and end, without
having any claim to be a divine book.

Spinoza (Tract. theol. pol., p. 15, 27) says of Solomon, that
" he excelled others in wisdom, but not in the prophetic gift;"
and he blames him, because he has taught that " everything is
vain."

All this amounts indeed to very little. We know from Sirach,
Philo, Josephus, and the early Christian writers, that Coheleth
belonged to the Jewish Scriptures in their times, *i. e.*, both before
and after the birth of Christ. It is critically certain that it was
included in the Scriptures sanctioned as divine by Christ and the

apostles. But as I have fully discussed this subject in my little work on the Canon of the O. Test., I need not repeat the discussion here.

It is true, indeed, that none of the N. Test. writers have quoted it; but equally true as to several other books whose *canonicity* cannot be questioned. The *argumentum a silentio*, we may again say, is of no value here. 'They did not cite it, because they did not need to cite it for their purpose,' — is a sufficient answer.

In like manner Christians of the earliest ages do not cite it, and for a like reason. At a later period, Gregory Nyss., Jerome, Olympiodorus, and Oecumenius, wrote Commentaries on Coheleth. Philastrius of Brescia (†387), and Theodore of Mopsuestia (†429), regarded it as savoring of Epicureanism, and as uninspired. But the Council of Constantinople (A. D. 553), at which 165 bishops were present, anathematized this position. Abul Pharagius, the Jacobite Maffrian (†1286), maintained that the book agrees with Empedocles, viz., that it declares there is no future state of existence.

The book remained without being seriously assailed, after the decision at Constantinople, until a period subsequent to the Reformation. The older commentators among the Reformers maintained the position, that it was written by Solomon, and they regarded all its words as indicative of his opinions, and did the best they could to reconcile them with each other, and with the rest of the Scriptures. If the subject were not of so grave a nature, many of their efforts at interpretation would provoke the smile of the interpreter at the present day. It is, indeed, a difficult task to make such passages as 4 : 19—21 speak *orthodoxy*.

Le Clerc threw out hints, calling in question the inspiration and authority of the book. He was answered by Witsius, Carpzov, and others. On the same side with the latter were S. Schmidt, Geier, Rambach, and many others. In recent times the book has undergone every kind of accusation and contumely.

Eichhorn, and even Jahn and Stäudlin, Augusti, De Wette, and others, accuse it now of immorality, of skepticism, and of Epicureanism, then of gloomy views, of contradictions, and the like. Knobel accuses it of *fatalism* and *skepticism*, as does Hitzig also ; but both allow that the book makes mention of many things which are not to be taken as the settled opinions of the author. Yet even these two last-named critics do not appear to have sufficiently considered the whole *plan* and *modus* of the book, as to its presenting doubts and difficulties, and then sooner or later solving them. If the author is allowed to be a man of acute and discerning mind (and most will allow this), then the supposition that all parts of the book, even those which contradict each other, are to be regarded as each giving alike the author's own views, is little short of an absurdity. No man of sense would contradict himself so often, within such narrow limits.

It is hardly necessary to give the recent history of the views respecting Coheleth, which have been entertained by many critics ; since their opinions have been sufficiently stated in the preceding pages. One thing undoubtedly is true, viz., that many Christians, and even many preachers of the gospel, seldom resort to this book for instruction, with the exception of a few favorite apothegms and sententious declarations. There are things in the book which seem to them plain ; and these they quote with the more pleasure, because they are so pointed and full of meaning. But in many parts of the book they fail entirely in discovering any thread of discourse, or the specific object which the writer has in view. The consequence is, that they look on the book much as they do on the Book of Proverbs. I mean that they regard it as having about as little of unity and connection as the latter book. When the author speaks of ' dead flies as causing the ointment of the apothecary to become offensive in smell ;' or when he speaks of 'a dulled tool which must be swung the harder in order to make it cut ;' they wonder what bearing this can have on the subject of religion, or even on the general theme of worldly *vanity*. And certainly this perplexity is not to be wondered at, considering the nature, plan, and course of thought in the book. It requires long and diligent study to discover all its bearings, after they have so long been overlooked, and nearly the whole of commentary has betaken itself to mere *moralizing* on some of the leading apothegms. A folio of *preachment* on Ecc. is rather a formidable affair to readers who have but little time at command. What they really want, is to get at the *thoughts of the writer*, and not merely to know what others have thought and said on certain ethical topics presented by him. Hence not a few of the folios which have been written, disappoint their hopes. More than most readers want, in respect to the views and reasonings of *commentators*, they can easily find; but of the *difficulties* in the text itself, whether of language or sentiment, they are still obliged to forego the solution.

Could the book be placed in its true light before the public mind, it would aid very much in restoring to it the usefulness which it is adapted to subserve. At all events, many of the difficulties would be removed which now embarrass and hedge up the way of the inquirer, and especially of the common reader. The writer of the following commentary would fain indulge the hope, that more satisfactory views of the book may be disclosed by the efforts which he has made to explain it. At least the student of *Hebrew* has a claim to expect that something more may be done to aid him than will be found in the great mass of even the recent commentators.

§ 7. *Ancient Versions of Coheleth.*

(I.) THE SEPTUAGINT. The most ancient version of the whole Hebrew Scriptures, of which we have any knowledge, is that of the *Septuagint*. That this work, as a whole, was made by different hands, is quite evident, from the variety of diction and style of translating in different books. Aristobulus says,

that the whole of the Hebrew Scriptures were translated during
the reign of Ptolemy Lagi and Ptolemy Philadelphus, his son
(323—246 B. C.); quoted in De Wette, Einleit. § 40, n. e. But
whether for the purposes of augmenting the far-famed Alexan-
drian Library, or to meet the religious wants of the Jews, is a
question not entirely settled. I see no difficulty in combining
both reasons. The two first Ptolemies treated the Jews with
great favor, and drew multitudes of them to Alexandria. They
might have procured the Sept. version to be made, as a designed
favor towards them.

Very diverse is the genius of translation in different books, as
I have intimated above. But this diversity could as well be
exhibited during the seventy-seven years of the reign of the two
Ptolemies, as in a longer and later period. If any one would
obtain full conviction of the discrepancies of the Greek, in
various books of the Sept., let him read Job and Proverbs, and
then come to the reading of Coheleth. Job and Prov., being
translated by a reader of the classics, afford evidence that the
author strove to exhibit classical Greek; especially in the Prov.
does he do this, even at the expense, not unfrequently, of the
meaning of the Hebrew. By his transpositions, his large additions, and his subtractions also, he has made the book quite
another thing than the original. But in Ecc., there is next to
nothing of all this; nor is there any aim at classic style. As a
whole, the version must be pronounced faithful, and in this respect, successful. There is a *literality* of translating, which
sometimes surprises, and sometimes (I had almost said) amuses
us. For example, the translation not unfrequently renders the
אֶת־, which marks the Acc. in Heb., by σύν in Greek, even when
the noun connected with אֶת is put in the Acc.; e. g., *I hated*,
אֶת־הַחַיִּים, is translated by ἐμίσησα σ ὺ ν τὴν ζωήν, 2 : 17; and
so in 3 : 17 bis.; 4 : 3; 7 : 30; 8 : 8, 15, 17; 9 : 15; 11 : 7;
12 : 9. Yet in other cases, the writer appears plainly to understand the true meaning of אֶת־, as marking the Acc. and being

equivalent to a demonstrative. But one would come to erroneous conclusions respecting the translator's Greek, should he judge of it by such a barbarism. The simple truth is, that, in his rigid effort to be as literal as possible, he has admitted σύν as a translation of אֶת־, because this word not unfrequently means *with* = σύν. He aimed to give what he thought to be the very shape of the Hebrew, even at the expense of grammatical propriety in Greek.

Servile imitations of the Hebrew double pronoun, *i. e.*, אֲשֶׁר־ with a subsequent pronoun, may be seen in 4 : 9, οἷς ἐστὶν αὐτοῖς μισθός. So in 6 : 2. But this is less frequent here than in some other books. In other cases, there is a servile literality in deference to etymology, without due regard to usage and proper sense ; *e. g.*, עַל דִּבְרַת, *on account of,* Sept. περὶ λαλιᾶς, making דִּבְרַת = דָּבָר, 3 : 18 ; 7 : 15. So in 8 : 9, בְּאָדָם, [*rule*] *over man,* Sept. ἐν ἀνθρώπῳ, ἐν being inapposite here, but still it gives the literal sense of בְּ. So 6 : 6, פַּעֲמַיִם, *twice,* Sept. καθοδόυς, *vices,* *i. e.*, *turns* or *returns,* which, although singular Greek here, still does not spoil the sense ; 10 : 17, בִּגְבוּרָה, *on account of strength,* Sept. ἐν δυνάμει, which gives an erroneous sense in this place, although literal. Instances not unfrequently occur, where what is *often repeated* or *habitually done,* is, according to the genius of the Heb. verb, expressed by the Greek Future, instead of the *Present. E. g.*, 10 : 6, יֵשְׁבוּ, *sit,* Sept. καθήσονται, *Fut.,* while it should be κάθηνται. So 11 : 5 ; 10 : 12 ; 10 : 4, al.

In not a few cases, the Heb. words were read by the translator by supplying vowels differing from those now employed, and in such a way as to make it plain that his copy had no *written* vowels ; *e. g.* סָכָל הוּא, *he is a fool,* Sept. ἀφροσύνη ἐστιν, *i. e.,* the translator read סֵכֶל הוּא, 10 : 3 ; so מִגָּבֹהַּ יִירָאוּ, *they are afraid of what is high,* Sept. εἰς τὸ ὕψος ὄψονται, *they shall see,* etc., *i. e.,* they read יִרְאוּ from רָאָה, 12 : 5. In the passage 12 : 9, is a peculiar example of this sort, viz., וְאִזֵּן וְחִקֵּר תִּקֵּן מְשָׁלִים הַרְבֵּה, *he weighed, and sought out, and arranged many apothegms,* Sept.

καὶ οὖς ἐξιχνιάσεται κόσμιον παραβολῶν, *i. e.*, *the ear searches out an orderly array of parables*, where the text must of course have been read וְאֹזֶן יַחְקֹר תַּכֵּן מְשָׁלִים, while תַּרְבָּה is joined by the translator to the following verse. In 2 : 12, הַמֶּלֶךְ, *the King*, is rendered τῆς βουλῆς, *i. e.*, it was read הַמְּלַךְ, which, as in Chaldee, probably meant *counsel*. In 10 : 4, ἴαμα is an example of the literal sense of מַרְפֵּא instead of the tropical one, viz., *gentleness*. In 10 : 17, we have οὐκ αἰσχυνθήσονται for the Heb. לֹא בַשֵּׁתִי, *not on account of drunkenness;* where, of course, the translator must have read לֹא בֹשֶׁת, *no shame*. Instead of simply saying, with the Heb. thus pointed, *no shame*, the Sept. now says : *They will not be ashamed.*

In other cases mistakes were made by *a wrong reading of consonants*. In 5 : 16, he renders רֹאכַל, *shall eat*, by ἐν πένθει, in mourning; *i. e.*, he read וְאָבֵל, putting ב for כ. In 6 : 12 (Sept. 7 : 1) for כַּצֵּל, *as a shadow*, he has ἐν σκιᾷ, exchanging consonants as before. In 8 : 6, for רָעַת, *evil*, was read דַּעַת. In 8 : 10, וְיִשְׁתַּכְּחוּ, *they were forgotten*, was read וְיִשְׁתַּבְּחוּ, and then translated by ἐπῃνέθεσαν, *they were praised*, by the same error of reading ב for כ. In 7 : 12 (Sept. 7 : 13), בַּצֵּל was again read כַּצֵּל, and translated ὡς σκία.

It seems, then, quite clear that the translator not only had no written vowels to guide him, but that the consonants ב and כ were often carelessly written, so that the distinction between them could be made only with difficulty. A fact like this shows, also, that the Hebrew alphabet must have then had the same *forms* of letters which it now exhibits.

In a few cases, *words in the text are overlooked; e. g.*, 3 : 20, הַכֹּל הוֹלֵךְ, which is translated only by τὰ πάντα. In 5 : 12, רָעָה is omitted. In 8 : 9, עֵת אֲשֶׁר is either omitted, or else read as כָּל אֲשֶׁר and translated τὰ ὅσα, *inasmuch as.* If there be any more omissions, they have escaped a careful perusal. These make quite an insignificant number.

ADDITIONS, however, amount to more than omissions. Yet

few are of any considerable importance. In 4 : 2, *all* is added to *the dead;* in 4 : 17, merely *thy* after *sacrifice;* in 5 : 1, *above* after *heaven;* in 7 : 15, *lo!* before the third clause; 7 : 22 (Hebr. 7 : 21), for *they say,* we have the phrase, *the ungodly say;* in 7 : 23 (Heb. 7 : 22), πλειστάκις πονερεύσεταί σε has no corresponding original; and in the next clause, רָלֵעַ was read for יָדַע ; in 7 : 27 (Heb. 7 : 26), καὶ ἐρῶ is not in the Heb.; the last clause of 8 : 17 is very paraphrastic, corresponding only in a remote way with the Heb. in 9 : 1; in 9 : 2, καὶ τῷ κακῷ is added after the Heb. טוֹב, apparently with good reason, if analogy in the rest of the verse be regarded; in 10 : 1, in the second clause, the sense is strangely missed, by rendering it τίμιον ὀλίγον σοφίας ὑπὲρ δόξαν ἀφροσύνης μεγάλην; 10 : 19, after יַיִן the Sept. has added καὶ ἔλαιον, and afterwards inserted ταπεινώσει; and in 11 : 9, the Greek says: "Walk in the way of thy heart *blameless* (ἄμωμος), and *not* by the sight of thine eyes;" the words *italicised* not being found in the Hebrew. It is evidently a loose paraphrase of the Hebrew, designed to save the credit of Coheleth's orthodoxy. In 2 : 15, διότι ὁ ἄφρων ἐκ περισσεύματος λαλεῖ is added to the text.

These are nearly all the *additions* made to the text, in the translation before us. They constitute but a small list, considering the length of the book; and they are of very little importance in a doctrinal point of view. Doubtless the translator, although he follows the Hebrew so closely in his version, did not feel himself bound to say, in all cases, exactly what the Hebrew says, and no more. Still, he would have done better to stick closely to his text; for his additions do not help the sense of the Hebrew, nor enable us better to understand it.

In some cases we find MISTAKES in the Greek version. In 3 : 16, we have εὐσεβής where we should have ἀσεβής (probably, however, a mere error of some transcriber); 4 : 1 is συκοφαντίας, *false accusations,* for הָעֲשׁוּקִים ; 4 : 4, ἀνδρίαν for כִּשְׁרוֹן ; 5 : 5, ἵνα μή for לָמָּה ; 5 : 6 he renders : *In the multitude of dreams, and of vanities, and of many words,* mistaking the relation of the

10

last two nouns. To save detail, I refer the reader to 1 : 17, 18 ; 2 : 12, 20, 25 ; 5 : 9, 10 ; 7 : 8, 13, 15, 17, 26 ; 10 : 19 ; 12 : 5, 11. This last-cited passage (12 : 11) is worth inserting, for its version of perhaps the most difficult passage in the whole book. It runs thus : λόγοι σοφῶν ὡς τὰ βούκεντρα, καὶ ὡς ἧλοι πεφυτευμένοι, οἳ παρὰ τῶν συνθημάτων ἐδόθησαν ἐκ ποιμένος ἑνός, i. e., "The words of the wise are as goads, and as nails driven in, which are given from the collections by one shepherd ;" almost as rendered by Hitzig, and with only a shade of difference from the version which I have given to it in the Commentary. One cannot well see why such strange translations should have been made of this verse, either in earlier or later times, with this model before the writers. The παρὰ συνθημάτων gives us a hint of the true sense of בַּעֲלֵי אֲסֻפּוֹת, the possessors of collections, and παρά here marks merely the relation of source, while σύνθημα means lit. things put together. The translator failed to discern that these Hebrew words are in the Nom., and constitute the subject of the second clause. See Commentary.

Besides this, there are other fortunate renderings. For example, in 5 : 8, Καὶ περίσσεια γῆς ἐπὶ παντί ἐστι, βασιλεὺς τοῦ ἀγροῦ εἰργασμένου, exactly true to the original, and quite plain, although endlessly varied in modern times. So the last clause of 5 : 19, ὁ Θεὸς περισπᾷ αὐτὸν ἐν εὐφροσύνῃ καρδίας αὐτοῦ. Here περισπᾷ means to divert one's attention from a thing, and so to divert it, in this case, from brooding over afflictions in past times. This is accomplished by the joyful state of mind now conferred. The Heb. מַעֲנֶה has more usually been rendered here by humble or afflict, while it means in reality, in the case before us, causes to answer or correspond with. In another way than by a literal rendering, the Sept. has hit upon the kernel of the thought, and very expressively given it. These may serve as specimens. To save room, I must merely refer the reader to other more or less happy renderings of difficult and controverted passages ; e. g., 6 : 3 ; 7 : 25 ; 10 : 10 (singularly curious, but not correct) ; 10 : 11 ; 12 : 11, which is given in full above.

On the whole, this version should be a *Vade mecum* with the student of this book. Even where he does not get light from it, he will feel an interest in it, and will be led to inquire *how* and *why* the writer departed from the apparent meaning of the Hebrew; and such inquiries will lead him to a more minute study of the Hebrew. The literal nature of the version in general is an admirable pledge for the correctness of the present Hebrew text, as compared with what it was in the time of the translator.

(II.) THE VULGATE. This is so commonly known, and so easy of access, that much need not be said here respecting it. Jerome, as every one will see who reads his work, translated from the original Hebrew. This he did, after having spent some twenty years in Palestine, in order to learn it thoroughly. He accomplished his object, beyond what we should have deemed possible, under his disadvantages. There were then no grammars, no lexicons, no commentaries, extant to guide him, unless we name the scanty remarks of Origen on the Hebrew a help of importance; which would surely be overrating them. But he had the Rabbies of Tiberias to give him instruction, among whom the Masora, if not the Talmud, was already concocting. It is plain that they possessed a good traditional knowledge of the Hebrew.

In translating Coheleth, Jerome doubtless made use of the same Sept. version that has been characterized above. His translation, rigidly as he professes to follow the Hebrew, has, on the whole, quite as many deviations from a literal rendering as the Septuagint. *E. g.*, the very difficult passage in 3 : 11, he renders thus: " Cuncta fecit bona in tempore suo, et mundum tradidit disputationi eorum, ut non inveniat homo opus quod, etc." How he disposed of בְּלִבָּם, to make *disputationi eorum* of it, one cannot well see. Rather better has he hit the spirit of 5 : 8 : " Et insuper universae terrae rex imperat servienti;" still, it is scarcely possible here to show how he disposed of the original Hebrew words, in order to make out such a version. The disputed 3 : 21, הָעֹלָה הִיא etc., he renders *interrogatively :* " Quis

novit si spiritus, etc.,;" as also the Sept. does. The controverted
8 : 10 he renders: "Vidi impios sepultos, qui etiam cum adhuc
viverent, in loco sancto erant, et laudabantur in civitate quasi
justorum operum." Nothing is plainer than that he did not understand the Hebrew here; or, at all events, it is clear that he
has not given us a picture which nearly resembles the original.
The very difficult 12 : 11, he has, by the aid of the Sept., hit
much nearer: "Verba sapientium sicut stimuli, et quasi clavi in
altum defixi, quae per magistrorum consilium data sunt a pastore
uno."

In general, as we might expect, Jerome follows closely the
Hebrew, and shows himself to be familiar with the idiom of the
book. But where one comes to a serious critical difficulty, which
nothing but a nicer knowledge of *formal* grammar and of syntax
will solve, he may usually expect to find Jerome halting. About
the same dependence can be placed on him as on the Sept.; and
neither of them will satisfy, in all respects, the present demands
of criticism. But still the Vulgate is well worth consulting; especially as showing the actual acquisitions of one of the Christian fathers in the Hebrew; and as the product of the only real
and thorough Hebrew scholar among them.

(III.) THE SYRIAC VERSION, OR PESHITO. This is, in
respect to time, the next after that of the Septuagint. This was
doubtless made directly from the Hebrew, because this language
was more easily understood by a Syrian than the Greek. Jerome
appears to have had no knowledge of this version; although he
might have been aided by it in a number of respects. But there
is no good evidence that he drew from it. In some cases, where
Jerome has a *peculiar* rendering, the like may be found in the
Syriac; which looks as if the former drew from the latter. But
here again we may without much difficulty suppose, if possible,
that Jerome of himself hit upon the same mode of paraphrasing
a difficult passage which the Syriac translator had adopted.

That the Syriac Peshito was made in the second century,

seems, from the recent investigations, highly probable. The name itself (ܦܫܝܛܐ *Peshito*) signifies *simple;* and it seems plainly to have been given to the translation as a simple and literal version, in opposition to, and distinction from, all paraphrastic and allegorical versions, for example such as the Targum below. Ephrem Syrus (flour. 350), who wrote Commentaries in Syriac during the fourth century, speaks of the Peshito as being *our translation* (Poc. ad Joelem, fol. 2): and he undertakes to explain a number of Syriac words in the version as being already *antiquated*, and unknown to common readers. *Tradition* among the Syrians goes back even to the apostle Thaddeus and king Abgarus of Edessa, as causing the translation to be made (Wiseman, Hor. Syr. p. 103). It is not contented even with this, but assigns the translation of a part of the Old Test. to the age of Hiram, king of Tyre, who, as it says, requested and obtained a translation of some books from Solomon (Wisem. ut sup. p. 97). At all events, considering how early Christianity was introduced into Syria, and how learning flourished at Edessa, we shall not be in danger of erring much if we assign the version before us to the second century, and perhaps even to the middle or earlier half of it.

Be this, however, as it may, nothing is more plain and certain than that the translation was made directly from the Hebrew. Jews in great numbers, who had been driven out of Palestine, had emigrated to Syria, and lived there, at the period in question. A *Christian* Jew was the probable author of the translation; for the manner of handling the Messianic passages shows clearly his *Christian* predilections. Whatever resemblances may be found in it to some peculiarities of the Sept., it is plain that they come from later interpolations, made with the design of conforming it to the Septuagint.

The following testimony of Hävernick respecting this version seems to me to be quite correct: "Among all the known ancient versions, no one attaches itself so faithfully to the original as the

10*

Peshito. Usually, it gives the sense of the ground-text very happily; and even where it indulges in explanation, it limits itself merely to what is necessary, and shuns all paraphrastic prolixity" (Einl. s. 95). The translator (doubtless of Jewish origin) stood in the same relation to the Hebrew as did the Sept. translators. But the former had one advantage over the latter, viz., that the idiom into which he translated was altogether a twin sister of the Hebrew, while the Greek was sufficiently remote from it. Hence the Syriac translator could give, and has given, a more exact picture of the Hebrew than the Sept. presents. The chief reason why appeal has not oftener been made to it in Old Test. commentaries, seems to have been a want of familiarity with it, and a want of knowledge as to its real worth.

(IV.) THE ARABIC VERSION, which appears in Walton's Polyglot, was partly made from the original Hebrew, and partly, as it would seem, from the Septuagint. So far as it respects Coheleth, it is by no means an unskilful version. It keeps close to the text, and indulges in no prolix or conjectural explanations, like to those of the Targum and the Midrashic commentaries. But the difficulty of reading it, and indeed of getting access to it, is such, that but little use has hitherto been made of it. *When,* and *by whom,* it was made, is unknown. So much seems probable, viz., that it was made by an Arabian Jew, who was probably a Christian.

(V.) THE TARGUM. Not long before the Christian era, most of the Hebrew Scriptures were translated into the *Chaldee* language, for the use of those who could not readily understand the original Hebrew. After the return from the Babylonish exile, the Jewish people in general spoke the *Chaldee,* which they had learned during the long period of their captivity. The Pentateuch was translated into this language by Onkelos; the historical and prophetical books by Jonathan ben Uzziel, who probably preceded Onkelos in respect to time; and here the work of translation, for a considerable period, ceased. At a later period, the books of Job, Psalms, and Proverbs, and finally, with the exception of Ezra, Nehemiah, and Daniel, all the rest of the Hagiography were translated or paraphrased into Chaldee. Ezra and Nehemiah were anciently counted as one book ; and, since a part of this composite book, and nearly half of Daniel, were originally written in *Chaldee*, no attempt has ever been made, so far as I know, to give the whole book a Chaldee translation.

The books of Ruth, Cant., and Ecc., were translated, as it would seem, last of all; but exactly *when*, or *by whom*, is not known. Since, however, in Cant., the Targums, and probably the Mohammedans are mentioned (Cant. 1 : 2 ; 5 : 11—6 : 7), it would seem that the version of the three books last named was *post-Talmudic.*

The internal evidence of *late* composition is made out, (1) From the kind of idiom (Chaldaeo-Rabbinic) which pervades them. (2) From the fashion of the *commentary* (as it might be called), or paraphrase, which shows that the *Midrash* (מִדְרָשׁ) or *allegorical commentary* had already been fully adopted (see Buxt. Lex. Chald. on the word). As we have scarcely any specimen of this kind of paraphrase or commentary which is accessible in English books, and as it is a matter of some interest that every Hebrew student should know what kind of a version or commentary he will find in a work written after the manner of a *Midrash*, I shall here lay before him a specimen (rather a prominent one) from the Targum, on Ecc. ii. The large type represents a close translation of the original Hebrew ; that which follows, in each case, in smaller letters, gives the Targum, which is as literally translated as the two idioms will bear.

ECC. II.

(1) I said in my heart : Come, now, let me try thee with pleasure, and do thou enjoy good ; and lo! even this is vanity.

I said in my heart: Come hither now, and I will try thee with pleasure ; and when distress and affliction came upon me, I said, by his word, Lo ! this also is vanity.

(2) In respect to laughter, I said: Madness! And in respect to pleasure: What avails it?

In respect to laughter, I said, in a season of distress: It is mockery! And in respect to pleasure : Of what use is it to the man who procures it ?

(3) I sought in my mind to draw my flesh by wine, and my mind continued to guide with sagacity; and also to lay hold upon folly; until I should see what is good for the sons of men, which they should do during the number of the days of their lives.

I sought in my mind to protract in the banqueting-house of wine my flesh, and my heart guided with wisdom ; and also to lay hold on the folly of the young, until I should try and see what there is of them which is good for the sons of men, which they may procure while they abide in this world under heaven, during the number of the days of their lives.

(4) I engaged in great undertakings; I built for myself houses, and planted for myself vineyards.

I multiplied goodly works in Jerusalem ; I built for myself houses ; the house of the sanctuary to make atonement for Israel ; and the house of re- freshment for the king ; the council-chamber, and the porch, and the house of judgment with hewn stones, where the wise men sat who exercised judg- ment ; I made a throne of ivory for the seat of royalty ; I made plantations for myself in Jabne for the sake of grape-vines, that we might drink wine, myself and the masters of the Sanhedrim and also make libations of wine new and old upon the altar.

(5) I made for myself gardens and pleasure-grounds; and I planted in them fruit-trees of every kind.

I made for myself watered gardens and pleasure-grounds ; and I sowed there all kinds of herbs, some of them for the use of food, and some of them for the use of drink, and some of them for a medicinal use, every kind of aro- matic herb ; I planted in them sterile trees, and all kinds of aromatic trees which the sprites and demons brought to me from India, and every kind of tree which produces fruit : and its boundary was from the wall of the city which is in Jerusalem to the margin of the waters of Siloah.

(6) I made for myself pools of water, for watering from them the forest shooting up trees.

I sought out a receptacle of water, such as is needful to water trees and herbs ; and I made for myself pools of water, from them also to water the grove producing wood.

(7) I procured servants and handmaids, and those born in the house belonged to me ; much property also in flocks and herds belonged to me, more than to all who were in Jerusalem before me.

I procured servants and handmaids, who were of the children of Ham and other foreign nations ; and stewards, appointed over the feeding of my household, belonged to me, for the nourishing of me and the men of my house, twelve months of the year : and one for nourishing me during the intercalary month ; moreover, I possessed cattle and sheep, more than all the dwellers who were before me in Jerusalem.

(8) I heaped up for myself silver and gold, and the treasures of kings and provinces ; I procured for myself singing-men and singing-women, and the delight of the sons of men, a wife and wives.

I heaped up for myself treasures of silver and fine gold, that I might make the weights and balances of justice out of pure gold ; and the treasures of kings and provinces were given to me for tribute ; I made in the house of the sanctuary instruments of music, that the Levites might make music with them, while presenting oblations ; and harps and pipes, that the singing men and women might make music with them in the banquet-house ; and the delights of the sons of men, warm baths and baths with tubes which poured forth tepid water, and pipes which poured forth hot water.

(9) And I waxed great and increased more than all who were before me in Jerusalem ; my wisdom also continued with me.

And I increased goods and added riches, above all the dwellers who were before me in Jerusalem ; my wisdom, however, remained with me and helped me.

(10) And all which my eyes sought for, I withheld not from them ; I kept not back my heart from any joy ; for my heart was cheered by all my toil, and this was my portion of all my toil.

And as to all which the masters of the Sanhedrim requested of me, in respect to purifying and polluting, to justifying and condemning — I kept not back from the explanation of things, I restrained not my heart from every joy of the Law; for I had an inclination of heart to rejoice in the wisdom, which had been given to me from God more than to all other men; and I rejoiced, and this was the goodly portion which was assigned to me, to receive on account of it a perfect reward in the world to come for all my toil.

(11) Then I turned towards all the works which my hands had performed, and towards the toil which I had labored to accomplish, and lo ! all was vanity and fruitless effort, and there is no profit under the sun.

Then I considered all the works which my hands had accomplished, and the toil which I had labored to accomplish ; and lo ! all was vanity and crushing of spirit ; for there is no profit in them under the sun, in this world, but there is a perfect reward for good works in the world to come.

(12) Then I turned to contemplate wisdom, even madness and folly ; for what shall the man [do,] who comes after the king? Even that which he did long ago.

Then I gave attention in order to see wisdom, and the commotions of the kingdom, and understanding ; for of what use is it to a man to make supplication after the decree of the king, and after retribution ? See ! long ago was the decision made respecting him, and it was done for him.

(13) I saw, moreover, that there is a preference of wisdom over folly, like the preference of light over darkness.

I saw, moreover, by the spirit of prophecy, that there is a preference of wisdom over folly, more than the preference of the light of day over the darkness of the night.

(14) The eyes of the wise man are in his head, but the fool walketh in darkness ; yet still I know, even I, that one destiny awaits them all.

The wise man sees in the beginning what will come to pass at the end ; and he prays and averts the decree of evil from the world ; but the fool walketh in darkness ; and I also know, even I, that if the wise man does not pray, and avert the decree of evil from the world, when retribution shall come upon the world, one destiny shall overtake all of them.

(15) Then I said in my heart: As is the destiny of the fool, so also will it happen to myself; and why then should I be overmuch wise? Then said I in my heart: This also is vanity.

Then I said in my heart, as is the destiny of Saul the son of Kish (the king who perversely revolted, and kept not the command which he had received concerning Amalek, and the kingdom was taken from him), so will it happen to me, and why then am I thus wise more than he? Then I said in my heart, that this truly is vanity, and there is nothing except the decree of the word of Jehovah.

(16) For to the wise man, with the fool, there is no remembrance forever ; because that long ago (in days which are to come) every one will have been forgotten. And — how dieth the wise man like the fool!

For there is no remembrance to the wise, with the fool, in the world to come ; and after the death of a man, that which was long ago in his time (when the days shall come which will be after him), even all will be discovered. Then why do the sons of men say that the end of the righteous is like the end of the wicked ?

(17) Then I hated life ; for the deeds that are done under the sun were odious to me ; for all is vanity and worthless effort.

Then I hated all of saddening life, because evil is upon me, even the evil work which is done against the sons of men under heaven, in this world ; because all is vanity and crushing of spirit.

(18) Yea, I hated all the toil which I had performed under the sun, because I must leave it to the man who shall come after me.

Yea, I hated all the toil which I had performed under the sun, in this world, because I must leave it to Rehoboam, my son, who will come after me ; and Jeroboam, his servant will come, and will take out of his hands the ten tribes, and possess half of the kingdom.

(19) And who knoweth whether he will be a wise man or a fool? And yet he will have power over all my toil which I have performed, and on which I have exercised my sagacity under the sun. This too is vanity.

And who knoweth whether he will be a wise man or a fool, viz., the king who will come after me? And yet he will have power over all the toil that I have performed in this world, and over all which I have acquired by my sagacity under the sun, in this world. And I was confounded in my mind, and I said again : This too is vanity.

(20) Then I turned to make my heart despair in respect to all the toil which I had performed under the sun.

Then I turned to make my heart despair respecting the toil to acquire, which I had performed under the sun; and because that I had been sagacious to make preparation under the sun, in this world.

(21) For there is a man who has toiled with sagacity, and with intelligence, and with dexterity, and to a man who has never toiled for it, must he leave his portion : This too is vanity, and a sore evil.

For there is a man who has toiled with wisdom, and with intelligence, and with justice, and he dieth without children; and to the man who has not toiled for it, must he give it to be his portion : This is vanity and a great evil.

(22) For what is there for a man in all his toil and strenuous efforts of his heart, which he has performed under the sun?

For what is there useful to a man, as to his toil and the worrying of his heart, which he has toiled for under the sun, in the present world?

(23) For all his days are grievous, and his employment harassing ; even by night his heart is not quiet.

For all his days are grievous, and his business makes vehement his indignation; even by night he sleeps not, because of the solicitude of his heart. Truly this is vanity!

(24) There is nothing better for a man than that he should eat and drink, and enjoy good in his toil ; even this I have seen to be from the hand of God.

There is nothing which is comely for man, except that he eat and drink and make his soul to enjoy good before the sons of men, that he may perform the commandments, and walk in the ways which are right before him, that it may be well with him on account of his toil; yea, this have I seen, that when a man prospers in this world, it is from the hand of God that this is decreed to be unto him.

(25) For who can eat, and who can enjoy himself more than I?

For who is he that will bestow labor on the matters of the Law, and who is the man that has solicitude concerning the great day of judgment which is to come, more than I?

(26) For to the man who is well-pleasing in his sight, hath he given sagacity, intelligence, and enjoyment ; but to the sinner hath he given the task of gathering and amassing, that it may be given to him who is well-pleasing in the sight of God. This is vanity and fruitless effort.

But to the man whose works are upright before Jehovah, hath he given wisdom and knowledge in this world, and joy with the righteous in the world which is to come; but to the man who is a sinner hath he given a grievous task, to amass riches, and to heap up many possessions, that they may be taken from him, and given to the man who is well-pleasing in the sight of God ; surely this is vanity to the sinner, and a crushing of his spirit !

From even a slight comparison of the Talmudic version with the original Heb., it is evident that the translator meant to act the *paraphrast* or *commentator*, as well as the Targumist. most of the additions consist of minute specifications of particulars, *e. g.*, as in v. 4, the simple word בָּתִּים, *houses*, and again, in v. 5, the words *gardens* and *pleasure-grounds*, are expanded into long detail derived from history or tradition. Besides this, many clauses are added throughout, for the sake of explanation, and sometimes to guard the reader against assigning to a word or a phrase a wrong sense. Thus, after the declaration of the text in v. 11, that *there is no profit under* the sun, the Targumist adds : *but there is a perfect reward for my works in the world to come.* This is a specimen of the *Hineinexegesiren* or *interpreting into the text*, rather than showing what the text of itself means. But this is not a practice limited to the Rabbins ; for it has come

11

down to the present hour, and is exhibited in all our homiletic commentaries. Where the matter thus added is good and true, there is no special objection to it in this species of commentary, provided the writers do not claim for their additions the same authority which the original text has. But this is too often the case.

One feature of the proper *Midrash*, the launching forth into the great abyss of ὑπόνοια, *i. e.*, an *under* or *secondary, occult, figurative*, and *symbolic* meaning is wanting in this Targum. We find a leaning towards this, as to some of the dilucidating particulars; *e. g.*, when, in v. 5, the Targumist mentions "the aromatic trees which the sprites and demons brought to Solomon from India." Bordering on this will be found the pregnant meaning assigned to the simple text in vs. 15, 18. The translator anxiously watches over every expression which might seem to be at variance with *orthodoxy. E. g.*, where (v. 14) Coheleth declares that one "and the same destiny awaits all men," both wise and foolish, the Targumist adds, that this will happen, *provided the wise man does not pray, and avert the decreed evil from the world when the retribution shall come;* a condition and mode of escape not provided for by the original author.

Among other things, the writer (as usual among the Rabbins) betrays his ignorance of historical geography. He represents (v. 4) Solomon as planting vineyards in *Jabneh*, a place on the Mediterranean sea belonging to the Philistines, until some 200 years later than Solomon's time, and taken from them by Uzziah about 800 B. C. But this is in good keeping with *Rabbinic* geography.

Diffuse as this Targumist is, on the chapter before us, it is nothing in comparison with what he has written on *Canticles*. There, as Jerome says of Origen, he has sailed *cum pleno velo*. On the words *Song of Songs* he has a full octavo page, giving an account of *nine* other songs mentioned in the Scriptures. It is easy to see what latitude a writer of his *Midrashic* spirit would take in paraphrasing such a work as the *Canticles*. But even here again he has his rivals in modern as well as ancient days. The Targumist rarely betrays an ignorance of the Heb. text. Yet in a few cases he seems to have been in total darkness ; *e. g.*, in v. 8, שִׁדָּה וְשִׁדּוֹת, *wife* and *wives*, which he renders, *warm baths and baths with siphons for tepid and hot water ;* which is hardly less ridiculous, however, than many other ancient and modern translations of the clause. The Sept. version has some more resemblance to a possible meaning of the Heb. original, viz., οἰνο-χόον καί οἰνοχόας, *i. e.*, *a butler and female butlers ;* deriving שִׁדָּה from שָׁדָה, *to pour out ;* for reading the text without vowels, they read the word שָׁדָה, without a Daghesh in ד. Jerome has another guess, viz., *scyphos et urceos, glasses and pitchers.* The Syriac and Arabic follow in the track of the Septuagint. It is but a short time, indeed, since the words in question were considered as presenting a problem not to be solved. Hitzig has made them quite plain.

Mixed, however, with a few *guesses* of a similar character scattered here and there, are many spirited renderings of the Heb. in cases where translation is not an easy task. If any one wishes to learn the genius of the *later* Jewish Targums, this on Coheleth may be recommended to him, as affording a fair specimen. It is easy to be read, with the aid given by the London Polyglott, provided the reader is somewhat versed in the Chaldee dialect. The idiom is thoroughly *Chaldaeo-Rabbinic.*

§ 8. *Modern Versions.*

Among these, in *Latin*, Arias Montanus, the *literalist*, whose version is mixed with the Hebrew, in the London Polyglott, may sometimes be of service to the learner. Among the best older versions is that of Junius and Tremellius. Dathe's, more recent, has some good qualities ; and so has the version of I. F. Schelling, 1806.

Among the *German* versions, that of Knobel and of De Wette are entitled to special preëminence; both of them made from a familiar acquaintance with the Hebrew. Hitzig and Heiligstedt, in their commentaries, have translated the greater portion of the book, although in a fragmentary manner. In both will be found some happy expressions of the spirit of the original; but most of all in Hitzig. The last-named writer possesses a knowledge of the Hebrew which seems to me quite rare, notwithstanding the many fine Hebrew scholars which Germany affords. De Wette, whose knowledge was of the highest cast, does not appear ever to have given himself very seriously to the study of Coheleth. Hence his somewhat barren chapter on this book in his *Einleitung*, § 282 seq.; and hence he was less fitted to render Coheleth with the best skill than either Knobel or Hitzig.

I know of no English version, lately made, which has any special claim on our attention. Our common English version is substantially good; but there are passages in Coheleth which were beyond the critical reach and power of the translators at the period when it was made. I would fain hope that the version given below will more accurately represent the original text, and specially in difficult passages.

§ 9. *Commentators.*

I deem it useless to aim at making a universal list of them. My design extends only to commentaries critical for the most part; and even of these I shall mention only a few, because, in the present state of Hebrew studies, only a few are worthy of particular consideration and study by him who is in pursuit of critical knowledge.

I. ANCIENT COMMENTATORS.

(1) Gregorii Thaumaturgi Metaphrasis in Ecc. Salom. in Greg. Nazianz. Opp. I, p. 749 seq. Par. 1609.

(2) Gregorii Nysseni Accurata in Ecc. Narratio, Tom. I, p. 373 seq., ed. Par. 1615.

(3) Olympiodori in Ecc. Comm. in Biblioth. patr. max. Tom. XVIII, p. 480, seq.

(4) Oecumenii Catena in Ecc. 1532.

(5) Hieronymi Comm. in Ecc. Opp. Tom. II.

These, with the exception of Jerome, must not be read with the expectation of much *critical* aid. In the main, it is more a matter of curiosity than of usefulness to spend time upon them.

II. OLDER PROTESTANT COMMENTATORS.

(6) Lutheri Ecc. Salomonis, Opp. Tom. III. 1532.

(7) Merceri Comm. in Job.; Ecc. etc. 1651.

(8) Grotii Annott. in V. Test. Opp.

(9) Rambachii Notae Uberiores in J. H. Michaelis's edit. of his Annott. Uberiores in Hagiôgraphos, 1729.

(10) Clerici Vet. Test. Libri. Hagiog. 1721.

(11) J. D. Michaelis Poetïscher Entwurf des Predigerbuchs Salomo, Götting. 1762.

(12) Döderlein Scholia in Lib. V. Test. 1784.

(13) Van der Palm, Ecclesiastes, Lug. Bat. 1784.

Here and there some good notes will be found in most of these. Such men as Grotius, Mercier, and Le Clerc, seldom wrote without suggesting something critically valuable.

III. RECENT COMMENTATORS.

(14) Umbreit Koheleths Seelenkampf. 1818.

(15) ———— Koheleth Scepticus de summo Bono, 1820.

(16) Kaïser Coheleth (as a curiosity).

(17) Rosenmülleri Scholia in V. Test. 1830.

(18) Köster, das Buch. Hiob und Prediger, 1831.

(19) Knobel Comm. über Coheleth, 1836.

(20) Hitzig der Prediger Salomo's 1847, in Exeget. Handbuch des Alten Test. Band VII.

11*

(21) Heiligstedt, in Maureri Comm. gramm. et. crit. Vol.
IV., 1848.

Nos. 19 and 20 are in reality original works, the fruit of much
and deep critical investigation. Knobel led the way in this.
Hitzig followed, although not exactly in his steps. The work of
the latter comprises but little more than 100 pages; but it is full
of remarks disclosing a most intimate critical acquaintance with
the Heb. language; and the author aims, more than any writer
to whom I have had access, to trace the *connection* of thought
and reasoning in the book, and with more success. Bating his
strong *neological* tendencies, his book is worthy of thorough study
and high regard.

The more recent work of Heiligstedt has some good traits.
He pursues criticism *grammatically*. But his work is lacking in
judgment as to the course of thought in Coheleth; and it contains
some striking conceits in respect to a part of the *difficult* passages.
It is in general very perspicuous and easily understood.

In a *critical* point of view, Knobel and Hitzig take the lead,
and are worth all the rest of the list.

Of the *preaching* or *homiletic* commentaries, there are many,
and some valuable English ones. But they do not come within
my present scope. The *preaching* pastor may consult some of
them to advantage on *ethical* subjects; but he must not expect
critical and hermeneutical aid from them. A work of a high
critical character, on this book, is as yet a *desideratum* in English.
It was with a hope of doing something to advance a critical knowledge of the book among us, that the present work has been
undertaken.

COMMENTARY ON ECCLESIASTES.

CHAP. I.

§ 1. Vs. 1—11.

THE leading and predominant design of the book, to show *the vanity of all earthly objects, pursuits, and designs,* and the apparent digressions from it, have been spoken of particularly in the account of the *plan* of the book in the Introduction (§ 2). The course of thought or argument exhibited in this first paragraph or section of the work, is as follows :

First the *title* of the book, as usual, is given, v. 1. Next comes the general proposition, which covers the whole ground of the work : VANITY OF VANITIES ; ALL IS VANITY. This is illustrated by the following course of thought : 'Man, by all his efforts, can attain to no stable and lasting condition of enjoyment ; for there can be no stability where one generation is constantly passing from the stage of action or enjoyment, and another is coming upon it. On the other hand, the world in which he lives is ever and always the same. The occurrences of the natural world all take place in one established and continual round, from which there is no departure or variation. The sun always rises and sets in the same manner ; the wind continually goes round its circuits in the same way. The rivers flow into the sea without filling it, and always are flowing back again to the source whence they originated. Language would fail to describe all of the like occurrences. They are so numerous, that no eye can ever be satisfied by a full sight ; nor ear so filled, that no more remains to be heard. Yet in all this countless variety of things there is nothing new, *i. e.,* no betterment, no improvement, no change. Any one who thinks that any new thing occurs, will find himself mistaken. There is the same unchangeable and ceaseless round of things forever repeated, so that no new sources of pleasure can be hopefully looked for in this quarter, vs. 3—11.

From this introductory statement it appears that the writer had in view some propositions of a general nature. These consist mainly of two things: first, that man can find no abiding good in the present world, because of his own frail and perishable nature; and secondly, that he cannot secure happiness by making any changes in the world, or in the state of things, in which sadness and suffering have been and are his lot, since they are fixed and immutable, and have been so ordered and arranged by a Power above him. Thus he finds himself helpless and hopeless. Such is the general course of thought in § 1. We come now to the examination of particulars.

(1) The words of Coheleth, the son of David, king in Jerusalem.

דִּבְרֵי קֹהֶלֶת, lit. *the words (or sayings) of Coheleth,* constitute the general title of the book. דִּבְרֵי does not mean specifically *doctrines* or *narrations,* but *things said,* or *words* in a generic sense. Thus we have *the words of Jeremiah* (Jer. 1 : 1); *the words of Amos* (1 : 1); and the title to the book of the Chronicles is דִּבְרֵי הַיָּמִים, *i. e., words in respect to the times.*

קֹהֶלֶת has the form of the Part. act. fem. in Kal. Knobel (Comm. p. 8) asserts that "*concrete* are converted into *abstract* nouns, by appending a fem. ending." This he represents as a universal principle. According to this rule קֹהֶלֶת, then, must of course here mean *preaching;* and the abstract being put for the concrete (which indeed is, in itself, a thing very common), he thus makes out the signification *preacher.* So Gesenius, in his Thesaurus. But the application of this principle to the Part. pres. is doubtful. Of the five examples of a fem. ending which designates an *abstract* meaning, as produced by Knobel, all but one come from masc. *adjectives;* as, e. g., אִוֶּלֶת, *folly,* from אֱוִל, *foolish,* etc. חֹבֶרֶת is the only Part. pres. form to which he adverts; but even this does not prove the point in question, for in Ex. 26 : 4, 10, where it is employed, its meaning is *socia,* and not the abstract *conjunctio.* Possibly, however, תּוֹעֵבָה, *abomination* (which is a frequent word), and חֹזֶה in Is. 28 : 15 = חָזוּת in v. 18, may support the allegation before us in a modified shape, viz., that *sometimes* the active Part. fem. has an *abstract* meaning. Beyond this we cannot safely go. But, leaving this view of the word as doubtfully established in such a way, we may illustrate it more satisfactorily by another view. The Hebrews were accustomed, in some cases, to designate men by the fem. name of the office which they held; e. g., פֶּחָה, *praefect*, Neh. 5 : 13; 12 : 26; Mal. 1 : 8, al.; בְּנָת, *colleague*, Ez. 4 : 7 (frequent in Chald.), סֹפֶרֶת, *scribe*, prop. name in Ez. 2 : 55; Neh. 7 : 57, and so פֹּכֶרֶת, Ez. 2 : 57; Neh. 7 : 59. Such a usage in Arabic is very frequent; as חַלִיפַת, *Caliph*, חַלִיקַת, *Creator*, and so (in fem. forms) advanced age for *old man*, story for *story-teller*, care for *curator*, service for *slave*, and the like. In some words, both the masc. and fem. forms are employed in the same sense, as *Aga* and *Agath*, signifying *defender*, *reprover*, etc. The general principle receives confirmation from other languages. Homer calls Oceanus θεῶν γένεσις, Il. xiv. 201, 302. Euripides puts ἀγεμόνευμα (*government*) for ἡγεμών, *governor*, Phoen. 1492; and νύμφευμα (*espousal*) for νύμφη, *bride*, Troad. 435. So in all the modern languages of Europe, we find such words as *majesty*, *excellency*, *highness*, *honor*, *grace*, *magnificence* (all feminines and abstracts), designating persons of a particular rank or office. Even we republicans call our governor *His Excellency*. It need not, and should not, seem strange to us, then, when we find the word קֹהֶלֶת employed to designate *preacher*.

But what means *preacher?* The root or stem-word, קָהַל, means to *assemble*, to *summon together*; but it is spoken only in reference to *persons*. Mostly, it designates summoning them together for religious purposes; and the assembly thus brought together is called קָהָל, and the discourse קְהִלָּה. Hitzig says (Comm. Ecc. 1 : 1) that "קְהֶלֶת cannot possibly mean *preaching* in the abstract;" to which (omitting the word *possibly*) I should fully assent. But preaching as an *act* it may mean, by a little deflection from its ordinary sense. The Latin *concionatrix*, by which it has often been translated, and the barbarous Greek word ἐκκλησιάστρια, in the Venet. Graec., are attempts to give the exact shade of the literal meaning; and in theory they are correct translations. Those who thus translate, however, refer the word (as fem.) to *wisdom* as the preacher. That the *discourse* in the present case (דִּבְרֵי) is not like a modern sermon is sufficiently plain. Equally plain is it, that what is said is not supposed to be addressed to a mass of men assembled. Nearly always the person addressed is of the singular number; *e. g.*, "Keep *thy* foot, when *thou* goest to the house of God;" "Rejoice, O young man, in *thy* youth, etc." But still, as the book is designed for general reading, and the writer often warns, reproves, and instructs, he might not unaptly call himself *preacher*. So far as Solomon is concerned, we know only of one occasion on which he addressed the great קָהָל, viz., at the dedication of the temple, 2 Chron. 6 : 1 seq. His proverbs, and songs, and botanical and zoölogical treatises, are mentioned in 2 K. 4 : 30 seq.; but nothing is said of his *preaching*. The name, קֹהֶלֶת, was not given subsequently to the author because of his writing the book so called, but he had the name already when the book was beginning to be written, Ecc. 1 : 1. If Solomon himself wrote the book, we can hardly make out a reason why he should style himself *Coheleth;* but if (as seems to be nearly certain) it was written at a later period (see § 5. Introd.), and Solomon's views and feelings were presented by the writer to the consideration of the reader, it was natural enough for the writer to call him *Coheleth*, in reference to what he had uttered. At any rate, the Sept. Greek ἐκκλεσιαστής, Jerome's Latin *Concionator*, Luther's *Prediger*, as well as our English *Preacher*, are generally acquiesced in, at present, as the appropriate meaning of the word. That the meaning is masc. is clear from the fact that in all cases the masc. verb is associated with it; for 7 : 27, אָמְרָה קֹהֶלֶת is no exception, since it should be read אָמַר הַקֹּהֶלֶת, as it is in 12 : 8. That Coheleth himself is represented as a *king*, is clear from 1 : 12.

The various, and sometimes even whimsical, meanings given

to this word, need not be formally discussed and refuted. Such
is *collector*, viz., of sayings and maxims; whereas קָהַל means
only to *collect men*. Then we have *assembly, academy, i. e.*, a
literary *consessus;* which meaning is defended by men of name,
as Döderlein, Paulus, Bauer, Bertholdt, Hartmann, and others.
But 1 : 12 decides this matter; for according to this exposition,
Solomon is made gravely to address his consessus, by saying:
" I, O Academy, was king in Jerusalem." Did they need to be
told this? And then, *was king* — when? Solomon was king to
the end of his life, and could never tell them he *was* once king,
which would imply of course that he is now no longer so. Next
comes *senex, the old man*, from the corresponding Arabic verb,
which, among other things, signifies to *grow gray*. But why go
to the Arabic in this case; above all, why go there, when we can
find in *senex* nothing specially appropriate to the book? Once
more, from the Arabic קָהַל, in the sense of *exaruit cutis*, is the
word derived, and so Coheleth means *the penitent*, who becomes
withered in skin by doing penance! Zirkel and others assert,
however, that the *fem.* ending is given by Solomon to Coheleth,
in order that it might mark gentleness and gracefulness in his
speech (like *Voltaire* substituted for Arouet). Others say it
sprung from the *effeminacy* of Solomon in his old age; others,
that Solomon's ghost is the speaker, and that the fem. ending is
given to show that ghosts have no specific gender (comp. Matt.
22 : 30). This last phantasy comes from Augusti, Einl. s. 242,
f. Jahn holds the ־ה final to be an *auxesis* to the force of the
word; for the like is often the case in Arabic. But such an
αὔξησις, if admitted, would strictly mean *preaching much*, not
preëminent preacher. But enough. We have no need of
guessing, in the present case. That Coheleth means one who
addresses serious discourse to his hearers, or rather to his readers,
is sufficiently plain. This, too, is in accordance with the nature
of the book, and with the character of the author. Happily, we
are not often called upon, at the present time, to notice and con-

tend against such phantasies as have just been brought to view. Their existence shows how unsafe and adventurous it is to for-sake the simple principle of grammatico-historical interpretation.

Son of David would not particularize enough for the writer's purpose, for David had many sons. Therefore he adds : *King in Jerusalem;* which words belong to David's *son*, and not to him, for they are epexegetical of *Son of David.* But why *King in Jerusalem?* Solomon himself, if he wrote the book, would natu-rally say : *King of Israel.* But in after times, when there were kings over the ten tribes of Israel, who were of a separate race, and had a different capital (Samaria), it would be natural to speak of a Heb. king either as belonging to Jerusalem, or else to Samaria, in order to distinguish accurately. That the writer of the book has here spoken in the usual manner which prevailed at a period later than that of Solomon, seems plain. And as only one of David's sons ever reigned at Jerusalem, Solomon is of course meant here.

(2) Vanity of vanities, saith the preacher, vanity of vanities ! All is vanity.

Here the main subject of the book is at once announced. *Van-ity of vanities!* An exclamation, and not a part of an ordinary complete sentence. The word הֶבֶל is one of the older Segholates, retaining its original Inf. form. In Hebrew this is rare, the com-mon Segholates (such as הֵבֶל) being substituted for such forms ; Heb. Gramm. § 83, II. 10.[1] Like to הֶבֶל are פְּאֵר, בְּאֵר, etc. ; but in Syr. and Chald. such forms are the usual Segholates. The unusual form in Hebrew seems to be chosen here for the sake of variety in diction, inasmuch as the plur. הֲבָלִים comes from the usual הֵבֶל. The root הָבַל means *to breathe;* hence הֶבֶל, *breath,* then *vapor,* and lastly, in a tropical sense, *nothingness, vanity, i. e.,*

---

[1] The Grammar referred to, where no title is given, is Roediger's edition of Gesenius's Heb. Grammar, translated by M. Stuart.

that which is altogether momentary and unsubstantial. The
meaning of the whole phrase is *most absolute*, or *extreme vanity ;*
see Gramm. § 117, 2. In אָמַר קֹהֶלֶת we see that the noun is used
as a *masculine*. The repetition of *vanity of vanities* gives the
highest intensity possible to the idea expressed. The extent of
its application next follows.

הַכֹּל must not be regarded here as = the Greek τὸ πᾶν, *the
universe*, as Rosenm. and others affirm; but it includes all the
efforts of men and all which befalls them. In other words, it
includes all that is done or happens *under the sun*, as the book
everywhere expresses it, see vs. 3, 9, 14; 2 : 14, 17—20, etc.,
passim. Neither divine operations, nor the great objects of
nature, are asserted to be vanity. In respect to the *work of God*,
the author never criticizes this, nor finds it to be defective. It is
the doings, purposes, designs, wishes, and strivings of men, which
he pronounces to be vanity, because all these never secure solid
and permanent happiness. The *article* is prefixed to כֹּל, because
it comprises a *universality* of efforts and events, a *tout ensemble ;*
and so it corresponds with the Greek article before πᾶς in a like
case. — הָבֶל for הֶבֶל, because of the pause-accent, Gramm. § 29,
4. In this last clause the copula (הָיָה) between subject and
predicate is, as usual in such cases, omitted; Gr. § 141.

(3) What profit is there to man by all his toil, which he laboriously per-
formeth under the sun ?

The question virtually contains the strongest kind of affirmation that there is *no profit*. In other words, it challenges all men
to show that there is any profit. And if none, then all is vanity
indeed. This verse also shows the extent of the ground which
הַכֹּל of the preceding verse is designed to cover. For מַה followed
by a Dagh. conjunctive, see Lex. מָה, Note *(b.)* at the close. —
יִתְרוֹן, from the root יָתַר, means literally *remainder, what remains*,
and then secondarily *gain, profit*. — לָאָדָם, with the article-vowel
under ל, § 35, B. *b.* Note 2 and § 35, 1. Here again the article

makes the word denote *the whole race of men,* the *genus huma-
num,* like our word *mankind.* It is the Dat. of appurtenance;
the copula being omitted, as usual. Or we may call it a case of
the Gen. made by prefixing לְ, Gr. § 113, 2. *In all his toil* is a
literal rendering of בְּכָל־עֲמָלוֹ, but the true sense of בְּ here is *by,
on account of,* or *in respect to,* Lex. בְּ, B. 10. The usual meaning of *in* would hardly make an intelligible sense here. The
suff. וֹ, appended to עָמָל, refers to אָדָם, which is in the sing.
number; but as the latter noun is generic, so also must the suff.
be.

In שֶׁיַּעֲמֹל, the common *abridged* form of אֲשֶׁר, שֶׁ is combined
with the verb. The א of the pronoun is dropped, because of its
feeble sound, and the ר assimilates to the letter which follows it,
and is expressed by a Dagh. forte in that letter. No book in the
Heb. Scriptures makes such a use of this abridged form, or employs
it with anything of the like frequency, as Coheleth. Early cases
of its use are rare, and mostly somewhat doubtful. It is found
mainly in Ecc., Cant., and some of the later Psalms. Its frequency in Coheleth even reminds one of the Rabbinic, and is one
of the distinctive characteristics of the peculiar diction of the
book. The imperf., as יַעֲמֹל, designates continued, repeated, customary action more frequently than any other tense; Gr. § 125,
4, 6. The Heb. much oftener than our own language, puts a
kindred noun after a verb to render the expression energetic.
We can say *run a race, fight a good fight,* etc., but our limits are
narrow as to this kind of diction. On the contrary, the Hebrew
extends this mode of expression very widely; as חָלָה, עָמַל עָמָל
רָעַע מֵצַה, חֵלִי, etc. To avoid saying (as the Heb. does) *toiled a
toil,* I have translated *ad sensum* by *toil which he laboriously per-
formeth;* see Gr. § 135, n. 1.

Under the sun occurs only in Coheleth; but here it is repeated
some twenty-five times, and constitutes a marked peculiarity of
the book. (See p. 11 for a list of the cases.) We convey the
same idea by calling things *sublunary* = under the moon. The

Heb. expression is more striking than ours. *Earthly* or *worldly* purposes, actions, and events are designated by assigning this predicate to them. — שֶׁמֶשׁ for שָׁמֶשׁ, because of the pause-accent.

(4) [One] generation passeth away, and [another] generation cometh: and the earth abideth forever.

The Heb. דּוֹר, without the article, is equivalent to *a generation*, or *one generation*. The latter is the preferable English here. — הָלַךְ is often used to designate *departure, going away;* and בָּא (Part. here) means *coming* in the sense of entering upon the scene of action. This going and coming shows the brevity and vanity of human life ; since there is nothing permanent or enduring in man ; and confirms the preceding verse, which denies that man has any solid and lasting good or reward in the present world. On the other hand, *the earth abideth forever*. The meaning here given to עֹמָדֶת (Qamets before pause) is by no means unusual; see Lex. s. v. No. 2. All three of the participles here employed are designedly used to express *continuance* of action. The sentiment is, that the earth is fixed and immutable, admitting no changes for the better, and, consequently, no hopes of lightening human misery by such changes. Man's condition in the world, and his relation to it, must ever remain the same. His frailty in himself on the one hand, and on the other the foreclosure against any change for the better in the things without, concur to show that he can find no permanent happiness here. Vs. 3 and 4 fall back upon, or stand related to, the assertion in v. 2, that "all is vanity."

(5) And the sun riseth, and the sun setteth, and to its place it hasteneth, where it ariseth.

Here בָּא (verb) is employed in a sense apparently the opposite of that in the verse above. The simple fact is, that occasionally the verb בּוֹא, whose usual meaning is *intrare, ingredi*, is also employed in the general sense of *ire*, viz., to go or move forward

in any direction; see Lex. Exactly to our purpose, is its meaning in Gen. 15 : 12. Perhaps (with Knobel) we may attribute
its use here, to an associated idea that the setting sun *enters* *(in-
greditur)* its subterraneous dwelling, viz., the ocean, according to
the view of the Hebrews. The greater distinctive accent on
מְקוֹמוֹ is not well placed; for this word is intimately connected
with שׁוֹאֵף. This last word literally means *to pant*, *e. g.*, as one
does in consequence of running swiftly. Figuratively it is attributed to the sun, in his race from the place of setting to that of
rising, in order that he may be ready to rise again the next
morning. I have given in my version the real meaning which
the word is designed here to express, viz., *hasteneth* instead of
panteth. The imagery is vivid. The sun must make *great haste*
(which occasions *panting*), in order to return, in a few hours, to
the place from which it arose. In what way the ancient Hebrews
conceived this return to be accomplished, whether by going *round*
the world, or *under* it, we are unable to say. In the Targum on
this verse (6th century), it is said, that ' the sun goes round by
the side of the north, in the path of the abyss.' But in the Heb.
Scriptures I can recall no passage which seems to designate the
common views of the ancient Hebrews on this subject. It must
have appeared very mysterious to a thinking man among them.

Where it ariseth, or *will arise.* As *habitual* action is here implied, the former is the preferable version. The clause is relative, and אֲשֶׁר is implied before זוֹרֵחַ, and therefore modifies שָׁם,
making it to mean *where*, Gramm. § 121, 3, comp. 1. The *present*
tense is formed most frequently of all, in this book, by the Part.
pres., which has often an accompanying pronoun, as here, זוֹרֵחַ הוּא.

(6) The wind goeth to the south, and turneth about to the north, turning
and turning it goeth, and to its circuits doth the wind return.

The Heb. *order* of words we cannot well follow here; for we
must then translate: *It goeth to the south, and turneth about to the*

north, turning turning goeth the wind. The Part. הֹלֵךְ does not
here indicate *departure*, as in v. 4, but *progrediens, progressing* in
any direction. *Turneth about,* or *circuiteth,* implies a moving of
the wind through the intermediate points, from the south round
to the north. But why these two points rather than *east* and
west? Evidently because the sun's rising and setting in the east
and west had already brought them to view, and the writer did
not wish to repeat the same points. There are *six participles* in
this verse, all indicative of continued successive action. — רוּחַ is
here employed as masc.; and so in Ex. 10 : 13 ; Ps. 51 : 12 ;
1 K. 19 : 11. It is fem. elsewhere. הָרוּחַ = ὁ ἄνεμος, *the wind.*
The repetition of סֹבֵב gives intensity to the description of the
turning, representing it as occurring in constant succession.

The wind returneth to its circuits, i. e., it turns until it reaches
the point from which it started, and then goes again upon the
like circuits. In other words, the same thing is repeated over
and over again continually.

(7) All the streams go to the sea, but the sea is not full; to the place
where the streams go, thither do they again return.

נְחָלִים, not specifically *rivers,* but *running* or *flowing water* in
streams large or small. Statistically accurate we need not require the writer to be ; for many brooks are lost in the sand, or
flow into the Jordan ; and even the Jordan itself flows into the
lake of Sodom. But in Hebrew, a lake is called a *sea.* The
usual fact as to the course of rivers, is enough for the writer's
purpose. How the rivers get back to their sources again, so as
to repeat the flowing into the sea, the writer does not intimate ;
even as before, he does not tell us *how* the sun gets back to his
place of *rising.* Probably underground channels were supposed
to exist ; comp. Gen. 7 : 11, where the *fountains of the great
deep* are said to be unstopped, in order to overflow the earth.
The fact that rain is formed by evaporation from the sea (by

12*

which the sea parts with as much as it receives and so is never full), seems hardly to have been known to the Hebrews, at least in any such way as we now understand the matter; although there is something like to this in the *earth-watering mist* of Gen. 2 : 6. — אֵינֶנּוּ is the negative of the verb to be, combined with הוּא, see Lex. אַיִן with the remarks on the suffixes. The negative before a def. *verb* would be לֹא; before a Part. it is אֵין. — מְקוֹם const. form before שֶׁ = אֲשֶׁר, Gr. § 114, 2. The article הַ, being a Guttural, does not admit the Dagh. forte that would normally follow שֶׁ. — שָׁם is rightly connected by the accent with the clause that follows it, and means *there* or (as we say in such a case) *thither.* — שָׁבִים Part., lit. *returning,* but it is here employed in the sense of *again* or *repetition;* see Lex. We might literally translate: *thither they repeat to go.* For לָ, *i. e.,* this prefix with Qamets before the fem. Inf. לָכֶת (root יָלַךְ), see Lex. לָ. The other Qamets, belonging to the verb, arises from the pause, § 29, 4.

(8) All words grow weary, no man can utter [them]; the eye is not satisfied with seeing, nor the ear filled so that it cannot hear.

The Part. יְגֵעִים belongs to an intransitive verb, and we may translate *grow weary* or *are wearied,* since יָגֵעַ is both act. and passive as to its form. The language is clearly tropical, but the meaning is plain, viz., that language would fail to tell the whole, or to tell it would weary out language. So the clause that follows, which affirms that no one can utter all the words necessary to tell the whole story. The article stands before דְּבָרִים, in order to show that the words or descriptions in question have relation to such things as are mentioned in vs. 4—7, = all words necessary to relate all such things. — יוּכַל, the Imperf. Hoph. of יָכֹל, lit. *shall be made able,* is in common use for Kal, which is unemployed in this verb. In לִרְאוֹת the לְ may be rendered *to,* or *in respect to.* I have adopted our more familiar phraseology —

satisfied with seeing.—Nor the ear be filled so that it cannot hear.
The מ before the Inf. has usually a *negative* meaning (see Lex.
מִן, 5, c.), *i. e.*, lit. it means *from, away from,* any thing or action,
and so a *negation* of it. The last two clauses are evidently a
commentary on the two preceding, designed to illustrate and confirm them. The eye is *satisfied,* only when it has seen all that
is to be seen. But this can never happen, for the things that
might be seen are at any time more than words can tell. So
with the ear. It can never be filled, so that there is not more
which might be told and heard. Hence מִשְּׁמֹעַ, *ita ut non audiat.*
Both of these cases show that the number of occurrences and
events is so great, that it is beyond the power of eye or ear to
see or hear of all. They are, as asserted above, more than words
can describe.

(9) That which has been is that which shall be, and that which has been
done is that which shall be done, and there is nothing new under the sun.

For מַה־שֶּׁ, *id quod,* see Lex. מָה, 2. This word loses its *interrogative* power, when combined (as here) with another word.
הָיָה, *has occurred,* or *taken place, accidit,* like γίνομαι. — הוּא
involves the copula *is,* and may therefore be literally translated
is that, or *is the same;* Gr. 119, 2. — נַעֲשֹׂה, verb Niph. The
Part. of this same form would be *fem.,* and so not accordant with
the masc. הוּא. — יֵעָשֶׂה, Imperf. Niph., Gr. § 62, 4. — For אֵין,
the const. form of אַיִן, see in Lex. — כָּל with short ŏ, because of
the Maqqeph. The first clause of the verse refers to things
which *happen,* occurrences; the second to things which are *done,*
actions. Of these it is said: " There is nothing new."

(10) Is there anything of which one may say: See, this is new? Long
ago was it, in ancient times which were before us.

דָּבָר, *matter, thing;* as often elsewhere; Lex. 3. The שֶׁ implies a preposition before it, בְּ or לְ, *concerning* or *in regard to,*
Gr. § 152, 3, יֹאמַר has no subject expressed, and has therefore

an indef. Nom. *one, any one.* — הוּא simply *is*, see Gr. § 119, 2,
and Lex. — כְּבָר, frequent in Syriac, but peculiar to Ecc. in the Hebrew. Hitzig has best illustrated it by the Arabic كَبِر (= כְּבָר)
which means *extreme old age*. Knobel doubts such a meaning
of the Hebrew, but without good reason. At any rate, it fits the
passage well. That עֹלָמִים often means *ancient times, days of yore*,
the Lex. will show. לְ before it, in such a case, is not unfrequent,
for this preposition is often prefixed to a word designating *time*.
Gr. 151, 3, *e.* The verb הָיָה, which follows, is *sing.*, while its
antecedent subject is plural. But like cases occur in respect to
this verb and some others; see in Ecc. 2 : 7; Gen. 35 : 26; 47 : 24;
1 Chron. 2 : 9; 3 : 1. Similar anomalies of הָיָה in respect to
gender also occur; comp. Ex. 12 : 49; Gen. 15 : 17. In fact,
then, הָיָה seems to be occasionally used in a kind of *impersonal*
way, so that the *sing.* number may be employed, even if the
noun to which the verb stands related is in the plural. It may
be, too, that אֲשֶׁר (in the present case), having a *sing.* form, even
when a plur. is designated by it (as here), may take after it a
verb of the like form. Ewald translates thus: *what happens
before our eyes*, making this clause the subject or Nom. to כְּבָר
הָיָה. But this would require לְפָנֵנוּ, and not admit of מִלְּפָנֵנוּ,
which means *from* [the time] *before us ;* see Is. 41 : 26.

The bearing of vs. 9, 10, on what precedes, is plain. The
writer had said that everything moved on in one perpetual circle
of repetition, the same things always occurring over and over
again. Here he confirms his assertion, by challenging any one
to point out a single thing which is actually new, *i. e.*, which is
an exception to what he affirms. Long ago did everything happen which now happens; therefore, there is one unvarying round
of occurrences.

(11) There is no remembrance of former things; and also in respect to
after things which are to come, there will be no remembrance of them among
those who will exist thereafter.

This verse assigns the reason why some err in supposing that something new takes place. Former occurrences are *forgotten ;* and, not recognizing this, some suppose that things happen which are really new. This will be equally true of things yet to come. Those who succeed the next generation will, in like manner, forget what preceded them. Consequently, there can be no proof that any new thing actually takes place.

The word זִכְרוֹן (from זִכָּרוֹן) is in the const. form; and it may be so, notwithstanding the לְ that follows; Gr. § 114, 1. But not improbably the apparent const. form here may, in reality, be absolute, like כִּשָּׁרוֹן, יִתְרוֹן, etc., as some nouns, we well know, have more than one absolute form. In לָרִאשֹׁנִים, the לְ has the *article-vowel,* and the article is employed before a word designating an entire totality. Lit. the word means *primus, first ;* but by usage (since there is no *compar.* form for adjectives in Heb.), it means *former, antecedent,* viz., former occurrences and actions. The same is true of לָאַחֲרֹנִים, which is generic, and designates all that will occur or be done thereafter. Of course the article may be used before it, as it is in לְ. — עִם, *with,* but also as *apud, among,* which is the better sense here.

§ 2. *Efforts to obtain Happiness by the Acquisition of Wisdom.*

[We have seen that § 1 contains an introduction, by proposing the theme, and pointing out the general sources whence the proof of that theme will be drawn, viz., from the brevity and vanity of human life, and the immutable and ever-recurring round of phenomena in the world about us and above us. A divine Omnipotent hand has enstamped these characters on everything ; and man, who is miserable now, cannot indulge any hope of bettering his condition by changes made in the order and influence of natural phenomena. Having thus introduced his reader to the outlines of his theme, the author proceeds to tell us who he is, and what experiments he has made in order to discover the secret of human happiness in the present world. His experience is very diversified ; and he shows us that, in whatever way he turned himself, he was always forced at last to the same conclusion, viz., that ALL IS VANITY.]

Chap. I. 12—18.

(12) I, Coheleth, was King over Israel in Jerusalem.

If, as Hitzig intimates (Vorbemerk. § 3), Coheleth be *Wisdom incarnate* in Solomon, and thus personified, how could the writer speak as he does here? In Prov. viii. and in the book of Wisdom, the personification of Wisdom is made plain and palpable to the reader. But here we have a personage, who is king over a particular people, and in a definite city. The designations in v. 12 would, indeed, seem very strange in the mouth of Solomon, on the supposition that he, in person, is addressing his contemporaries. Did they need to be told that he lived at Jerusalem? Above all, those who think Coheleth means a literary academy, or consessus, are forced to an almost ridiculous translation here. So Döderlein: "I, O academy, was king, etc." The language seems to be explicable only on the ground that the book was composed when the nation had been divided, and there were two kings and two capitals in Palestine. *Israel* is a name applicable to the whole nation, or to the ten tribes, or, finally, to the two tribes of Judah and Benjamin. Here it has the latter meaning. The emphasis laid on *was*, by expressly inserting the verb הָיִיתִי, shows that the day had passed by when Coheleth was king. This was not the case with Solomon while he lived, for he was king to the time of his death; and therefore he could not speak of himself as a *past*[1] king. The plural (or dual) form of יְרוּשָׁלַיִם probably took its rise from the upper and lower parts of the city; like מִצְרַיִם, *the two Mitzars*, or Egypt, upper and lower.

But why does the writer bring this to view? Plainly because that *wisdom*, the first special and individual topic of discussion, belonged preëminently to Solomon. If any one could find happiness in the pursuit of it, he surely was the man.

---

[1] Too much stress seems to us to be laid on this form of the verb, both here and in the Introd., § 5, p. 68, where see note. — Ed.

(13) And I gave my mind to seek out and make careful investigation, by wisdom, concerning all which is done under heaven; this is an unhappy employment which God has given to the sons of men, to occupy themselves therewith.

The verb דְּרוֹשׁ means *to seek after, to seek out.* תוּר means more than this, viz., it literally signifies *to go round and round a thing,* in order closely to inspect it; hence it means, in its secondary sense, to *investigate carefully and closely.* The first verb designates looking up the object, the second means carefully prying into it and minutely examining it. The בְּ (prep.) marks the instrumentality employed, or the manner in which the investigation was conducted. The Pattah under it is the article-vowel; and rightly does it stand here, for הַחָכְמָה means *the wisdom* requisite or appropriate to such an investigation. *Everything which is done,* refers to the *actions of men,* and not the objects of nature; for he could not well say of them what he affirms in v. 14, viz., that they were all vanity and an empty affair. Their immutable order and ever-recurring and uniform phenomena, however, render them incapable of control by man, as vs. 4—8 show; and therefore they are incapable of being so used by him as to prevent all his inconveniences and sufferings. Yet the things in themselves are beautiful and good, as 3 : 11 declares. It is the vanity of human effort after knowledge, *i. e.,* such knowledge as will secure and render stable our present happiness, which the writer is going to discuss. He declares at the outset that this employment is an unhappy one, although Providence has seen fit to discipline men thereby.

הוּא *it is,* or *the same is,* § 119, 2. — עִנְיָן, *business, occupation,* in the const. state before רָע, which is here a noun used for an adjective, § 104, 1. The distinctive accent (Rebhia) gives the form with Qamets, instead of the original Pattah, רָע. Such a grammatical relation of nouns connected intimately, is not unfrequent; see Ecc. 4 : 8; 5 : 13; Ezek. 11 : 2; Prov. 6 : 24; 24 : 25; 28 : 5, and compare Gr. § 104, 1. The meaning of the word מִנְיָן here, and in several other places in Ecc., viz., *occu-pation, business*, is peculiar to this book alone in the Old Testa-ment. In Rabbinic, the like is very frequent. It comes from the meaning of No. II. under עָנָה, which is *laborem impendit*, followed by בְּ before the object on which the labor is bestowed; see the end of this verse. The same meaning and construction is common both to the Syriac and Arabic. Specially is the word applied to a *toilsome labor* bestowed on anything; which is just the case before us. Before נָתַן the pron. אֲשֶׁר is implied, § 121, 3. *God has assigned to the sons of men*, is designed to show that an overruling Providence controls all such things, and there-fore that men should not murmur because this is their lot. No-where does the writer cast imputations upon Providence for its allotments; but still, he fully states the trials and grievances of man, under the immutable arrangements of Providence. — עֲנוֹת in the like sense as מִנְיָן.

(14) I considered all the works which are done under the sun, and lo! all is vanity and fruitless effort.

רָאִיתִי is used to designate *mental seeing* or *consideration* (so here), as well as corporeal seeing. *Works* are here the same which have before been brought to view. הַכֹּל with the article, because it designates an entire class of things. — רְעוּת רוּחַ some translate *affliction of spirit*, deducing the word from רוּעַ or רָעַע. But this cannot be done; for such verbs do not yield the form in question. Another class render it *feeding of the wind*, deriving it from רָעָה *to feed*, and comparing Hos. 2 : 2. But the noun is abstract in its present form, and will hardly bear this verbal active sense. It should be רְעוֹת, an Infin. *nomen actionis*. The word seems best derived from רָעָה as equivalent to רָצָה, *to take pleasure in, to will* or *desire*. So the Chald. רְעָה means. We may translate: *studium venti, i. e., a windy affair*, or *a worthless business*. Considering how much of the diction of the book consists of the later Hebrew, which approaches to the Chaldee, such a use of the word is not improbable. But this use, however, in Hebrew, is to be found only in Ecclesiastes. This sense harmonizes well with עִנְיַן רָע, in v. 13. So Knobel, Ges., Rosenm., and Heiligs.; and to this I see no weighty objection. The form is like שְׁחוּת from שָׁחָה, Gr. § 84, V.

This result shows why, in the preceding verse, he declares the undertaking of a close investigation to be an עִנְיַן רָע, *a disagreeable occupation.*

(15) That which is crooked cannot be straightened, and that which is wanting cannot be numbered.

Here is the ground of the sentiment in v. 14. Human efforts are vain and fruitless, because they cannot change or amend the constitution and course of things. In 7 : 13, the מְעֻוָּת is attributed to God as a work of his, or something which he has made. The idea here is, that there are numerous causes of human misery and suffering, which lie under no control of man. Many things are lacking which might administer to his comfort, that cannot be at all supplied by any human effort. Hence the efforts of man, in pursuit of gratifying his desires, are a רְעוּת רוּחַ. The Part. מְעֻוָּת is in Pual of עָוַת, with וֹ as a reg. consonant. — תְקֹן is neut. intrans. verb, *rectus fuit,* and so it may be rendered passively, as above. חֶסְרוֹן instead of חֶסֶר or חָסֵר, shows the tendency, in the later Hebrew, to forms of this kind. — הִמָּנוֹת, Inf. Niph. of מָנָה, *to number.* When the parts of a thing can be *all numbered,* everything is there which makes a complete whole. The lack, in the present case, shows imperfection; and one which no man can supply or make up.

(16) I spake in my heart, saying: I, lo! I have increased and added to wisdom beyond all who were before me at Jerusalem — and my mind has considered wisdom and knowledge very much.

To speak in the heart, means to commune with one's self, to
13

reflect or deliberate upon. The אֲנִי which stands before הֶפָּה is designed to give special emphasis to the clause. The shape of the Heb. is such as I have given to the Eng. translation above. הִגְדַּלְתִּי, in Hiph. means *to make great, i. e.*, to increase, to enlarge. — הוֹסַפְתִּי, Hiph. of יָסַף, *I made addition to; i. e.*, he increased the wisdom which had before become great, he added to it still more by his strenuous efforts. The second עַל, before the name of a place, means *at;* see Lex. עַל, 3. — הַרְבֵּה, Inf. Hiph., lit. *multiplicando.* In meaning = מְאֹד (not used in this book), and sometimes both are united in the Hebrew for the sake of intensity. Its adverbial use, as here, is very common everywhere, Gr. § 98, 2, *d.* — חָכְמָה וָדַעַת, the first word means *practical* or *prudential wisdom*, while דַּעַת designates *theoretical knowledge* or *sagacity;* like the Greek σοφία and γνῶσις. For the first Qamets in וָדַעַת, see Lex. ו; for the second, Gr. § 29, 4. The form is the same as that of the feminine Infinitive of יָדַע; but the meaning is *abstract*, and it is not, like the Inf., a mere *nomen actionis*.

All who were before him in Jerusalem, cannot mean all persons of every class, but *all kings*. See Introd., § 5.

(17) And I applied my mind to know wisdom, and to know madness and folly ; I perceived that this also is fruitless effort.

For the ה־ in the first verb, see § 48 b, 2, *a.* — וְדַעַת, with לְ implied, as in the preceding case it is expressed, viz., in לְדַעַת. For the pointing of לְ, see Lex. לְ. — הוֹלֵלוֹת, Plur. of הוֹלֵלוּת (10 : 13), and much oftener employed, because it is intense = *ravings.* — שִׂכְלוּת with *Sin;* more correctly is ס put for שׂ in 2 : 3, 12, 13 ; 7 : 25 ; 10 : 1, 13 ; for ס follows the true etymology. — הוּא, *is*, as before. — רַעְיוֹן רוּחַ the same as רְעוּת רוּחַ in v. 14. It is from the same root (רָעָה), and differs merely in form from the other, § 83, 15, 16.

(18) For in much wisdom is much irritation ; and he who addeth to his knowledge, addeth to his sorrow.

The reason is here given of what is asserted at the close of the preceding verse.   *Irritation* or *vexation* results from the often-disappointed hopes and efforts to extend one's knowledge. *Sorrow* may refer to the depression of mind which often succeeds intense study and efforts to acquire knowledge, or possibly to the bodily indisposition which commonly attends such exertions.   When the pursuit of wisdom, and the efforts to separate it from folly, result in this state of mind and body, it becomes plain that it is a fruitless pursuit, in respect to attaining to solid and permanent happiness.   In accordance with this sentiment Cicero speaks: Videtur mihi cadere in sapientem aegritudo, Tusc. III. 4.   So Montenabbi: "Destiny contends with the preeminent; by the side of greater knowledge marches greater grief ;" in Gynsburg's Geist des Orient, s. 144.

§ 3. *Efforts to obtain Happiness by the Pursuit of Pleasure.*

Chap. II. 1—11.

[These are presented in a variety of particulars. Coheleth indulged in mirth and wine ; in building and planting; in parks and pleasure-gardens ; in the possession of many servants and of many flocks and herds; in heaping up gold and silver; in procuring singing men and women ; in marrying a wife and taking many concubines; and finally, in everything which could gratify either the eye, or the ear, or any of the senses. At last, he found all these indulgences to be utterly incompetent to afford the happiness which he sought, vs. 1—11. In 1 : 17 he says that he sought out both *wisdom* and *folly*. Of his ill success in the former pursuit, he has already told us ; he is now going to tell us what resulted from the *folly* of pursuing pleasure.]

(1) I said in my heart : Come now, let me try thee with pleasure, and do thou enjoy good ! And lo ! even this is vanity.

This form of monologue with one's self is not without parallel in the Heb. Scriptures ; see Ps. 42 : 6, 12; 43 : 5, perhaps Ps. 16 : 2, comp. Luke 12 : 18, seq., " I will say to my soul: Soul,

thou hast many good things," etc. (for לְכָה, לְכָה emphatic prolonged Imper., *come thou!* — אֲנַסְּכָה, Piel of נָסָה with suff. having ה paragogic: *Let me try thee.* Both suffixes refer to לֵב =
נֶפֶשׁ, for both occasionally = *self.* — בְשִׂמְחָה, *with joy, i. e.,* pleasure of every kind. — וּרְאֵה, *and enjoy thou ;* but the form is
Imper. *masc.* in reference to לֵב. Some translate: " Thou shalt
enjoy, etc." But this is less energetic than the Imper. form of
the Hebrew. *To see* is often used in the Old Test. and in the
New for *perceiving, enjoying ;* comp. 6 : 6. — גַּם, *also, likewise ;*
i. e., found this to be vanity as well as the matter set forth in
1 : 17. — הִנֵּה, *see here, lo!* calling special attention. — הוּא,
This is.

Such is the general proposition of § 3. The proofs and illustration of what is here laid down are detailed in the sequel.
The *good* in question is not *moral* or *spiritual*, but natural physical good, *i. e.,* pleasure or enjoyment. The writer intends to
show that all the sources of it fail to produce the desired end,
i. e., solid and lasting happiness.

(2) In respect to laughter I said : Madness ! And in respect to pleasure :
What avails it ?

לְ, *in respect to,* see Lex. לְ A. 5. —מְהוֹלָל, Part. Poal, neut.
gender, *silly stuff,* or *a stupid business.* By *laughter* is meant
boisterous or noisy mirth, *i. e.,* unrestrained and immoderate
rioting. But שִׂמְחָה designates pleasure in general, comprehending all and every kind of it. Respecting this he asks: *What
does it avail,* or *yield ? i. e.,* it yields nothing of solid and lasting
worth. — זֹה is fem., and peculiar to this book only as to frequency. It belongs to the later Hebrew, and seems to be an
apoc. form of זֹאת, like גְּלֹת out of גָּלְיַת ; for examples of it, see
5 : 15, 18 ; 7 : 23 ; 9 : 13. — עֹשָׂה Part. fem., with meaning as
in עֹשָׂה פְּרִי, *to produce fruit ;* which meaning is very common.
For the Dagh. conjunc. in ז, see under מַה in Lex.

(3) I sought in my mind to draw my flesh by wine, and my mind continued to guide with sagacity; and also to lay hold upon folly, until I should
see what is good for the sons of men which they should do under heaven,
during the number of the days of their lives.

The לְ here before the Inf. might have the same sense that I
have given to it in the preceding verse, viz., *with respect to;* but
the version above is more congruous here. The preceding verb,
תַּרְתִּי, means to *investigate*, lit. *to go round and round* a thing in
the mind; with the design of preparing for action. Erroneous
is the version : " I determined in my mind to confirm or attract,
etc." The meaning is, that Coheleth often and seriously reflected on the doings in which he was about to engage. — לִמְשׁוֹךְ
here has long been an *offendiculum criticorum.* The literal
meaning of the verb is *to draw, drag along, draw out* in the
sense of *extracting*, or (in case of sound) *protracting.* These
meanings exhaust the legitimate sense of the word ; the rest assigned to it are factitious, and made out from the apparent stress
of the occasion. Ges. renders : *firmavit, strengthened*, because
the corresponding Syriac verb has the sense of *induruit.* But
this meaning is inapposite here ; for it is *pleasurable indulgence*
in wine which is the immediate subject-matter of the discourse,
and not wine used as a tonic or medicine, *i. e.*, to strengthen.
We are not at liberty to appeal to the Syriac, if we can do as
well without it. Knobel : *festhalten*, in the sense of *holding fast
to, i. e.*, retaining and not remitting the use of wine. But so the
proper order of things would be reversed. It is the drinking of
it that comes first in order; the *holding on* to drinking is a *subsequent* matter, and therefore should not be placed first. Heiligstedt : *trahere, i. e., attrahere, to attract, i. e., allure*, which surely
is not the meaning of מָשַׁךְ. Then it requires בַּיַּיִן to be translated *to wine* (*attrahere ad vinum,* as he renders it), which is out
of the question here, because wine is the *instrument* or *agent* by
which the drawing is done. J. H. Mich. (in Bibl.) : " *ut pro-
traherem, i. e.*, paullo diutius detinerem ; " a sense which would

13*

give to the wine-drinking a *medicinal* object and aspect here, instead of a pleasurable one, as the text demands; and this would
be inapposite. Besides, *diutius detinerem* is a sense that the verb
will hardly bear. But after rejecting all this, what have we left?
Hitzig has given a new turn to the matter. He puts מְשׁוֹךְ in
relation with the following נֹהֵג; the one *draws* the chariot in
which the man (בְּשָׂרִי) is seated, while the other *drives* or *guides*
it. He compares with it the phrase: *to support* or *prop up the
heart with bread.* In this last phrase, bread is represented as
holding up or *supporting.* So *to draw* or *carry along* by the aid
of wine, he thinks to be a parallel mode of expression. Wine
"keeps the machine in motion." But this seems rather far-
fetched, at first view. *To draw along the body* or *flesh* is, at
least, a metaphor elsewhere unknown. *To protract the flesh*
would be less strange, if it could have any other meaning than a
medicinal one, *i. e.*, prolong its continuance. *To draw out*, in
the sense of *widening* or *expanding*, would be inappropriate.
Coheleth surely could not expect pleasure from making his body
huge and unwieldy. Still, that נֹהֵג has a relation to מְשׁוֹךְ, seems
to be altogether probable. They are correlates, in a like way as
coach and *driver.* Urged by this apparent correlation, and by
the difficulties of the other and different versions, we can hardly
refuse to conclude that the first expression regards men as moving along on the journey of life, while wine is, so to speak, the
drawer of their chariot. But such a steed is often furious, and
so it needs a נֹהֵג endowed with *wisdom*, *i. e.*, skilful *leader* or
driver. And such a driver Coheleth employed. In other words:
he did not go into excess in drinking wine, and thus injure or
destroy himself; but when he indulged in it, he took חָכְמָה for
his guide; *i. e.*, discretion, wariness, or sagacity. In this way he
might proceed some length in his experiment, without material
harm. — בְּשָׂר is the *corporeal me*, the *physical self.* — נֹהֵג means
literally *panting;* then *making to pant, to agitate*, or *urge*, and
so the Part. means, *one who urges*, etc., *e. g.*, as a driver urges

his team, or a shepherd his flock.   The discretion of Coheleth in providing such a guide or coachman (so to speak) as חָכְמָה, when wine was carrying him along on his journey, is very apparent.   On the whole, there can be no doubt that the sense thus given by Hitzig is significant, and to the writer's present purpose. The main difficulty is the seeming strangeness of the figurative or symbolical representation.   But we now and then are compelled to admit, in other cases, imagery not elsewhere employed, on the ground of securing congruity in the sense.   Must we not acquiesce in this here, inasmuch as it does not violate the principles of lexicography, while it makes the passage altogether significant?

— לֶאֱחֹז connects with לִמְשׁוֹךְ, and both fall back on תַּרְתִּי.   He resolved in his mind the project of *laying hold* on folly, *i. e.*, to grasp it and keep hold of it, until he could thoroughly examine it.   In the preceding chapter, we are told how he had been disappointed in the pursuit of wisdom.   Now he is making a new sort of trial.   He mixes wisdom and folly together; *i. e.*, he gives up himself to indulgence in wine, but takes care not to lay aside discretion in the matter.   The drinking is the matter of folly; and this is what he designs to investigate.   *Until I might see what is good*, etc., אֵי const. form of אַי, and usually connected with a pronoun of some kind.   Originally it means *where;* but secondarily it occupies the same place as אֲשֶׁר, and has a like sense.   It is the sign of a question before pronouns and adverbs; and this, whether the question be direct, or (as here) indirect. We may therefore translate it here by *what*, as do Hitzig, Knob., and Heiligs. — טוֹב here, as usual in this book, means what is *useful, pleasant, promotive of enjoyment.* — אֲשֶׁר יַעֲשׂוּ, *that they should do*, not (as many) *what they do;* see Lex. אֲשֶׁר, B. 2. The object of Coheleth was to see, by experiment, what could be done to advantage, or so as to secure true enjoyment in respect to the matter before him. — מִסְפַּר is translated by De Wette, Knobel, and others, *few* (lit., as they aver, *fewness*).   But no case occurs of מִסְפָּר, in the const. state as here, with such a meaning. All the cases, e. g., Gen. 34 : 30; Deut. 4 : 27; Jer. 44 : 28; Ps. 105 : 12; 1 Chron. 16 : 19; Job 16 : 22, et al., are cases where the form is מִסְפָּר, which is in the Gen. after another noun, and thus meaning *fewness*, it becomes an adjective = *few*, § 104, 1. Lit. it designates *that which can be numbered*, and of course comparatively *a few*. But it also means *number* simply considered; and such is the meaning here, it being in the Acc. of *time how long*; we must then translate thus: *during the number of the days*, etc. See § 116, 2.

Sentiment: 'I revolved in my mind the effort, to make the journey of life by the aid of wine to carry me along, associated with sagacity as my conductor or guide; and thus to subject to examination the apparent folly of drinking wine, until I should come to see how far it might promote our present enjoyment. In this meaning we may acquiesce, undisturbed by any incongruity excepting the apparent singularity of the imagery employed. I feel philologically compelled to assent to this; at least, until more light is thrown upon the doubtful clauses. The *new* meanings given to the word מָשַׁךְ do not make an apposite sense here; and therefore it is better to abide by the old one if we can.

(4) I engaged in great undertakings; I built for myself houses, and planted for myself vineyards.

The first clause, lit. *I made great my works*, is a general introduction to what follows; which consists in designations of the specific undertakings that constituted his works. לִי is the *Dat. commodi*. Solomon was thirteen years in building his own magnificent house; he also built a like one for his Egyptian wife, besides his "house of the forest of Lebanon" (1 K. 7: 1, 2, 8), not to mention the temple, 1 K. 9 : 19. His *vineyards* are mentioned in Cant. 8 : 11.

(5) I made for myself gardens and pleasure-grounds, and I planted in them fruit-trees of every kind.

גַּן is from גָּנַן ; hence the Dagh. forte in the plural. The verb means *to protect;* and therefore the Heb. idea of a *garden* is that of an *enclosed* or *protected place.* —פַּרְדֵּס is a foreign word, found elswhere only in Cant. 4: 13. Neh. 2: 8. The latter passage shows that large trees belonged to such a paradise. The Greeks transplanted the word, through Xenophon, into their language — παράδεισος ; Xen. Cyrop. I. 3. 5. 12. Oecon, 4. 13. In Armenian, *pardes* signifies a *garden close to the house,* filled with herbage, flowers, and grass. Hitzig and Heiligs. derive the word from the old Sanscrit *pradeça,* which means an *enclosure,* like the Heb. גַּן. Still, a *pleasure-ground* would be enclosed, and would naturally contain trees and shrubs of every kind, and specially *fruit-trees.* The Arabians use the word, and the Persians seem to have derived it from them. It belongs only to the later Hebrew. In the older Heb., גַּן עֵדֶן designates the place where Adam was originally stationed. Gen. 2 : 8, 10; 13 : 10.— בָּהֶם, *in them,* denotes that both the gardens and pleasure-grounds were planted with fruit-trees; comp. Cant. 4: 13.

(6) I made for myself pools of water, for watering from them the groves shooting up trees.

בְּרֵכוֹת with ◌ָ immutable in regimen, § 93. 1, in e. g. The first meaning of בָּרַךְ is *to kneel,* so that בְּרֵכָה lit. designates a *kneeling-place,* viz., for camels when they drink. Hence a *pool,* a *watering-place.* The design of the pools is described in the sequel, viz., to supply water for the trees. See the *pool of the king,* Neh. 2 : 14, which the Jews held, and not improbably, to have been constructed by Solomon.— צוֹמֵחַ is properly a neut. intrans., but still it is followed by the Acc. עֵצִים, which is often employed to designate the object *in respect to* or *as to* which the assertion of the verb or Part. is made, § 117, 3. Comp. Prov. 10 : 31; 24 : 31; Is. 34 : 13, for like specimens of the Acc.

(7) I procured servants and handmaids, and those born in the house be-longed to me; much property also in herds and flocks belonged to me, more than all [possessed] who were before me in Jerusalem.

קָנִיתִי often means to *buy* or *purchase,* which I take to be the sense here, although my translation does not imply it of necessity. בְּנֵי־בָיִת, *sons of the house,* was the softer Heb. appellation of *slaves.* It designates such as were born of bond-women in the houses of their masters; for, by universal custom, the children followed the condition of the mother; Gen. 14 : 14; 15 : 2, 3. Sometimes they were called יְלִידֵי בָיִת; at others, בְּנֵי אָמָה. — הָיָה לִי, lit. *there was to me* = I had, or possessed. On this ground, *i. e.,* because the meaning of a verb active is really designated, the Acc. *(sons of the house)* is placed after הָיָה; see like cases in Gen. 47 : 24; Ex. 12 : 49; 28 : 7; Num. 9 : 14; 15 : 29; Deut. 18 : 2; 2 Chron. 17 : 13, where הָיָה *disagrees* with its subject, either in number or gender; *i. e.,* it is used in a kind of *impersonal* way. — צאֹן, rendered *flocks,* includes both *sheep* and *goats. Above all before me,* etc., *i. e.,* above all *kings* who were before him. See the remarks on 1 : 16, and reference. For the illustration of *abundance* in such possessions, see Gen. 12 : 16; Job 1 : 3.

(8) I heaped up for myself both silver and gold, and the treasures of kings and provinces; I procured for myself singing-men and singing-women, and the delight of the sons of men, a wife and wives.

Riches were of course to be expected among the train of ex-periments. In these Solomon abounded above all. *The treas-ures of kings,* viz., such as are brought to view in 1 K. 5 : 1; 10 : 15; 4 : 21. *And provinces,* viz., such as the twelve prov-inces mentioned in 1 K. 4 : 7 seq., comp. v. 20, which were divis-ions of the kingdom for the purpose of collecting revenue. מְדִינָה is a word belonging to the later Hebrew only. The article before the plur. in the text refers to well-known provinces; comp. 1 K.

20 : 15, and Ps. 45 : 17 (16). As to *riches* in general, see 1 K.
10 : 27 seq.; 2 Chron. 1 : 15; 9 : 20. *Singing-men and singing-women* were a part of the usual accompaniments of feasting;
2 Sam. 19 : 35. Compare the allusions to the like custom in Is.
5 : 12; Amos 6 : 5, 6.

שִׁדָּה וְשִׁדּוֹת has been the theme of much conjecture and dispute.
Still, it would seem that a plain path has at last been opened by
Hitzig. It is certain that תַּעֲנוּגִים, in Cant. 7 : 7, refers to *amorous delight* (as the Latins sometimes use *deliciae*), to which
Solomon, beyond any other Jewish king that we know of, was
addicted; see 1 K. 11 : 3; Cant. 6 : 8. Again, this kind of
pleasure is nowhere referred to in the context; and we can
hardly conceive that it would be entirely omitted in such a case
as his, for he had seven hundred wives and three hundred concubines. Moreover, the singular here (שִׁדָּה), and then the plur.
שִׁדּוֹת, agrees well with the fact, that there was one, the *proper
queen*, who was Solomon's שֵׁגַל (Ps. 45 : 10), *i. e.*, *spouse*, in the
higher sense (see 1 K. 3 : 1; 7 : 8), and that he also had many
subordinate *wives*. In accordance with the characteristic traits
of Solomon's life, this circumstance is put last, as being the highest point or summit of his efforts to obtain enjoyment. The stem
of the word appears to be שׁנד, from which the derivate שִׁדָּה comes,
with נ assimilated and expressed by Dagh. f., as elsewhere often.
This verb is used in Arabic, and in the third Conj. (= שׁאנד) it
means *to take into one's arms, to embrace, to enclose around the
neck*, etc. The derivate noun, with מ prefixed, means, in Arabic,
bolster, pillow, and then is figuratively employed, as in our text.
So the Greek λέχος, *a couch, a marriage-couch*, also *a spouse*.
The endless conjectures of commentators respecting these words
are hardly worth recounting and refuting, since, as the words are
ἅπαξ λεγόμενα, it is proper, of course, to resort to a kindred language for illustration; and the meaning thus obtained fits the
passage exactly, and supplies a necessary *desideratum* in the list
of objects which had been pursued.

(9) And I waxed great, and increased more than all who were in Jerusalem before me; my wisdom also continued with me.

Waxed great in the same sense as in Gen. 24 : 35 ; 26 : 13 ; Job 1 : 3 ; *i. e.*, in the sense of acquiring *large possessions* or *property. Above all before me in Jerusalem*, see on v. 7. — הָיָה sing. because כֹּל is so. — עָמְדָה, *continued*, stood firm, *abode*, Ps. 102:27 ; Jer. 48 : 11, seq.   In v. 3 he tells us that he indulged in wine under the guidance of *wisdom* or *discretion.*   Here he tells us that his *discretion* was ever retained in the midst of all his various indulgences.   In other words : He never gave himself up to immoderate and excessive indulgences, but acted as a sober man, earnestly making experiments in order to learn what the true good is.   Tempered by this same discretion were his indulgences at large, which he next describes.

(10) And all which mine eyes sought for I withheld not from them ; I kept not back my heart from any joy ; for my heart was cheered by all my toil, and this was my portion of all my toil.

Sought for, lit. asked for, demanded.   Of course he means, when he says *I kept not back*, to designate indulgence only in such things as were within his power. — לְבִּי (from לֵב) is hardly represented, as to its Hebrew meaning, by *heart*.   It means *the source of sensations, affections, and emotions.*   We have no one word that corresponds wholly to it.   *Soul, mind*, which לֵב sometimes means, is not congruous here.   It designates *the self that feels and enjoys.* — שָׂמֵחַ, Part. of a verb intrans., § 43, 1, § 49, 2. *a.* — מִכָּל, מִ, *i. e.*, מִן *by, by reason of*, מִ before a noun designating the cause or source of the joy in question ; comp. for the like sense, 12 : 12 ; Ps. 28 : 7 ; 2 K. 6 : 27 ; Prov. 5 : 18 ; 1 Chron. 20 : 27.   *By all my toil*, *i. e.*, his toil was the ground or source of his enjoyment.   He sought not for pleasure beyond those things on which he bestowed time and pains.   He was not a mere reckless debauchee or Epicurean. — חֵלֶק means *that which is apportioned* or *allotted* to any one. — מִכָּל here means *of* or *from* all, מ again denoting *source*, quasi *out of*.

(11) Then I turned towards all my works which my hands had performed, and towards the toil which I had labored to accomplish, and lo! all was vanity and fruitless effort, and there is no profit under the sun.

One may supply the verb *to look* (from v. 12) after פָּנִיתִי. Plainly, the Hebrew expression is elliptical ; but that ellipsis is immediately supplied in the sequel. *The toil*, etc., Heb. lit. *the toil which I had toiled to accomplish.* Our idiom hardly permits in this case such a mode of expression. *There is no profit,* etc., a general proposition ; for if such things as he had pursued ; would not afford any substantial good, then nothing else earthly could do it, and the proposition is generally true.

§ 4. *The Advantage of Wisdom over Folly is of little Account, and does not exempt from the common Lot of Suffering and Sorrow.*

II. 12—26.

[The writer has now come to the end of his experiences in regard to the means of happiness. Neither efforts to acquire wisdom, nor folly in indulgence, will secure this, nor even these combined, vs. 1—11. He comes then deliberately to inquire whether *wisdom* in itself has any preëminence over folly. In some respects, he says it has ; but still, these are not sufficient to exempt it from the imputation of being *vanity;* for, first, it dies with every man who acquires it, and passes not on by heritage to another. Every one must begin *de novo* to acquire it for himself. Next, it does not exempt the wise man from the same common lot with the fool. All are the sport of accident alike, and all die at last alike, and are equally forgotten. Thirdly, a repulsive aspect is given to life by the fact, that all which one has laboriously and skilfully toiled to acquire, passes, at his death, to others of whom he cannot know whether they will be wise or foolish. What good, then, can come to him, which will compensate for all the toil and suffering and wakeful nights which he has endured in order to obtain substance ? Who can look on all this but with feelings of despair?

14

The conclusion, then, to which he comes is, that the only real good to be derived from all is that which we enjoy, from day to day, in the gratification of hunger and thirst, and other appetites which are the sources of present pleasure. This is our own, and we may regard it as a kind of good. But even this, to whatever it may amount, comes all from the hand of God. Such as are *good in his sight, i. e.*, the objects of his favor, may sometimes be permitted to enjoy what the sinner, his enemy, has labored to provide. But, after all, even this will not exempt the whole from the category of *vanity and empty pursuit*. Such pleasures are too low and fleeting to confer substantial good on rational beings.]

(12) Then I turned to contemplate wisdom — even madness and folly ; for what shall the man [do] who comes after the king ? Even that which he did long ago.

Evidently a new aspect of the subject is introduced by this verse. I have therefore rendered וֹ as a transition-particle, as it often is, like καί in καὶ ἐγένετο, etc. — חָכְמָה here, and generally through this book, has the sense of *sagacity, discreet wariness,* or *dexterous management,* whilst in the Book of Proverbs it often has a sublimer *moral* sense, designating sagacious, religious, and moral demeanor. This makes one point of palpable distinction in the *usus loquendi* of the two books. The explanation of the words וְהוֹלֵלוֹת וְסִכְלוּת is attended with some difficulty here. We may regard them as *coördinates* with חָכְמָה and in the Acc. after the verb, רְאוֹת, and *objects* of the action expressed by the verb. But in 1 : 17 the writer, to avoid any misunderstanding, has repeated the verb before the last two nouns. Not so here, however. Moreover, if we adopt this exegesis, we only make him to repeat here what he has already said in 1 : 17. In the mean time the context shows that he had done what was proposed in 1 : 17. Why should he speak here as if he were now about to commence the process, when in fact he has already been through it? It would rather seem, then, that some *result* of his investigation is here designated ; for the clause that follows shows that no other person can do anything more than the king has done ; for such person can only repeat what has already been done, and done so as to come to a result. This result, then, must stand, if the investigator is competent ; and it is to be regarded as correct. It has been suggested that *folly* is here a *second object* in the Acc., so as to give the clause this turn: *to contemplate wisdom as folly ; i. e.,* to regard it in the light of folly. The whole of the first clause would then signify that he addressed himself to the effort of considering wisdom in this light. But to be told that he set out with such design in view, sounds rather strange. He may come to such a result, but would hardly propose it beforehand as an object or design which he had in view. Moreover, the double Acc., in such a case, seems doubtful, if we compare Judg. 9 : 36. It appears more probable that *madness and folly* are the *result* which he finds in respect to the *wisdom* here spoken of; comp. Zech. 14: 6; Is. 66 : 3 ; Jer. 17 : 2, for like cases of *result.* Such wisdom ends in nothing essentially better than *folly.* And so the sequel goes oᴸ to show. All would be plain if there stood before וְהוֹלֵלוֹת וְסִכְלוּת the usual גַּם זֹאת or הֵנָּה. But brachylogy or pathos may have occasioned the omission of them. In the sequel, the writer has shown that although *wisdom,* in itself considered, and regard being paid only to its proper nature, is preferable to folly, yet in its *results* it has nothing to boast of. This the various considerations subsequently suggested plainly serve to show. We have then this sense : *To consider this wisdom (which is even madness and folly) ; for,* etc.

The last half of the verse has received a great variety of expositions. The history of them would not be very instructive. Enough, if the sense can be made plain. — כִּי is *causal,* as usual ; *i. e.,* it assigns a ground for admitting the preceding declaration. It is as much as to say : This is true, *for* no one can better investigate, or better come to a conclusion, in regard to this matter, than the king (Coheleth, 1: 12), who has already examined it. — מֶה הָאָדָם, *what shall the man* [do], etc., plainly implying the

verb יַעֲשֶׂה, as in Mal. 2 : 15 it is of necessity implied.   If *who*
were the sense required, then should we have מִי instead of מֶה .
This last is the Acc. after the verb implied.   The article here
stands before אָדָם, regarded as a specific individual, viz., the king's
successor, *i. e., he who comes after the king.*   The question is,
whether he can do anything better than has already been done
by the king before him, and so make out a different result.   The
answer follows : *Even that which he long ago did; i. e.,* he can
only repeat the same process, and come to the same result. —
עָשׂוּהוּ may be disposed of in two different ways.   Usually, it is
taken (as it is pointed) for the third pers. plur. impersonal, *what
they did, i. e.,* other men — a verb with an indef. Nom. § 134. 3.
This would be well enough, if in it were contained a good reason
why wisdom is found to be folly.   But the simple fact that nothing new can be done, has no direct bearing on the proposition
to be established.   But if the writer can bring forward his own
experience, after such long and thorough trials as he has made
in regard to this matter, then the conclusion to which he has
come would seem to be stable.   Accordingly, we may (with Hitzig) point thus : עֲשׂוֹהוּ.   That the *Inf. const.* of this verb, in several cases, omits the usual final ה, and is pointed as a regular verb,
is clear from Gen. 50: 20 ; Prov. 21 : 3 ; Ps. 101 : 3 (followed by
a Gen.), and Exod. 18 : 18, where the very form in question
occurs with a suffix, in the same manner which is now proposed.
We then obtain for the meaning: *the doing of him, i. e.,* what
he did.   The אֵת אֲשֶׁר of course is in the Acc., and is dependent
on יַעֲשֶׂה implied.   So: [He shall do] *what long ago was his*
[the king's] *doings.*   In other words: He may repeat the experiment, but can never alter the conclusion, for he can never
repeat it to any better advantage.   Consequently, the conclusion
indicated by the first clause must remain unshaken.   Heiligstedt,
in his recent commentary, comes out with this strange result : ' I
compared wisdom and folly, in order to know what sort of a foolish man he would be who should succeed the king, *in compari-*

son with him (אֵת אֲשֶׁר) whom they long ago made king;' which he explains by saying, that the design is to point out Rehoboam, the successor of Solomon, who was long ago made king, and who, as he strongly suspects, will overturn his father's wise institutions. This seems, to me at least, to be almost " a new thing under the sun." And yet he even has the assurance to say, at the close: " No one of the other interpretations of this verse *aptum sensum habet*." But to refute his interpretation would be little less than a loss of time, and to small purpose, since the language and drift of sentiment in the text are so utterly at variance with him. Hitzig has ably defended the sentiment which I have given above.

From the view thus taken of *sagacity* or *wisdom*, considered in respect to its power of conferring solid and lasting happiness, the writer turns, for a moment, to the consideration of the natural and essential difference between wisdom and folly in themselves considered, or viewed merely in respect to their proper nature. This difference he has expressed in the sequel.

(13) I saw, moreover, that there is an excellence of wisdom over folly, like the excellence of light over darkness.

In taking another view of the matter, he felt himself compelled to yield to the superior claims of wisdom, in respect to its nature. It gives insight into things, and explains many of them which must remain dark to folly. — יִתְרוֹן *profit, excellence*, lit. *something over and above.* — מִן *in comparison with, more than, over.* The *light* and the *darkness* are both specific and monadic objects, to which the article is properly prefixed, *ad libitum scriptoris;* in English it is quite useless here. The preëminence asserted is illustrated and confirmed by the next verse.

(14) The eyes of the wise man are in his head, but the fool walketh in darkness; yet still I know, even I, that one destiny awaits them all.

14*

To say that *one's eyes are in his head,* means that his eyes are in their proper place, and will be appropriately employed, *i. e.,* in seeing. But the fool, who has no mental eye, who is אֵין לֵב, must of course walk in darkness. So far as there is naturally a יִתְרוֹן then, it is on the side of the wise man; for who does not prefer light to darkness? Yet the latter part of the verse dashes down, in the main, the hopes which any one might be inclined to cherish, from the circumstance of the essential difference between the two. *One destiny awaits all; i. e.,* they have after all a common lot; all are subject to toil and suffering and death, to loss of property, loss of friends, and loss of hopes. — יִקְרֶה, *overtake, happen to.* — כֻּלָּם *all of them,* viz., both the wise and foolish. The Hholem in כֹּל goes into the short vowel Qibbuts in the suff. state, § 9. 10. 3.

(15) Then I said in my heart : As is the destiny of the fool, so also will it happen to myself; and why then should I be wise overmuch ? Then said I in my heart : This also is vanity.

אֲנִי *I,* prefixed to the verb which has the suff. of the same pronoun. נִי — *me,* after a preceding אֲנִי, is a construction which we cannot imitate. The force of it, however, is expressed in the translation *myself.* It makes the word *me* very emphatic. See the like in Gen. 24: 27 ; Ezek. 33 : 17, al. saepe. — אָז *then,* Hitzig remarks, refers to the close of life, when all his experience has been had. But it is enough to assume a point when his convictions are full. *This also is vanity,* viz., the strife to become *overmuch wise, i. e.,* wiser than all others. I take אֲשֶׁר (שֶׁ) to be here only the sign of quotation, like ὅτι in Greek. The next verse adds a new reason for the conclusion to which he has come.

(16) For to the wise man with the fool there is no remembrance forever, because that long since (in days that are to come) every one is forgotten. And how dieth the wise man like the fool !

In the phrase *with the fool,* עִם *with* designates not merely a

communion of *association*, but lot or condition. We might translate *as well as*, or *as*, see Lex. עִם, B. 1. e. — לְעוֹלָם . . . . אֵין =
never, so that we might translate : *There never will be any remembrance*. The כְּבָר *long ago, long since*, applies to a stand-
point in future time, *during days that are to come*, as this future
is expressed in the Hebrew. That is, in future time the day will
arrive when both the wise and the foolish will have been long forgotten. — הַיָּמִים הַבָּאִים are the Acc. of time, § 116. 2. — אֵיךְ for
אֵיכָה, made up of אֵי and כָּה *quo modo, how* or *alas!* an exclamation of grief. — יָמוּת Imperf., to designate what is continued or
often repeated. The consideration of such a matter forces a
sigh from the writer, which is expressed in the exclamation that
he utters. It is as much as to say : ' Alas! that all should share
the same destiny!'

(17) Then I hated life, for the deeds that were done under the sun were
odious to me ; for all is vanity and worthless effort.

The phrase רַע עָלַי lit. means *an evil upon me*, where the עַל
indicates the *burdensome* consequence of the evil, *lying upon* him,
or pressing him down. רַע is by no means confined to *moral*
evil. It designates anything *grievous* or *incommodious*. *Deeds
that were done*, viz., such things as men are engaged in doing ;
comp. 1 : 14. The *doings of God* are not included in these. To
these the author assigns another and a different character ; see
3 : 11, 14.

(18) Yea, I hated all the toil which I had performed under the sun, because I must leave it to the man who shall be after me.

עֲמָלִי means, *what I have acquired by toil* here, inasmuch as
this only could be inherited by posterity. — עָמֵל Part. for verb,
as frequently everywhere in this book. Moreover, the Part.
best designates continued action. — אַנִּיחֶנּוּ from נוּחַ with suff.,
see Lex. in Hiph. B. For suff., see Parad. p. 289 ; — אַחֲרָי in

Pause. This evil of transferring to another the fruits of toil, is aggravated by another circumstance, which he proceeds to name.

(19) And who knoweth whether he will be a wise man or a fool? And yet he will have power over all my toil which I have performed, and on which I have exercised my sagacity under the sun. This too is vanity.

The ו before יִשְׁלַט I have rendered, as the sense requires, by *and yet*— a meaning not unfrequent of ו. The two verbs that follow might be well rendered: *have sagaciously labored;* § 139. 3. That a fool should have the disposal of property acquired by sagacity, makes the toil doubly a vanity. The writer of this book plainly does not hold fools in much estimation. For the pointing of הֶ interrog. in הֶחָכָם, see Lex. הַ, Note d.

(20) Then I turned to make my heart despair, in respect to all the toil which I had performed under the sun.

סַבּוֹתִי is *turning* from one occupation in order to engage in another, while שׁוּב and פָּנָה mean, *turning* in order to see or behold anything; see 7: 25; 1 Sam. 22: 18, for the first case. For the two latter verbs, see v. 12, 4: 1, 7; 9: 11. Disappointed in all his toil, and in view of what was speedily to become of that which he had acquired, he set himself to *despair* of the whole matter. — יָאֵשׁ is Inf. Piel of יָאֵשׁ; for form see § 63, 3. His despair he proceeds to vindicate by the mention of an additional evil, described in the next verse.

(21) For there is a man who has toiled with sagacity and intelligence, and with dexterity, but to a man who has never toiled for it must he leave his portion; this too is vanity and a sore evil.

The idea that one who never made an effort to acquire is to bear rule over what another has acquired by his sagacious and successful toil, is very grating to a sensitive mind. It gives a despairing aspect to human effort. The writer feels it deeply, and names it רָעָה רַבָּה, an intensity of expression not before employed.

(22) For what is there for a man in all his toil and the strenuous effort of his heart, which he has performed under the sun ?

What is there, etc., there is nothing — חֹוֶה Part. of הָיָה, later Hebrew, or Aramaean, = הָיָה. — רַעְיֹון is intensive here, as it is designed to be climactic.

(23) For all his days are grievous, and harassing his employment; even by night his heart is not quiet. This too is vanity.

Hitzig and Ewald take כִּי here in the sense of *truly, surely ;* a meaning that it sometimes has, where *it is true,* or *it is so,* etc., may be easily supplied. If the preceding question, however, is regarded as a *negative* (and so I have taken it), then is כִּי *causal,* as it assigns a good reason for the negative. It is, in one aspect, a new suggestion. The question might be asked, whether men might not enjoy themselves in their labor and their efforts ? The verse before us seems to answer this question : *All his days are sorrows,* i. e., sorrowful, grievous. *And vexation* or *harassing his employment ;* i. e., instead of comfort and ease, his efforts have been sources of suffering and vexation. His solicitude will not even let him sleep at night. His mind is disquieted with plans and disappointments. But surely this proposition must appertain only to such excessive and ambitious pursuits as make life a bustle and a scene of disquietude. Occupation, business, of some kind or other, is essential to man's being, or at least to his *well-being.* "Labor ipse voluptas." Coheleth, then, must be regarded as having special reference here to a bustling life, engaged in by reason of ambition or avarice, or with erroneous expectations of finding solid and lasting happiness in worldly concerns.

(24) There is nothing better for man, than that he should eat and drink, and enjoy good in his toil ; even this I have seen, that it is from the hand of God.

The shape of the first clause shows that the sense is such as

I have expressed in the version above.—טוֹב as in the compar.
degree, should be followed by מִ. So in 3 : 22, טוֹב מֵאֲשֶׁר יִשְׂמַח
better than that he should rejoice. The reading required here
seems to be מִשֶּׁיֹּאכַל, and the מִ may have been dropped in tran-
scribing, because another מ immediately precedes. In בָּאָדָם
the בּ takes the same place which לְ elsewhere sometimes occupies in this book; 6: 12; 8 : 15. So is it with בּ in 3 : 12, בָּם,
for them; and so is it twice with בּ in 10: 17. *Make himself
happy in his toil,* lit. make his soul to see good. Comp. on 2 : 1.
Even this (זוֹ fem. and neut.) *is from the hand of God; i. e.,* even
such enjoyment is not secured by our own efforts. God alone be-
stows all blessings. Without his favor and aid all human efforts
are הֶבֶל. Comp. 3: 13; 5 : 18.

(25) For who can eat, and who can enjoy himself, without him ?

The Heb. text, as it now stands, says, in the last clause, *more
than I?* That is : ' Who can better say what the good is of
eating, etc., than I, who have had so much experience, and enjoyed so much?' But if, with the Sept., Syr., Jerome, Ewald,
Heiligs., and Hitzig, we adopt the reading מִמֶּנּוּ, *without him* (as
I have done), the sense is seemingly more appropriate. It runs
thus: ' Who can enjoy the good of his labor *without the divine
blessing?*' He had just said, that to God, and not to his own
efforts, this enjoyment was to be attributed. This latter translation, also, better suits the sense of חוּץ, which means *extra, without, i. e.,* apart from him. See Lex. for חוּשׁ and also חוּץ. The
union of חוּץ מִן occurs nowhere else in Heb.; but it is frequent
in the Talmud, and among the Rabbins.

(26) For to the man who is well-pleasing in his sight hath he given
sagacity, and intelligence, and enjoyment; but to the sinner hath he given
the task of gathering and amassing, that it may be given to him who is well-
pleasing in the sight of God. This too is vanity and fruitless effort.

Well-pleasing, טוֹב does not mean *good* here in the sense of *holy*, but designates merely the idea of one regarded in a favorable light; so in Neh. 2 : 5 ; 1 Sam. 29 : 6.   Of course, חוֹטֵא, the opposite here of טוֹב, means in this case one who is *offensive* to God ; for לְפָנָיו is of course implied after it. — לָתֵת lit. *for the giving*, Inf. of נָתַן.

But what is it which is vanity and a fruitless affair?   Surely, not the distribution which God makes; and not the scraping together of treasure, for this has already been denounced in vs. 17, 18.   We can therefore do no less than fall back on v. 24, and refer it to the effort to obtain enjoyment in the way which is there spoken of; not, indeed, an enjoyment which is altogether satisfactory in itself, but only such as is more promising than that obtained by other efforts and pursuits.   But even this, although *the portion which God gives*, and although it is to be gratefully received, is still, compared with good which is great and true and lasting, little less than vanity and a fruitless affair. Under the circumstances before us, we can, of course, give to these last words here only a limited and *comparative* sense.   *Absolute vanity* the enjoyment of the fruit of one's labor is not; but in comparison with the enjoyment which a rational and immortal being is capable of, in comparison with a happiness uninterrupted, solid, and lasting, all this is vanity.

Thus we are brought, step by step, after passing prominent particulars in review, to the general conclusion, that no possessions or pursuits of men secure the good which they need and seek for, and that the most we can make out of all these is the enjoyment which we experience from the actual satisfying of the wants and cravings of our physical nature.   Even this is not the result of our own efforts merely, but is bestowed upon us by the special favor of God.

Such is the conclusion of a most acute observer, a man endowed with high intellectual powers, and who sought for wisdom and knowledge in all the various ways practicable at the time when he lived.   Different, we may well believe, would be the conclusions of the same investigator, in some respects, and to a certain extent, were he now to reäppear and come among us, and again make his experiments. In his day, all that science could offer of satisfaction to its votaries, was meagre indeed, and very unsatisfactory to an active and inquisitive mind. The *ne plus ultra* would soon be reached, and might well be called *vanity* and an *empty pursuit*. But at the present time the same inquirer might turn in scores of directions, and find enough busily to engage his whole life, and much more, in any one of the numerous sciences. Put such a man as Coheleth, at the present time, in the position of a Newton, Laplace, Liebig, Cuvier, Owen, Linnæus, Davy, Hamilton, Humboldt, and multitudes of other men in Europe and in America, and he would find enough, in the pursuit of *wisdom and knowledge*, to fill his soul with the deepest interest, and to afford high mental gratification. "To eat, and drink, and enjoy the good of one's toil," while it is always a grateful blessing, would not even be named in comparison with pursuits like theirs. How would every true votary of science now look down on mere sensual gratifications (important and even necessary as they might be in their proper place, and in their appropriate measure), compared with the delight which he would experience in his literary and scientific pursuits! But it does not follow that Coheleth felt wrongly or wrote erroneously, at his time, in respect to these matters ; his conclusions, made in view of his experience, are altogether sober and correct, although, as has been said, if they had been made in circumstances such as ours, his estimate of the pursuit of *wisdom and knowledge* would have been very different in many respects. I speak in this manner only in reference to the *present world*, and the means of promoting worldly happiness or temporal enjoyment. But if we take a stand where we must look beyond this, and have regard to the *immortal soul* of man and the happiness of the world to come, then all the delights of even science and philosophy, ardently pursued, dwindle down to insignificance in comparison with hope animated by a living faith. All the science or philosophy of the world has never made, and would not and could not make, one *good man*, in the gospel-sense of this word ; and all, therefore, which they could bestow on us, or encourage us to hope for, would be mere *vanity of vanities* in comparison with the possession of such a faith and such a hope.

I must add a word in order to prevent any misconception of the object of these remarks. I believe Coheleth to be one of the genuine books of the holy Hebrew Scriptures. I believe it to have been in the Canon of the Old Test. when this was sanctioned by Christ and his apostles ; and therefore, that it is to be numbered among the inspired books. But inspired books may have a *plan* in view, and carry one into execution, as well as other books. The Book of Job has a *plan;* and the Book of Proverbs, and that of Canti-

cles, have each a *plan* at their basis.   I take the plan of Coheleth to be, *a relation of what passed in the mind of a reasoning man of his time, a man ardent
in the pursuit of finding out what are the principal means of happiness in the
present world, and how one must demean himself amidst the incidents and trials
of life, in order to secure some good degree of enjoyment and preserve a conscience
void of offence.*   That the author has a deep and abiding sense of the divine
power, and sovereignty, and wisdom, and goodness, is everywhere apparent
(see Introd. § 2, p. 30 seq.).   Not a word, amid all his complaints, respecting
the vanity and uncertainty of terrestrial things ; not one word in derogation
of a superintending Providence; not a word of apology for mistrust or want
of submission.   But all this is the result of conclusions to which experience
had led him when he sat down to write his book.   Yet still, while he gives
us these conclusions, he tells us also, at the same time, of the doubts and
difficulties with which he had to struggle in his own mind before he came to
them.   He lays open to our view the process through which he had passed.
The book is, in fact, a kind of monologue, or self-dialogue.   The mind, in
some past attitude, has suggested things which, in themselves, are far from
being correct and true ; but, in another and better attitude, it now suggests
things which remove doubts, or at least extract from objections their sting,
and, in many cases, even annul all their force.   One must hear him to the
close before he can fully decide what his creed was ; for he, like Paul, often
introduces the objector to his doctrines, without giving any notice that he is
going to do so.   The objections with which he has struggled are related, and
in due time are answered ; not, it may be, in our way of attack and defence,
under the guidance of modern systematized logic and method, but in a way
altogether accordant with the taste and genius of the Hebrews.   If, now, the
interpreter undertakes to make *orthodoxy* out of these objections, which are
contrary to it, then surely he undertakes a task which is desperate indeed.
But if he allows the writer to present a picture of the operations of his own
mind, when in a doubting and inquiring state, then he must concede to him
the right of presenting the objections which once wrought upon him, and
filled him with perplexity.   From this poison he now extracts potent medicine.   He settles down, at last, on a solid and immovable basis, not likely to
be again shaken.   But one must follow him through his book, with his eye
on all this, before he can fully attain to the writer's *ultimatum.*

    This picture of a struggling mind, which comes off triumphantly at last,
and settles down on "fearing God, and keeping his commandments," as the
way to happiness, and as the sum of human duty, will be felt, by multitudes
of like struggling and inquiring minds, to be a resemblance of what passes
within themselves.   They may therefore draw from the contemplation of

15

such a picture, much important instruction. But to make it truly interesting and profitable, it must be placed in an appropriate light, and contemplated from an advantageous station.

Thus, in reviewing the ground so far passed over, we must look at the writer in the state in which he truly was, with regard to the pursuit of wisdom and knowledge, in order to sympathize with him in respect to the acquisition of these. In our day, the pleasure or good that towers high above all other mere worldly enjoyments and pursuits, and ranks as inferior only to true piety, is the *pursuit of knowledge.* This is the high prerogative of man ; his excellence above all the creation around him. It would be impossible for *us* now to reason as Coheleth seems to do, in respect to this ; and equally impossible to deny the truth of what he said, at the time when he wrote the book which bears his name. And even now, the *spirit* of what he said is applicable to all science and all knowledge of a mere worldly nature, when we bring them into competition with that knowledge which concerns the life to come. " *This is eternal life, to know thee, the only true God, and Jesus Christ whom thou hast sent.*"

We have no good ground, then, in view of the whole, to take offence at what Coheleth has here advanced. He turns it all, at last, to good and proper account. He shows, in a vivid and impressive manner, how impossible it is for the world, and all which is therein, to give enduring peace and joy to the soul of man, which the inspiration of the Almighty has breathed into him, and thus exalted him to a rank that makes him aspire to something more elevated, more holy, and better than all which the world can bestow.

§ 5. *Dependence on Providence of Everything which can happen, or be done, or enjoyed. All is fixed and immutable, beyond any Change by the Power of Man.*

Chap. III. 1.—15.

[The prolonged title given above shows the nature of the next section. Vs. 24—26 of chap. ii. above give express intimation that whatever good there is to be enjoyed results from the interposition and favor of God. The mind of the writer seems to be conducted by those thoughts to the contemplation of the extent to which this interposition goes. It extends, in his view, to everything. All events, and all the actions and efforts of men, are under the surveillance and guidance of a Being who is wise and good ; vs. 1—8.

God has given employment to men; he has given them intelligence to discern his works; and he has made these his arrangements permanent. That they have any enjoyment, comes from him, and is to be viewed as his gift. God has prescribed bounds to all these things, which we can neither enlarge nor diminish, for the purpose of inspiring men with reverence and awe of him. He steadily pursues his course, and causes the circle of events, once gone over, to be renewed, so that all may recognize his continual providence, and know what they are to expect from the invariable course of things which he has established; vs. 9—15.]

(1) To everything there is an appointed time, and a season for every undertaking.

לַכֹּל *to everything*, i. e., as the sequel shows, to all human actions and conditions. The article (which the pointing לַ shows) is employed because of *totality*, like τὸ πᾶν. — זְמָן, used only here and Neh. 2 : 6; Esth. 9 : 27, 31. It designates a defined, appointed, or certain time. — עֵת means specially *opportune season* or *time*. — חֵפֶץ, *negotium, business, undertaking*. In this sense it belongs rather to the later Hebrew. The sentiment is, that the *when* and the *where* of all actions and occurrences are constituted and ordained of God. They are not within the power of man, and cannot be controlled by him. What is thus announced here in the way of a general proposition, is confirmed by the particulars that follow in vs. 2—8. The series of them begins with the birth and death of every man, and proceeds with recounting some of the more striking actions and occurrences of human life.

(2) A time for birth, and a time for death; a time to plant, and a time to pluck up that which is planted.

לֶדֶת, Inf. nominascens, *birth*; indicating, however, *parturition* by the mother, and not = הִוָּלֵד, Inf. pass. *being born*. The לְ prefix prep. in both cases is so pointed because it stands before a tone-syllable; see Lex. לְ. What birth and death are to man, *planting* and *being plucked up* are to plants and trees.

(3) A time to kill, and a time to heal; a time to break down, and a time to build up.

The *killing* and *healing* relate to men; the *pulling down* and *building up* have respect to structures, such as houses, etc.; what the former doings are to men, the latter are to edifices, etc.

(4) A time to weep, and a time to laugh; a time to mourn, and a time to dance.

Weeping and *mourning* stand connected with the dying and killing of the preceding verses. *Laughing* and *dancing* are exhibitions of mirth, and stand opposed to mourning. — רְקוֹד instead of שָׂמַח, because of its assonance with סְפוֹד. The לְ is omitted before the last two Infinitives for the sake of variety in the construction.

(5) A time to cast abroad stones, and a time to gather up stones; a time to embrace, and a time to remove from embracing.

Probably, the first half of the verse refers to *casting stones*, by an invading enemy, over arable land, in order to render it unfit for cultivation (see 2 K. 3: 19, 25); to *gather them up*, is to restore the land again to its useful state; see Is. 5: 2. — חֲבוֹק probably designates *amorous embrace*; comp. Prov. 5: 20. *To refrain* from this in due time is necessary, if one would guard against enervating indulgence.

(6) A time to seek, and a time to lose; a time to preserve, a time to cast away.

To seek, viz., with the prospect of finding; which is the opposite of what follows. — As אָבַד in Kal is intrans. and sometimes means, *to be lost*, so Piel (אִבֵּד) means, *to lose* anything. The translation by *destroy* here interferes with vs. 2, 3, inasmuch as it would thus make a virtual repetition.

(7) A time to rend, and time to sew together; a time to be silent, and a time to speak.

The *rending* probably refers to the rending of garments, on the receipt of bad news, or on the part of mourners. The *sewing together* is mending such rents, *i. e.*, it indicates the time when mourning is past. *The time to be silent* probably refers to silence observed through excessive grief; see Job 2 : 13. Of course, the *time to speak* designates the period when that excess is past, and speaking is resumed.

(8) A time to love, and a time to hate; a time of war, and a time of peace.

From *hatred* proceeds *war*. *Peace* follows war, at last; and with this the author ends his list of particulars. He has marked it, moreover, by adopting *nouns* in the last couplet, instead of the Inf. mode, which is employed in all the cases preceding. He now resumes his general declaration, so often made respecting things which he had tried by experience.

(9) What is the advantage of the doer, in that for which he has toiled ?

It was for the sake of raising this question, and of the answer which it elicits, that he introduced the preceding list of doings and occurrences, which are prominent among human efforts and affairs. He proceeds immediately to the answer. — הָעוֹשֶׂה, participial noun, *doer*, having the article.

(10) I have considered the task which God hath given to the sons of men, to busy them therewith.

All these things in which men are engaged, and by which they are affected, proceed from divine arrangements. Nothing can be done out of the time allotted by God, and all must be done or take place when his time comes. So, more clearly, in what follows.

(11) Everything hath he made beautiful in its season; moreover, he hath put intelligence in their heart, without which no man can find out the work that God doeth, from beginning to end.

The idea here depends mainly on the interpretation given to מִבְּלִי אֲשֶׁר לֹא. I cannot assent to most of the recent translations of this, although by the hand of masters. Ges.: *so that not;*

15*

Herzfeldt, *that not;* Knobel, *without that;* Ewald, *only that not*
— none of which can well be made out from the language. If
מִבְּלִי means *not,* then how could the לֹא follow? מִן of itself may
mean *without,* as in Job 21: 9; Jer. 2: 15; 48: 45, al. But מִן
has many other meanings. In order to make the *privative* meaning certain here, בְּלִי seems to be added; but בְּלִי is merely an *accessory,* and not the leading part of the word. For מִבְּלִי as meaning *without,* see also Zeph. 3: 6; Job 6: 6 — very plain cases.
In the same way אֵין is put after מִ, when it means *without,* see Is.
5: 9. Cases of מִבְּלִי where the מִ means *on account of, because of,*
such as in Ex. 14: 11; 2 K. 1: 3, do not compare with the case
now before us. *Only that* would in Heb. be אֶפֶס כִּי , and cannot
be expressed by מִבְּלִי אֲשֶׁר; see Amos 9: 8; Judg. 4: 9; 2 Sam.
12: 14, al. The writer could not say מִבְּלִיו (as Ges. intimates in
Thes.), in order to designate *without,* for בְּלִי admits of no suffix.
He could not well employ מֵאֲשֶׁר, because the word would then
present a sense doubtful at first view. It seems, then, that מִבְּלִי
אֲשֶׁר is the most plain and specific of all. Indeed, we may come
to the meaning *without,* in another way. Lit. מִבְּלִי אֲשֶׁר means
from the lack of which, or *by reason of the failure of which,* which
is = *without which.* This fully vindicates the translation, and
is satisfactorily sustained by Zeph. 3: 6; Job 6: 6. But to
what does אֲשֶׁר relate? Not to לִבָּם, surely, but to הָעֹלָם; to which
some such sense must of course be attached, as will make it designate the organ or instrument employed in acquiring a knowledge of what God has done.

עֹלָם (or rather עוֹלָם) is a frequent word, always bearing the
sense of *remote* or *obscure* or *indefinite time* or *age,* past or future,
except in this place. Much controversy has been made about
the meaning here. The Sept. and Aquila translate it by αἰών;
the Vulg. and some moderns, by *mundus;* Bauer, Rosenm., Mich.
et al., by *eternity;* Ges., De Wette, Knobel, by *Weltsinn,* or *mun-
dorum rerum studium,* which may mean *a love for* or *attachment to
the world,* or *the desire of searching out* or *investigating worldly*

things. But in the some three hundred or more examples of עוֹלָם in the Heb. Scriptures, not one of them approaches such a sense as *world* or *world-sense ;* and plainly it is the mere offspring of a supposed *exigentia loci.* What is more still, it *disagrees* with the contex. עֹלָם must, from the nature of the case, be something *without which* men cannot investigate the works of God, and something therefore *with which* they can investigate them. But a *Weltsinn* (world-sense) cannot aid in such an investigation, if we understand by it *love of the world;* and as to a *desire of searching out worldly things,* even the German word *(Weltsinn)* cannot well have this meaning, and much less can עֹלָם have it. But even if it be admitted, it would be incongruous. *The searching after worldly things* is not the way of finding out the works of God from the beginning to the end. Gesenius (in Thes.) renders : " God hath put into their heart the desire of worldly things, so that man cannot find out," etc. Here man is represented as being *hindered* by his *Weltsinn* (studium mundanum), instead of being *aided* by it ; and the Divine Being is brought before us as giving to man such a *worldliness* of mind as to defeat his efforts to acquire knowledge ; — a degrading view of Providence, which cannot well be put to the account of Coheleth. To translate by *world* simply, is liable to the same objection ; for it either has no tolerable sense in itself, or else it has one wholly inappropriate, viz., *love of the world.* To translate by *eternity* is equally incongruous, in case we render מִבְּלִי אֲשֶׁר לֹא by *so that not ;* for if *eternity* here means (as it must if it have any tolerable sense) *eternitatis studium,* then this would *aid* investigation, instead of being given to *defeat* it. If *eternity* simply be meant, then no appropriate sense whatever can be elicited from it.

Another and different rendering has, in view of these difficulties, been proposed by Gaab, Spohn, and recently by Hitzig. This is *intelligence,* or *the active faculty of knowing.* To justify this they resort to the Arabic عَلِم = עֶלֶם, meaning *wisdom, under-*

standing, etc.; which is altogether appropriate. In Ex. 36: 2, we have נְבַן חָכְמָה בְּלִבּוֹ in just the same way, and probably with the same meaning. That the Heb. word, as now written, was not designed to bear the usual sense, seems probable from the *form* itself. In some two hundred and ten cases of עוֹלָם, *eternity*, *age*, the ו is inserted throughout. In fourteen cases with the article, only one (1 Chron, 16: 36) besides that before us omits the ו. It is only when an accessory syllable follows (as in עֹלָמִים, עֹלָמוֹ) that the ו is left out, as in 1: 10; 12: 5. In Ecc. we have, excepting such cases as those, and also the one before us, always the form עוֹלָם; see 1: 4; 3: 14; 9: 6. Is it not fair, then, to draw the conclusion, that in the case before us ו is designedly omitted, in order to advertise the reader of a different meaning? The punctators, indeed, read and pointed it as ═ עֹלָם. But the passage seems not to have been understood by them, and, being in doubt, they followed the common analogy. I hesitate not to prefer (with Hitzig) the pointing עֶלֶם, as the Masorites are of no binding authority. Gesenius and Heiligst. disclaim the meaning of *intelligence*, because such a case as this is nowhere else to be found in the Hebrew Scriptures. But where else do they find their admitted sense of *mundus* in Heb.? It is only in the late Talmud and among the Rabbins, that this can be found. Of course one may make the same objection against their view as they make against ours. Ges. also says that it can in no way be rendered probable that מִבְּלִי אֲשֶׁר ever means *without*. The examples given above fully disprove this, and show plainly that it sometimes does so mean: and the context shows that עֶלֶם, in the sense of *studium mundanum*, is wholly inapposite. That we may resort to a kindred dialect, as to the Arabic here, to illustrate the meaning of a word which common Heb. analogy does not explain, is conceded on all hands, and is often done. There are a goodly number of words in Hebrew which are best illustrated in this way.

In further confirmation of this view, we may refer to Sir. 6:

22, Σοφία γὰρ κατὰ τὸ ὄνομα αὐτῆς ἐστι, καὶ οὐ πολλοῖς ἐστι φαν-
ερά, *i. e.*, For wisdom is according to her name, and is not manifest to many." The name then, here alluded to, must of course
be a name indicating some concealed or hidden thing. Plainly,
there is an allusion here to Job 28 : 20, 21, which runs thus:
" Whence does wisdom come? And where is the place of understanding? For she is *concealed* from the eyes of all the
living." Here the word *concealed* is in Heb. וְנֶעֶלְמָה, from עָלַם, *to
conceal.* The declaration of Sirach, that *according to her name*
she is *not manifest* = *concealed*, seems plainly to be built on the
verb עָלַם, as here applied to her; and this of course is the root
of עֶלֶם. It would seem that Sirach understood this noun, which
might be literally rendered *concealment*, to be one of the appellations of wisdom. It is a significant way of indicating that wisdom is something recondite, deep, and difficult to be discerned.
If so, it gives a Heb. interpretation of עֶלֶם in his time, and helps
to illustrate and confirm the one just given.

We come then to this result: ' God has made everything goodly
or appropriate (יָפֶה) in its proper time; and not only so, but
he has given to the mind of man *intelligence*, without which no
one can scan the work which he has done from the beginning to
the end.' In other words : In their proper season, all his arrangements are fitting or goodly, and he has enabled men to find out
this by their intelligence. But chap. 8: 17 seems to gainsay this;
for it *denies* that men can seek and find out the work of God.
But there the subject-matter is different. The writer is treating
of the fact, that no difference is made between the righteous and
the wicked in this life, and that one and the same destiny awaits
all. This mystery is too deep for him. He declares that he
cannot *find it out.* But, in our text, it is *the fitness of things in
their appropriate season* which men's understanding can search
out and see. Yea, the whole course of things, *from beginning to
end*, as it respects this matter, may be understood by the עֶלֶם,
intelligence, of man. If one is not satisfied with this method of

conciliation, he may betake himself to another mode of explanation, viz., that the writer, in 3 : 11, throws out an erroneous view,
viz., that of an objector, which is corrected in the progress of his
work, *i. e.*, in 8: 17.   So Hitzig; but I prefer the former.

(12) I know that there is no good for them, except to rejoice and to procure happiness during their lives.

בָּם, *for them*, see remarks on בָּאָדָם in 2 : 24; בְּ and לְ are not
unfrequently used, in the like sense, in the later Hebrew.   The
plur. suff. refers to הָאָדָם, *mankind*, in the preceding verse, which
is a noun of multitude.   At the end of the verse, in בְּחַיָּיו, is a
suff. sing. refering to the same noun in its sing. form. — טוֹב,
happiness or *enjoyment*, as usual in this book. — לַעֲשׂוֹת טוֹב, not
to do good in a moral sense (as many construe it), but *to make*,
i. e., *to acquire*, or *procure* happiness; comp. 2 : 24; 3 : 22; 5 : 17;
8 : 15 ; 9 : 7, which make this meaning clear.   Here the writer
recapitulates the sentiment already expressed in 2 : 24, from
which he started in this present section.   The next verse is, in
like manner, a repetition of 2 : 24*b*.

(13) And moreover, as to every man who eateth, and drinketh, and enjoyeth good in all his toil, the gift of God is this.

In 2 : 24 he says: *This is from the hand of God*. — הִיא *this
is*. — מַתַּת noun from נָתַן with נ assimilated, a formative מ, and
the fem. ending ת.   So entirely dependent are we on the Divine
Being, that even the little which we enjoy, is not secured by our
own plans and efforts, but by God's own arrangements.   He has
constituted the perpetual circle and order of all things.   We can
neither hasten nor retard his designs.   We can neither add to his
work, nor diminish from it.   It remains ever the same.   He
keeps all things evermore at his own disposal, in order that, from
our dependence on him and a sense of our own weakness, we
may regard him with reverence.   So the sequel.

(14) I know that all which God doeth, the same shall continue for ever; to it there is no addition, and from it there is no excision ; and God so doeth, that they may fear before him.

It shall be forever, i. e., his *doing* will always be the same. No one can add to it or abridge it. He is a sovereign, and "doeth all things after the counsel of his own will." *God so doeth,* lit. *has so done ;* but as he remains ever the same, so he is still doing, and will continue to do, the same. *That they* [men] *may fear before him ;* not *in order that,* or *for the purpose that,* but he is sovereign and uniform in his doings in such a way that men do and will fear before him, or have reason to fear. *Fear,* in Heb. usage, when it has respect to God, implies what we name *reverential awe.* The construction of אֵין here twice before the Inf. made with לְ, is rather aside from the common usage. Usually, it stands before nouns, pronouns, and participles ; but sometimes before the Inf. *gerundial* or Inf. *nominascens,* as in the present case. The two Infinitives may be regarded as virtually in the Gen. here ; § 113.

(15) That which is, was long since; and that which is to come, was long since ; and God seeketh out that which is past.

The first הָיָה here, although in the form of the Praeter tense, includes a *present* sense (as the Praet. often does), viz., *which was and is.* The sequel shows this to be necessary. So, what is and what will be, happened long ago, see 1 : 9, 10 ; in other words, "There is no new thing under the sun." *God seeketh out that which is passed,* נִרְדָּף, Part. Niph. of רָדַף, which means, *to follow after, to chase away.* The idea of the writer is, that one thing or occurrence follows after or upon another, and expelling it (so to speak), occupies its place or rather *time.* What has thus been thrust away by more recent events, God seeks out again, *i. e.,* he does this in order to renew and repeat it. Thus the generic sentiment of the first two clauses is developed in the last clause. And this completes the view which the writer takes

of the fixed, established, and invariable sequency of things which
God has ordained in the world, and so arranged that no efforts
or toil on the part of man can change his ordinances, or arrest
the course of things. *Man is thus impressively taught how dependent he is, and of how little avail it is to repine and murmur
at the irresistible will of an overruling Providence.*

§ 6. *Objections against the Assertion that God has made Every-
thing goodly.*

CHAP. III. 16—22.

[The manner in which this section commences (רָאִיתִי), shows that it stands
connected with the preceding. An objection to a previous assertion, that all
is made יָפֶה occurs to the writer's reflection, viz., that wicked instead of good
men occupy places of judgment. The answer to this is, that such things
continue only for a time, and are brought speedily under inquisition. Again,
his mind suggests to him that there is one and the same lot or destiny for
man and beast. That all die alike; they return to dust alike; and, so far
as we can see, we cannot discern whether the spirit of man goes upward, or
the spirit of a beast downward. What else is left for us, in this predicament,
but to enjoy what we can of the fruits of our toil? These last doubts or difficulties, however, are but partially solved here. The suggestion is made at
the outset (v. 18), that the object of such an arrangement is *to try men*, and
see whether they will *act* like the brutes, which, as to their destiny, they
seem so much to resemble. The writer gives full scope to the doubt or difficulty, without further answer here than what is implied in the assertion
that all is for the trial or exploration of them. But he draws from the statement thus made the conclusion that, since the matter of fact is thus, one
must do what he has repeatedly advised men to do (2 : 24 ; 3 : 12, 13, 22 ;
5 : 18 ; 8 : 15), viz., enjoy the good of his toil, and, at all events, make sure of
that. So much, at least, can be said with propriety, whether we know or do
not know what the future will be. The general view and conclusion to
which he ultimately comes is not given here, but toward the close of his
work. Objections (as here) are sometimes brought forward, which are not
immediately and fully answered. The sequel usually develops the answer.]

(16) And further, I saw under the sun the place of judgment, there was
injustice; even the place of justice, there was injustice.

וְעוֹד shows a transition to another subject, and has reference to v. 10, which commences with רָאִיתִי. — Not מְקוֹם alone is the object of the preceding verb, but the thing or fact described in the whole verse, viz., the occupation of the place of justice by injustice. מִשְׁפָּט means here both *power of deciding* and *obligation to a just decision.* The tribunal is occupied by רֶשַׁע, lit. *improbity, injustice;* here the latter, because it stands opposed to צֶדֶק, *justice.* The article before an abstract noun is a very common usage in Heb., § 107. N. 1. *c.* That the concrete, however, viz., an *unjust judge,* is here meant, is quite plain. The spectacle adverted to is one to which this book frequently adverts: (4 : 1 ; 5 : 8 ; 6 : 7 ; 8 : 9, 10) ; too frequently to leave us at liberty to suppose that it could have been written in the time of Solomon, when such things did not occur ; see 1 K. 10 : 24 ; 3 : 12 ; 13 : 28.

(17) I said in my heart, the righteous and the wicked God will judge; since a time for everything and for every work he hath appointed.

God will judge, i. e., he will pass sentence on each man according to his deserts. He will do so, because he has appointed a time when every deed and work will be judged. In most of the versions, שָׁם is regarded as an *adverb,* which some translate *there,* and some *then.* That it may designate either *time* or *place,* is familiar to every reader of Hebrew. But if it mean *there,* then a difficulty is easily raised by asking, *where?* No place has been adverted to in the context. If we render it *then,* we naturally inquire, of course, *when?* No time has yet been mentioned, to which *then* can refer. Besides, if *there* be the meaning, שָׁם should be placed earlier in the clause: see in Ps. 36: 13; 53 : 6, for a different position. There are other difficulties, moreover, which are serious. עֵת *time* — time for what? Not a time appropriate for the doing of any or every action, as in v. 1 ; for this would be merely a repetition of v. 1. Besides, that there is such a time, would not help to prove that God will judge the righteous and the wicked. Nor can *time* here mean a *limited*

16

time beyond which the wicked will not be tolerated; for then it must apply to the righteous as well as the wicked. Such a meaning cannot ever be urged upon עֵת לְכָל־חֵפֶץ, for this means *opportunity* to do this thing or that, and not a *brief space*, beyond which *doing* cannot extend. We must seek, then, for some other meaning. This is easily found. Houbigant, Döderl., Van der Palm, and Hitzig, point the last word שָׂם (not שָׁם), which means *to appoint, constitute.* The version which this would require is given above. The course of thought, then, runs thus. ' God will judge all men, for he has appointed a time [of judgment] for everything which they do.' This gets rid of all the doubt about the *where* or the *when.* The only difficulty that remains is, whether לְ and עַל can well mark the same relations. But this too is easily removed. Ges. (in Lex. עַל, 4, c.) says : "Non raro ponitur pro לְ et אֶל," as in Esth. 3 : 9 ; Job 33 : 23 ; 22 : 2 ; 6 : 27; 19 : 5; 30 : 2; 33 : 27; 38 : 10, al. Of course, then, we need to say no more here, than that עַל is employed merely in the way of varying the diction. But in this way of construing the clause, it follows that the verb שָׂם is rather unusually separated from its object עֵת. Yet cases of the like kind are not very rare. *Time,* i. e., a judgment-time, is made emphatic by standing first. The greater concinnity of the meaning thus elicited must be quite evident to all.

But when is this עֵת = *opportune time* to come? Is it in this world, or in the next? Hear Knobel : " The *last* judgment one must not here think of, but hold fast to the idea in general of a retribution some time or other to be made," *i. e.,* in the present world. Of the same opinion is Hitzig, Heiligstedt, De Wette, Ges., and many others. But they extend the same rule of exegesis to all the passages in the Old Test. which speak of a divine judgment respecting the doings of men. Heiligs. has appealed to more than twenty passages, all which (and many more besides), as he says, refer only to the present life. Therefore (such is his reasoning), Coheleth knew nothing of a *future* judgment. One might object that this is a *non sequitur* here ; but still, it could hardly be made probable, unless the language is very cogent that the author knew so much more than all his fellow Hebrews. That

there are things in this book, which, if taken as the established opinion of
Coheleth, would show that he doubted or denied a future existence, cannot
well be gainsayed. So vs. 18—20 below, where he seems to doubt, or ignore any knowledge of, the spirit of man after death, viz., whether it goes
upward, or not. In 9 : 5 he says, that " the dead know nothing, and have
no reward." In 9 : 6 he says : " There is no work, nor device, nor knowledge, nor wisdom, in the grave, whither thou goest." Certainly, these things
cannot be fairly disposed of by any one who maintains that the writer gives
everywhere his settled opinion, instead of communicating sometimes the
doubts he had experienced in a course of philosophical inquiry. They are
forced, in his way, to admit contradictions in the book, by their mode of
exegesis; and if not, then they have to put the author's words on the rack,
to make them confess what they themselves wish. On the other hand, admitting the expression of such doubts and objections, the question remains:
Has the writer developed anywhere his *ultimate* and settled opinion ? In regard to the point now before us — the judgment of men's actions — it seems
to me quite clear that he has. I bring out this conclusion by means of
several things which lie on the face of his book.

(1) The present life presents no important distinction between the righteous and the wicked as to their condition and destiny. The wise and the
foolish have the same experience of the evils of life, 2 : 14, 15. Even that
which befalleth the beasts, befalleth all men in common, 3 : 18—21. The
oppressed have no comforter; the dead, yea the unborn, are in a more desirable condition than the living, 4 : 1—3. What hath the wise man more than
the fool ? 6 : 8. The just perish in their righteousness, and the wicked prolong life in their wickedness, 7 : 15. There are just men to whom it happeneth according to the work of the wicked, and there are wicked men to
whom it happeneth according to the work of the righteous, 8 : 14. All
things come alike to all; there is one event to the righteous and to the
wicked, to the clean and to the unclean, 9 : 2. No man knoweth either love
or hatred by all that is before him, 9 : 1. Time and chance happen to all, 9 :
11. Thus we have, according to the simple tenor of these words, complete
doubt, or rather direct denial, of any distinctions in the present life between the
righteous and the wicked. If now we take these declarations as evidence of
Coheleth's settled opinion, it is idle to talk of reward and punishment as
applicable to men in this world. On the other hand, if we regard all declarations of this kind as indicative merely of a doubting state of mind, or as
related simply to those misfortunes and sufferings of all men, which are in
common while they are in their temporal condition, neither of these positions
will go to disprove a *future* judgment. At all events, it is in sober earnest

that Coheleth maintains the lot of all men, without distinction, to be one of misery and death. In this respect all are alike, for there is no distinction. But,

(2) He still holds fast the idea that there is a *retribution* to the righteous and the wicked.

God is to be feared, 3 : 14. His worshippers are to avoid offending him, by the most scrupulous attention to their religious duties, lest he should be angry, 5 : 1—7. He that feareth God, shall come forth out of all harm, 7 : 18. God made man upright, but they have sought out many evil inventions (7 : 29), and consequently deserve chastisement. Wickedness shall not deliver those who are given to it, 8 : 8. It shall be well with them that fear God, ... but it shall not be well with the wicked, 8: 12, 13. Remember thy Creator in the days of thy youth, 12 : 1 (with the implication of reward for so doing). Fear God, and keep his commandments, 12 : 13 (with the same implication).

Here then, in Nos. 1. 2, are diverse and *opposite* sentiments — *opposite*, in case we maintain that there is no retribution beyond the present life in Coheleth's view ; as most neological critics and some others do. First there is no distinction, in the present life, as to the condition of the righteous and the wicked ; " all things come alike to all." Secondly, " it shall *be well* with them that fear God ; it shall *not be well* with the wicked." — When ? Not in this world, according to the preceding view, for, according to that, " all things come alike to all." If, then, the second class of texts be true (and why should we call this in question ?), it must be that a *future* retribution awaits men. We come now to our text again.

(3) There is, then, *a time for judgment,* according to this text, when distinctions will be made, and retribution will follow. There is "One higher than the highest," who will punish oppressors, 5 : 8, and vindicate the oppressed, who " had no comforter" here, 4 : 1. He that feareth God shall be delivered, 7 : 26. The young may rejoice in their blessings, and live cheerfully ; but they are to remember always that " for all these things God will bring them into judgment," 11 : 9. " God will bring to judgment every work, with every secret thing, whether it be good, or whether it be evil," 12 : 14. This last passage forces even Knobel to acknowledge its reference to a *future* judgment. He assigns two reasons ; the first, that *everything* is to be brought into judgment ; the second, that even *every secret thing* is to be judged. This formula, as he well remarks, is always applied to a *judgment after death ;* see Rom. 2: 16 ; 1 Cor. 4 : 5 ; 1 Tim. 5 : 24, 25. He then goes on to say : " Neither of these two expressions could be expected if the writer were speaking merely of the natural consequences of human actions as a

retribution;" see Knob. in loc. This is ingenuous; but what next? Knob.
says, that "such being plainly the sentiment of 12:14, it could not possibly
have been written by Coheleth, and must have another author." In like
manner, Döderlein, Schmidt, Bertholdt, Umbreit, etc. Of all these assail-
ants of the genuineness of the passage, Heiligstedt well says: *Authentiam
argumentis infirmissimis et inanibus impugnarunt.*

I see no way of consistency, then, but that of supposing a *future* judgment
and retribution. The motives to piety without this are inert and powerless.
If you say that the prospect of a judgment during the present life is sufficient, we may well ask how that can be, when Coheleth tells us that "there
be wicked men to whom it happeneth according to the work of the righteous,"
(8:14); and that "all things come alike to all," 9:2? What *retribution* is
there in all this? All exhortations to "fear God, and keep his commandments," are fruitless on any other ground than that of a judgment after
death. *Retribution* is the very soul of all. He that cometh unto God must
believe that he is, and that he is the *rewarder* of them that diligently seek
him," Heb. 11:6.

And when we are told so often and so confidently that the ancient Hebrews had no idea of a future state and a future judgment, and therefore
Coheleth could have no reference to either, we must crave the liberty of
hesitating before we receive this. What did the Hebrews think had become
of Enoch and Elijah, after their translation? What is the meaning of being
gathered to one's fathers? Gen. 49:29; Judg. 2:10. Ges. says: "It is spoken
of the entrance into Orcus, where the Hebrews supposed their ancestors to
be assembled." (Lex. אָסַף, Niph.) Then what means: "In thy *presence*
is fulness of joy; at thy right hand are pleasures for ever more?" Ps. 16:
11. What shall we say of Ps. 17:15, "I shall be satisfied when I awake
in thy likeness"? And Daniel, not improbably a contemporary of the real
Coheleth — what means he when he tells us that "many of them that sleep
in the dust of the earth shall awake, some to everlasting life, and some to
shame and everlasting contempt"? Here is not only *futurity,* but a *resurrection* of the body itself. Isaiah, too, has added his testimony: "Thy dead
men shall live: with my dead body shall they arise. Awake and sing, ye
that dwell in dust [*i. e.,* ye dead]; for thy dew is as the dew of herbs, and
the earth shall cast out [*bring forth,* in the Heb.] the dead," 26:19. Beautiful imagery this: in which the grave is represented, like the grass on which
dew falls, as fructiferous, and bringing forth its dead as the fruit. This is
now generally admitted to refer to the *resurrection.* And when the Saviour
says, respecting the God of Abraham, Isaac, and Jacob, that "he is not the
God of the *dead,* but of the *living,*" does not he suppose the Jews, with whom

he was reasoning, to believe in a future state? All this, and more which might be easily adduced from the Old Test., makes me hesitate to receive the neological doctrine in respect to the subject before us. How can any man reasonably suppose that the Hebrews, with Moses, and Samuel, and David, and Solomon, and Isaiah, and other highly distinguished men to teach them, and above all if we believe them (as I do) to have been *inspired* — that the Jewish nation, after all, knew less than the Egyptian and other heathen nations around them, about a future state of existence? The idea is all but preposterous in my view. Still, I would not claim for Coheleth more than his book will justify. Those who find *gospel-clearness* in the Old Test., on such subjects, seem to forget that Paul has assigned to the gospel of Christ the high prerogative of "bringing life and immortality to light." It has brought out into noonday splendor what before was seen only in the twilight.

A more inconsistent man than Coheleth it would be difficult to find, putting all his views side by side, provided he has abjured all *futurity*, and yet insists on *retribution* to the righteous and the wicked, while he at the same time has again and again declared that " all things [in this world] come alike to all," and that " no man knoweth either love or hatred from all that is here before him." But when we view him in the light of proposing the doubts and difficulties which perplexed his own mind, and sooner or later as *solving* them, then we meet with no very serious embarrassment in the plain and straight-forward grammatico-historical interpretation of the book.]

(18) I said in my heart, on account of the sons of men, in order that God might search them, and that they might see for themselves that they are beasts.

On account of the sons of men — what is it which has been done, or is to be done, on their account? This verse is *coördinate* with v. 17, both beginning in the same way, and both equally having relation to v. 16. There we have the declaration, that *injustice* occupies the tribunal of *justice*. This is suffered or permitted, partly in order that men might be brought to see how brutish their conduct often is. *God searches them* by such a dispensation, and makes them conscious, in this manner, how wickedly they can demean themselves. — לְבָרָם, Inf. of בָּרַר, with pref. לְ and suff. ם-ָ. The Inf. ending with ר takes Pattah, like verbs ל Gutt.; and the usual Dagh. forte of verbs Ayin

doubled, is inadmissible in ר § 66. 3. Of course, the Pattah goes
into Qamets, § 22. 2. ם‑ is the usual Suff., here in the Acc.
after בַּר. The verb בָּרַר = בּוּר in 9 : 1, and means here *to ex‑*
plore, to search; see Lex. The subject of the Inf. (הָאֱלֹהִים) fol‑
lows the verb as usual, with the Acc. pronoun suff. inserted be‑
tween them. The לְ before the verb designates *purpose* or *design.*
Sentiment: 'It is for their sakes, or on their own account, that
God sifts or explores them.' Why? *That they might see,* etc.
Here, as אֱלֹהִים is not repeated after לִרְאוֹת, so as to designate a
subject for the Inf. verb, we must supply one from the context.
This gives us *sons of men.* It is that *men* (not God) *may see*
how brutish they are, in placing and continuing *injustice* on the
tribunal of justice. They are thus made *to perceive for them‑*
selves that they are beasts. — שֶׁ instead of שֶׁ = אֲשֶׁר, is perhaps
shortened because of the Maqqeph that follows; once, however,
שֶׁ occurs in 2 : 22, without Maqqeph, but with variations, as some
Mss. have שֶׁ. — הֵמָּה *are* simply a copula, § 119, 2. — לְהֶם gives
intensity to the expression of the subject *that they themselves*
might see, or *that they might see for themselves,* § 119. 3.

The writer next proceeds to give a reason why he has be‑
stowed on mankind the degrading appellation of *beasts.* He
points out the resemblance between them and the beasts.

(19 For as to the destiny of men and the destiny of beasts — there is even
one destiny for them; as dieth this, so dieth that; there is one breath to all;
and excellence of man over beast there is not; for all is vanity.

As to *sentiment,* comp. 9 : 2, 3 ; 2 : 14, 15 ; Ps. 49 : 13, 21. In
the first clause מִקְרֶה, as now pointed, is Nom. absolute. In וּמִקְרֶה,
the ו is climactic, § 152. Vav, B. 2. The *copula,* as usual, is
omitted in all three clauses, § 141. — מוֹת may be Inf. *nominas‑*
cens, or a noun in the const. state before זֶה, lit. *as is the death*
of this, so is the death of that. That רוּחַ means *vital breath* here
is plain; for this *breath* belongs in common to both, and is desig‑
nated in each case by רוּחַ; comp. Gen. 2 : 7 ; 6 : 17 ; 7 : 15, 22,

where the idea is fully expressed by רוּחַ חַיִּים. Sometimes the word designates *anima*, also *animus* and *intellectus*; see Lex. — בַּכֹּל, with the *article*, because of universality. *No excellence of man over beasts, i. e.*, none in regard to the thing which he has in view. One and the same destiny, viz., *suffering and death*, equally awaits all. — אַיִן *is not*, its subject is מוֹתַר. All are to be placed alike under the general category of *vanity*. The writer next proceeds to confirm v. 18 by other facts.

(20) All go to one place; all sprang from the dust, and all return to the dust :

הָיָה = ἐγένετο, *originated, came into existence* — שָׁב, 3 Praet. of שׁוּב, and not Part., comp. הָיָה in the preceding clause. — הֶעָפָר article before the name of a well-known substance, § 107. 3. N. 1. *b*. For the vowel (Seghol), see Lex. הֶ, Not. 2. *c*. Beasts are from the dust, Gen. 2 : 19 ; 1 : 24 ; and so is man, Gen. 2 : 7 ; 3 : 19. Both return to dust, Ps. 104 : 29 ; 146 : 4. Thus far the bodies only of each party are compared ; for of these only is the assertion true. But what of the רוּחַ, *the animating breath of life?* This is not *material* or *corporeal.* Whither, then, does it go ?

(21) Who knoweth the spirit of the sons of men, whether it ascendeth upward, and the spirit of beasts, whether it descendeth downwards to the earth ?

הַעֹלָה, the הַ is rendered as the article-pronoun (§ 107. 1) in our version, viz., *that* = which. But all the old versions make it the *interrogative* הַ, viz., Sept., Vulg., Syr., Arab., Chald., and so Luther and others, with nearly all recent critics. Even the present pointing does not decide against this, for הַ interrog. not unfrequently takes a Dagh. after it, like the article ; *e. g.*, in Job 23 : 6 ; Lev, 10 : 19 ; Is. 27 : 7 ; Ezek. 18 : 29, al. Here, as the Dagh. is suppressed, because of the Guttural, the short vowel becomes long, as in case of the article. So also in הַיֹּרֶדֶת, where the Dagh. is inserted, as stated above. Besides הַ *pronoun* does not couple with הִיא which here follows. It must be אֲשֶׁר, in such a case. Moreover, *who knoweth?* implies the indirect interrogative *whether* after it, *i. e.*, who knoweth *whether* it is so, or so? The doubt which is suggested here about the *spirit of man* is not answered for the present, but is fully answered in 12: 7, where we are told that "the spirit returns to God who gave it." Comp. Job 33: 28—30; 34: 14; Ps. 104: 29. As to the *spirit of beasts*, the question is not one of the same interest; no answer to it, therefore, is anywhere given. It would seem that the common impression about the entire extinction of beasts at their death, is tacitly admitted to be true. The הָיָא, in both cases, answers the purpose of the substantive verb in forming the participles so as to make them into verbs, § 119. 2. § 131. 2. *c.* It is *fem.*, because רוּחַ is usually so. — מַטָּה probably from מַט *depression*, with ה- parag. — לָאָרֶץ makes the meaning still more express and emphatic.

That an opinion was entertained by some around him, when Coheleth wrote his book, that the *spirit of man goes upwards, i. e.*, returns to God (12: 7), is clear from his putting the question. The idea was not new to him. But here, in his doubting and desponding mood, he makes it a question by asking: *Who knoweth?* That is, he here intimates that this matter is doubtful. It is to his purpose here to leave it so; for this brings man and beast into a closer resemblance, and his present concern is to make out this. The whole passage (vs. 18—21) shows that when the writer penned it, he was in that perplexed state of mind which is so often developed in the book, before we come near to the close of it. There the mist begins to dissipate, and he sees many things in a truer and more cheering light than before. Hesitation and skepticism are overcome, and his manful struggle to obtain light and truth becomes triumphant. But, taking things as they now appear to him, he comes once more to the former conclusion, viz.

(22) Then I saw that there is no good other than that a man rejoice in his

doings, since this is his portion ; for who shall bring him to look upon that
which shall be after him.

The same sentiment above, in 3 : 12, 13 ; 2 : 24. — מַעֲשָׂיו *his
doings*, not merely *toil* or *labor*, but all his actions and efforts.
Let each one take all the enjoyment which his efforts can secure.
Rational and moderate enjoyment, not Epicureanism, is doubtless
to be understood here ; see 2 : 9, 3. — For suff. נוּ- in יְבִיאֶנּוּ, see
Par. of Suff. p. 289. — רָאָה בְּ means, *to look intently upon*, i. e.,
with interest or pleasure. Sentiment: ' Seize on the present,
and enjoy what you safely and reasonably (בְּחָכְמָה) can ; for the
future no one can disclose with any certainty.' In other words :
' Make the best of what is now at your command, and trust not
to the uncertainties of the future.' Confining our view merely
to the world of sense, this advice is beyond all doubt correct and
proper. Every being instinctively desires enjoyment ; and Coheleth would have him secure what he can derive from his efforts,
but enjoy it with moderation and caution. Such advice is far
enough, indeed, from any monkish asceticism. Coheleth, for the
present, is looking only at this mutable and transitory world, and
inquiring what good it can afford which is worth striving for.
He comes repeatedly to the conclusion that all is mutable, evanescent, unsatisfactory, and not to be depended on, since we have
no control over it. To satisfy our innocent natural appetites, and
supply our wants, is all to which we can attain in the present
world. This he urges all to do, in order, as it plainly seems,
that they may be more contented and happy and cheerful. But
it would be a great mistake to cite from this book passages in
order to encourage men to become Epicureans, or, on the other
hand, to be gloomy and discontented Fatalists. Coheleth was
neither the one nor the other.

In my remarks above, on v. 17, I have stated the views of most of the
recent German commentators respecting the opinions of Coheleth as they
regard a future state. The doubt expressed about the final destiny of רוּחַ ,

in v. 21, they are well satisfied to accept as evidence of his skeptical views concerning the future. But 12 : 7 stands somewhat in their way. " The רוּחַ *returns to God* who gave it." The explanation which they give of this is, that ' God takes back the *breath of life* (רוּחַ) which he originally gave.' Hitzig asserts that the writer, in 12 : 7, has declared this to be true of the רוּחַ of both man and beast. If so, however, it does not lie in the words of 12 : 7, for there the רוּחַ of *man* only is spoken of. But Ps. 104 : 29 seems adapted to sustain his position. The Psalmist is speaking of all the animals, great and small. He says respecting them : " Thou takest away their רוּחַ, and they expire," *i. e.*, breathe out their vital breath, יִגְוָעוּן. In Job 34 : 14, 15, occurs the like expression respecting man : " He [God] taketh to himself *his spirit* (רוּחוֹ) and his breath ; all flesh perisheth together, and man return-eth to dust." In 33 : 30, this is expressed by לְהָשִׁיב נַפְשׁוֹ, *to take back his soul* or *life*. It is clear, then, that רוּחַ may be and is employed to designate *vital breath*, both of man and animals, and that the *taking away* of this brings on natural death. But when, as in 12 : 7, it is said of the רוּחַ itself, that *it returns* (תָּשׁוּב) *to God who gave it* (Gen. 2 : 7), it is doubtless the same רוּחַ, of which (Gen. 6 : 3) it is said : *It shall not always be humiliated* (יָדוֹן from דוּן = Arab. ‎دَانَ‎ *to humble*) *in man ; i. e.*, God will speedily recall it, or take it back, since it is so degraded. It is said *to return to God*, in our text. But how did the Hebrew conceive of such a *return* ? Was it a reäb-sorption into the source whence it came, and was *the breath of life* regarded as something material, *e. g.*, like to our atmosphere ? I know not how we can answer this question with entire confidence ; for a minute knowledge of Heb. speculative philosophy, with respect to such a point, we do not possess. Yet Job 4 : 15, 16, gives us an important hint : " Then a *spirit* passed before my face ; the hair of my flesh stood up. It stood still, but I could not dis-cern the form thereof ; an image was before mine eyes ; silence, and then a voice," etc. In other words, a shadowy, undefined something was before him, visible as distinguished from other things, and yet not defined in the detail. Here then is a רוּחַ diverse from vital breath. It seems, in the speaker's view (Eliphaz), to be the visible symbol or representative form of something which was immaterial in man, viz., the breath of life. This then, as it would seem, does not dissolve and perish like the body, and with it. It *goes back to God*, who gives to it this subtile and unsubstantial form. With this agree the words of Jesus (Luke 24 : 39) : " A spirit (πνεῦμα = רוּחַ) hath no flesh and bones, as ye see me have." The two passages let us into the porch of Jewish pneumatology ; but do not lead us into the *adytum* of the building. What *returns* to God, what he *takes away* (אָסַף), seems not to be absorbed in him, but to take to itself as it were a shadowy form, capable of motion and development. Nor does this stand in opposition to Ecc. 9 : 10, which declares that " in Sheol, there is neither work, nor device, nor knowledge, nor wisdom." The meaning of this is, that the dead cannot perform the functions of the living ; but it does not decide that there is no future existence, no surviving of a human being in any sense, in and by something which belongs to man.   There may be a רוּחַ, like that described by Eliphaz and by Christ, and yet all the actions of the common physical man be unsuitable to be ascribed to it. Nor can we appeal with confidence to Is. 14 : 9, 10, where the רְפָאִים (umbrae) in Sheol are represented as in commotion, to meet the approaching ghost of the Babylonish monarch and deride him ; for this picture has its basis merely in the popular views respecting שְׁאוֹל, like those among us about ghosts. Hitzig, on Ecc. 12 : 7, says that Coheleth represents the רוּחַ " as a particle of the divine breath, or worldsoul, which at decease is reäbsorbed." · With all due deference, I would suggest that a *world-soul* belongs to Greeks and Romans, but not to the Hebrews. God, a *personal* God, infinitely above all matter, separate from it, is an unvarying doctrine of the Hebrew theology.   " God is a spirit," is a declaration of Jesus (John 4 : 24) ; but evidently a declaration which develops only the common Jewish sentiment.

The question, then, What becomes of the רוּחַ *physiologically* which *ascends upward* — which *returns* to God who gave it? is one on which no portion of the Old Test. Scriptures directly passes sentence. It must be made out from *inference*, if made out at all. An incorporeal being Eliphaz saw ; one that hath neither flesh nor bones, Jesus decides a *spirit* to be. But beyond this, who can with certainty affirm ?   The word רוּחַ means *breath* of the mouth or nostrils ; then *breath of the air,* i. e., wind ; then *breath of life*＝נֶפֶשׁ (No. 2 Lex.), and ψυχή, or *anima ;* then *the seat of sensations, affections, and emotions ;* then *the love* or *temper of these,* and specially *the will and purpose* of the soul ; and lastly, *intellect, intelligence.* For the last we have a notable passage in Job 32 : 8 : " There is a *spirit* in man, and the inspiration of the Almighty hath given him *understanding.*" The two clauses are parallelisms, and of the like meaning. See also Job 32 : 18 ; Is. 29 : 24 ; 40 : 13 ; Ps. 139 : 7. Yet none of all these meanings compare with our English word *soul* in the higher sense, viz., a *spiritual incorporeal being,* having a separate and personal existence. Has the Old Test. disclosed such an idea, except it be obtained by implication ?   That the later Hebrews believed in something of this nature, is clear from the parable of the rich man and Lazarus, and from the words of our Saviour to the thief on the cross : " This day shalt thou be with me in Paradise," Luke 23 : 43 ; which is confirmed by Heb. 12 : 23 ;

Rev. 5 : 8—13 ; 6 : 9, 10, al. So too angels are *spirits*, and demons are *spirits*. But there is nothing so express as this in the Old Test. When the divine Being is called "the God of the spirits of all flesh" (Numb. 16 : 22 ; 27 : 16), the meaning is simply that he is supreme over all men that live or have *vital breath ;* comp. Job. 12 : 10 ; Is. 57 : 16.

We must give up, then, the idea of finding exactly the *pneumatology* which is taught by our philosophical systems in the Old Test. An incorporeal *personal* being after death, we cannot find expressly and definitely in the Jewish Scriptures ; *i. e*, this is not formally and directly developed there. But is it not a matter of fair inference from what is there said ? At the close of Coheleth, when the writer brings old age to view, and death as its proximate sequel, he announces the latter by saying, then " shall the spirit return to God who gave it." But what says he a moment after this ? "For God will bring to judgment every work, with every secret thing, whether it be good or whether it be evil. " But how shall the spirit which has returned to God be *judged*, if it be absorbed in him as the *anima mundi* (Hitzig), or as a part of his subtile impalpable essence ? How can it be *judged*, without any personality, or any identity of being with the former man ? How can it have " fulness of joy in God's presence" (Ps. 16 : 11), or be " satisfied, when it awakes in his likeness" (Ps. 17 : 15), without *personality* and real existence of its own ? In Dan. 12 : 2, and Is. 26 : 19, a *resurrection of the body* is taught ; so that we cannot appropriately appeal to those texts as to the point now before us. But the other passages just quoted, and Ecc. 3 : 17 ; 11 : 9, viewed in the light which they afford, seem to lead us to the conclusion, that while רוח, in far the greater number of cases, means *breath*, *breath of life, the seat of affections and emotions. and understanding* or *intelligence*, the use of it in some cases, like that of Ecc. 12 : 7, imports a surviving of the germ or source of those affections and of that intelligence. That the Hebrew pneumatology was well defined as to this point, that ancient metaphysics made it out as plainly and fully as ours under the teachings of the gospel, no considerate man will assert, who has well studied the subject. The *judgment*, the *reward*, the *retribution*, still were realities in the view of the Hebrews. At least this seems to be plain in the way of inference. And athough Coheleth here appears to doubt this (3 : 21), he plainly quits all his doubts in 12 : 7, and speaks decidedly.

17

§ 7. *Difficulties in respect to Enjoyment. Toil and Disappoint-
ment consequent on Plans to be rich or powerful.*

CHAP. IV. 1.—16.

[The writer has just been urging the present enjoyment of one's labors and
efforts. Difficulties that lie in the way of this now seem to start up and present themselves. Oppression is rife, and even carried so far as to make life
disgusting. All one's efforts are frustrated by it, so that the pursuit of good,
in this way, turns out to be vanity, vs. 1—6. One sets out to accumulate
much wealth; he even lives a solitary life in order to avoid expense; yet
this lonely condition is attended with inconvenience and harm, vs. 7—12.
One born poor is presented as striving to obtain even a throne; he succeeds,
to the prejudice of the old king; but at last his own disappointment and disgrace follow, vs. 13—16.]

(1) Then I turned and saw all the oppressions which are done under the
sun; and behold! the tears of the oppressed, and they had no comforter;
and from the hand of their oppressors was violence, but to them no comforter.

The wound of oppression, disclosed in 3:16, dwelt so on the
mind of the writer, and was so aggravated by his own experience,
that it breaks out afresh here, and he suggests the subject as
practically connected with the preceding advice about enjoyment.
This he thinks is impossible while things remain as they are.
— עֲשֻׁקִים, *committed, perpetrated.* — דִּמְעָה, const. sing. being a
collective noun. We must render it by the *plural,* because our
idiom does not employ the sing. in such a case. The second
עֲשֻׁקִים is Part. pass. — כֹּחַ, *power* in malam partem, *i. e., force,*
violence. The three participles here well designate the *continued*
action which the case presents.

(2) Then I praised the dead, those who long since died, more than those
who are living unto the present time.

שַׁבֵּחַ most critics regard as a Part. with מ dropped; which
sometimes occurs, perhaps, in Part. Piel, Zeph. 1:14. Knobel
has cited four examples in proof of this usage, every one of which

belongs to *Pual*, and not to Piel. Hitzig denies such a usage in
Piel; and Ges. has noted none in his Grammar.   Hitzig says
that we must make it in the Inf. absolute, which may follow a
definite verb, and continue the construction as though it were a
definite mode, 1 Chron. 5: 20.   In like manner, on the other
hand, the def. mode may follow the Inf. abs. in the same construction, Job 40: 2 ; Gen. 17 : 10.   But in Chron. 5 : 20, the Inf.
abs. is not followed (as in our text) by a Nom. or subject of the
verb, which seems to make a difference.   The אֲנִי, in our text
seemingly requires a Part., or else the def. verb שִׁבַּחְתִּי must be
implied.   Yet cases of the Nom. or subject in the *third* person,
may be found in Job 40 : 2.   Ezek. 1 : 14 (see § 128. 4. n. 1),
joined with the Inf. abs.   We may, therefore, accept this solution.
The making an *adjective* of שֻׁבַּח, as some have done, the meaning of the word puts out of question. — מֵתוּ declined with the
Tseri of the ground-form, מֵת. — חַיִּים adj. from חַי. — הֵמָּה *are*,
§ 119. 2. — עֲדֶנָּה, compound particle from עַד־הֵנָּה, *unto here*, either
as to place or time.   The ה- is local and paragogic, the root being הֵן.

(3) And better than both of them is he who hath not hitherto come into
existence, who hath not seen the evil deeds which are done under the sun.

מִשְּׁנֵיהֶם, lit. *than the two of them*, the dual Nom. is שְׁנַיִם. —
אֵת אֲשֶׁר, Acc. governed by שֻׁבַּח implied, and to be deduced from
the preceding verse.   Some make it the Nom., for אֵת is sometimes found before the Nom. (see Lex. אֵת, 2. *a.*) ; but this is unnecessary.   Still, I have made the translation as if it were in the
Nom. ; for literally rendered as *Acc.*, it would run thus : *And as
better than both of them* [I praised] *him who*, etc.   The version
above is more facile. — עֲדֶן, apoc. form, without the parag. ה-.
— הָיָה is a real Perf. here, and should be rendered, *has not been ;*
and so of רָאָה. — הָרָע adj. here, final Qamets made by the pause-
accent, from רַע. See a different construction in עִנְיַן רָע (1 : 13),
where רַע is a noun in the Genitive.

The pressure of the times must have been grievous to call forth
such a sentiment as this. We cannot imagine anything like to
this in the days of Solomon. The connection of vs. 1—3 with
what immediately precedes, is such as serves to show that the
·advice given in 3 : 22 could not be followed, at the time then
present, so as to secure the enjoyment in question; and as this
was the writer's last hope respecting earthly things, and this hope
was now frustrated by oppression, Coheleth despairs of life, and
wishes rather for death. He pushes the matter even to the highest extreme. 'It would be better,' he says, 'never to have been
born, than to come into life, and undergo such vexations and disappointments.' Thousands, every day, now sympathize with him.
The only mystery about the matter is, that he does not here say
one word about a *future* world; for a lively hope of happiness
there ought, full surely, to make him patient and submissive.
But, alas! as he has told us, " There is not a just man on earth,
that doeth good, and sinneth not." Job, with all his patience, in
a moment of exasperation, "cursed the day of his birth," 3 : 1
seq. Moses wished rather to be "blotted out of the book of God,"
i. e., to be erased from the catalogue of the living, than that the
request which he made should be refused, Ex. 32 : 32. Elijah,
when hotly persecuted by Jezebel, wished heartily to die, 1 K.
19: 4. Jonah was doubtless a good man; but when under disappointment, he gave expression to the wishes similar, Jon.
4 : 3. If, then, we allow Coheleth the same latitude which sacred
history shows us was tolerated in others, we cannot be at all sur-
prised at his impatience : especially if we regard his views of the
future at that time as somewhat unsettled and vacillating. We
need no Procrustes' bed for the text. We are not bound either
to approve of or to follow Coheleth's conclusions when he was
in his perplexed and unsettled state, but rather to take warning
from them, and seek to avoid them. Any other ground for the
exegesis of this book puts many parts of it on the rack, and even
then we cannot make it intelligibly confess what we desire. Very

different from all this is the close of the book, where he develops the *ultimatum* to which his mind comes. Christians have a spontaneous feeling that such a state of despair is wrong; ànd yet, under the full blaze of gospel-light, and all its revelations of the future, more or less of them indulge, at times, the like feelings with those of Coheleth. More pardonable and less strange were they in him, because, at the best, he could only see by twilight. The full strength of Christian sentiment we see in Paul and Peter, and others of similar hopes. " All things shall work together for good," sustained them in their most dark and dismal hours. Coheleth comes, at last, to the same conclusion; but the process in him was slower, and attended with more difficulty, than in their minds. Thus much for the dark cloud which oppression threw over him. Will the amassing of wealth serve to heal the wound? We shall soon see.

(4) Then I considered all toil and dexterity of doing, that it becomes matter of jealousy toward a man on the part of his neighbor; this too is vanity and fruitless effort.

When one strives to outdo his neighbor in his efforts to be rich, he often becomes an object of that neighbor's jealousy or envy; and this is a passion so bitter, that all pursuits which excite it become worthless by reason of it. Most render כִּשְׁרוֹן here *emolument, profit.* But in 2 : 21 it has the sense assigned to it in the version above, and the connection and sentiment seem to be alike in both passages. Indeed, *dexterity* is more *enviable* than wealth. — כִּי stands connected with רָאִיתִי, *I saw . . . that,* etc.; is not *causal.* — הִיא is fem., and is usual when the neuter (*id*) is required. It means, *it is,* or *it becomes.* But what is the *it,* which is matter of jealousy? The answer is, both the toil and the dexterity. These are included under הִיא = *that thing.* — קִנְאַת, most explain by *object of jealousy;* for toil and dexterity are not, themselves, jealousy. Hitzig, however, insists on *Beneiden, the envying* (active), not *the being envied.* In this case, we

17*

must give to הִיא the sense of *it occasions* — a possible, but not very facile meaning. — אִישׁ מֵרֵעֵהוּ, if we adopt Hitzig's view, is more readily explained, מִן often standing before the *author* or *cause* of anything; and so we may translate: *of envying by his neighbor.* The sense is good; but the other mode of interpretation makes it equally so. מֵ would then mean *from* or *on the part of*, designating the source of envy or jealousy ; a meaning not unfrequent of this particle. (See Lex. A. 2. *c.* For the suff. ‑הוּ to the noun, see § 89. § 91. 9.) If such be the consequences of dexterous toil to grow rich, it may well be said : *All is vanity and an empty pursuit.* That such is often the case every day bears testimony. But to the author's view some one may object (in the words of an old proverb), that still none but *fools* are inactive and lazy. So the next verse :

(5) The fool foldeth his hands, and consumeth his own flesh.

To fold the hands, is to assume the position of one unemployed and idle. — *And consumeth his own flesh,* not — sucks his own fat, and lives on it, like the bear — but *destroys himself.* In other words, through idleness he lacks the means of healthful nutriment, and his body pines away under its deprivations. He is *felo de se ;* comp. Ps. 27 : 2 ; Mic. 3 : 3 ; Is. 49 : 26 ; Num. 12 : 12. Such, then, are the consequences of laziness ; and if so, how, it is asked, can dexterous toil be *vanity*, which supplies the wants of the body ? Such seems to be the objection made to the preceding view of Coheleth ; and by the *activity* which he mentions, it is implied that some serious advantage is gained which the foolish *idler* must forego. Idleness is its own punishment; therefore activity, which makes provision for want, is not altogether *vanity*, as Coheleth had called it. Such is the logic of the objector. To this, an answer is made forthwith :

(6) Better is a handful of quiet, than two hands full of toil and fruitless effort.

The reply does not commend the course of the idle or foolish man; how could it? But it decides that quietude in life, with a *modicum*, is better than to have a double portion, or *both hands full*, which turns out, after all, to be but vanity and fruitless effort. In other words: It is better to be contented with what can be obtained in a quiet way, and without bustle and strenuous effort, than to toil incessantly in order to get both hands full, *i. e.*, an overflowing abundance. Coheleth would choose, for himself, neither the extreme of the bustling covetous man, nor yet that of the idle man, whose inaction must bring him to want. *In medio tutissimus.* Strive for a sufficiency, and be content with that; for this can be procured consistently with quiet. Therefore neither overdo, nor be idle. Both are vain and fruitless in their issue. — מְלֹא is Inf. nominas. followed (as often) by a Genitive. נַחַת, in the Acc. governed by מְלֹא, § 135. 3. *b.* Qamets on the penult here, on account of the pause. חָפְנַיִם, used only in the dual, lit. *both fists* or *clenched hands*, referring to the grasping of an object with both hands in order to hold it. — עָמָל, etc., both nouns in Acc. by reason of מְלֹא, as above. The folly of a greedy pursuit of wealth is still further illustrated by the sequel.

(7) And I turned and considered a vanity under the sun. (8) There is one man, and no second; moreover he has no son nor brother; and yet there is no end to all his toil; his eyes also are not satisfied with riches: " For whom then [saith he] do I toil, and deprive myself of enjoyment? " This too is vanity, a sad undertaking is it.

The discourse is climactic. Beginning with the vanity of excess in toil in order to acquire, it goes on here to illustrate the extreme folly to which this passion will lead. The writer begins, in v. 7, by calling it a *vanity*, he ends (v. 8) by calling it a *sore evil.*

And not a second is exegetical of the emphatic meaning of אֶחָד, viz., *one only.* — אֵין, being in the Const. state, it implies after it one or each of the two preceding nouns. — עֵינָיו takes a

sing. fem. verb after it, being the plur. of *things*, and not of
persons, § 143, 3; see 1 Sam. 4 : 15; Ps. 37 : 21; Jer. 2 : 15.
There is no need of the *Qeri* עֵינוֹ. — עֹשֶׁר, Acc. § 135, 3, *b*. —
And from whom, etc., *i. e.*, the miser is introduced as exclaiming
thus, אָמַר being omitted, as often in other cases. The statement
is thus rendered more vivid and striking. — נַפְשִׁי is as often =
myself. — עִנְיַן רָע, the first is in the Const. state, and lit. we must
render : *an undertaking of sadness* or *misfortune.* — הִיא, *is it*
as usual, fem. for neut., and *it* means the whole business, or the
whole affair in question.

Having adverted emphatically to the *loneliness* of the miser,
he pursues this view of the subject further, and describes the
evils that result from such an insulated position.

(9) Two are better than one, because they have a good reward on account
of their toil.

Heiligst. says that אֲשֶׁר does not mean *quia* here, but is to be
referred as a relative pronoun to the preceding שְׁנַיִם. But the
verse then would run thus : *Better are two than one, to which*
[two] *there is a reward*, etc. But this would defeat the speaker's
object, for it would limit *better* only to such two as might have a
reward. The assertion is more general. — אֲשֶׁר, *because*, is a
very common use of the word, see Lex. B. 3. What the
reward in question is, he now goes on to illustrate by some
particulars.

(10) For if they fall, the one shall raise up his fellow, but woe to him —
the one who shall fall — should there then be no second to raise him up.

If they fall, that is, either one or the other ; but not both at
the same time, for then no helper is left. — אִילוֹ is two words
compounded, viz., אִי לוֹ, *woe to him.* הָאֶחָד being in apposition
with the pron. in לוֹ, by implication the לְ prefix is carried on
mentally, so as to stand before it. *Falling* need not be confined
merely to stumbling *physically*, but may be extended to any case
where a *friend in time of need* is a good.

(11) Moreover, if two lie together, then they have warmth; but to one alone, how shall there be warmth?

The nights in Palestine, when the cold is nearly approaching to frost, become to the feelings severely cold, by reason of the warmth at mid-day. It would seem, from Ex. 22 : 26, that a man's cloak or outer garment was all the covering usually provided for sleeping. The point aimed at in the text becomes, in this view, quite conspicuous. With us, provided as we are with abundance of covering, the allegation of the verse seems comparatively tame. But the Hebrews slept on a floor-mat at the best, and not on feather beds; and they had few if any blankets, made for the purpose of procuring warmth by night. Many refer the text to *conjugal* union in sleeping; but the sentiment is more general, and the writer is not discussing the subject of matrimony. The object is merely to illustrate the sentiment he designs to confirm, by examples taken from the common occurrences of life. — וְחַם, lit. *then is it warm*, for וְ *then*, see § 152, B. *d.* — יֵחַם, Imperf. with A. of חָמַם, *Qamets* by reason of the pause; see § 66, Note 3, also 5, *e. g.*

(12) And if one prevails over him who is alone, two shall stand firm before him; and a threefold cord is not hastily broken.

The verb. יִתְקְפוֹ is here impersonal, and therefore requires the indefinite *one, any man*, before it. — הָאֶחָד is exegetical of the preceding suff. וֹ — used anticipatively, and means the *lonely one*. *Stand firm before him* is used to express successful resistance; see 2 K. 10 : 4; Josh. 10 : 8. — הַחוּט, designating a particular substance, it takes the article. — הַמְשֻׁלָּשׁ, *trebled*, Part. Pual of the denom. verb. — בִּמְהֵרָה, *with haste*, used adverbially. That is, if it be an advantage that two should combine, still more may be expected from the addition of a third. The last clause was doubtless a common proverb.

Thus much for the advantages of *society* or *union*. The lonely miser fails of securing these. His wealth, gotten by the relinquishment of the assistance and consolation which he often needs, is indeed but vanity.

But how fares it with the *ambitious* man? Do the honors which he covets, and which he successfully strives to win, render him secure, and stable, and renowned? We shall soon see.

(13) Better is a youth indigent and sagacious, than a king old and foolish, who cares not to be any more admonished.

חָכָם, *sagacious, cunning,* the secondary and lower sense of the word. — יָדַע, not only *novit, scivit,* but also *to care for, to have regard for;* see Lex. No. 7. All sorts of kings, from Nimrod down to Rehoboam, and even to Joash, have been conjectured here, in order to make out the *old king* mentioned. It is not absolutely necessary, indeed, to make out any other than merely a case supposed by way of illustration. If, however, any suppose that Solomon should be regarded as the author of the book, is it not very improbable that he would characterize himself as *old and foolish*? But a later writer, who read such an account of Solomon as is given in 1 K. 11 : 1—13, might well deem him to be old and foolish, and disinclined to hear wholesome admonition. It was not enough to have seven hundred wives and three hundred concubines, many of them heathen, but Solomon built heathen temples in the face of the temple of God, and *worshipped* in them, 1 K. 11 : 5. The young sagacious man seems not improbably to be Jeroboam, as we shall see in the sequel. יָדַע לְ, lit. *cares not in respect to.* The טוֹב, at the beginning, does not mean *better* in a moral sense, but *more fortunate.*

(14) For from the house of fugitives he goes forth to reign : for in his own kingdom he was born a poor man.

הָסוּרִים, as appears by the הָ (article with Qamets) was doubtless understood by the punctators as put for הָאֲסוּרִים, *the imprisoned.* Hence our version *out of prison;* and so most of the critics have translated. That א is sometimes dropped in such

cases, is clear from 2 Chron. 22 : 5, comp. with 2 K. 8 : 28 ; Is.
13 : 20. But if אָסַר is the stem of the word, we might expect
אֲסִירִים here, as in Judg. 16 : 21, 25 (Kethibh), and Gen. 39 : 20
(Qeri). On the other hand, no change in the text is really
needed ; for סוּרִים gives an apposite sense ; see in Jer. 17 : 13 ;
2 : 21, where it means *departed from.* The general sense of סוּר
is *to turn away, recede,* either to avoid danger, or to seek a place
of safety. *Fugitives* is our nearest word ; for men become so in
order to avoid danger, or to find safety. If, now, Jeroboam be
the *cunning youth* in question, the language applies fitly. He
fled to Egypt for safety, 1 K. 11 : 40. Moreover, Egypt was
the common asylum of fugitives from Judea, Jer. 26 : 21 ; 24 : 8 ;
and in later times, Joseph with Mary and the child Jesus went
thither, Matt. 2 : 13—22. From Egypt did Jeroboam come to
reign over *ten* tribes in Israel. He was born in Judea, and his
mother, at the time of his flight, was a widow, 1 K. 11 : 26. As
he was a *servant* of Solomon, he was probably poor ; but his
sagacity soon gave him the place of an officer under him. When
he " lifted up his hand " against the old king, Solomon sought to
kill him, and he fled to Egypt, the *house* or *asylum of refugees,*
1 K. 11 : 26, 40. The second כִּי is *causal* here, stating a ground
or reason of his flight. *In the kingdom* over which he afterwards
reigned, he was born *poor,* and so had not the means, at first, of
exciting and carrying out a revolt. On this ground he became a
fugitive, until opportunity of returning with a prospect of success
occurred. On his return, the people, disgusted by the new king
and his exactions, hailed Jeroboam with joy. So the sequel.

(15) I saw all the living, who walked beneath the sun, with the youth, the
second, who stood up in his room.

Living, i. e., living men, those who lived at that period. *All
the living,* is hyperbole in form ; but every reader feels at once
that it is merely a strong expression of the idea of great numbers, yet still such as belonged to Palestine, and not all the living

of the whole human race. See the like in Matt. 3 : 5. *Walked under the sun*, moved hither and thither on the earth. — עִם, *with*, in the usual sense of *association*. Heiligs. takes עִם in the sense of comparison — *the living compared with the youth*, etc. But what sense can be made of this I do not see. Clearly the meaning is, that he saw the populace thronging around the youth who was to be *second*, i. e., to be successor to the old king, instead of his own son, who retained only two tribes. The article in הַיֶּלֶד makes it plain that the יֶלֶד of v. 13 is referred to here. So הַשֵּׁנִי, in apposition and explicative, also takes the article. The *second king* may mean the next which follows the old one, or comes after him in the throne; but a somewhat different sense will be adverted to in the sequel, v. 16. *To stand up*, is *to stand firm, to establish* one's self. *In his room*, i. e., in the room of the old king.

(16) There is no end to all the people, to all before whom he was [whose leader he was]; moreover, those who come afterwards will not rejoice in him. Truly this also is vanity and fruitless effort.

Before whom he was. He is describing the popularity of the young king. He has just said that all the people are *with him*, and now he adds that he is leader — *is before* — a mass of men not to be numbered — *there is no end to them*. That the Heb. idiom readily admits this sense, may be easily shown. In 1 K. 16 : 21, it is twice said that *half of the people were after* such and such a one, i. e., followed him as their leader. In Num. 27 : 17, the leader is characterized by saying: "He shall go out *before them* [the people], and come in *before them*." The same is said of David, 1 Sam. 18 : 16; also of Solomon, 2 Chron. 1 : 10. אֲשֶׁר makes the suff. pron. הֶם a *relative*, § 121, 1. — הָיָה relates, of course, to the young king. Thus we gain a consistent and continuous sentiment; and so Hitzig and Knobel, while Ewald and Heiligs. refer לִפְנֵי to *time*, which appears to be altogether irrelevant. — הָאַחֲרוֹנִים, *the after-comers*, i. e., those who came on the stage of action after the elevation of the young man to the

throne, will take a different course from that of those who surrounded him with huzzaings at the outset. Such was the case
with Jeroboam. The terrible message communicated to him by
the prophet Abijah (1 K. 14 : 7—16), and the testimony concerning him in 2 K. 17 : 21, show that with all the good and
pious among the ten tribes, he must have been held in abhorrence
for his gross idolatry. While the mourning of Israel over the
grave of his infant child is particularly related (1 K. 14 : 18),
not a word of this nature is spoken about him, on the occasion
of his death. The opposite of regret is implied in 1 K. 14 : 10,
11. The wars which he waged (1 K. 14 : 19) must have occasioned heavy taxes to be laid upon the people, and this would
render him odious; for in the light of a *conqueror* he is not presented, and *conquest* only could secure popularity in such a case.
So we may conclude, with our text, that *they,* viz., the people
who lived under him, *would not rejoice in him. This, too, is
vanity;* truly so, because the object of his rebellion and treason
was not attained, viz., a quiet settlement on a throne. Such is
the end of all projects of mere ambition. It is *fruitless effort.*
The כִּי before the last clause has made some difficulty. But it
is unnecessary. — כִּי, at the head of a sentence or clause, not
unfrequently is an *intensive* (§ 152, II. d. Lex. כִּי, 6 c.), and is
equivalent to the Lat. *imo,* or the German *ja, i. e.,*=*yea, indeed,
truly;* see Is. 32 : 13; 15 : 1; Ps. 71 : 23; 77 : 12; Ex. 22 : 22;
Job 8 : 6. So Ewald, Gramm. § 320, *b.* (fifth edition), who has
finely illustrated this use of the particle, which is imperfectly
treated of in Ges. Gramm. and Lex. — גַּם denotes *addition,
cumulation; also this,* or (as we must express it here in our
idiom) *this too, this also, i. e.,* this matter must be added to the
list of vanities. Ambition, then, comes out badly at last.

If we are correct in referring the *old king* to Solomon under
the guidance of his heathen wives, and the *young man* to Jeroboam, there still remains some difficulty in the case. Rehoboam,
Solomon's son and successor, is, to all appearance, not brought

18

to view; and this seems somewhat strange. Perhaps, however, there is in reality a reference to him implied by the יֶלֶד, which designates Jeroboam in v. 15. I have supposed above (on v. 15) that it may mean the *successor of Solomon*, as king to the great mass of the Hebrew nation. But I do not see, on the whole, why we may not suppose that יֶלֶד designates Jeroboam, and refers to Rehoboam, as being implied by the *first*, because his birth and rank gave him the lawful title to the kingdom. A *second* יֶלֶד would seem to imply that there was a *first* יֶלֶד ; and if so, this must have been Rehoboam.

Hitzig concedes the applicability of vs. 13—16 to Solomon and Jeroboam; but the fact that *Rehoboam* is not adverted to, he thinks so strange, that we must seek elsewhere for an explanation of the passage. Accordingly, he goes down to the time of Ptolemy Euergetes, king of Egypt (fl. 246—221 B. C.), and finds that the high-priest of that time, Onias, is represented as old and foolish by Josephus (Antiqq. xii. 4), and that his nephew, Joseph, is described as being a shrewd manager, who wrested his office from his uncle, and then, in consequence of being farmer of the Syrian tribute revenue, he afterwards became unpopular. He even finds in Φιχόλα, Joseph's native place, another form of *Phigela*, an Ionian town built by *fugitives*, as the name imports. This, then, as Hitzig supposes, is the בֵּית הַסּוּרִים from which the young man comes. All this is ingenious, no doubt, yet not very satisfactory ; for first, there is no evidence, worthy of credit, that any part of the Jewish Scriptures was written so late as 246—221 B. C. ; and secondly, Onias was *not king*, while the *old and foolish man* of our text *is king;* nor was Joseph a *king*, who ousted and succeeded him. Still, it is mainly on this ground that Hitzig puts the authorship of Coheleth down to the time of Euergetes (Vorbemerk. § 4). Surely this has slender support, and is, on the whole, a real רְעִיּוֹן רָע. Nothing but desperation in neology, as it seems to me, could have contrived such an interpretation as this. In fact, a con-

summate Hebrew philologist, as Hitzig clearly is, ought not to
risk his reputation on such a fantasy. How could he reasonably
expect that others who should investigate for themselves would
be satisfied with such a criticism? I trust that few of such will
be brought to believe that the office of a *priest* and a *king* is the
same. And whoever looks at Josephus's account of *Joseph* will
find a very different character from that of the רֶלֶךְ.

§ 8. *In what Way, under such Circumstances, a Man ought to
demean himself in respect to the Ordinances of God.*

CHAPS. IV. 17—V. 6.

[Thus far all has been *description* of the evils and disappointments of life,
interspersed with a few incidental remarks. A new turn is now given to the
discourse. It becomes *preceptive* and *monitory.* The first great question for
a man who reverences God is : "How shall I demean myself toward him,
when his providence has placed me in the midst of such trials and disappointments, from which there is no escape ? Shall I shun his presence, and
cease to worship him, since I despair of any solid good in the present life ?
If not, how can I propitiate him, or how worship him acceptably ? " This
brings the question to a point where Coheleth feels it needful to interpose
and give his advice. He addresses the questioner in the way of precepts
and precautions. Hence the *second* person (which has not before appeared)
in the precepts that follow. As the transition is so great from 4 : 16, with
the preceding context to the subject in 4 : 17, it is wonderful that those who
divided the Hebrew Scriptures into *chapters* should not have joined 4 : 17
with what follows in Chap. V., as is done in our English version. The
present division in the Hebrew helps to bewilder the reader.]

(17) Keep thy foot when thou goest to the house of God ; and to draw
near to hear is better than the sacrificial feast which is given by fools ; for
they know not how to be sad.

In רַגְלֶיךָ, the vowels are adapted to the sing. רַגְלְךָ, as the
Masoretic marginal note indicates. With the latter agree the
versions of the Sept., Syr., Vulg., and most of the modern critics.
See the sing., also, in like cases, in Prov. 1 : 15 ; 4 : 26. *Keep*

thy foot = look well to thy going; seek to go safely and surely by looking well to thy steps. *Goest to the house of God*, seems to imply that both the adviser and those whom he designs to instruct live in the vicinity of the temple, where they often and habitually worship. It seems probable from this that the author wrote this book at Jerusalem, or in its vicinity, or at least had lived there. — וְקָרֹב, Inf. abs. Piel, and so it may be of any mode or person, § 128, 4, 6; here it means the *approaching* or *drawing near*. Here, too, it is the *subject* of the sentence; which is rare, § 128, 4, n. 1. comp. Job 40 : 2; Ezek. 1 : 14. The object is to show what *keeping the foot*, etc., signifies. *An approaching to hear*, denotes entrance into the interior temple, where the priests read the law, and uttered their exhortations; see Deut. 33 : 10; Mic. 3 : 11; Mal. 2 : 6, 7, comp. Acts 3 : 11. — מִתֵּת, *i. e.*, מִן before the Inf. תֵּת (from נָתַן), which is a contraction of תֶּנֶת fem. Inf. Before this word (מִתֵּת) טוֹב is plainly *implied* (because מ is comparative, § 117, 1), but it is not here expressed; as, *e. g.*, in 9 : 17; Ezek. 15 : 2; Is. 10 : 10, al., where it is omitted. Accordingly I have rendered it — *better* than the instituting or giving by fools of a sacrificial feast. הַכְּסִילִים (article before a whole class) is the agent or subject of תֵּת; but as it is impossible, in our language, to imitate the Heb. construction, I have designated the agency in the translation thus: *by fools*. That זֶבַח (in Pause זָבַח) may and does often mean the *feast* on a part of the victim which is offered, is plain; see Lex. and comp. Prov. 17 : 1; Is. 22 : 13; Deut. 33 : 19. Here, as the *offerers* are plural (fools), and the *feast* singular, it is probably indicated that while one victim is sacrificed and feasted on, there is a *company* who sit down at the feast upon it. Such, indeed, was the usage; comp. 1 Sam. 9 : 13; 2 K. 1 : 9, 41. If this were not meant, we should expect זְבָחִים in correspondence with הַכְּסִילִים. The כִּי *causal*, that begins the last clause, indicates a reason why the *offerers* in the preceding clause are called *fools*. When they go to the temple, instead of going

there to be instructed, instead of entering the inner court and
listening to prayers and instructions, they content themselves
with staying in the outer court, and there holding their sacrificial feast, accompanied by their friends, for the sake of social
enjoyment. There they eat and drink for pleasure, and are
merry withal. This the writer opposes to, and contrasts with,
that *sadness* which becomes a penitent who goes to the temple to
confess his sins, to offer sacrifice for expiation, and to hear the
monitions of divine truth. All this imports godly sorrow and
penitence, with desire to be corrected. But fools neglect this
part of duty. They go to the temple to keep up appearances as
worshippers, but mainly for the pleasure of the social feast.
This is the doing of *fools*, and not of men who act reasonably.
They are full of exhilaration and merriment, and do not feel or
exhibit any of the sadness which contrition occasions. That רַע
(in pause רָע) often means *sadness* is made clear in Lex. Cases
in point, which cannot be mistaken as to the meaning of עֲשׂוֹת
רַע, may be found in 2 Sam. 12 : 18 ; and the opposite, viz., עֲשׂוֹת
טוֹב, in Ecc. 3 : 12 above. As the latter clearly means to *enjoy
good* or *procure pleasure*, so the former means, lit., *to make sad*,
i. e., to demean one's self with sadness. The idea of a suffering
condition stands connected with it ; for sadness comes through
this. But it is by no means confined to *physical* suffering ; it
extends to mental. Fools know not how to sorrow for the sins
which occasioned the זֶבַח in question. But he who *keeps his
foot* — *i. e.*, looks well to his goings — will avoid their folly.
He will go up to the temple with becoming solemnity, and will
be *sorrowful* or *sad* for his sins, and listen to admonition.

This explanation I owe to Hitzig. Its correctness, as to truly
representing the Heb. idiom, cannot well be questioned. But
others translate differently, and after the old fashion : Knob. :
That do not concern themselves about evil-doing ; Ewald : *Because
they know not that they do evil;* Heiligs. : *Nam nesciunt se
facere malum.* But what is the *evil*, in this case ? Not the

18*

mere offering of sacrifice; for that the Law commands. If *real ignorance of evil* is implied by the last clause, would not this palliate instead of enhancing their fault? To put them in fault, they must neglect some *known* duty. When they feast and carouse, and sorrow not for sin, they neglect the obvious duty of one who brings a sacrifice. Therefore they act foolishly, and therefore are they called *fools*. The word יוֹדְעִים is not confined to mere mental perception; for the word also means *advertere animum, providere, curare, to take knowledge* of a thing, in the sense of looking after it and caring for it; see Lex. s. v. No. 7. The above modes of exegesis, then, are conformed neither to the Heb. idiom, nor to the exigencies of the case. In the other mode of interpretation, we obtain an excellent sentiment: ' When thou goest to worship God, go not to indulge in levity and mirth, but to humble thyself and be *sad* for thy sins. Fools stay in the outer court, where they can indulge in the first; go thou into the inner one, where thou canst be made better by sadness.' See this sentiment fully and explicitly repeated and confirmed in Ecc. 7 : 3—6. It is, indeed, plain that men are not fools for offering an appointed sacrifice; nor yet from mere ignorance about its true value; but they are fools for refusing to receive the obvious instruction which such a transaction implicitly gives, viz., that the offerer should be penitent, and desirous of admonition.

Chap. V.

(1) Be not hasty with thy mouth, and let not thy heart urge thee on to utter words before God; for God is in heaven, and thou art on earth, therefore let thy words be few.

The preceding verse brings to view the subject of *sacrifice;* but here we have the duty of *prayer,* which would naturally follow on. Caution is given against hasty and thoughtless utterance of words in prayer. *Be not hasty with thy mouth,* עַל פִּיךָ,

like עַל לְשׁוֹנוֹ, Ps. 15 : 3, lit. means, *on thy mouth.* We say : Let
no slander be *on thy tongue;* but the Hebrews have extended
the usage further, and speak of the mouth in general as the seat
or source of utterance, or on which utterance rests. — דָּבָר, *a
word, i. e., any word,* any one thing in thy prayer. *Before God,*
here means in the temple where he peculiarly dwelt; but the
spirit of the precept will apply to prayer anywhere, or at any
time. *God is in heaven and thou on earth; i. e.,* God is infinitely
exalted above all created things, but thou art only one of the
latter, and on his footstool; comp. Ps. 115 : 3. *Let thy words
be few; i. e.,* do not speak much and at random, as men in light
and free conversation with familiar friends and equals are apt to
do. Speak as penetrated by reverential awe of the exalted
majesty and power of God. — מְעַטִּים, a Pilel form from מָעַט,
fewness; used only in the later Hebrew.

(2) For a dream cometh with much occupation, and the voice of a fool
with a multitude of words.

עִנְיָן (not מַעֲשֶׂה), not *hand-labor,* but *occupation* in business
that tries and perplexes the mind. Common experience shows
how often the fact here stated is verified. *And a fool's voice,*
etc., *i. e.,* only the foolish prattle and outpour a flood of words.
The two parts of the verse include a *comparison,* for the Hebrew
often makes a comparison with only וְ between the members of
it, which in such cases may well be rendered *and so,* or *and thus;*
§ 152, B. 3. If the phrase were filled out, כְּ or כֵּן would be
inserted between the two parts. The intimation of the verse is,
that dreamy visions have as much substance as the prattle of
the fool; or, in other words, overdoing in business or in talking
is followed by a dreamy sequel.

The two preceding verses are not directed against earnest,
repeated, or even long prayers, where they proceed from the
heart, and are uttered with holy earnestness and fervor. The
Saviour's words in Matt. 6 : 6—13 are a good comment on the

true meaning. It is much, and light, and thoughtless loquacity before God, which is disapproved and rebuked, as showing want of due reverence. This is the ground or reason (כִּי at the beginning of the verse) why the words should be few.

(3) When thou shalt make a vow unto God, make no delay to pay it, for there is no pleasure in fools ; whatever thou shalt vow, pay it.

That is, only fools delay to fulfil or to pay their vows ; do thou not be one of them. *Make a vow*, we say in English ; but the Hebrews said, *vow a vow*. We can say the same, but commonly do not. *No pleasure, i. e.*, there is *no complacency* on the part of God toward the conduct of such as neglect their vows. — תִּדֹּר, Imperf. of נָדַר, answers to the conditional future here.

(4) It is better that thou shouldest not vow, than that thou shouldest vow and not pay.

In other words: As vows are a *voluntary* thing, and not a prescribed duty, it is much better to forbear making them, than to make and then violate them ; for by this one incurs the guilt of falsehood or perjury. — מִ, מִשֶּׁתִּדּוֹר is the comparative = *than;* שֶׁ == אֲשֶׁר, as often in this book. All three Dagheshes arise from omitted letters, viz., נ, ר, and נ.

The two preceding verses have respect to what often took place among worshippers. They asked certain things of God, and vowed to render certain offerings of gratitude in case they obtained them. It was natural to associate such acts with the subject of prayer, as all belonged to the subject of religion.

(5) Let not thy mouth bring punishment upon thy flesh ; and say not before the messenger that it was an error. Why should God be displeased on account of thy words, and destroy the work of thy hands ?

Nearly all the expositors translate לַחֲטִיא by *cause to sin*. To this there are several objections: (1) The Old Test. does not employ בְּשָׂר in the sense of σάρξ in the New Test. ; the *flesh*, in

the Heb. Scriptures is not the sinner, but the *mind, heart, soul,*
are the sinners. (2) This mode of explaining does not well
coincide with the last part of the verse, which appears to ask
the question (in the way of remonstrance) why the punishment
in question need be incurred. *The destroying of one's handi-
work,* seems to aim at expressing, for substance, the same thing
as *the punishment of the flesh.* Ges. (Lex.), under Hiph. of the
verb, has not, indeed, given the meaning assigned to it above;
but under חַטָּאת (the noun) he has given us *poena, calamitas,*
as one of the meanings, *i. e.,* the consequence of sin. The same
is the case with עָוֹן, which signifies *crimen,* and very often also
poena, calamitas. And so פֶּשַׁע, *delictum,* and also *poena.* This
gives us a clue to the Hiph. of the verb, הֶחֱטִיא; it may mean
either *to cause to sin,* or *to subject to punishment, i. e.,* to the
consequences of sin, having the same twofold sense as the noun.
The mouth that speaks much and at random, and utters false
vows, is of course the cause of the *punishment* that follows.
The *sinning* is described in vs. 1—4; the *consequences* in v. 5;
for this does not describe a *new* sin, but adverts to those already
described. — בָּשָׂר is the *animal man* as the seat of feeling, the
body which suffers penal consequences in the present world;
comp. Job 14 : 22, which gives the exact idea of the word in such
a connection. — הַמַּלְאָךְ, the *messenger, i. e.,* the person commis-
sioned to explain the law of God, and propound it to the people,
i. e., God's *ambassador.* In the present case, the *priest* of course
is meant, before whom confession of sin is to be made. The
same sense of the word in Mal. 2 : 7. But in neither case
should we translate by *priest.* How the priest was concerned
with vows, may be seen in Lev. 27 : 2 seq. — כִּי here merely
introduces direct speech, like ὅτι in Greek. — שְׁגָגָה well characterizes the sin in question here, for the root means : *to commit
a fault through error or imprudence.* Hitzig translates : *Unbe-
sonnenheit, i. e., an act of inconsideration;* altogether *ad rem,*
for hasty vowing is still in the view of the writer. We cannot

hit the mark quite so well in English. The design of the whole
clause is not to prohibit confession before the priest, after a fault
has been committed, but to teach that a man should avoid the
necessity of making a confession, by avoiding the sin which will
demand one. — אַל before the first two clauses is the negative
before a *hortatory* verb = the Greek μή, while לֹא is positive and
= the Greek οὐ. — הִיא, *it was*, viz., the thing done was. — לָמָּה,
for what? why? It is the intensive interrogative of one dissuad-
ing or rebuking. — קוֹלֶךְ (־ with a pause-accent), קוֹל כְּסִיל in
v. 2. It means words uttered by or with the voice, or what the
voice declares, and thus it is of a *generic* sense. I have therefore rendered it by *words*. *The work of thy hands*, means any
active employment or business in which a man is engaged. His
undertakings may be frustrated or *destroyed* in a great variety
of ways, by sickness, by untimely accidents, or by misfortune
(as we say) of any kind. Such is the threatened punishment,
which, like the threats in the Pent., and nearly throughout the
Old Test., has a reference primarily, to chastisements in the
present world. It is rather by *inference*, than by direct and
plain words, that a state of *future* punishment is disclosed in the
Hebrew Scriptures.

(6) For in a multitude of dreams there are indeed vanities; and so [in]
many words: but fear thou God.

This verse is a general summary of vs. 1—5, making a conclusion of the paragraph. One must refrain from idle prattling
in prayer, and from false vows; because, like dreams, they come
to nothing, or are of no avail. The כִּי at the outset is *causal*,
since a reason is given for refraining from the things before
specified. The וְ before חֲבָלִים is intensive, § 152, B. 2. The וְ
before דְּבָרִים means *and so*, because comparison is made by it,
§ 152, B. 3. The בְּ in ברב is by implication carried forward to
דְּבָרִים, as translated above. — כִּי, before the last clause, is disjunctive and adversative = *but;* see Lex. כִּי, No. 6. —*Fear thou*

the God (lit.), where the article marks the only living and true
God, τὸν θεόν. The word יְהוָֹה never occurs in this book. At
the period when this book was written, the ὄνομα ἀφωνητόν began
to be disused; and it is everywhere dropped in the version of
the Seventy, who always read (as the Jews now do) אֲדֹנָי in the
room of יְהוָֹה. Sentiment: 'Many words, like many dreams,
come to nothing; fear God, so as neither to speak lightly or
vow falsely.'

§ 9. *Supplementary Reflections on various Topics, which lead to the same general Result as before.*

Chap. V. 7—19.

[The topic of *oppression*, made so prominent in 3 : 16; 4 : 1, is here
brought again to view, and some mitigation of the evil is suggested. The
Most High will watch and oversee rulers, vs. 7, 8. The covetous can enjoy
no real good; they can only look at their wealth. The industrious laborer
has much the advantage over them. Wealth often injures its possessors, and
perishes by adverse occurrences, so that it does not continue even for one's
own children. At the most, the rich can carry away nothing with them at
their death; and while they were living, much vexation ensued from the
acquisition of wealth and the safe guarding of it; vs. 9—16. To enjoy the
fruits of labor as they are gathered, therefore, is fit and proper, and this
must be regarded as the gift of God; for men could not, of themselves,
attain even to so much. A man who enjoys this, will in a good measure
forget his sorrows, while God makes all things respond to the joys of his
heart; vs. 17—19.]

(7) If thou shalt see oppression of the poor, and robbery of judgment and
justice in the province, be not astonished concerning such a matter, for
there is one high above him who is elevated, a watchful observer; yea, there
are those high above them.

And robbery of judgment and justice, צֶדֶק is in the Gen., as
well as the preceding noun, and both stand related to גֵּזֶל. Oppressive magistrates often refuse trial of the causes of the poor,
from motives of haughtiness or self interest; and when they do

try them, they rob them of their just rights by a wrong decision. *In the province, i. e.,* in the particular province to which the person seeing belongs: see on 2 : 8, and comp. Est. 1 : 1. The Hebrew kingdom was divided into *provinces* for the sake of collecting imposts and revenues. — תִּתְמַהּ, *astounded,* here reg. with ה Mappiq, *i. e.,* vocal as a consonant, at the end, and therefore a regular guttural verb. — הַחֵפֶץ, *the matter,* as several times before. The art. is prefixed, because it refers to the particular matter just mentioned. — גָּבֹהַּ, *elevated, high.* — מֵעַל, lit. *on the part of,* over, *i. e., above;* see עַל, B. in Lex. The second גָּבֹהַּ designates the oppressive magistrate who is *elevated* to office; the first גָּבֹהַּ designates his superior in office, *i. e.,* one *above him* in point of rank. This superior magistrate is a שֹׁמֵר, *one who watches over* any things or persons, and observes all actions in order to take cognizance of them. The implication seems to be, that in such a case he will call to an account the oppressor. But if not, then, as an ultimate resort, there are גְּבֹהִים, lit. *elevated ones* over them both. I take the last word, in the plural form here, to relate to *God, the Most High,* the plur. being intensive (§ 106, 2, *b.*), and so like to other plural participles and adjectives applied to the Supreme Being; *e. g.,* קְדֹשִׁים, Hos. 12 : 1 ; Prov. 9 : 10; 30 : 3 ; בֹּרְאִים, Ecc. 12 : 1 ; עֶלְיוֹנִין (Chald. plur.), Dan. 7 : 18, 22, 25, 27. The last clause of the verse before us contains a reason why one should not be astonished, since it is introduced by כִּי. Sentiment: 'When inferior magistrates are oppressive, and in the habit of robbing and plundering the poor, do not regard this as a perplexing, inexplicable, and hopeless matter. An appeal lies to a higher court (see Acts 25 : 11) ; but if the matter still goes on adversely there, then remember for your comfort that there is *One superior to all,* who will bring all into judgment.'

Hitzig makes three orders of magistrates, all concurring in, or conniving at the same injustice and oppression. But how would a knowledge of this lessen the astonishment of the beholder?

Oppression and injustice from any judge of causes is always a matter of astonishment to the good and upright; and if so, a regular series of them, from the lowest to the highest magistrate, would be still more so. Coheleth advises the person astonished to consider the matter in its ultimate results. Apparent inconsistencies in the government of Providence will then be much diminished, if they do not entirely disappear. With Hitzig's exegesis one cannot well rest satisfied, because in 3 : 16, 17, the same complaint is made as here, and the answer to it is, *that God has appointed a time for judging all.* This is too plain to be misunderstood ; and this of course makes plain the verse under discussion, which is of a parallel nature. It is difficult to see how so sharp-sighted a critic as Hitzig could overlook this obvious auxiliary in interpreting the verse before us.

(8) Moreover, an advantage of a land in all this, is a king to a cultivated field.

A text which has occasioned no little difficulty and perplexity among critics. Our first object is to obtain a right view of the grammatical sense. The proposition is a general one ; for he says not *the country* or *the land,* but simply אֶרֶץ, *a land, any land.* The Kethibh should of course be pointed thus : בְּכָל הִיא, *i. e., in all this.* The pointing in conformity with the Qeri would be thus : בַּכֹּל הוּא. We must, then, translate the latter as follows : *The advantage of a land — in everything is it.* But first, this is not only in itself an extravagant assertion, but irrelative and incongruous with respect to the context, which affords no reason for saying this. Next, the *position* of הוּא is very strange, on the supposition that the Qeri is the right reading ; for then הוּא is a *copula,* and should be placed immediately after the subject, and not, as here, after both subject and predicate. Besides, a copula in this case is unnecessary, § 141, since no emphasis is demanded. The Kethibh, therefore, viz., בְּכָל־הִיא, is undoubtedly the true reading. Compare בְּכָל־זֹאת in Is. 9 : 11, 20 ; 10 : 4,

for this latter expression can mean only : *in all this;* and בְּכָל
הִיא is virtually the same, for this means : *in all of that thing*
(the fem. represents the neuter).   But what is *that thing?*   It
is what is described in the preceding verse, viz., the need of
protection from the highest ruler, the king, against oppression.
An advantage to a land is it, to have a king endowed with power
and will to interfere and protect.   This cannot be a king who
through oppression lays waste a land, by causing its poor laboring men under his yoke to despair of obtaining anything for
themselves; but it must be a *king to a cultivated field-land;* a
king, therefore, who renders justice to the poor, and encourages
the laborer to continue his toils, instead of despoiling him.   That
לְשָׂדֶה נֶעֱבָד means a *cultivated field,* or *champaign,* is rendered
clear by Ezek. 36 : 9, 34; Deut. 21 : 4; and so the Sept. translate.   The word שָׂדֶה has no article, because אֶרֶץ has none, and
both mean substantially the same thing.   The proposition, therefore, is general and indefinite.   Sentiment : 'To any land
exposed to oppression and injustice, it is an advantage to have a
king who reigns, not over a country made desolate by oppression, but *over a cultivated field-land.*   Justice will then be so
administered, that the country will pour forth an abundance by
reason of the poor laborer's toil in cultivating it; and this is
an advantage.'   See Prov. 14 : 28.

I merely mention some of the renderings of the last clause
here.   Rosenm. : *rex est agro addictus.*   Herzfeld : *the king is
subject to the field.*   Ewald : *a king is set over the country.*
Knobel : *a king honored by the land.*   Heiligstedt : *a king is
made for the field.*   Eng. version : *a king is served by the field.*
Not one of all these accords with the grammatical meaning of
the Hebrew.   Rosenm. makes the king only a lover of agricul-
ture; Hertz., the king to be a servant of the field; Ewald, a king
set over the field (a meaning that נֶעֱבָד never has); Knob., a
king honored, etc., while the proper word for this is מְכֻבָּד;
Heiligst. (like Ewald), a king *terrae praefectus;* the Eng. ver-

sion, *a king served by the field,* which is nearer than any of the others to the Hebrew, but still gives an irrelevant sense. To what direct purpose is all this, or rather, are all these views? while that which is given above commends itself by its concinnity with the context. Rulers may be oppressive; they often and usually are so; but it is an advantage to any land, where the poor are exposed to oppression, to have a king who will not suffer any to lay waste his domain by oppressing, but will cause it to be cultivated by dealing justly with all.

The verse is probably a side-blow at some tyrant of the day, whose measures had made the country a comparative desolation. A striking illustration of the effect of such a government on the country is found by casting our eye over Palestine and Asia Minor; the latter of which once had an immense population, but now has not one twentieth part of the numbers which it could support. Scarcely any region of the earth is capable of supporting more inhabitants on its soil. Yet Turkish despotism has made it a waste. The Sultans have never aimed to be kings over *cultivated fields*, and have been something very different from a יִתְרוֹן to the land. Coheleth seems to have lived under some prince of such a character; and while he complains of oppression, and reminds the גָּבֹהַּ, or *king*, that he should look to his under-officers, he reminds him also of his responsibility to a higher King, and that he would be a blessing to his realm, if by his justice and equity he would convert the whole country into a cultivated field. It is comforting to the oppressed when such admonition is faithfully given.

These views in respect to *avaricious* and *rapacious* magistrates naturally led the mind of the writer to the consideration, once more, of riches, and of the strife to acquire them. His views in the sequel are more general, and are not confined to magistrates, although *they* are doubtless included. The subject lay heavily upon his mind. In 2 : 7—9 he has spoken plainly respecting *regal wealth.* In 4 : 8 he returns again to the subject, and takes a more general view. But now, when occasion again prompts, he comes out more fully still, and contemplates the subject from various points of view.

(9) He who loveth silver shall not be satisfied with silver; and whoever loveth wealth shall not [be satisfied] with revenue; this too is vanity.

Silver was the most common coin, and therefore is employed here as the representative of all wealth. The second כֶּסֶף is in the Acc., after a verb of *filling*, § 135, 3, *b*. — בֶּהָמוֹן, with the article, as the vowel under ב shows; for pointing, see Lex. הַ; the word being abstract, it naturally takes the article in Hebrew, § 107, n. 1, *c*. For ב, after אָהֵב, see in Lex. s. v. That יִשְׂבַּע is implied after לֹא is quite plain; and I have translated accordingly. תְּבוּאָה is Acc. after this verb implied. Here a new shape is given to the *vanity* in question. The eager pursuit of wealth enkindles desires that never can be quenched or allayed. Of course it is truly a tormenting הֶבֶל.

(10) By the increase of goods, they who consume them are increased; and what advantage is there to their owner, except the looking on with his eyes?

חַטוֹבָה, sing. generic, while our exactly corresponding English word *(goods)* is employed only in the plural, in the sense here required. I have translated in accordance with our idiom. The article is put here before a word designating a *class* of things, § 107, n. 1, *b*. The suff. to the Part. (הָ-) is sing. in order to correspond with the noun to which it relates. The same with the suff. in לִבְעָלֶיהָ, from בַּעַל — כִּי אִם, see in Lex. — רְאוּת has vowels belonging to the Qeri רְאוּת. Which form is preferable, it would be difficult to decide, since both are good. Both of these forms are *nouns* of the Inf. formation; while רְבוֹת, at the beginning of the verse is Inf. *nominascens*. That כִּשְׁרוֹן does not here mean *dexterity* (as in 2 : 21), is plain from the context, which requires such a meaning as I have given in the version

above. Great wealth must needs be furnished with a large
retine, to guard it and to add to it; comp. Job 1 : 3. These
must consume much; so that the owner can do no more than
gratify his eyes for a time, by looking at his treasures. — עֵינָיו,
his eyes, but ו *sing.* refers to the preceding apparently plur.
noun. But still, as the plur. of this noun (like אֱלֹהִים) has
always a sing. meaning (see Lex.), the concord *ad sensum* is
complete, § 107, 2, *b.*

(11) Sweet is the sleep of the laborer, whether he eat little or much; but
the abundance of the rich man does not permit him to sleep.

Here is another defect in riches. The poor laborer has quiet
sleep, and is so hardy that whether he has more or less food it
does not disquiet him. The rich are kept awake through fear
of losing their riches ; or perhaps the writer alludes to the
satiety of the rich in their food, which disturbs their sleep.
Observe that עֹבֵד, Part. *(laborer)* has a different meaning from
עֶבֶד, *servant.* — הָשָׂבָע with the art., it being abstract. This word
is in the abs. state, and of course the following noun is in the
Dat. of appurtenance, having the force or meaning of a Gen.
§ 113, 2. The article (its vowel is under לְ) is put before a
whole *class.*—מַנִּיחַ, Part. Hiph. of the form B. or No. II. (Lex.),
from נוּחַ, *concessit.* By a little change in the version we can
imitate the Heb. לֹו that follows ; *e. g., does not afford leave* or *permission to him,* etc. — לִישֹׁון, Inf. with לְ of יָשַׁן ; for the first
vowel, see § 24, 1 (לִי for לְיָ).

(12) There is a grievous evil which I have seen under the sun, riches
kept to the owner's harm.

Hitherto the *negative* side of the evil has been presented to
view. Now comes the *positive. There is a grievous evil,* etc.,
excites attention in the reader to a new attitude of the thing
considered. — חוֹלָה, fem. Part. of חָלָה, used adjectively. Before
רָאִיתִי the pron. אֲשֶׁר is implied, § 121, 3. — בְּעָלָיו with sing.

19*

meaning as before. — לְרֵעָתוֹ with sing. suff. accordingly. The lit. Heb. here runs thus: *for its owner, to his harm.* I have abbreviated the expression in my version. The proposition made by this verse he now goes on to illustrate by particulars.

(13) And those riches perish by luckless undertakings; and he has begotten a son, and there is nothing in his hand.

עִנְיַן רָע, lit. *an affair of evil,* which is not limited to bad bargains only, but extends to any unfortunate occurrences in business which call for a sacrifice of property. *He hath begotten a son,* viz., while he was rich. *And there is nothing in his hand.* Whose hand? Some say, the *son's;* others, the father's. I agree with the latter; because the writer seems desirous to convey the idea that, having begotten a son, he now has nothing to bestow upon him. This is a *sore evil* to paternal feeling. — אֵין, const. form, is connected with מְאוּמָה. This last word is compounded of מָה וּמָה = *quid quid.* The negative אַיִן or לֹא before it, makes it mean *nothing.*

(14) As he came forth from the womb of his mother, naked shall he again depart as he came, and nothing shall he receive by his toil, which he may carry away in his hand.

He shall go out of the world as he came into it; he brought nothing into it, he shall carry nothing out of it. — שֶׁיֹּלֵךְ, as pointed, is in Hiph. Imperf., which means, among other things, *to take with one, to carry away with one.* The Imperf. Hiph. is from יָלַךְ. Hitzig insists on pointing the word יֵלֵךְ (Kal. Imperf.), and then translating thus: *his toil, which goes through his hand; i. e.,* either which his hand performs, or which *escapes* through his hands. But I know of no case in Hebrew where such a manner of expression occurs. *Persons go,* or *cause to go,* not things. Nor can I see any objection against the meaning given above, which is of serious import. *Minutiae* of manner in coming and departing are not aimed at. The general and obvi-

ous sense is given above. The verb שׁוּב here signifies *again*,
see Lex. — כְּשׁ = כַּאֲשֶׁר, *as*.

(15) And this too is a sore evil, that altogether as he came so shall he
depart; and what advantage is there to him who toils for the wind?

This second *sore evil* is not merely like that just mentioned,
viz., of coming into the world without anything and leaving it
without anything, but in addition to this part of troubles comes
what is mentioned in the next verse. Both vs. 15 and 16 describe the second *sore evil*, as כָּל between them shows. — כָּל־עֻמַּת,
altogether as, like as, עֻמַּה (like עִם) is literally a noun, meaning
conjunction or *communion*, root עָמַם. As a prep., it always takes
this const. form. In שֶׁבָּא, the אֲשֶׁר (שֶׁ) is superfluous for us.
Lit. the three words mean *altogether like that.*—יֵלֵךְ often means
depart, as here. *To toil for the wind,* is to toil to no purpose.

(16) Also he consumes all his days in gloom, and is much irritated, and
his infirmities are matter of indignation.

יֹאכֵל *(to eat)* has often a tropical sense, as *to devour, consume,*
etc. So here. The literal meaning would only say, that he,
during all his days, takes his meals in a gloomy state of mind;
but the tropical meaning gives us the idea, that all his time is
spent in gloom. So *darkness* is not literal here, but = *gloom,
sadness.* The rest of the verse is difficult, and has given rise to
a variety of interpretations. Taking the text as it stands, כָּעַס
is a neut. intrans. verb, and may be rendered passively, as above.
וְחָלְיוֹ וָקֶצֶף, *and his infirmity is even indignation,* is the literal
version. The first part of the verse discloses his gloomy state
of mind; the second, his bodily infirmities and their consequence,
viz., *excitement, indignation.* I take וְ before the last word to be
a note of *intensity,* § 152, B. 2. Sentiment: 'His infirmities
excite him to anger or strong indignation; *i. e.,* he is impatient,
and frets while they are upon him.' I have rendered חָלְיוֹ by
the plur. *(infirmities),* because it is an abstract noun (of the

Inf. form, § 84, V.), and denotes a *state* or *condition of infirmity;*
which same thing is designated more usually with us by the
plural, for the sing. has respect commonly to some specific
malady. As to the ו before the last noun, in many cases it is
put before a noun which makes an accession to what precedes, in
the way of explanation, or of comparison, or for the sake of
adding a stronger or more explicit word. Thus Zech. 14 : 6 :
" There shall be no light, קָרוֹת וְקִפָּאוֹן, *coldness, even ice* [shall
there be "]. Here the latter noun designates the *intensity* of
the cold. To translate ו in such a case by the simple *and,* would
make the sentiment tame. As rendered above, the words convey
the same idea for substance, as *very cold;* for when ice is formed
in Palestine, the sensation of cold is extreme. As the words
are now we have a fine poetic substitute for the prosaic מְאֹד,
very much. And in such a light I regard our text. I take the
writer to be showing the usual concomitants, or rather the consequences, of wealth which procures the means of living luxuri-
ously. The temptation to such living is very great, and in its
train it usually brings the evils here mentioned, viz., *gloom of
mind, irritability, prolonged infirmity,* with *impatient and angry
fretting* under it. All this is indeed what the writer calls it —
a sore evil.

In this way of interpretation, no change of the text is needed.
Hitzig thinks the text to be so corrupt, that he ventures to re-
fashion it thus : וְכַעַס הַרְבֵּה בְּחָלְיוֹ וְקָצֶף. He then makes כַעַס the
Acc. after יֹאכַל implied, which must be rendered : *devours violence;* and this he explains or illustrates by a reference to שֹׁתֶה
חָמָס, *he drinks in violence* (Prov. 26 : 6), and by the Latin
aegritudinem devorare. He might have added to the last :
devorare molestiam — ineptias — libros — pecuniam, etc. But
the Latin verb means both *to devour, to eat up,* and also *to sup-
press, to keep under.* But the expression in Proverbs means
receiving or *suffering much violence* = drinking a large draught
of it. It is possible that יֹאכַל כַעַס may be construed in like way;

but it is hardly probable. There is 'nothing like it elsewhere. *Devouring* or *destroying* is the prominent *tropical* meaning of אָבַל, and this would make no sense in the passage before us. Hitzig gives the verb the sense of *swallow down;* but that belongs rather to שָׁתָה. No *analogon,* then, can be found in Hebrew to support his view. As to the verb כָּעַס, it is by no means unfrequent; and it is employed here in 7 : 9. Hitzig says that the text as it stands must refer the suff. in חָלְיוֹ to *covetousness* as implied in the preceding context. But this would be singular, indeed, to personify that covetousness, and then apply to it the word *infirmity*. To us, *sick covetousness* sounds strangely. What need of this? The same person who *consumes his time in gloom,* who *is irritated, i. e.,* the greedy and covetous man, is the person referred to by the suff. in חָלְיוֹ. Why perplex that which gives a good sense as it stands? Indeed, the changes in the text proposed by Hitzig are too numerous to be credible; and clearly they are unnecessary. Heiligstedt pursues the same course, without either explaining or defending the necessity of it. Surely, it is not a safe course to pursue, when we not only transform the text, but also assign to it a meaning new and strange. All this is easier, indeed, than to enucleate the somewhat obscure declaration of Coheleth, simply in the way of grammatico-critical investigation. But after all, labor laid out on artificial exegesis is an עִנְיַן רָע, to say the least of it. Seldom, indeed, does Hitzig take such liberties; and here we may well dispense with them.

We come, now, after this repeated survey of oppression and avarice, by placing them in some new positions, to the same general conclusion as before:

(17) Lo! what have I seen which is good, what comely; to eat and to drink, and to enjoy good for all one's toil which he hath endured under the sun during the number of the days of his life which God hath given him; for this is his portion.

אֲנִי may be regarded as *emphatic* here — ' I, who have so long

reflected on this matter, 'have come to this conclusion.' It is
usually (but not always) emphatic when *expressed* as the subject
of a verb, § 134, 3, n. 2.   Before טוֹב the pron. אֲשֶׁר seems to
be implied, with the meaning *which is;* for the same is inserted
before יָפֶה, which is in the same predicament.   This latter word
means *comely, decorous,* etc. ; *i. e.,* enjoying the fruit of one's toil
is not only a pleasure, but one which is *becoming* and *proper.*
The לְ before the three Infinitives = *ut, that;* and so we may translate : *that one should eat,* etc.   Our simple *to* before the Inf.
answers the same purpose as to meaning. *See good;* see remarks
on 2 : 1. — בְּ, *on account of,* in the sense of *for;* see Lex. ב B.
9. — שֶׁיַּעֲמֹל, lit. *which he toils.*   We can say *toil a toil,* but we
do not.   We substitute *endure* or *undergo* in lieu of employing
the correlative verb. — מִסְפַּר const. and in the Acc. of *time.*   It
is only when 'it is in the Gen. after a noun, that it means *few.*
Which God hath given him, I must refer to the allotted time of
man, and not (with Hitzig) to the enjoyments before named.
For this is his portion ; i. e., it is good to eat, etc., because this is
the portion, and our only one, *allotted to us by God,* in order that
we might have enjoyment.   To the same conclusion which this
verse expresses, the writer has repeatedly come before; see
2 : 24; 3 : 12, 13, 22.

(18) Moreover, as to every man to whom God hath given riches and
wealth, and hath given him power to eat thereof, and to take his portion, and
to rejoice in his toil — this is the gift of God.

כָּל־אָדָם is Nom. absolute, suggesting the main subject of the
sentence, but having no verb.   I have translated accordingly.
Riches and wealth, two synonymes, and therefore the meaning is
abundant riches. — הִשְׁלִיטוֹ, lit. *made him to have control.* — מִמֶּנּוּ,
of it, viz., of עֹשֶׁר. — שֵׂאת, contracted fem. Inf. of נָשָׂא, put for
שֵׂאֶת. — מַתַּת contract of מַתְּנָת, from נָתַן. — הִיא, *is,* as often before.   He means to say that it is a good gift, so far as it goes.
He proceeds to assign a reason for so saying :

(19) For he will not much remember the days of his life, when God shall cause [things] to correspond with the joy of his heart.

Much remember, etc., where *the days of his life* seems to refer to his *past* life, which had so often been checkered with sorrow. Now, in the enjoyment of the special gift of God, his reflections on the sombre past, or on the shortness of his days, will cease to be painful and disturbing to him. The reason is more explicitly stated in the last clause. — מַעֲנֶה, Part. Hiph., has made not a little difficulty here; but without adequate cause. — עָנָה is *to respond to, to chime with*. Here the writer asserts that *God will cause a response*, viz., in the things around him, to the tone of the man's mind who is enjoying. The *things* are not named, for they are indefinite and unlimited. *All things* may be understood. In the version, I have supplied an Acc. In Hos. 2 : 21, 22, is a passage which well illustrates this: "I will *answer* [אֶעֱנֶה, the same verb as here] the heavens, and they shall *answer* the earth, and the earth shall *answer* the grain, etc., and that shall *answer* Jezreel;" *i. e.*, everything shall be ready and *responsive* to its proper purpose. So in the verse before us: 'God will cause everything to respond to the *joyful state of mind* which follows his gift. Hope and pleasing anticipation shall prevail.' As to the phrase *joy of heart*, see it in Cant. 3 : 11 ; Jer. 15 : 16 ; Is. 30 : 29, comp. Ps. 21 : 3. In this way, no change in the text is needed.

It is needless to repeat here what has been already said (on 2 : 3, 24) concerning the prudent and cautious indulgence which *wisdom* demands. Coheleth is no Epicure. Specially is he remote from *Epicurism*, as it concerns the acknowledgment of a God, and gratitude to him for his blessings. Most earthly pleasures he finds at last to be altogether empty and vain ; but the enjoyment of the fruits of one's industry, he repeatedly declares, is a good, and the only good that promises much, while even this is short-lived and transitory. But whatever there is in it of satisfaction, this is God's gift, and not procured by ourselves. A

deep and reverential feeling toward God must have prompted
such a sentiment in such a connection.   Providence is not taxed
with injustice, nor is unbelief in it excited, on account of the
apparently undistinguishing distribution of good and evil in the
world, or because of the untoward events of life.   All good comes
from God, and demands thankful acknowledgment.   Suffering
and sorrow, when they come on all alike, are mysteries not to be
explained, but not things which give us any right to complain.
It would seem that the writer had drunk deep of the spirit of the
Book of Job, and perhaps it is probable that he lived near the
time when that book was written.   We shall see that he quotes
or alludes to it in the sequel.

§ 10. *Disappointments frequent, in respect to attainable Good;
they come both upon the* WISE *and the foolish, and no one can
control Divine Arrangements.*

CHAP. VI. 1—12.

[The declarations in 5 : 17—19, respecting our highest attainable earthly
good, give occasion to further consideration of the subject.   There are men
who lose this good.   Their lot is an unhappy one.   It would be better had
they never been born.   And even if one lives to old age, he must at last die
like others.   All toil is for sustenance, and yet the appetite is never satisfied.
Both the wise and foolish are subjected to the same law of never-satisfied
craving.   Experience of enjoyment would be better than the wanderings of
desire; but the order of Providence cannot be changed, which has definitely
fixed and limited circling events.   Who, then, can point out any stable good
for man, in days yet future?]

(1) There is an evil which I have seen under the sun, and heavily does it
lie upon man.

רַבָּה, lit. *great, much*, but connected as it here is with עַל *(upon)*,
the indication is that it *bears heavily on* him, *i. e.*, so as to grieve
or oppress him.— עַל often indicates *uvon* in the sense of *a burden,*

a grievance; § 151, 3, *b.* The transition by יֵשׁ at the outset, marks an advance to a new phase of the subject.

(2) There is a man to whom God hath given riches, and wealth, and splendor, and he lacketh nothing for his soul of all which he desireth, and yet God hath not given him power to eat thereof, but a stranger eateth it; this is vanity, yea, a grievous malady is it.

Riches and wealth, i. e., great riches, as in 5 : 18. — כָּבוֹד may mean either the *splendor* connected with wealth, or the *honor* of elevated rank. The former seems more congruous here. — חָסֵר Part. of a verb final Tseri, § 49, 2, *a.* — נֶפֶשׁוֹ means the physical animal man, with his appetites and desires. — מִכֹּל, the מ being connected with חָסֵר and naturally following it, מִן = *part, portion,* רְתְאַוֶּה, reg. Hithp. with ו consonant in the root. — מִמֶּנּוּ, *of it,* viz., of his wealth which he has acquired. *A stranger eateth it, i. e.,* his unknown heir ; see 2 : 18. The case of the man here presented is different from that in 5 : 12, 13 (Eng. 13, 14), inasmuch as he keeps in possession of his property through life, but has no disposition to enjoy it, while the man described in 5 : 12 seq., loses his estate. But even the power of enjoyment depends on God — *God hath not given to him,* etc.

(3) If a man beget a hundred [children], and live many years, and the days of his years that are to come are multiplied, and his soul is not satisfied with good, and moreover there is no burial to him, I say : Better than he is an untimely birth.

The word *beget* carries with it of course the implication of *children,* which I have supplied in the version ; see the like ellipsis in 1 Sam. 2 : 5 ; Jer. 15 : 9, al. — שָׁנִים fem. with masc. form, as רַבּוֹת shows. — רַב appears to be a *verb* used impersonally here (root רָבַב), for if it were an adjective, the plur. רַבִּים would be necessary in order to agree with יְמֵי, *days.* The Heb. cannot be closely followed in the translation, as to its order ; but the sense of the clause is presented in the version above. Literally

20

rendered, it would run thus : *And if there be much which shall be
the days of his years.*

Two circumstances of his misery are developed; first, *his soul
is not satisfied with his portion,* because God has not given to
him power to be satisfied (v. 2) ; and secondly, he dies without
the honors of a burial. The fact that he was too covetous to
appropriate his wealth to his own enjoyment, renders it probable
that he makes no provision for an honorable or expensive funeral
or monument, such as becomes his rank. His heir, if a *stranger*
(as he is named in v. 2), would not be anxious to do at his own
expense, what he had left unprovided for. We are not, however,
to take קְבוּרָה in the sense of mere *sepulture* (for no man would
be left unburied, in the midst of society and in a time of peace),
but in that of *sepulchre* (Gen. 35 : 20 ; 47 : 30), or else in that
of *funeral, i. e., burial* with customary and expensive cere-
monies. The meaning of *sepulchre* is rather preferable, because
this is an *enduring* monument of the man who is laid in it and
has his name inscribed on it. To leave the dead *unburied* is a
disgrace inflicted only by the most hostile enemy; see in Is.
14 : 18, 19. For disgraceful burial without expense, see Jer.
22 : 18, 19. The feelings of the Hebrews in respect to the
decorum of burial, are well developed in Gen. 23 : 3—13. In
Coheleth's view, that man's lot is sorely grievous, who is very
rich and yet so miserly as to dispense with the comforts of life
for himself, and who dies unnoticed, and unhonored by a sepulchre befitting his condition. "Better," he exclaims, "is an
untimely birth, than such a person." The reason of this declaration is given more fully in the sequel.

Hitzig finds great difficulty in this verse, and thinks it partly
spurious. The clause about *burial,* he thinks, has a wrong loca-
tion, and should be put before נַפְשׁוֹ, with the omission of לֹא.
The clause would then run thus : "And moreover should be
buried, and his soul not be satisfied with good," etc. From a
strange hand he thinks the latter part of the verse, as it now is,

must have come, and that it should be stricken out. He represents the words of Coheleth, now in the text, as comprising or implying the sentiment, that if the circumstance of being *unburied* were omitted, then the case of the miser would be better than that of the untimely birth. But on this, as it seems to me, he lays more stress than the writer intended. His renunciation of comforts through life, and then his death unmourned and as it were unnoticed, are both combined in the writer's mind, while the latter is only the climax of the former. That the poor and friendless should die unnoticed and unhonored, would be nothing strange in such a world as this; but when the honors of a tomb or a funeral are withheld from a rich man, his case must be grievous in the view of the public, and one which shocks the common sensibility. Other commentators have not found, and none need to find, such difficulties as Hitzig; and his allegations seem hardly to justify a charge of surreptitious addition to the text, or a violent dislocation of it.

(4) For it cometh in nothingness, and it departeth in darkness, and in darkness is its name concealed.

In nothingness, בַּהֶבֶל, *i. e.,* it has no real life, no proper existence as a human being, or none to any purpose. *In darkness it departeth, i. e.,* it perishes unseen, before it sees the light. It does not even obtain a *name* = *a remembrance.* There is nothing to call or remember it by. For the article before הֶבֶל as abstract, see § 107, 3, n. 3, *c.;* before חֹשֶׁךְ the article stands also, because it is either a kind of abstract, or the name of a special substance so considered, ib. *b.*

(5) Moreover, it hath not seen the sun, nor had any knowledge; quiet hath this rather than that.

Hitzig translates: *It hath not seen and hath not known the sun.* But I apprehend that this version falls short of the writer's meaning. *It hath not seen the sun,* alludes to its death before its

birth; while וְלֹא יָדַע goes further, and declares that it has not
had any kind of knowledge. This verb not unfrequently is used
as intransitive, *i. e.*, without an object after it, and so means *to
possess cognition* or *knowledge.* This surely makes the text
more significant. *Quiet has this,* viz., this untimely birth, which
so prematurely perishes, *rather than that,* viz., the miserly man
without a sepulchre. Not more quiet after both are dead,
for then the case is the same with both; but quiet on the
whole ; quiet considered in opposition to the turmoil and vexation of the rich man. *Quiet* is a thing which stands high on
the list of oriental enjoyments, and is regarded as a matter of
eager desire. The *rest* in heaven, and in the land of Canaan,
borrows a part of its intense significancy from this circumstance.

(6) And even if he live a thousand years twice told, and enjoy no good —
do not all go to the same place ?

אִלּוּ, contraction of אִם לוּ, both of which mean *if.* In this case
of highest doubt as to the possibility that the case stated should
be realized, the double *if* makes the expression very congruous.
We may translate by *even if.* The וֹ before the particle has an
influence on the following חָיָה, and makes an Imperf. or Fut.
sense. — פַּעֲמַיִם, dual, *two times,* used adverbially, like our *twice.*
הֲלֹא with הֲ interrog. *One place,* viz., *Sheol, the grave.* — הַכֹּל,
the whole mass, the totality, and therefore it takes the article, § 107,
3, n. 1, *b.* — הוֹלֵךְ, *depart, go away,* as very often in this book.
The question here asked is easily understood, and is equivalent
to a strong assertion. The idea is: 'Live he ever so long, yet
he goes at last to the same place as the untimely birth, *i. e.*, to
the region of the dead;' so that "one destiny awaits all," without distinction, 3 : 19. In 9 : 4 and 11 : 7, our author speaks
of the high value to be set upon life, and the pleasure derived
from beholding the light. But in these passages a contrast is
made with *death,* and the latter is rendered the more bitter
because it cuts us off from enjoyment. But in the text before

us, *life* is not asserted to be of no value, but the gist of the
assertion is, that, be it ever so long, it saves us not from going
to the same place where an untimely birth has gone, *i. e.*, the
grave. In itself, the enjoyment of what one has acquired is a
good which is desirable; but the time is at hand when this enjoyment will be no more, and our condition will then be the more
annoying, because of what we have lost.

(7) All the toil of man is for his mouth, and yet the soul is not satisfied.

This connects with the preceding context. There it is declared, that however long life may be, yet at last it comes to
vanity. All must go down to the grave. Long life, therefore,
will not secure a *permanent good.* All the toil of man can do
no more than procure the means of eating and drinking — it is
all for his mouth, *i. e.*, all which promises enjoyment. But even
here our hopes are in a measure dashed. The author has too
often elsewhere commended eating and drinking, *i. e.*, the enjoyment of the fruits of toil (see in 2 : 24 ; 3 : 13 ; 5 : 17 ; 8 : 15),
wholly to decry it here. But even the privilege of this enjoyment has its drawbacks. The appetite (הַנֶּפֶשׁ, *the animal soul*)
is never satisfied so that it does not return. The same want and
necessity press us again, which we felt before eating and drinking. Stable, abiding good, then, is not to be looked for even
here. Too much must not be expected from this source. — גַּם
here means *yet, tamen;* see Lex. גַּם, No. 5.

(8) Then what advantage is there to the wise man over the fool, and what
to the poor man who knoweth how to walk before the living ?

כִּי is variously rendered ; Knobel : *doch, still;* Heiligs.: *immo,
tamen;* neither congruously. It is the כִּי *apodotic, i. e.*, such as
is employed in sentences of this nature : *If* — so and so ; *then*
(כִּי) this or that is the consequence. I understand the question
here to be a kind of apodosis to the preceding verse. *The appetite is not satisfied; — then* (asks the inquirer) how do the wise

20*

have any more advantage than fools, for both have the same appetite? The last part of the verse merely sets the חָכָם in a special light. He is regarded as being a עָנִי, *a poor man*, but dexterously conducting himself. *To walk before the living*, is to behave with propriety and discretion before men. "Enoch *walked* with God," Gen. 5 : 24; "I am God . . . *walk before me*, and be thou perfect," Gen. 17 : 1. — יוֹדֵעַ, as agreeing with הֶעָנִי (having the art.), we might expect would also have the article-pronoun הַ; but the Part. of itself contains or implies the pronoun (§ 131, 2, n. 2), and the repetition of it is not necessary. In Greek, it is much oftener omitted in the Part. than in adjectives. — הַחַיִּים is used in this book frequently to designate *men on the stage of action*. Only such can witness one's demeanor. Sentiment; 'If what you have said about desire never satisfied be true, what advantage is there in superiority of knowledge, or in sagacious correctness of demeanor?' This question is not directly and explicitly answered here. It has already been answered in one respect, in 2 : 14—16. But the following verse suggests a species of answer:

(9) The sight of the eyes is better than the wandering of desire; this too is vanity and fruitless effort.

To see good is, as we have seen, usually put *tropically* for the enjoyment of it. *The wandering of desire*, in the Heb. מֵהֲלָךְ, is Inf. with ŏ because of the Maqqeph that follows; the מ is the sign of the comparative after טוֹב. The verb הָלַךְ means *to go* in any direction, *to progress;* and here it designates the *fluctuating* or *going forth* of desire from one thing to another, or the continual *motion* of it. In other words, Coheleth concedes the evil of *desiring continually*, and says that it *is vanity and fruitless effort;* but still, he maintains that there is some good in present enjoyment. The זֶה refers to the מַהֲלָךְ-נָפֶשׁ. The use of לַהֲלֹךְ in the preceding verse, probably occasioned the employment of the same word here. But it is in the way of *paronomasia*, the meanings in the two cases being quite different.

The writer betakes himself once more to his usual resort, when evils come up that cannot be shunned. Providence, says he, has arranged all these matters. There is an *established* order and succession of things, and it is of no avail to quarrel with it. Man cannot strive with his Maker.

(10) That which is, was long ago called by name, and it was known, because he is man, that he is unable to contend with him who is stronger than he.

The Perf. הָיָה is here used as an abstract Pres., including what *was and still is*, § 124, 3. *Its name was called, i. e.*, it had a *name*, and therefore an *existence*, long ago. — אֲשֶׁר, *because*, or *since*, introduces a circumstance which serves to explain the *inability* that is asserted in the sequel. — הוּא, *he is*, as often elsewhere. *Man, i. e.*, a frail and dying creature, springing from the dust, and returning to the dust. — וְלֹא־יוּכַל connects with נוֹדָע, *it was known . . . . . that he will be unable*, § 152, B. *e.* שֶׁהַתַּקִּיף is said, by the Masoretic note in the margin, to have a *superfluous* ה, and accordingly it has no vowel-point assigned to it. But there is no need of this criticism. It may be read and pointed שֶׁהַתַּקִּיף, *i. e., him who is the mighty One, the Almighty*, of course with the article. This is the very idea that the writer meant to convey, but which the Punctators failed to discover. שֶׁ, *him who.* — מִמֶּנְהוּ = מִמֶּנּוּ, *than him*, not *than us*. Here the sentiment comes out so fully, that striving against the arrangements of Providence can be of no avail. The *presumption* of so doing is also implied.

(11) Truly, there are many words increasing vanity; what advantage is there to man?

כִּי here is clearly not *causal*, but *intensive*, and so I have translated it. It might be well rendered by *however*, and then the shape of the discourse would be thus: 'However, I will say no more, since much speaking has already been condemned;'

see 5 : 6, and remarks on 4 : 16. — מַרְבִּים, Hiph. Part. of רָבָה.
What advantage to man? *i. e.*, no number of words, however
great, can disclose a permanent and immutable good for him, in
the present world. Words, therefore, are *multiplied* in vain.

(12) For who knoweth what is good for man in life, during the number
of the days of his vain life, since he spends them as a shadow; so that who
can tell man what shall be after him under the sun?

The כִּי at the beginning may be rendered *for* (causal), and
then its connection stands thus : '*What advantage is there to man?*
[I ask this question] *because* (כִּי) *who knoweth,*' etc.; *i. e.*, 'because no one can know and tell. No one can point out any
stable good, not even in the *future;* for who knoweth the future?
In life; *i. e.*, while a man is living. — מִסְפַּר is Acc. of measure
or time, and needs no prep. or verb. The indication is that of
a *definite number* told or appointed. — חַיֵּי חֶבְלוֹ, *his vain life*
(§ 104, 1), *i. e.*, life which yields no solid good. — וְיַעֲשֵׂם, *since
he spends,* or with וְ intensive: *he even spends them.* That עָשָׂה
may mean the same as ποιεῖν χρόνον, *to spend time,* is plain from
Lex. 2, *g.* This usage is even somewhat frequent. The suff.
them refers to the preceding *days.* — כַּצֵּל, *as a shadow,* for the
article here, see § 107, 3, n. 1, *a.* It is inadmissible, however,
in such a case, in our language. The idea is, that the days of
man pass quickly or swiftly away, as a shadow does (comp. 8 : 13
Job 14 : 2). — אֲשֶׁר, here (as often) is like כִּי, *so that,* see Lex.
אֲשֶׁר; No. 10. *Who can tell,* etc.; *i. e.*, his days are so fleeting
and short, that no one can gain a knowledge which will enable
him to see and foretell future things. — אַחֲרָיו may be rendered
after him, or *after it,* viz., the *number* of his days. What is
beyond is unknown to all; so that the question : *What advantage
is there for man?* (in v. 11) must remain without any answer
which is wholly satisfactory.

[In such a state of mind as is here described, it seems strange to us that
the inquirer did not look *beyond* those dark and gloomy scenes around him.

How spontaneously would the Christian, in like circumstances, now look by faith, beyond the veil of time, to that blessed world where all is peace and joy, and where is no vanity nor vexation, where "there shall be no more pain, and no more death!" The circumstance above adverted to is of itself a very significant commentary on the declaration of Paul, that "*the gospel has brought life and immortality to light.*" Surely, if Coheleth enjoyed the full vision of this immortality which Christians now enjoy, he must have spontaneously looked for the adjustment in another world of all the seeming difficulties, and contradictions, and mysteries that are apparent in this world. Everywhere does Paul rise superior to his sorrows, when he directs his eye to the glories of the upper world. His afflictions are " light," his sufferings "only for a moment," when he is anticipating "the glory that is to be revealed." And so, we are ready to say, must Coheleth have felt and acted, had he cherished such a strong belief as Paul's. But are we not somewhat hasty in reasoning thus from the one case to the other? When one sees as clearly as Paul did, he may well exult in hope, and forget all his sorrows. But can the same animation and hope be expected from one whose lot it is to live only in the twilight, as from one who looks on the meridian sun? It must be a rare case, if indeed any who grope their way by the glimmerings of twilight, yet move as rapidly and cheerfully as those who travel by broad daylight.

But at all events, Coheleth does not stand alone. Where, we ask again, is the appeal, in the Book of Job, to a future adjustment of all the difficulties and troubles that assailed him? Read Job 14 : 7—14, and then say whether the patriarch felt as Paul did when he was suffering; *e. g.*, as described in 2 Cor. 4, 5. The celebrated passage in Job 19 : 25—27, will hardly stand the test of criticism, if brought to support such an appeal. And in all the laws of the great Jewish legislator, where is the appeal to a *future* judgment, a heaven, and a hell? The Hebrews had not even a word in their language, at least as known to us, which corresponded to the *Gehenna* of the New Testament. שְׁאוֹל is either *grave, sepulchre*, or else *world of the dead, region of death* (as in Is. xiv.), but never *Gehenna*. The *future judgment* I have already discussed, under 3 : 17 above. If at all taught, it is mostly by *implication;* and by that very seldom. Read through all the prophets, *i. e.*, the *preachers* to the Hebrews. Promises of reward, and threats of punishment, are everywhere abundant; but where, except in Is. 26 : 19, and Dan. 12 : 3, is there anything which is *patent* respecting the future state? Many are the promises and threats in the Psalms and Proverbs; but where, excepting in Ps. 16 : 11, and 17 : 15, is there anything which necessarily respects the *future* world? *We* bring it out, indeed, from the Jewish Scriptures, by

transferring our New Test. ideas to the exegesis of the Old Test.; but did
the *Jews of old* so construe their Scriptures? To say this, would be attributing to them more than Paul is willing to allow, 2 Tim. 1 : 10, and more
than John would be willing to concede, John 1 : 17, 18. The simple truth
is, that we must come at last, in the way of exegesis, to the concession that
the Mosaic dispensation was only *preparatory* to the gospel; it was "only
the shadow of good things to come." There was enough in it to encourage
the obedient, and to lead to faith and trust in God. And in the case of
Coheleth, the latter part of his book shows that he attained at last to a steadfast condition of mind, and that all his inquiries terminated in leading him
to a belief in a future judgment, and to a deep conviction that to "fear
God, and keep his commandments," is the great end of man's being, Ecc.
12 : 13, 14. Through how many doubts and difficulties he had to pass with
his busy and inquiring spirit, the book before us shows. But let us not
understand him as having come to a real *ultimatum* before he gets through
the contest with his doubts and difficulties. We have, specially in the
chapter above considered, a despairing and hesitating frame of mind; a
state which bounded his circle of vision by narrow limits for the time being;
one which made life a burden to him; one from which he found no escape,
and for which he could find no substantial alleviation but in the unques-
tioned and unquestionable supremacy of the Divine Being. Whatever is
wrong in men, and however much of evil is done, he still believes that "God
made man upright," while "the evil inventions" are his own. Must it not
be conceded, then, that there was in him a strong and active principle of
living faith, which could support him amid such trials and such inquiries,
and keep him steadfast in the attitude of reverence and submission? It
would really seem, after all, that while he had far less *light* than we have, he
had more of *filial reverence* and *submission* than most of us would venture
to claim. Who can help feeling the deepest interest in the struggles of
such an inquiring, sensitive, and anxious man? He does, indeed, at times
seem to succumb, and to wish for death. So did Job; and so did Jonah.
But, after all, the tenor of his book is far from inculcating gloom and
reckless despair. Cheerfulness and sober enjoyment are everywhere
commended, when he comes to advise and to give precepts. All impiety,
lightmindedness, murmuring, and distrust of God's justice or goodness, are discarded by him and condemned, even in the midst of all the
temptations to indulge such feelings, while one is under hopeless suffering
under an oppressive government, and has only glimpses of the world of
future happiness. To any one who reads the book intelligently, who looks
at the condition, and sees the design of the writer, such a struggle in regard

to the most interesting question man can ask: viz., *How can I find true and lasting happiness?* — to such a one a picture is presented, to be contemplated with the most lively emotions. It is only when we mistake the tenor and object of the book, and look for and demand that which is not in it, nor in any other book of the Old Test. (except as stated above), — it is only then, that we meet with insoluble difficulties at every turn. No one who gets an enlightened view of the whole book can feel that a straight going exegesis will endanger our faith. Quite the contrary. We are led to see, step by step, what the mind can struggle with and overcome, where there is an unshaken confidence in God at the bottom of the heart. If one in ages past, before the Sun of Righteousness arose in his full splendor, could thus struggle and thus triumph, shame and reproach to us, who live under the full blaze of gospel light, if we doubt, and grow cold, and murmur when the ways of Providence are mysterious and afflictive to us !

That Neologists should exult in the alleged scepticism of this book, is no wonder indeed ; but I cannot think it to be indicative of much candor and liberality of feeling. Coheleth is an ardent inquirer, and in one respect, if I may be allowed to say it, he is like them, *i. e.*, he is a *philosopher.* But Coheleth's philosophy begins with doubts, and ends with deep conviction of truth, and with reverence for God and his commandments. Their course is usually the reverse of this. Kant's last words are said to have been, " All is dark." And so indeed it is, where the Bible is superseded, and one's own reason becomes the supreme arbiter of all things. Even if Coheleth be in reality a doubter in immortality, it would not prove that all the Hebrews were so ; it could not disprove the assertion of Paul, that Abraham " looked for a city which hath foundations, whose builder and maker is God," nor could it convict him of error when he declared that other patriarchs did " seek a better country, even a heavenly one," Heb. 11 : 10—16. Such critics mistake the doubts suggested in the process of investigation in this book for the confirmed opinions of the writer himself, and thus they argue against all knowledge of the future among the Hebrews from his alleged views. They seem to ignore the fact that what the writer undertakes in this book is not to discuss the doctrine of the soul's immortality, or the existence of a future world, but to ask, and if possible answer, the question, *Is there any solid and lasting good attainable in the present world?* They may wonder, and so may we, that the author rarely steps beyond the boundaries of this question, until near the close of the book. We can scarcely repress the feeling that views of the future must have thrust themselves in as the means of solving many a *nodus* which is presented. And we have that same feeling when we read the Book of Job, which in many respects has resemblances to Ecclesiastes. Yet, in cases of this kind, very much depends on the special object which the writer had in view, as well as on his state of knowledge. Inspiration does not put a man out of the age and country in which he lives. The *circumstantials* of a writer remain the same, whether inspired or not. And these always affect the costume of his work. Let Coheleth be judged, then, by his time, his circumstances, and the object he had in view; and if so, his book need not fear the tribunal of criticism. The work is far enough removed from the gloomy conceptions and views of a hopeless sceptic, and from the tame and dull truisms of a wiseacre. It is full of vivacity, of deep feeling, and of a pervading spirit of submission to God in all his doings. If we do not profit by it, the fault is our own.]

§ 11. *Alleviations in various distressing Circumstances. Caution as to Demeanor toward Oppressors and Rulers. Our Miseries are not from God, but from the Perversion of Men.*

Chap. VII. 1—29.

[Left in despair of any adequate remedy for the evils of life, or of attaining to wisdom adequate to point out true and lasting good, the writer declares death to be preferable to life. Death is indeed an evil, but not unmixed with good; for some advantage, in such a case, may accrue to mourners, and the wise may profit by being among them. Fools only desire continual merriment: vi. 1—4. But even the rebuke of the wise, well administered, is better than the merry shouts of fools, which are short-lived, vs. 5, 6. Still, the *wise* are sometimes thrown off their guard by *passion*, which causes much misery, and makes even the wise grow mad under it. But they ought to wait with patience for the end of such things, and see how Providence disposes of the issue or sequel, and not to be impetuous in their feelings, nor to complain of the badness of the times, vs. 7—10. After all, wisdom, as well as a heritage, is of some profit, although imperfectly attained, and liable to be blinded for the moment by untoward circumstances. Both wisdom and money are at times a protection, vs. 11, 12. Still, we must remember that God has ordered all matters, and that we ought to submit to his ordinances, v. 13. Agreeably to his ordinance. we may rejoice in prosperity; but we should also consider well in the day of adversity. God disposes of both these in the way of alternation, and in such a way that we cannot scan his doings, v. 14. All this Coheleth has reflected upon while engaged in his vain pursuit. Nor does the mystery stop even here. The righteous sometimes perish through their probity, and the wicked enjoy long life through their improbity, v. 15. To this the writer brings forward a kind of reply, or at least an attempt at explanation. It comes in the form of a precept, the purport of which is to tell how the evil in question may be shunned. One must not be rigidly unbending in his righteousness, carrying the matter to severe excess. Nor should he sedulously endeavor to show how wise he is, for this will make him singular and cause him to be deserted. Nor should he be very wicked, since this would show him to be a fool; for it brings on a premature death. It is good to attend well to both these cautions, for he who fears God will proceed with both in his eye, vs. 15—18. That this comment on the destiny of the righteous and the wicked (v. 15), and on the wisdom here aimed at (v. 16), is not satisfactory to the writer, will appear in the sequel. For the present, as *wisdom* has been spoken of in the attempted reply, as a means of *destroying* or making one *desolate*, he contents himself with remarking that wisdom is a more effectual *security for protection* than ten military chieftains with their forces. In respect to such protection wisdom does at times what virtue fails to do, because all men sometimes *sin*, and then not their virtue but their *skill* protects them; vs. 19, 20. If one makes an effort to act wisely, he will doubtless set in motion the tongue of slander; but he must give no heed to it, for it is not worth minding. If you are over-eager to listen, you will hear something to your own disadvantage, even from servants. Besides, you yourself have sometimes indulged in such scandal, and you must therefore expect it from others, vs. 21, 22. Coheleth now sums up by saying that he has with wariness subjected to trial the wisdom of which so much is said, in order to discover its true nature, and tried to become wise in this matter. But he has found the thing too remote and deep to be probed, vs. 23, 24. He has pursued the investigation of *wisdom* by considering it as contrasted with *folly* and *madness*, v. 25. Of this folly, he has sought out the most prominent and conspicuous sources and exemplars. He has found these in the ensnaring women of his time, whose seductive appearance and demeanor are so alluring and fatal, that only those specially favored of God escape from them. He has desired to find some abatement of this charge, but he cannot find one in a thousand who is to be excepted. Among men the case is somewhat better. But even there examples are very rare, vs. 27, 28. But whence come such abounding perversity and wickedness? God made man upright; therefore it is not to be put to his account, but to the account of man himself, who has degenerated, v. 29.

This chapter may be numbered among the most difficult in the book. There is less of orderly sequency and of close or discernible connection. Actual *digressions*, indeed, are not exactly to be found in the chapter; but transitions from one subject, or one aspect of a subject, to another are frequent. To a mere cursory reader much of the chapter has the appearance of apothegms or sententious sayings, like the Book of Proverbs. But a closer examination dissipates this illusion, and shows, in the main, a connected undercurrent of thought. Still, it is miscellaneous. The writer goes, for example, from the subject of *death* and *mourning* to that of *oppression*, and strives to present some alleviations and administer some cautions in both cases. Once more he resumes the oft-considered topic of *wisdom*, and also glances again at that of *wealth*. Both of these things have their value in some respects; but they cannot reverse or stay the ordinances of Providence. God has designed to hide some things from our view, and therefore we cannot search them out; but our safe course is to yield implicit submission to his will. Some things take place which confound us; the righteous suffer the doom of the wicked, and, *vice versa*, the wicked prosper as if righteous. This cannot be explained by putting it to the account of excess in the righteous, and of small sins in the wicked. Excess in either is not the ground on which this matter rests. As to wisdom, it often serves for a *defence*, even where virtue would not or could not, because it is so imperfect. Let no one be dissuaded from laboring to attain wisdom, by the tongue of slander and scandal. Give no ear to it, and thus escape the mortifications of it. As to the *essential nature* of wisdom, what it is in itself, and whence it originates, we cannot develop these matters as we may wish. But something we may know by looking at and considering the *opposite of wisdom, viz., folly*. The most striking examples of this are among enticing women; examples of virtue, moreover, are very rare, even among men. So much at all events, is clear, amid all that may be doubtful, viz., that *God made man upright, and that he has corrupted himself.*

Such is the tenor of thought, briefly expressed, and divested of all its circumstantial *minutiae*. This is a *discursive* method of writing, beyond any doubt; but still, *discursiveness* and free latitude in thinking pervade the book, and designedly so. Yet it is far from being a second book of Proverbs. Single and unconnected apothegms are rare indeed in it, and in fact never appear, as has already been said, except for the purpose of illustration. But to claim for it the regular series of a continuous logical process throughout, would plainly be to make an extravagant and inadmissible claim. Such is not the manner of Hebrew writing anywhere. Paul himself, though a master logician in fact, with few exceptions, never presents us with a regular and continued series of ratiocination. The times, the style, the genius of the Hebrew people neither required nor admitted this. But Coheleth has a wide field before him, which he explores in search of some solid and abiding earthly good. When he viewed some of the leading pursuits of men in one light, and dismissed them as disappointing our hopes, on another occasion something brings them to his view in another attitude, and he again contemplates them, and then decides as before. It is in this way that the seeming repetition occurs ; but excepting his repeated final conclusions, it is rare to find the same thing looked at again in the same attitude and in the same light as before. Free digressive remarks often spring from ideas associated with something which he mentions, and called forth by that something ; and one must narrowly watch for this, who desires to explore the course of thought and the connection of topics. He must not think of binding him to the *consecution* of a Paley or a Whewell. He must rather read the *Consessus Hariri*, or the *Gnomes* of some of the oriental philosophers, or the book of the *Wisdom of Solomon,* if he wishes to obtain light on the question of *method* in the book before us. It is through and through *oriental,* and has some strong resemblance in more than one respect, to some parts of the Mishna. Withal, it is *verily Hebrew* in its manner and method ; but not Hebrew history, or prophecy, or Psalms. It is Hebrew *philosophizing,* and at least as intelligible as that of our *cousin-Germans.* Perhaps parts of it have been as little understood as some of their works. But patience is said to master even their works ; perseverance and a good knowledge of the Hebrew idiom will make most of this book, if not all, quite intelligible. We now come to the detail.]

(1) Better is a good name than precious ointment, and so the day of one's death than of his birth.

The first טוֹב is predicate, and so (as usual for a predicate adjective) it stands first, § 141. — שֵׁם of itself may mean *good name,* by established Heb. usage, Prov. 22 : 1 ; Job 30 : 8. The second טוֹב qualifies שֶׁמֶן, and shows that it means *perfumed* or *precious ointment.* The writer introduces this merely for the sake of throwing light, by *comparison,* on the sentence that follows ; *i. e.,* the day of one's *death* is as much better than that of his *birth* as a good name is better than good oil. Doubtless illustrations as striking as this might have been selected from other objects. But this bears every mark of being a common

apothegm ; and it was probably chosen on this ground. — הִוָּלְדוֹ,
Niph. Inf. Nominas. of יָלַד, lit. *of being brought forth.* The suff.
here indicates that there is an implied suffix after הַמְיָת ; which
I have given in the version. In this case וְ as often is equivalent
to *and so,* or *and thus;* see Gram. § 152, B. (3). The verse
before us reasserts in another form the sentiment of 6 : 3. New
reasons for despair, exhibited in 6 : 4—12, have made Coheleth
more sick at heart than ever. He does not say merely that he
would as willingly die as live, but that *death,* the termination of
life, is altogether better than *birth,* the commencement of it.
But if death be not at present attainable (he never once speaks,
and never appears to think, of *suicide*), then the next most
mournful concern, attendance on the death or burial of others, is
most in unison with his then present feelings. In point of fact,
indeed, a man may be profited by resort to the house of mourning.

(2) It is better to go to the house of mourning than to go to the house of
feasting, because this is the end of all men, and the living will lay it to
heart.

The word מִשְׁתֶּה, *banquet,* is often employed in the more general sense given to it here, *i. e., feast.* — הוּא, *this is,* § 119, 2.
סוֹף, *the end,* but the article required is put before the Gen. noun
that follows, § 109, 1.—אָדָם, *man, mankind,* or *every man,* generic.
הַחַי, sing. generic, and designating a class, it takes the article ;
§ 107, 3, n. 1, *b.* *Lay it* or *put it to heart,* is the familiar phrase
in Heb. to designate the *consideration* of a thing ; for this meaning of נָתַן, see Lex. It is *placing the thing before the mind,* in
order that it may be the object of consideration. Hitzig says
that there are two benefits designated here as belonging to the
house of mourning : the one, which the author claims for himself, since he cannot himself die, the pleasure of seeing others
permitted to die ; the other, the sober reflection which is occasioned in all, and is useful to them. The first of these reasons
appears strained and unnatural, too much so to be admissible ;

the second is enough to establish the *better* in the case which is asserted. *This is the end* — what? The answer must be, that the *house of mourning is, i. e.*, represents, symbolizes in an expressive manner, *the end* or *death* of all men.

(3) Better is sorrow than laughter; for by the sadness of the countenance the heart is made glad.

כַּעַס, *aegritudo, moeror, grief* or *sorrow;* often it means *vexation, irritation,* but not so here, as the antithesis shows. — שְׂחוֹק, lit. *laughter,* but this is merely the expression here of *merriment,* the opposite of sorrow. — רֹעַ, *sadness,* see Lex. — יִיטַב, Imperf. with Pattah, § 69, 1. *The heart is made glad;* Hitzig: *is made sound.* But plainly *soundness* is not the opposite of *sadness;* and טוֹב, moreover, has all along the sense of *enjoyment, gladness.* Usually, the countenance expresses the state of the heart, and when that is sorrowful, we conclude the heart to be so ; see in Neh. 2 : 2. But there the writer employs an *Oxymoron,* in order to express himself with point (see this word explained in New Test. Gramm. p. 300). We might say, with something of the like point: The look is *sad,* but the heart *not bad.* — יִיטַב need not be regarded as implying mere ordinary merriment here, but the *pleasure* derived from sober reflection. The whole verse is only an extension of the thought in v. 2. In v. 4 we have an exhibition of the part which *wisdom* will act.

(4) The heart of the wise is in the house of mourning; but the heart of fools in the house of merriment.

For the reasons above stated, we may anticipate what part the wise will act. They will frequent *the house of mourning,* for the solid profit which will accrue ; but fools, who love laughter, will prefer *the house of merriment. Heart,* in the text, means *inclination, feeling,* which prompts the course in question.

(5) Better is it to hear the rebuke of a wise man, than that one should hear the song of fools.

21*

This is partly digressive. The writer pursues the idea of the difference between the foolish and the wise, beyond the matter of mourning and rejoicing. So much more highly are the wise to be held in estimation, that one had rather suffer even *rebuke* from them, than to hear the *plaudit-song* of fools. As *song* here is the opposite of *rebuke*, so *encomiastic* or *plaudit-song* is plainly meant. In other words: Rebuke from the wise is more tolerable than the eulogy of fools. — שֹׁמֵעַ, Part. *auditurus*, or it may merely express the *repeated act* of hearing, *i. e.*, what one habitually does ; which is a special office of the participle. The Heb. runs thus, lit.: *than a man, the hearer of a song*, etc. The plaudit-song of fools is, indeed, noisy enough, but very short-lived and insignificant. So the next verse :

(6) For as the noise of thorns under a pot, so is the laughter of the fool. This too is vanity.

There is a kind of *paronomasia* or *assonance* in this verse. The preceding verse has כְּסִילִים, and this הַסִּירִים (art. generic) ; In v. 6 itself, הַסִּיר follows הַסִּירִים ; words evidently selected for the sake of *assonance;* for this is often employed to give point to a sententious saying. The state of Palestine as to *fuel*, makes plain the expression, *thorns under the pot*. Bushes are the only fuel, and the thorn of the desert, often employed in cooking food, blazes and snaps fiercely, and makes much noise for a little while, and leaves few if any coals behind. Of course something more substantial is needed for convenient use. So is it with the noisy merriment — the laughter and song of fools. We have a vulgar proverb of nearly the same tenor as that here quoted : *Great cry and little wool.* The כִּי at the beginning of the verse, shows that the design is to give the *ground* of the preceding declaration. — וְגַם, *this too, i. e.*, this as well as other things before mentioned.

(7) But oppression rendereth mad a wise man, and a gift corrupteth the heart.

Rendereth mad, i. e., foolish; in other words, the practice of oppressing will soon bring a wise man to act as a fool. The author refers to the practice of the magistrates of that day, of which he so often complains. As to *making mad,* comp. Is. 44 : 25. As to the character and effect of the *gift* (bribery), see Deut. 16 : 19 ; Exod. 23 : 8. — וִיאַבֵּד, in Piel, either *leads astray,* which is the original idea, or *corrupts,* in the moral sense. לֵב, *heart, i. e.,* mind or soul. In Arabic, *Hakem* (= חָכָם) means *magistrate,* and not improbably it does so in the passage before us; for it is the *corruption* of a *judge,* to which the gift (bribery) refers. In such a case, there would be an exception to the value of a rebuke from a חָכָם, as mentioned in v. 5 ; and perhaps the writer means to produce an oppressive חָכָם here in the way of an exception to the general principle.

(8) The end of a matter is better than its beginning; forbearance of spirit is better than haughtiness of spirit.

The first part of the verse seems at first view to be a kind of parallel to v. 1. But in v. 8 it stands in a different connection. Both parts of the verse are doubtless *proverbial* sayings, applied by the writer to the case in hand. What he means is, that the *end* of this matter of oppressing will show at last the true state of the thing; and that it is better to wait — to exercise *forbearance of mind,* than *haughtily* to resent the injuries received. We might expect קְצַר רוּחַ, *hastiness of spirit,* in contrast with אֶרֶךְ רוּחַ. But *haughtiness* is the passion which most and quickest of all resents oppression, being very sensitive to indignity. The caution is, not to move too hastily in such a matter, but to wait, and see how it will turn out in the sequel. That such is the indication, may be seen by what follows. — אֶרֶךְ is probably the const. form of אָרֵךְ (adj.), according to the vowel-points. The sense is better, at least more expressive, if pointed אֹרֶךְ (as a noun) ; and so גְּבֹהַּ (Infin. noun) may be regarded as a parallel construction with אֹרֶךְ.

(9) Be not hasty in thy spirit to be irritated, for irritation dwelleth in the bosom of fools.

This repeats the sentiment of the preceding verse, with an additional reason. Avoid an irritable temper of mind, for only the foolish indulge it. 'Embroil not yourself with the oppressive ruler, by reason of hasty vexation or sudden passion,' is the substance of the sentiment. — יָנוּחַ, Imperf. of נוּחַ, indicating (as often) habitude, § 125, 4. *b*.

(10) Say not, Why is it that former days were better than these? for thou dost not inquire wisely respecting this.

הָיָה, *was and still is.* — שֶׁ, *that.* — מֵחָכְמָה, lit. *from wisdom,* i. e., it comes not *from wisdom* as its source = *wisely.* — עַל־זֶה, *concerning this,* viz., concerning the superiority of former times over the present. This has a bearing on the then present state of things. Men are presented as groaning under oppression; and present evils are always magnified in the view of sufferers. Hence it is natural to praise *former times,* as if they were exempt from evils, when in fact their evils are merely forgotten. Every day, even now, furnishes us with examples of this kind. Coheleth means to say that 'such comparisons will provoke the rulers as well as help to aggravate our evils, and thus increase the difficulties which they occasion. Therefore be *wise,* and refrain from this.' That this is implied, seems to be clearly shown from the next two verses, which speak in praise of *wisdom,* i. e., discretion or sagacity.

(11) Wisdom is good as well as an inheritance, specially to those who see the sun.

In other words: 'Act *wisely* in respect to rulers; for wisdom will protect you as much as money. It is of great benefit to those who are in active life.' — עִם נַחֲלָה, *as well as wealth;* for that עִם may and does have such a meaning, is clear; see 2 : 16, and remarks there, and also Lex. עִם, B. 1. *d.* The word *in-*

heritance has here a more generic sense, meaning *wealth* of any kind. Besides, in the next verse, *wealth* or *money* is made coördinate with *wisdom*, not subordinate to it. The sentiment drawn by many from this verse, viz., that 'wisdom is good if you have money with it,' is both tame and untrue in its implication; for the implication would be, that wisdom is not good unless accompanied by wealth. — יוֹתֵר, an adverb here, viz., *very, very much, abundantly;* see in 2 : 15. Sentiment: 'Wisdom is good as well as wealth, and especially good for those on the stage of action.' *Those who see the sun,* means living men abroad in the world of action; comp. 6 : 5; 11 : 7. So the Greeks: 'Ορᾶν φάος = ζῆν; and so the Latins: *Diem videre.*

(12) For wisdom is a defence, and silver is a defence; but a preëminence of knowledge is wisdom, which preserves the lives of its possessors.

In בְּצֵל, the בְּ is the so-called בְּ *essentiae,* and therefore need not be translated, indeed cannot be, so as truly to represent the Heb. idiom. See Lex. בְּ, D., and compare בְּטוֹב in v. 14 = טוֹב. See in Job 23 : 13; Gen. 49 : 24, al. in Lex. — צֵל, lit. *shadow.* In the glowing east, *shade* is a most grateful and salutary protection. The Scriptures often employ the word as here; Is. 30 : 2, 3; 32 : 2; Num. 14 : 9; Lam. 4 : 20. A *preëminence* or *excellence of knowledge* is the predicate in the second clause; and so I have translated. It is put first, for the sake of emphasis. 'That wisdom,' says Coheleth, 'which preserves life, must be regarded as an excellent knowledge,' having the preëminence even over money; for this, although it may and does at times shield us, is still liable to be lost, for it is exposed to robbery, to accident, and to ill success in business, etc.

All this looks back to the case of demeanor under the oppression of rulers, and is designed to show the importance of acting *discreetly,* that our safety may not become endangered. Wisdom here is truly a יִתְרוֹן.

(13) Consider the work of God; who can make straight that which he hath made crooked?

That is, in all these troubles and perplexities, remember that
there is an overruling Providence, whose arrangements cannot
be opposed or disturbed. When the will of God is ascertained,
bow to it in quiet and silent submission. — הָאֱלֹהִים, like Θεός in
Greek, used either with or without the article. Here emphasis
is intended, and the article becomes necessary. — כִּי (causal),
stands before a reason for considering well how much of present
trouble results from the unchangeable ordinance of the power
above. — עִנְּתוֹ, Piel with suff., root עָנָה with movable ו.

(14) In the day of prosperity be joyful, and in the day of adversity consider; moreover God hath arranged this in connection with that, in order
that man should not discover anything which will be after him.

Whatever may be the confusion and disorder of the times,
when good and evil alternate and are fluctuating, it is plain that
nothing forbids your enjoyment of *prosperity*, when it is your
lot; and when *adversity* comes, make good use of that by exer-
cising sober reflection and consideration. — טוֹב == בְּטוֹב, with בְּ
essentiae; see on בְּצֵל in the verse above. *Consider,* instead of
which we should have expected הֱיֵה בְרָע, *be sad,* as the opposite
of בְּטוֹב. But רְאֵה gives a more expressive and useful counsel.
Men do not need exhortation to sadness, when misfortunes come
upon them. God has arranged these alternations in such a way,
and so entirely are they under his own control, that we can never
predict the future with certainty. We know, indeed, that alternations must needs take place; but 'how and when, are beyond
our ken.' — לְעֻמַּת, *together with,* or *in connection with.* — עָשָׂה,
arrange, constitute, a frequent meaning of this word; see Lex.
עַל דִּבְרַת שֶׁ (const. form of דִּבְרָה), *on the ground that, in order
that* (not merely *so that,* as many translate). The sentiment
plainly is, that God has so arranged the alternations of good and
evil, that no man can know the future with certainty; and in all
this he has a design. He does not mean to admit man to pry
into the secret things which belong to him alone.

The mass of commentators are content with this view; but
Hitzig, ever watchful to detect and bring to view any scepticism
in the Hebrews, finds this sentiment: '*To the intent that he shall
seek for nothing after death.* God leaves good and evil to alternate here, in order that nothing may be expected or found after
death.' He adds: "This sense of the passage interpreters *en
masse* have failed to discover." But it seems to me no matter
of wonder that they have failed to see what was not to be seen.
Hitzig gets his view by a *Hinein-exegesiren,* and not by a *Her-
aus-exegesiren.* The writer has said again and again, that good
and evil are *not* duly rewarded in the present life. His greatest
complaint is, that they are not. How, then, can he be made to
say now that good and evil are awarded here, and are so dispensed that no further award is to be expected?

(15) All this have I considered in the days of my vain efforts; there is a
righteous man who perisheth through his righteousness; and there is a
wicked man who prolongeth [his days] by reason of his wickedness.

אֶת־הַכֹּל, lit. *the all,* but the article makes כֹּל refer to something
which precedes, viz., what is contained in vs. 13, 14, *all this.*
He means to say that the subject of the mysterious alternations
of good and evil he has often considered *in the days of his* הֶבֶל,
i. e., of his vain efforts in trying to solve the problem. As to
the mere fact of *being vanity,* personally considered, *i. e.,* a frail
dying creature, that was as true when this was uttered as it ever
had been. This was not something which had passed, and therefore this was not the kind of vanity meant in the text. But
there is a new attitude in which the subject may be placed, which
will show more fully still that there is a mystery respecting the
dispensation of good and evil, which is more perplexing than
their mere alternations. 'Right fails, and wrong prospers.'
The righteous sometimes perish (instead of receiving a reward)
for the very reason that they are righteous; while the wicked
enjoy the benefits promised to the righteous, by means of their

wickedness, בְּרָעָתוֹ. The wicked often prolong their days by the
acquisition of various comforts and means of promoting health,
through gains wickedly obtained; or it may be that they escape
penal justice by means of bribery. How Providence could
permit this, was a great mystery, and one which Coheleth thinks
has not been uncovered. Of some attempts to account for this
he has indeed a cognizance; or it may be that he tells us what
once passed in his own mind, *in the days of his vanity.* As to
the fact, "persecution for righteousness' sake" has always existed
in some shape; so that a man may perish בְּצִדְקוֹ, *by* or *through
his righteousness,* not merely *in it.* After מַאֲרִיךְ the word יָמִים
is implied; for the full expression of this see 8 : 13; Deut. 4 : 26,
40; 5 : 30; Josh. 24 : 31; Prov. 8 : 16, al. For the elliptical
expression as here, see Prov. 28 : 2. Long life is everywhere
counted among the Hebrews as a blessing, Ex. 20 : 12; Deut.
11 : 9, 21; Is. 65 : 20; Ps. 49 : 10; Prov. 28 : 16, al.

(16) Be not righteous over much, nor display thyself as being wise; why
shouldest thou make thyself to be forsaken?

In other words, a course too exact, rigid, and severe, occasions
the misfortunes of the righteous. They *overdo.* And so also
they show themselves as wise, or *demean themselves as claiming to
be wise,* תִּתְחַכַּם Hith., *i. e.,* wiser than others; and so, by carrying these things to excess, they cause themselves to be *deserted*
or *forsaken,* תִּשּׁוֹמֵם, Hithp. for תִּתְשׁוֹמֵם, *make thyself desolate* or
lonely. Like Job in 16 : 7 (on which passage the writer perhaps
had his eye), friends forsake him, and leave him to his fancied
superior sanctity and wisdom. But the verse above speaks of
his *perishing.* This also may be involved in תִּשּׁוֹמֵם, or at least
the consequence of it. — יוֹתֵר is evidently adverbial here (see in
v. 11), and corresponds to הַרְבֵּה in the first clause. The next
verse continues the comparison.

(17) Be not wicked over much, and be not foolish; why shouldest thou
die before thy time?

That is, *great wickedness* only leads to destruction, and makes a man a *fool*. All men sin some, and sometimes act unwisely; but it is only when they become abandoned, and turn fools, that they perish. *Excess* in both cases *destroys*. Those who are righteous in a moderate measure, may remain safe; and so with the wicked who observe moderation. — בְּלֹא עִתֶּךָ, lit. *in thy not time, i. e., untimely.*

This 17th verse evidently does not correspond exactly with the last clause of v. 15, *prolongeth his days by wickedness*. It merely maintains that *excessive* wickedness *destroys* instead of preserving. But by implication it admits that wickedness short of this may consist with prolongation of days. In other words, the statement in v. 15 is limited and softened down by vs. 16, 17; for it is here suggested that only *excess* in righteousness causes the mischief complained of, and that prosperity in wickedness cannot truly be affirmed of such as are very wicked. Verses 16 and 17 do not directly deny or contradict v. 15, but they qualify and diminish the force of its expressions. The inference is, that the objector in this case (no matter whether the objection comes from Coheleth's own deliberating mind, or is suggested by another) — the objector intends to say, that the proposition of v. 15 cannot be admitted in its full latitude. There is evidently an attempt to diminish the force of the objection against the mystery of providential arrangements. What is said in v. 15, is assumed as applicable only to cases of excess in righteousness, or to a low or small degree of sin.

Nor has the objector yet done. He goes on to show the importance of his suggestion in the following verse :

(18) It is good that thou shouldest keep hold of this, and also not let go thy hand from that; for he who fears God will make his way with all of them.

Keep hold of this, refers to the precept he had given respecting *excess* in righteousness; *not let go thy hand from that*, means that

22

he should also observe due caution in regard to excess of wickedness. By a wary observance of these cautions, he will be safe.
And *he who fears God, i. e.*, fears to incur his displeasure, will
go along the path of life associating these maxims with all his
steps, so as not to depart from them.   It seems plain to me that
this verse comes from the same quarter as the last two verses
which precede it.   It is an attempted confirmation of what is
there said. — מִזֶּה is put at the head of the second clause, in
order to make the contrast with בָּזֶה more striking. — הַנִּחַ, Hiph.
apoc. of נוּחַ; see Lex. B.   *Will make his way with both*, usually
rendered: *Will escape both.*   But how can יֵצֵא be made to govern the Acc.?   It is an *intransitive* verb in Kal; and the cases
appealed to in Gen. 44 : 4; Ex. 9 : 29, 33, etc., are not parallel
with the present.   With that sense it would be followed by מִן,
from; see Jer. 11 : 11.   As the phrase now stands, it designates the idea that he who will go safely so as to avoid the
divine displeasure, will make his way as it were in company
with both the cautions given, or (in other words) he will take
them along with him.   These cautions are expressed by כֻּלָּם, *all
of them,* viz., *all* of the things he had just said.   In the other
mode of rendering, the meaning of *all of them* must be, *all of
the disasters.*   The sense would be well enough, if we could
make יֵצֵא govern an Acc.   As we cannot, we must adopt the
other method ; which Hitzig does in his Comm.

(19) Wisdom strengthens a wise man more than ten chieftains who are in
a city.

In v. 12 above he has said of *wisdom,* that it is a *defence.*   It
cannot indeed overleap the bounds which Providence has set to
the achievements of man, but it can do more than riches, and be
available where they are not.   The intermediate matter (vs.
15—18) is a partial digression from his immediate object, which
is to set forth the various advantages connected with *wisdom* or
sagacity.   A seeming exception to its claims is, that the right-

eous and the wicked sometimes take each other's place in the
award that follows their actions. After suggestions in the way
of opposition, that some abatement must be made from this statement, or some qualification of its terms, and an assertion that
shunning all excesses will keep every man in safety, the writer
resumes the subject of *wisdom,* in the verse before us. It will
be seen, of course, that he does not immediately answer or oppose
the suggestions that had been made, although it would seem,
·by the sequel, that he does not wholly accede to the views advanced in those suggestions. For the present, he has further to
say of *wisdom* that in the way of *protection* it often answers
purposes that power or force cannot answer; yea, which even
piety itself cannot; since all men, even good ones, commit more
or less of sin, and then they are exposed to its consequences.
תָּעֹז, not *is strong,* but actively here, viz., *gives strength, makes
strong,* or *strengthens.* The לְ before the object marks the direction, and so conveys the sense of *imparting to.* The vowel
(Seghol) belongs to the suppressed article. — מֵעֲשָׂרָה, noun of
number in the abs. state, see Parad. in § 95; also, for construction with the abs. noun that follows, consult § 118, 1, *b,* and
No. 2. — שַׁלִּיטִים, here *chieftains* of troops, as the nature of the
case demands, for what is said refers to *defence.* — שַׁלִּיט is one
who *rules* in any way. *Sultān* is an Arabic form from the root
of this same word. The *chieftains* include by implication the
forces which they lead. The noun of number is Nom. sing. in
form, but a *collective* plur.; see Gramm. § 95. — הָיוּ, *are,* § 124, 3.
What he means is, that there are times when *sagacity* is of more
avail than force of arms; for the latter can be repelled by like
force, while the former makes calculations for safety, which
cannot always be anticipated or adequately met. *Ten* is not
here designed to mean just this number; but (as often elsewhere) for the designation of a *considerable number.*

(20) For there is not a just man on earth, who doeth good, and sinneth
not.

Apparently the sentence is *causal*, for it is preceded by כִּי.
But what reason is contained in it to establish the validity of
the preceding remark? A question that has much perplexed
the commentators, who have answered it very variously. The
true exegesis of it, as it seems to me, has already been hinted in
the remarks on the preceding verse. Apparently it amounts to
this: After saying that *wisdom* is a *protection* more to be relied
on than wealth, and even more than military force, he now
suggests that even *righteousness* may sometimes fail its possessor
as a means of preservation, because it is not constant and uniform, but at times is interrupted in all men by sin; when, of
course, its protective power for a time must cease. If כִּי be
rendered *truly, surely*, the verse is then made into an apothegm,
true indeed, but *irrelevant*. If we interpret it as just proposed,
the *relevancy* of it at least seems to be discernible.

It is possible that Heiligs. may be in the right, who makes a
transition here in the discourse, and supposes the writer now to
be intent on chastising the spirit of those who are prone to find
fault with others, by suggesting to them that they should keep
in view the fact that no one is perfect, and therefore should be
kind and candid. Perhaps the next verse favors this, which, it
cannot well be doubted, has a reference to rulers, *i. e.*, to the
reports of men respecting them. But as there is no *particle* at
the beginning of the verse which indicates a new turn of the
subject, but is indicative merely of the reason for what has been
said, and as the sentiment adopted by Heiligs. appears somewhat
abrupt without some indication of transition, the former method,
defended by Hitzig, seems rather preferable. It must be owned,
however, that some obscurity rests on the exact aim of the
author here. But the whole chapter has more of the apothegmatic character than usual.

Were it not for the כִּי, we might give the verse another turn.
In vs. 7—12 above he has introduced the subject of oppressive
magistrates, and cautioned against dealing hastily or haughtily

with them. He has commended the wisdom which enables one
to steer safely without provoking them, or without coming into
offensive contact with them. If now he be viewed here (in v.
20) as intending to soften down the irritated feelings of the
oppressed against their rulers, by suggesting that all men, even
the best, are liable to sin, and that therefore we should not be
too severe in our judgment of them ; then would the verse be a
good preparative for what follows, the design of which is to show
that hasty and exaggerated or slanderous reports should not be
readily admitted and believed. This would add to the cautions
already given above ; and with this the subject is here dismissed.
The reader can choose for himself. The כִּי in question seems to
stand in my way with respect to adopting the view last suggested ; although I do not think it an insuperable obstacle, because it sometimes stands at the head of a new discourse (see
Is. 15 : 1 ; 8 : 23 ; Job 28 : 1), and then means *verily, surely,
immo;* see on 4 : 16.

(21) Moreover, give not thy mind to all the words which are uttered, in
order that thou mayest not hear thy servant cursing thee.

That is, listen not to tale-bearers and slanderers. Magistrates
are specially exposed to assaults in this way. But if you indulge
the disposition to hear such things, you who are a *master* may
be very likely to hear them from your *servants,* who stand in a
relation to you like that in which you stand to your rulers. Men
in such a relation are apt to be hardly judged and talked about,
as experience shows. This is the reason why *servants* are here
mentioned as examples for warning. They are often prone to
tattle and to find fault with their master ; and such is the case of
others in respect to their civil rulers, who exact tribute of them.
Now, as you dislike such slander against yourself, and often feel
that it is groundless and wanton, so may your civil masters feel
in respect to their detractors. — יְדַבְּרוּ (in pause) is 3d Plur.
impers., there being no subject expressed. Of course it may be

translated as virtually a *passive* verb, and so I have rendered it; § 134, 2. *Give not thy mind* means, 'Do not deem it an object worthy of serious attention, nor one that ought to occupy the mind.' — אֲשֶׁר, *that, so that.* — מְקַלְלֶךָ, Part. Piel, with suff.; Dagh. omitted in the first ל, as oftentimes, § 20, 3, *b.* — ךָ, suff. in pause; see p. 288, Par. col. A.

(22) For thine own heart also knoweth many times when even thou thyself hast cursed others.

As a proof or ground of what he had just said, he now appeals to the experience of the individual addressed. He suggests that he himself must be sensible that he has exercised the temper which would lead him to curse others; and why may he not expect the like from them? There is nothing strange in it. פְּעָמִים, fem. with a masc. form, as רַבּוֹת shows, § 105, 4. It means here *cases*, or what we usually call *instances;* and it is in the Acc. governed by יָדַע. So Hitzig. — אַתְּ = אַתָּה, as the Qeri shows; see in Neh. 9 : 6; Ps. 6 : 4 al. Such being the proneness of human nature to think and speak ill of superiors, one needs to be well guarded against this vice.

(23) All this have I tried by wisdom. I have said : Let me become wise now; but it was far from me.

He means to say that he had made a discerning and sagacious trial of the much talked-of *wisdom.* He had applied practical wisdom in order to search out and investigate the true nature and essence of *wisdom;* for this seems to be the object now before us. Already has he told what practical wisdom achieves. But now he wishes to go deeper, to inquire into and search out its real nature and essence. — אֶחְכָּמָה, Imperf. hortative, § 48, 3, with parag. ה. — הִיא, *this thing*, viz., the becoming wise, fem. for neuter, as usual. *Far from me, i. e.,* out of his reach, he could not attain to it. Viewed in the light in which it is now placed, this verse is not a contradiction of the asserted value of

wisdom, already made in various ways. It is designed to show
that beyond the point of that value, *i. e.*, beyond its *practical*
effects, he could not successfully pursue inquiries so as to discover
its real nature or essence. The next verse shows how fully he
was persuaded of this.

(24) That which is far off and very deep — who can find it out?

Not with Herzf. : *far off remains, what was far off;* nor with
Ewald : *far off — what is it?* nor with Rosenm. : *that is far off
which before was present* (?) — מַה־שֶּׁהָיָה, *that which is.* The
predicate רָחוֹק is placed first for the sake of emphasis. — עָמֹק is
made emphatic by repetition, § 106, 4. — נּוּ verbal suff. The
whole hangs on the רחוקה of v. 23. The gender of the adjectives is changed in v. 24, because the proposition there assumes
a more generic form. Indeed, it appears like a common collo-
quial apothegm; and here it is cited probably in the way that
accords with its usual popular form. Sentiment: 'What I
sought was exceedingly beyond my power to attain.'

But although he discovered thus much, as to the way in which
he had been investigating, yet he did not wholly abandon the
pursuit. He tried the matter once more in the way of examining the *opposite* or *antithesis* of wisdom, in order that he might
thus, *i. e.*, in the way of *antithetical* comparison, discover something more of the true nature of that which he was investigating.

(25) I turned myself, and my purpose was to acquire knowledge and to
investigate, even to seek out wisdom and intelligence, and to know wickedness as folly, and folly as madness.

וְלִבִּי has been an *offendiculum criticorum* here. Knobel,
Heiligs., and even Hitzig, with others, make it the instrumental
Acc., and translate : *with my mind,* as if it were בְּלִבִּי (as a number of Codices have it). But וְלִבִּי cannot be here translated *with*
or *by my mind.* If this were the meaning, the וְ must of course

be *omitted*, and לְבִּי be taken as the Acc. of manner or instrument (116, 3) = *intelligenter*. But as the text is, לִבִּי must be the subject of the clause ; the copula (הָיָה or הוּא) is implied, and the Infinitives (nominascent) that follow are the complement or predicate. That לֵב may mean *desire, purpose, wish*, admits of no doubt; see Lex. לֵבָב, d. — וּבַקֵּשׁ וּ׳ forms a new clause, to distinguish which the לְ before the Inf. is omitted. The clause is epexegetical and supplementary, inasmuch as the first clause says nothing more than that he addressed himself to acquiring knowledge and investigating, but without saying what it was which he investigated ; while the second clause tells us what the objects of inquiry were, and בַּקֵּשׁ sums up and comprises the meaning of the two preceding verbs. Hitz. puts לָדַעַת and לָתוּר in the Acc. after בַּקֵּשׁ, and of course translates thus : *And with my mind to seek to know and to investigate*. The sense in itself is well enough, but one of the two *Vafs* must be ejected in this case from the text, either that before וְלִבִּי or else that before בַּקֵּשׁ. It is unnecessary and inexpedient to do this. Heiligs. moves on without the least notice of any difficulty in the text, and says nothing of the וְ in question. Knobel recognizes it, but ejects the first וְ *sans ceremonie*. None of these plans admit and explain the text as it is. But surely there is no necessity of changing it, as the version above shows. In the case of וּבַקֵּשׁ, I have rendered וְ by *even* (§ 152, B. 2), which is the proper translation before an epexegetical clause designed rather to explain than to add anything new. — חֶשְׁבּוֹן is another term for *wisdom*, designating it as *meditating* or *excogitating*. Both terms increase the intensity of expression = wisdom in the highest sense. It is the *nature* of this which he is now *seeking out*. — רֶשַׁע כֶּסֶל, not *the wickedness of folly* (for this would be רֶשַׁע הַכֶּסֶל), but *wickedness as folly*. *And folly as madness*, the same construction as before, the latter noun having no article and no וְ, and thus showing that it is subordinate and explanatory, and not a case of const. noun with a Genitive after it. In

הַסִּכְלוּת, the article merely points to the preceding כֶּסֶל, and is as much as to say: *that folly.* So that from both clauses we obtain the sentiment that wickedness is both folly and madness; which surely is a sound doctrine of the Scriptures. The word סִכְלוּת is merely a variation in *form* (not in meaning) from the preceding כֶּסֶל. Thus much for the grammatical part of our investigation.

The occasion of what is here said seems to have been taken from v. 17: *Be not wicked overmuch, nor be thou foolish.* It seems to be there assumed that it is only a *high degree* of wickedness (הִרְבָּה) which makes a man *foolish;* that is, he may be somewhat wicked, and yet be wise. Coheleth is not satisfied with such a view of the subject, although the sentiment which it conveys is designed to apologize or account for the mysterious providence described in v. 15. He thinks all wickedness to be *folly,* and that this folly is, moreover, a *lack of reason,* or *madness.* He had sought to discover the nature of true wisdom contemplated by itself; but this was far away and deep. He now makes another effort; and this is, to seek out what wisdom is by searching into its opposite or antithesis, viz., *folly.* This is equivalent to *wickedness,* and also to *madness.* True wisdom stands opposed to all three. All sin, then, in his view is folly; and not merely an *excess* of wickedness is sin, but every degree of it. Consequently, to be *wise* is to refrain from all sin; for the commission of it, in any manner or measure, is folly and wickedness so far as it goes.

What follows I regard as designed to exhibit how widely sin and folly are diffused abroad. Examples on all sides are before him, and he can easily discover what *folly* is by observing and examining these examples. And if *folly* can be fully seen, then its opposite, viz., *wisdom,* may of course be better understood. Withal, the reader should compare the verse before us with 1:17 and 2:12—15, where he speaks more despairingly of acquiring an adequate knowledge, and thinks it to be כִּרְעיֹן רוּחַ.

(26) And I found more bitter than death the woman whose heart is nets and snares, whose hands are chains; he who is pleasing to God shall be delivered from her, but the sinner shall be caught by her.

This is truly *oriental* in its conception. Women, it seems, are the examples most in point of the *folly* in question. The low estimate in which females are held throughout the east, even down to the present day, never associating nor even eating with men, being moreover without education or any true dignity of character, and reckoned as mere menial instruments of man's pleasure, leads of course to degradation and depravation of character. Here, then, Coheleth seeks his most striking examples of folly, either in its mental or moral sense. How different is the case in those countries on which the light of the gospel has dawned! Were we now to make the same inquest which he did, we should first betake ourselves to the male rather than the female sex, in order to light upon those where wickedness more fully abounds. So much has Christianity done for women. But still, Coheleth's proposition cannot, as many suppose, be a general, or rather a universal, one in respect to the sex. Plainly, he speaks only of those women who employ their arts and charms to inveigle paramours. He likens these arts to *nets* and *toils*, which inclose and secure their prey; and their clinging hands he calls *chains*, because they hold fast the victim. Highly favored of God is the man who escapes their enticements, and only those who are displeasing in his sight, *i. e.*, sinners, will be ensnared by them. This is a high although not directly designed encomium on chastity in men; and it shows that the writer was no mere voluptuary. What he says of women bearing the character here described, we may fully accede to, even at the present time; and among them we might say as he afterwards says, that there is not one in a thousand, *i. e.*, one example of wisdom in its true sense. — אֶת־הָאִשָּׁה, Acc. after מִצֵא; which last word is pointed, as to its final vowel, in the Syriac fashion, instead of taking the usual Tseri; see § 74, VI. n. 21, *a*. So הוֹצֵא, in this

same verse, is written חׂזֶּה in 8 : 12 ; 9 : 18. There is some
difficulty in the construction of אֲשֶׁר־הִיא here. The most facile
method of rendering the clause is to put together אֲשֶׁר . . . לִבָּהּ,
and translate: *whose heart.* The only objection to this is that
made by Hitzig, viz., that if לִבָּהּ were the subject or Nom. of
the clause, then the fem. הִיא could not be employed, but הוּא
must be inserted. But this rests simply on the ground that לֵב
is masc., and that consequently the pronoun must be of the same
gender. But this is far from being certain. — לֵב makes its plur.
לִבּוֹת; which Fuerst says (Concord.) must come from לִבָּה, fem.
But why? Are there not many nouns of *comm.* gender which
have a masc. form for their singular; *e. g.*, נֶפֶשׁ, plur. נְפָשׁוֹת, a
word of kindred meaning with לֵב. So the fuller form לֵבָב has
masc. and fem. forms both in the plural, indicating a *common*
gender of the singular. Adopting this view here (Ges. Lex.
says nothing about the gender), then הִיא is in due order. But
it is a mere *copula* here $=$ *is*, as often elsewhere in this book.
In this way the version above is justified. But we may take.
another way, and yet arrive at a like conclusion. We may
translate thus : *who is nets and snares as to her heart, i. e.*, לֵב is
in the Acc. of the *manner* or *the respect in which* she is snares,
etc. So Herz.; although he prefers making אֲשֶׁר־הִיא the Acc.,
and rendering it thus : *in respect to whom.* — טוֹב, goodly, pleas-
ing. Caught by her, refers to the *nets and snares.* The *hands*
are called *chains*, for the obvious reason that they are employed
in fondling and embracing, and thus bind the captive paramour.

(27) See! this have I found, saith Coheleth, [adding] one to another in
order to find out the computation.

רְאֵה demands special attention $=$ *look well* to what follows.
It is stronger than הִנֵּה, *ecce!* — זֶה, *this*, viz., what follows in
the next verse. — אָמְרָה קֹהֶלֶת is in all probability wrongly
divided. The ה should be attached to קֹהֶלֶת, as it is in 12 : 8.
Being an *appellative*, it may take the article, if the writer pleases,

for the sake of emphasis; and being used as a proper name, the
article may as is usual be omitted. It is without it in 1 : 1, 2, 12 ;
12 : 9, 10.   But it is always *masc.*, which speaks decidedly
against אֲמָרָה, and shows that the verb should be אָמַר. — אַחַת
לְאַחַת lit. *one to one*, without anything to connect or govern the
phrase.   It is employed adverbially therefore (like our *one by
one*), and of course implies before it a verb or Part. which signifies *adding* or *joining*, e. g., שָׂם. — לִמְצֹא, *in order to find*,
where לְ has a special significance, indicating object or design.
חֶשְׁבּוֹן speaks for itself here, by reason of the context.   It means
account, reckoning, or *computation*. This he has disclosed in
the next verse.

(28) What my soul has hitherto sought, and yet I have not found (one
man of a thousand I have found), but a woman among all these have I not
found.

My soul hath sought, intensive, *the inner man*, differing however from *I* only in intensity of expression. — בִּקְשָׁה, in Piel,
but the Dagh. in ק is omitted, because of the vocal Sheva it
would make, § 20, 3, *b*.   A rapid or abridged enunciation is the
object of such omissions, as we say *honor'd* for *honored*. Instead of saying immediately what that is which he has *not* found,
he throws in the cutting or ironical remark, in the way of paren-
thesis, which tells us what he has found, viz., *one man of a thousand*.   Of course he means one *upright* man, one who is not a
fool.   *But a woman*, וְ adversative, § 152, B. 1, *b*. Lex. וְ 2.
Among all these, not among all these thousand men, for there of
course he would not look for the woman in question, but *among
all this number*, or *such a number*, viz., among a thousand.   As
אָדָם means a *just man*, by the exigency of the passage, so אִשָּׁה
(= אֲנָשָׁה fem. of אֱנָשׁ) means an *upright woman*.   Sentiment:
' Just men are exceedingly scarce ; just women still more so.'

[That Coheleth means here to include all women, and to pass such a
judgment on all, should not be admitted unless his language obliges us to

admit it. He was too keen an observer not to know that a sweeping proposition of this nature cannot be true. Certain it is that the women described
in v. 26 are such as are given to amorous dalliance. And among these it
would be difficult at any time to find *one good woman*. Such indeed may
become *penitent*, but then they no longer belong to the class described.
Who, then, are the *thousand*? Specially as applied to *men*, to what sort or
class of men do the *thousand* belong? Nothing is said to show this. Are
they then, like the women, of that class which are given to wantonness?
If so, how could even one just or good man be found among them? This
consideration seems to compel us to conclude that the thousand men are
such as belong to ordinary men. We say in like cases: ' We must take
them as they come.' But still, this is not quite so certain here as it seems
to be. In the East, where polygamy and concubinage have ever been prac-
tised and ever stood even in high repute, there might be men of strong sexual propensities, who still did not violate any law of the land, or even law
of Moses, in indulging them somewhat freely ; for these allowed *polygamy*,
and did not condemn except indirectly, the practice of even *concubinage*. It
was not, therefore, in the eyes of men any sacrifice of character with them,
when a man gratified to a large extent his sexual propensities. Some
among this class of men might be found of a character otherwise substantially good. · But very different was the condition of *women*. They must
adhere to one man, and could not have intercourse with any others without
a total loss of character and standing. Among these, amorous dalliance
with many showed an unspeakable debasement of character. It might be,
then, a matter of course that Coheleth could find no one of a good character among them. But with *men*, to whom variety of paramours was no
reproach (I speak only of intercourse with wives and concubines by com-
pact), his experience, or the result of his investigations, was different. I
do not see to what רַק־אֶלֶה can refer, except to the women described in
v. 26. Certainly they are the class who, of all human beings, are the most
conspicuous examples of folly ; and for examples of this sort Coheleth is
seeking. With the men, too, of similar propensities, the case is not much
better. *One for a thousand* is a small proportion indeed. Of course, however, the exact number makes nothing here ; for the real idea to be conveyed is simply that examples of righteousness or goodness are exceedingly
rare among men ; and among women of a particular class they are not at
all to be found.

Such, then, is the result of his בַּקֵּשׁ in order to find out the nature and
extent of *folly.* Hitzig seems to represent him as expecting to find at least
some of a good character among women, and as being disappointed in not

23

finding them. Says he, *more suo:* "Er denkt zu. fischen und krebst," *i. e.*, *he designs to catch fish, and catches crabs.* But, levity apart, his disappoint-ment could not be great, at not finding them among the class of women whom he describes. He was *grieved* rather than disappointed. Grievous, too, the result of his search among *men* must have been. Yet if *wisdom* can be better known by comparing its *opposite*, he has found full scope in this case for the investigation of it, for *folly* in abundance did he meet with.

The use which has sometimes been made of vs. 26—28 (by applying them to all of the female sex in the way of reproach, or else for the purpose of showing the extravagance and paradoxical character of the book before us) seems to have no solid ground. The writer designs to say that when he searched after *folly* and *madness,* which is *wickedness* (רֶשַׁע), he found the most complete exemplification in wanton *women,* and that he met with little better success as to finding any that were good and just among *men.* Some refer the thousand women to Solomon's seven hundred wives and three hun-dred concubines, 1 K. 11 : 3. But then, who are the thousand *men* in such a case? Coheleth might indeed look to the harem of Solomon with full confidence of finding folly there in its highest measure, specially after what is told us concerning his heathen women, in 1 K. 11 : 1—8. But I appre-hend the use of *thousand* in this case is only in the common way, often met with, of designating a large and indefinite number.

But whence this overwhelming and universal extension of folly and prof-ligacy? Is this one of the *arrangements of Providence,* so often spoken of and appealed to by him? This is a question which he meets by strong denial.]

(29) See! this only have I found, that God made man upright and they have sought out many devices.

In the Heb. the *order* in the first clause is different from that of the version. It runs thus: *Only see! this have I found,* רְאֵה being a parenthetic interjection. — לְבַד seems to be placed first here in the Hebrew, because of its emphatic meaning. *This* refers to what follows. — הָאָדָם, generic, *mankind.* — יָשָׁר is truly given by *upright.* It means *justus, probus, integer. They have sought out, i. e.,* men, mankind have, etc. — בִּקְשׁוּ, without Dagh. in ק; see above on v. 28. — חִשְּׁבֹנוֹת, has probably a Dagh. *dirimens* or *euphonic,* as it is called; for nouns of this form do not elsewhere exhibit such a Dagh., *e. g.,* זִכְרֹנוֹת, etc.

This Dagh. is inserted where a sharp tone of the preceding syllable is required, so that Dagh. causes the final consonant of that syllable to be more distinctly pronounced, § 20, 2, comp. Ewald, Gramm. § 92, 1, c.'a. Gesenius (Lex.) has not noticed the Dagh., and of course he regarded it as belonging to the proper form itself of the word. It may be so, but from analogy it seems hardly probable. *Devices* means of course here *evil devices, artes malae.* To himself alone then must man look as the source of all his follies and sins. God has indeed arranged all things and made them what they are; and one of these things is, that men should be *free agents,* and therefore the authors of their own wickedness. How it came that God created man peccable is a question which Coheleth does not bring to view, and probably one on which he did not speculate. It might be well for the church, if there were more who followed his example.

§ 12. *Men sin from a Variety of Causes; Punishment will not always be delayed.*

CHAP. VIII. 1—17.

[If men are not made sinners by their Creator, then how came men to sin? This question naturally arises at once in the mind of the reader. There seem to be three reasons given in the sequel why they fall into sin; (1) Men often sin through fear of rulers, by obeying their unjust commands when they know them to be so, vs. 1—5. (2) They sin because judgment and punishment are delayed, v. 11, seq. (3) They sin because oftentimes the wicked fare as well as the just, v. 14, seq. In regard to this last matter there is undoubtedly a mystery of Providence which is beyond the limits of our inquiries or knowledge, vs. 16, 17.

The course of thought more minutely investigated, runs thus: Truly wise must he be who can explain difficult matters, viz., such as he had been stating But there is a *spurious* wisdom This bids unreserved submission to the commands of rulers, whether they be good or evil. Resistance, it suggests, is dangerous; prudence, therefore, dissuades from it, vs. 1—4. But it should be remembered that there is a judgment-period hanging over all evil-doers, although no one can tell *when* it will take place. Death is inevitable to all, and wickedness cannot rescue the sinner from it, vs. 5—8. The wicked do indeed sometimes reign over and oppress the good. Yet still, they will die and be buried without the city, and will be soon forgotten. Oppression is grievous. But although judgment slumbers, and men grow bold in sin because of this, yet let the wicked do wickedly ever so long, it shall be well with the righteous at last, and to the wicked it shall be ill, vs. 9—13. To this an objection immediately presents itself: 'The righteous share the doom of the wicked, and to the wicked falls the lot of the righteous.' There is nothing left then for the latter but to enjoy all they can of the good things of life, vs. 14, 15. But in procuring the means of this enjoyment, much and grievous toil is necessary, so that it is of little account, v. 16. This the writer concedes must be acknowledged; and he allows that we can offer no adequate solution of the mystery, because the ways of Providence are beyond our knowledge, v. 17.]

(1) Who is like the wise man? Who understandeth the explanation of a saying? The wisdom of a man maketh his face to shine, but haughtiness disfigureth his face.

Hitzig thinks that the first clause is the language of exultation over the discovery he had made, as announced in the preceding verse. My convictions are of a different kind. It seems to me more natural to suppose that the difficulties which he had just been stating, and had left unsolved, moved him to exclaim as he does. The questions seem to amount to this: ' Who, like a wise man, can explain the difficulties or solve the questions that arise in respect to wisdom?' — כְּהֶחָכָם, usually written in such cases, as כֶּחָכָם, *i. e.*, the article is usually dropped, and the כ normally takes its vowel, § 35, n. 2. See like cases of this punctuation in the *later* books (for in them only, almost without exception, is it found), *e. g.*, Ezek. 40 : 25 ; 47 : 22 ; 2 Chron. 10 : 7 ; 25 : 10 ; 29 : 27 ; Neh. 9 : 19 ; 12 : 38. The article specifies a particular man, viz., the man wise enough to make explanation. But of what? Of a דָּבָר, *word, maxim, apothegm*, etc. But

ECCLESIASTES VIII. 1. 269

what one? I see no answer to this but one, viz., the דָּבָר exhibited in the sentence or apothegm (such I take it to be) that follows. What follows this apothegm does not point us to any explanation of *preceding* difficulties, namely, those in Chap. VII. *Wisdom*, then, will be shown in case a proper explanation of the apothegm can be made out. In fact, it needs some wisdom to make it out, as the endless variety of opinions about the latter clause may serve to show. *Maketh his face to shine, i. e.*, exhilarates him, makes his face to glow with pleasure and satisfaction; comp. like modes of expression in Num. 6:25; Ps. 4:7; Job. 29 : 24. — עֹז פָּנָיו has been long debated. The Hebrews used עַז פָּנִים to denote a man of *impudent face* or of *stern visage;* also הֵעֵז פָּנִים to signify: *he made up an impudent face* (as we express it). — עֹז is from the same root (עָזַז) and might have the same meaning also, if this word and the next after it constitute a common case of const. and Gen. after it. But this we cannot well admit, for פָּנָיו here makes a relative meaning by virtue of the suffix, quite different from that which פָּנִים alone would have. The conclusion then must be that עֹז is *Nom.* and *subject*, and that פָּנָיו is Acc. governed by the verb which follows. Then we take the two last clauses as constructed alike, and we have a facile sense: *The wisdom of a man enlightens his face, and haughtiness* or *impudence disfigures his face.* — יְשֻׁנֶּא, as pointed is in Pual Imperf., the א being used for ה; for so in 2 K. 25:29, we have יְשֻׁנֶּא for יְשֻׁנֶּה, and in Jer. 52 : 33 (the same expression). See § 74, vi. n. 22. The Seventy translate μισηθήσεται, *shall be hated*, and so must have read יִשָּׂנֵא (in Niph. and with *Sin* instead of *Shin*). The true pointing seems plainly to be יְשַׁנֶּא (Piel of שָׁנָה), with א for ה as above stated. The comparison, or rather the antithesis, shows that, as in the first case the action of the verb falls on פָּנָיו, so in the second case the same is to be said as to the second פָּנָיו. The one *brightens*, the other *disfigures*. The antithesis is not indeed closely pressed, for then we should have as the opposite of תָּאִיר, the verb תַּחְשִׁיךְ, *darkens*.

23*

Nor is the meaning, as found above, to be confined to a *physical*
change of the countenance, although the trope is borrowed from
this. By the *light* which wisdom sheds, we may well understand the *light of life;* comp. Job 33 : 20 ; Ps. 56 : 14; comp.
also Ecc. 7 : 12. On the other hand עֹז (*haughty disregard*),
destroys, see v. 8 below. So in Job 14 : 20, מְשַׁנֶּה פָנָיו refers to
the *change of countenance* which takes place after death ; and
this is a striking illustration of our text from a writer contemporary, or nearly so, with Coheleth. Sentiment: 'Wisdom preserves life, or imparts the light of life, while haughtiness brings
on the disfigurement of death.' This gives to the whole apothegm a spirited tone and significance far above the merely
physical sense. But it needs, as the author intimates, some
understanding in order to make out a פֵּשֶׁר. It has indeed a kind
of *esoteric* meaning, while the literal sense is merely exoteric,
and would present no mystery. The whole conception seems to
have sprung from Job 16 : 15, 16, q. v.

Knob. renders: *the gloom (?) of his countenance is changed.*
Ewald: *the splendor of his countenance is doubled,* making the
verb from שָׁנָה, *to repeat* (but *splendor* is a *manufactured* sense
for עֹז) ; Herzf.: *his stern visage is changed;* all of them mistaking the relation of עֹז and פָּנִים. Hitzig adopts the meaning
given above, and to him I owe the best arguments in its favor.
He has not, however, sufficiently indicated the bearing of the
sentiment on what precedes, or its relation to it. If the reader
will look back to 7 : 11 seq., 19, 25 seq., he will readily perceive
how often and earnestly *wisdom* is discussed. In the verse
before us, at the close of these discussions, he will see that for
wisdom is still claimed a high place, like to that asserted in 7 : 12,
but it is here more vividly described. As the opposite of this is
the עֹז (*haughty perseverance*) which refuses to receive and obey
instruction, we might perhaps expect סֶכֶל instead of עֹז, since it
is the direct antithesis of חָכְמָה. But עֹז better characterizes the
temper of mind which leads men "to seek out many evil devices."

To all this the writer now subjoins the counsel which a timid and counterfeit wisdom gives; for this by contrast sets off true wisdom to advantage. Let us hear this *worldly-wise man*:

(2) I keep the commandment of the king; and so, because of the oath of God.

פִּי, const. of פֶּה, lit. *mouth*, then what the mouth utters, *command;* see Lex. — שְׁמֹר, as pointed, is an Imper.; but then one must of course supply אָמַרְתִּי after אֲנִי. With Hitzig, I would point the word שֹׁמֵר, as in v. 5 below. — וְעַל, the וְ I have rendered *and so=and I keep it because of,* etc., § 152, B. 23. — דִּבְרַת =*propter*, when עַל stands before it, see Lex. *The oath of God,* means an oath in which God is named and called to witness the transaction, so as to give to it the highest and most solemn sanction. Hitzig says that no such oaths of fealty to rulers are anywhere mentioned in Hebrew antiquity. But 2 K. 11 : 17 mentions a בְּרִית *(covenant)* between the king and people; could this be made without the sanction of an oath? Ptolemy Lagi exacted an oath from the vassal Jews, Jos. Arch. XII. 1. Oaths, we know, were very common among the Jews when great and solemn transactions were engaged in; see Gen. 24 : 2, 3, comp. Gen. 47 : 29; 1 Sam. 12 : 5. Here, then, religion is called in to give color to the obligation of obedience and loyalty. But this view of the matter is repelled in v. 5. I see nothing here to determine whether the king is a foreigner or indigenous; nothing either Persian or Egyptian.

(3) Do not hastily depart from his presence. Do not make delay in regard to a command which is grievous; for all which he desireth he accomplisheth.

The two verbs תִּבָּהֵל and תֵּלֵךְ are so united in the expression and qualification of one idea (there is no וְ between them), that the first is used *adverbially,* and so I have translated it *hastily;* see § 139, 3, *b.* — תִּבָּהֵל is in Niph. Imperf., and is reflexive =*do*

not hurry thyself. — מִפָּנָיו, *from his presence* or *his face.* It is
not the same as *Do not make revolt from him,* or *Do not make
defection.* It applies to such as have personal intercourse with
him, and dissuades them from testifying dislike or impatience at
his commands or orders by an abrupt departure which will of-
fend him. — תַּעֲמֹד, *delay, stand still,* not an unfrequent sense of
עָמַד; see Josh. 10 : 13; 1 Sam. 20 : 38; Ezek. 21 : 35, Lex.
No. 2.   So Sept. also. — דָּבָר here is the same as פִּי in v. 2, viz.,
command. — רָע means *grievous,* on whatever, or on any ground.
Here the implication, if we advert to v. 5, seems to be that the
command is both *wrong and burdensome.*   Sentiment: 'Treat
not lightly any command of the king, and hesitate not to obey it
forthwith, let it be what it may.'   Then follows a reason for
prompt obedience: 'The king has unlimited power to enforce
obedience.'   See like descriptions of power applied to God in
Jon. 1 : 14; Job. 13 : 12.

(4) Where there is the word of a king there is power; for who will say
to him: What doest thou?

This repeats in another form the sentiment of the preceding
clause.   It reminds the reader that when the king utters any
word, *i. e.,* command or sentence, there is lodged with him power
to enforce its execution; and therefore resistance or neglect
would be folly.   For the last phrase which challenges all opposition, see again Jon. 1 : 14; Job 23 : 13.

Thus far the man of *prudential* wisdom.   We shall now see
in what estimation Coheleth holds such reasonings.

(5) He who obeyeth the command will have no concern about the grievous word; but the heart of a wise man will take cognizance of time and
judgment.

שׁוֹמֵר, being a participle, supplies its own subject, *he who,* or
whoever, any one who. — מִצְוָה, *command, mandate,* explains the
preceding דָּבָר. — יֵדַע means in both clauses, *to take knowledge*

of, in the sense of *caring for, having regard to*, or *looking well to;* see Gen. 39 : 6 ; Prov. 27 : 23, which make this meaning very plain. — וְיֵצֵא, וְ, *but*, adversative, see Lex. וְ No. 2. *Time* means of course some future time, which will bring *judgment* with it. See the same declaration in 3 : 17 ; and virtually the same in 5 : 8 ; 11 : 9 ; 12 : 14. The wise man who anticipates this will not yield obedience to commands which bid him to sin, דְּבַר רָע. He fears divine displeasure more than a monarch's frowns. There is no true wisdom in doing evil to please a king who is but an erring man, when that deed displeases the King of kings.

I forbear to discuss the various opinions in relation to this passage, which may be found in Knobel, Heiligst., and others. They are too loose and conjectural to need confutation. Hitzig seems to have hit the true mark ; at least, my own views coincide with his.

(6) *For to every undertaking there is a time and judgment; for the evil of man is great upon him.*

הֵפֶץ, in the same sense as in 3 : 1, viz., *undertaking, negotium.* The existence of an appointed time for judgment, assumed in the preceding verse, is affirmed here. But the latter part of the verse presents some difficulty. *The evil of man,* means here that which he commits or does; for cognizance in judgment concerns only this, and not the evils which befall him. *Is great upon him* means, *weighs heavily upon him;* for רַבָּה, in such a connection, is explained in Gen. 18 : 20 by כָּבְדָה מְאֹד, *is very heavy;* and so in Is. 24 : 20, *transgression* כָּבַד עָלֶיהָ, *is heavy on it,* viz., the land. In Gen. 4 : 13 Cain says that "his iniquity is greater מִנְּשׂוֹא, *than he can bear* or *carry.*" All these phrases render the design of our text clear. Sentiment: 'There will be a time of judgment, because the evil which man commits is so great that it presses heavily upon him.' — עָלָיו indicates what is *burdensome* to one, Lex. עַל, 1, γ. The כִּי, at the beginning of the clause, is of course *causal; i. e., judgment* is necessary *because evil-doing is so frequent and excessive.* The scriptural idea of the appropriate time for punishment is this, viz., that it is the period when *iniquity is full* or *heavy;* comp. Gen. 14 : 16 ; Dan. 8 : 23 · Matt. 23 : 32 ; 1 Thes. 2 : 16. It is the same in our text.

(7) For no one knoweth what shall take place; for who can tell him when it shall take place?

The ground of the connection with the preceding verse by the causal כִּי is not discerned at once by the reader. But a little consideration seems to show what that ground is. Evidently, the writer means to show the sinner that there is no chance of escape from the *judgment* in question; for since no man can know the future, he cannot know that the judgment will not come ; and since he cannot know *when* the judgment will come, therefore he cannot take any precautions to avoid it. The כִּי before the last clause is also *causal,* and may be regarded as *coördinate* with the כִּי preceding, or as growing out of the clause immediately preceding it. If we choose the latter, the sentiment would stand thus : 'The future no one can foretell, *for* (כִּי) he cannot even name a time when this or that shall happen.' But as this does not run quite smoothly in respect to logic, perhaps the other method of coördination is to be preferred. So Hitzig. כַּאֲשֶׁר, *when,* which meaning is quite common; see Lex. The next verse asserts still more positively the punishment of the sinner.

(8) No man hath power over the wind to restrain the wind ; and none hath power in the day of death, for there is no discharge in this warfare, and wickedness cannot deliver those to whom it belongs.

רוּחַ here has more usually been rendered *spirit.* But if this were meant, it must be written בְּרוּחוֹ, *over his, i. e.,* his own *spirit,* and must then mean either his *vital breath,* or *the spirit of life* which animates him. But if *spirit* mean, as is commonly supposed, his *immaterial soul*, the passage must be understood to apply only to his final departure, and to mean that power is wanting to keep back the soul when it is about to take its flight; for in many other respects man has power over his spirit, for "*he ruleth it,*" Prov. 25 : 28 ; 16 : 32. As to having *power over the wind*, see in 11 : 5 ; Prov. 30 : 4 ; John 3 : 8. The same word (רוּחַ) means both *wind* and *spirit;* which may be a reason for fixing upon this object of comparison, viz., the wind. The course of thought seems to be this : 'If you have no power over the natural רוּחַ, how can you have any over the more subtile and invisible רוּחַ of a human being. If you cannot keep back the former, how can you expect to restrain the latter?' — שִׁלְטוֹן is the later form of שַׁלִּיט, and used in the way of variety. *Day of death* means of *decease, i. e.,* of natural death. So *his day* is used in Job 15 : 32; 1 Sam. 26 : 10. — הַמָּוֶת, lit. *of the death* = his death, and being a particular specific day, it takes the article. So the Greeks often substitute the article in place of a pronoun. *No discharge in the warfare* (lit.) = *this* or *his warfare;* for so the article makes it mean. In other wars there are frequent furloughs and dismissions ; here, none. The design of all this figurative language comes out at last in plain words at the close : *Wickedness cannot deliver its possessors,* viz., those to whom it belongs, or (in other words) those who commit it.

(9) All this have I seen, and I gave my attention to every deed which is done under the sun : there is a time when one man ruleth over another man to his own harm.

All this, viz., what is stated above in vs. 2—4, with respect to rulers. — נָתוֹן אֶת־לִבִּי, *to give* or *set one's heart, i. e.,* mind, to a thing. The verb is Inf. abs. employed as a definite verb in the Praeter tense, § 128, 4, *b.* The רָאִיתִי here may be taken for *seeing* in the natural sense, *i. e.,* all this is what I have been witness to with my own eyes. — עֵת, *a time* = sometimes ; of course יֵשׁ is implied. — לֹו, to the harm of the *ruler*, or (as in the version) *to his own harm*. In other words: 'He has seen rulers insisting on obedience to evil commands; and this at last, to their own hurt.' It is shown above, v. 5, that obedience to such evil commands is sin, and that it brings evil upon him who executes them. Now he subjoins, that such commands injure those also who give them. — רָע in this case means *mischief, harm;* as often elsewhere.

(10) And then I saw the wicked buried, for they had departed, even from a holy place did they go away, and then they were forgotten in the city where they had so done; this too is vanity.

Of the numerous explanations (widely differing) which are before us I need not give an account, as it would occupy much time and space. Enough, if adequate reasons can be given for the one which is here adopted. The subject of vs. 2—13 is plainly *one* and the *same*, in different aspects which, as we have already seen, lay very heavily upon the mind of Coheleth, viz., *the oppressive conduct of rulers.* He blames men for flattering them by readily executing their wicked commands, and indicates that this is a *sin* that will certainly meet with condign punishment. In v. 9 seq. he turns to the rulers themselves who enforce obedience to such commands. His proposition (v. 9) is, that it will occasion their *own harm*, as well as that of others. The verse before us gives a picture of the consequences which follow such conduct. — וּבְכֵן, lit. and *in the so, i. e., and then*, or *in that state* in which he was while contemplating their conduct as mentioned in the preceding verse. See a clear case of such a meaning in Est. 4 : 16, see also Ges. Lex. כֵּן, 3, *b.* He sees the wicked rulers dead and *buried;* which does not necessarily import (as some would have it) "with funeral honors," for it is said of all, of good men and evil men, of those honored and those dishonored, that *they are buried.* So Ahab and Jezebel, Gog and Magog, *are buried.* To lie *unburied* is indeed *dishonor;*

but *buried* is not the necessary antithesis to this, in such a way that it must mean *honorably buried.* It means merely and simply *inhumed, entombed.* — וּבָאוּ, *for they had departed, gone away;* Pluperf. § 124, 2. — בּוֹא is frequently used to designate the *setting* of the sun, and is so generic that *progress* or *motion* in any direction is occasionally designated by it. It may be that בֵּית עוֹלָם (see 12 : 5) is implied after it here, *i. e., the perpetual home* to which they go; but this is not necessary in order to make out the sense. Like הָלַךְ, it may sometimes mean *departure,* viz., to another world; as is plain in the case of applying the word to the *setting sun.* The common idea of the verb בּוֹא is that of *entering into* any house (for example) or city, place, etc. ; and such an implication is probably designed for the word here. *The wicked had gone* [to their final abode]. The idea of entering into *rest* (as in Is. 57 : 2) is not at all implied here ; for there it is predicated expressly of the *righteous,* and שָׁלוֹם follows on after the verb בּוֹא. The whole phrase is exactly like our *buried and gone, i. e.,* finally quitted all earthly scenes. I have rendered the וְ before בָּאוּ by *for,* as standing in a kind of apodosis, and being equivalent to *nam* or *quia;* see Lex. וְ, No. 4. *Even from a holy place did they go.* Not from the *temple,* for then we should have הַקֹּדֶשׁ, but from *a holy place* (the article being omitted in order to avoid giving a wrong sense). The next clause shows *holy place* to be the *city, i. e.,* Jerusalem (called, down to the present hour, *the Holy* by all its neighbors). יְהַלֵּכוּ (in pause), Piel, which in actual usage differs, as to sense in this case, nothing from the conjugation Kal ; generally Kal and Piel are the same here, and there is only now and then a case of the latter, where *habitude* or *intensity* is implied. Hitzig proposes יֵהָלְכוּ (Kal), and to translate it *perished.* But there is no need of this new pointing ; nor does the meaning seem to be what he makes it here. The clause is a climactic one. Not only did they *depart,* but *even from the holy city,* where they had lived, and reigned, and oppressed, *they went away; i. e.,* their

24

departure was made from *the city*, by their being carried out of
it in order to be buried; as indeed all the dead were. *And then*
(וְ, *and so, and then*) *they were forgotten in the city;* in other
words, no monument was erected to them, no lamentation made
over them, and therefore they were forgotten; see 2 Chron. 35 :
24, 25, and comp. Jer. 22 : 18, 19. — אֲשֶׁר may be rendered
where (Lex. s. v. No. 6), or *who.* I prefer the former. — כֵּן־עָשׂוּ
with a Maq., showing that the two words are closely united, and
thus deciding that כֵּן, in the view of punctators, is the particle
so here, and not כֵּן *right* or *just.* The clause *they had so done,*
refers to what is said of them in vs. 2—4, where the subject
commences. In other words : Their oppression prevented the
erection of a monument to their memory by the hatred which it
excited, and caused them to be *buried in oblivion.* "The tri-
umphing of the wicked is short."

This interpretation not only makes the whole passage plain
and perspicuous, but it falls in entirely with the tenor of the discourse. Hitzig and others render כֵּן־עָשׂוּ by *had done rightly* or
justly, and thus make two classes of men to be mentioned in the
verse. Nothing calls for this, and the tenor of the context is
clearly against it. Our English version favors the meaning which
I have given. The writer designs to say that even in Jerusalem
he had found examples of oppression among rulers, and had seen
the consequences of it in the dishonor and oblivion which they
brought upon their own name and memory.

(11) Because sentence against an evil work is not speedily executed, therefore the heart of the sons of men within them is fully set to do evil.

פִּתְגָם is *masc.* (see the foreign origin of this late word in the
Lex.), and therefore demands the preceding word to be pointed
נַעֲשָׂה, *i. e.,* the Part. (and not a verb in the Praet. as נַעֲשָׂה is).
As this word is preceded by אֵין, it *must* be a *participle*, for אֵין
stands not before *definite verbs*, and so it must be נַעֲשָׂה. Then
again, פִּתְגָם has a pause-accent on it, and it stands in the abs.

form, whereas the sense shows that it is the *const.* before the
following Gen. noun, and therefore should be written פְּרִגַם, and
of course not have a pause-accent on it. *Sentence against an
evil work* is our English mode of expression; *sentence of a work
of evil* is the Hebrew one here, which means of course what I
have expressed in the version. — הָרָעָה is a noun in the Gen.,
and has the article because it is an *abstract* noun, § 107, 3, *c.*
Of course מַעֲשֵׂה is of the const. form, while it also is a Gen.
after the preceding noun; for the *const.* form may be in the
Nom., Gen., or Acc., as the case may demand. *The heart* (לֵב),
i. e., the heart as the seat of *thought, will,* or *desire.* It strengthens the assertion of proneness to evil. — מָלֵא, Part. adj., lit. *is
full, i. e.*, full of *inclination* or *desire,* or (as we say) *fully set.*
רָע, the adj. neuter here, and therefore used as a noun; it is in
pause, and its normal form is רַע.

The proposition in this verse is to all appearance general or
generic; but under this lies special reference to oppressive and
tyrannical rulers. Because punishment is *protracted,* they are
emboldened to continue their doings. What is said here of
them, however, is true of others also; but this need not hinder
a special application of the words to them. And so of the sequel.

(12) Although a sinner doeth evil a hundred times, and prolongeth [his
days] for himself, yet I certainly know that it shall be well to those who fear
God, who continually fear before him.

אֲשֶׁר, *although,* which, however, is not a usual sense of the
word when a case of concession occurs (Lex. s. v. B. 4); yet it
is sufficiently vouched for by proximate meanings elsewhere.
חֹטֶא (Seghol for final Tseri), see § 74, VI. n. 21, *a;* the same
form is also found in Ecc. 9 : 18. Elsewhere it is חֹטֵא. — עֹשֶׂה,
Part. instead of the verb, but in the same sense as the verb, and
governing the Acc. after it, instead of being put in the const.
state, § 132, 1, *a. b.* — מְאַת has the const. form, and is an adverb.
Some few other cases occur of the like kind, *e. g.,* רַבַּת, etc.

מַאֲרִיךְ, Part. Hiph., but absolute, *i. e.*, without a complement.
What then is implied as to its complement? In the next verse,
מַאֲרִיךְ יָמִים would seem to answer the question, and make the
word mean the *prolonging of life*. But לֹו, it is said, stands in
the way of this. Moreover, it is not by his own efforts that life
is prolonged; but in this case it seems to be said that *he pro-
longs something for himself, i. e.*, by his own efforts. Still, as
the Dative is often used after verbs (*e. g.*, like לֶךְ־לְךָ, Gen. 12 : 1)
which have no complement, it may possibly come under this category, if the Hiphil sense does not prevent it. Hitzig supplies
for the Acc. here, the עֲשׂוֹת רָע of the preceding verse. In favor
of the other construction is the same elliptical use of מַאֲרִיךְ in
7 : 15, where יָמִים must plainly be the supplement; and the full
form occurs here in v. 13. Conceding this, לֹו must be regarded
as a *Dativus commodi.* — כִּי, *yet, still;* see Lex. — גַּ, *profecto,*
qualifies יוֹדֵעַ (as the Maqqeph shows), and renders it intense =
I certainly or *truly know. It shall be well,* טוֹב, lit: *there shall be
good. Who fear before him* repeats the idea of the preceding
clause, for the sake of intensity. The one is a participle, and
the other a verb in Kal. Imperf. of יָרֵא. Both therefore denote
continued, habitual action. The repetition, then, must be for the
sake of intensity. Both phrases = *those who truly and habitually fear God.*

In other words: 'Whatever advantage oppressors may gain,
and however great the evils which they occasion, it remains true
after all, and it is a consolation for the oppressed, that those who
fear God shall sooner or later obtain their reward.' In *this*
world? The tenor of the book is plainly against this, for it is
often repeated that "all things come alike to all," and that "the
wise man and the fool die alike." That it is in *another* world,
then, seems to be the necessary implication; although it seems
strange to us that it is not spoken out more plainly and frequently, since we are prone to forget that "The gospel [only]
has brought life and immortality to light."

(13) But to the wicked it shall not be well, nor shall he prolong his days; as a shadow is he who doth not fear God.

This is the *antithesis* of the closing part of v. 12. 'The wicked shall be punished; they shall not prolong their days.' The accents join כַּצֵּל to the preceding clause, much to the injury of the sense. Altogether preferable is it to join (as I have done) כַּצֵּל to the closing part; and so Hitzig. The *copula* is of course implied after this word, so that the sense is as the version above expresses it. *As a shadow,* means and designates the idea of what is brief and fugitive, or evanescent, and also unsubstantial. *Shadows* are constantly varying, and at most continue but a little time. Such will be the condition and destiny of the sinner, and specially of oppressive rulers, for he has them still in his eye.

Here, then, seems to be a very full and firm conviction of the doctrine of a *retribution,* both for the good and for the evil. To this, however, an objection rises up when we come to the examination of actual occurrences. He goes on fully to state it.

(14) There is a vanity which is done on the earth; there are righteous to whom it happens according to the doing of the wicked; and there are wicked to whom it happens according to the doing of the righteous; I said that this surely is vanity.

יֵשׁ belongs to all numbers and genders. — מַגִּיעַ, Hiph. Part. of נָגַע, *pervenit, advenit, comes, happens.* The sentiment coincides with 2 : 19—21, and specially with 7 : 15. The fact itself cannot indeed be denied. The writer does not attempt to deny or evade it. Still, he does not take back what he has said in vs. 12, 13. But if what he meant to say there was to assert the doctrine of complete retribution in the present world, then how could he speak as he does here? We are forced then to conclude, on the ground of consistency, that he must have meant something more. And now, without denying the allegation made in the verse before us, he goes on to prescribe what must be done

24*

in order to obtain any enjoyment in a world where such things
are constantly occurring.   He comes again to the oft-repeated
conclusion, viz., that we must seek for enjoyment in the sober
and prudent use of such good things as our toil may procure.
After all, however, even this toil, if rendered strenuous, may
annoy us more than the good is worth which it acquires.   Moderation in this is necessary.   He finds his ultimate refuge, then,
in implicit submission to an overruling Providence, whose ways
are utterly beyond our investigation.   This thought is expanded
in the coming chapter.

(15) Then I praised enjoyment, because there is no good to man under
the sun but to eat, and to drink, and be joyful; for this will cleave to him
for his toil during the days of his life which God hath given him under the
sun.

אֲשֶׁר, *because,* as it often means, see Lex.   *Under the sun, i. e.,*
in the present world. — כִּי אִם, *but, except,* see Lex. s. v. B. 2.
שָׂמוֹחַ, neut. intrans. verb, as also the preceding verbs are in this
connection. — יִלְוֶנּוּ, Imperf. Kal of לָוָה with suff. נּוּ־, Gramm.
p. 289.   The ו is a consonant throughout. — בַּעֲמָלוֹ, *for his*
labor, or *in respect to* or *on account of his labor.*   We have seen
(on 2 : 24) that בְּ in this book and in the later Hebrew not
unfrequently coincides with לְ in regard to meaning. — יְמֵי, Acc.
const., the Acc. of *time,* § 116, 2.   Compare with this what has
before been said on passages of the same tenor, viz., 2 : 24;
3 : 12, 13, 22; 5 : 18.   The reasoning stands thus: 'Since virtue
and wickedness are both treated in a way that reverses their
tendency and natural consequences, it follows that virtue does
not afford the certain means at all times to procure happiness in
the present world.   But still, this does not forbid the enjoyment
of all the comforts that toil can procure.   Of this one can make
sure.'   Yet the next verse throws in a caution against too much
reliance even on this.

(16) When I gave my mind to know wisdom, and to consider the busi-

ness which is done on earth — that even by day and by night one enjoyeth
no sleep with his eyes;

The verse is a *protasis* to the next verse, and inseparably connected with it thus: ' When I did so and so — then I perceived,
etc. — לָדַעַת, *to know*, here *in order to know, i. e.*, acquire knowledge of. —הָעִנְיָן (as before) *negotium, business, i. e.*, whatever is
undertaken to be done. Specific here, and therefore it has the
article. Before כִּי the preceding verb רָאוֹת is implied, but it
should be put in the past tense, viz., [*I saw*] *that*, etc. — שֶׁנָּה,
Acc. placed first in the clause on account of the stress here laid
upon it. — רֹאֶה, lit. *seeth*, but here *experienceth* or *enjoyeth*, as
often elsewhere. But *who* seeth no sleep? Plainly it is the
man who is deeply engaged in the עִנְיָן (*business*) mentioned
above. In other words: ' Even the enjoying of the fruit of toil
is often marred by engaging too earnestly in it.'

(17) Then I saw all the work of God — that man cannot find out the
work which is done under the sun : in that which a man may toil to find
out, he will still make no discovery; and even if the wise man should say
that he knows it, he will not be able to discover it.

וְרָאִיתִי, וְ, *then*, here introducing the *apodosis* or after-clause.
Work of God, is what he does. In the second case, where, after
work, God is left out, it is still the same מַעֲשֵׂה, as the article
shows, which refers to the first מַעֲשֵׂה. Therefore נַעֲשָׂה, *done*,
means *done by God* who doeth all things; see 9 : 1. — בְּשֶׁל =
בַּאֲשֶׁר לְ, but as it is followed by another אֲשֶׁר, the meaning is
somewhat embarrassed. Ewald and others read בְּכָל־אֲשֶׁר, instead of both words now in the text; a more facile text, no
doubt, but not the true one on this account. — בְּשֶׁל is used twice
in Jonah, viz., 1 : 7, 12, comp. v. 8, where it is explained as =
בַּאֲשֶׁר לְ, and means in each case *because of, on account of*. We
might so translate here, and the clause would run thus : *because
that whatever a man may toil to find*, etc. But it may also be
rendered as in the version, which runs somewhat easier. — אֲשֶׁר

is Acc. governed by רַעֲמֹל. — וְלֹא, וְ in the apodosis, *yet, still.*
Not even הֶחָכָם, *the wise man,* the article by way of eminence.

In other words, this matter of the righteous and the wicked,
as having their respective lots reversed, and the insufficiency of
an attempt to enjoy the fruits of labor — all this is a matter too
deep for us to fathom. God has kept the grounds of this mysterious dispensation to himself. "Who can by searching find out
God?"

§ 13. *Suffering and Sorrow the common Lot of All, both Good and Bad.   We should look at the brighter Side of Things, and enjoy what we may.*

CHAP. IX. 1—10.

[The ninth should not have been dissevered from the preceding chapter,
with the close of which it is most intimately connected. The author had
said that God's work is inscrutable, and to him must be attributed the arrangement of all events. He now says that the righteous and the wise, and
all their doings, are at the divine disposal, and subjected to the will of God.
All have one common lot, whatever their character may be, v. 1. All men
have more or less of folly, and all die alike (vs. 2, 3), and when dead all
enjoyment ceases, and they know not anything more, vs. 4, 5. All sensation ceases, and they have no more a part to act in life, v. 6. The only
alleviation is that one should betake himself to enjoy all the innocent pleasures he can while Providence is smiling upon him, for this is all the earthly
portion allotted to him, vs. 7—9. Let him do this with energetic effort, for
such and all action is speedily to cease, v. 10. Neither strength nor skill
will always command success; that is at the disposal of a power above,
v. 11. Man cannot foresee his misfortunes, and is often and unexpectedly
overtaken by evil, v. 12. There is one thing more, however, to which some
preëminence must be given, viz., *wisdom*, v. 13. This sometimes contrives
to prevent threatened evil, even when superior force is employed to inflict
it, vs. 14, 15. Wisdom, then, is better than power, although some despise it,
v. 16. The noiseless persuasion of wisdom is better than the vociferous
boasting of fools, v. 17. Wisdom is better than weapons of war, and one
unskilled in it may do much mischief.]

(1) For all this have I considered, and searched out all this; that the righteous, and the wise, and their works, are in the hand of God; neither love nor hatred doth any man know; all is before them.

The בִּי here Hitzig renders *ja, truly, verily.* Of course he disconnects this from the preceding verse. But it seems to me a plain case of a *causal* meaning. In 8 : 17, it is said that no man can fathom the mystery of the exchange of lots by the righteous and the wicked. The grievous part is assigned to the righteous. Now, he gives a reason why this cannot be investigated by men, viz., that all is at the divine disposal, which has so ordered matters that what happens is not an index of approbation or disapprobation as to persons. *To put to heart* is *to consider, to revolve in one's mind;* as often before. — לָבוּר, Inf. const., but filling the place of an Inf. absolute, which sometimes continues a discourse after a finite verb, in the same manner as if it were itself finite. For an example of the Inf. abs. so employed, see Is. 42 : 24, comp. with Ezek. 20 : 8. For the like of the Inf. *const.*, see 1 Sam. 8 : 12, three Infinitives with לְ. In Is. 44 : 14, 28 ; 38 : 20 ; 10 : 32 ; Jer. 19 : 12 ; 2 Chron. 7 : 17, we find the Inf. const. with לְ employed as a definite verb in discourse. — לָבוּר is employed in the same way as if it were בַּרְתִּי, *i. e., I sought out* or *explored*, root בּוּר. *All this,* in the second clause, is a repetition designed to specify his *entire* investigation, and to add intensity to the affirmation. It refers to what is said in vs. 14—17 of Chap. VIII. *The righteous and the wise* are the party for whom the writer is most deeply concerned, and therefore they only are mentioned here. *In the hand of God, i. e.,* they and all their doings are in his power, and at his disposal. *Neither love nor hatred,* Knobel takes in the passive sense, *i. e.,* neither love nor hatred on the part of another toward the righteous, etc., not that which they themselves exercise. Herzf., Heiligst., and Hitzig, however, understand the latter ; which can make sense only by interpreting it as meaning that men do not know whether they are hereafter to love or to

hate, since God directs all. This seems to me tame and insipid.
The writer is laboring to show (at least the objector whom he
here personates is doing so) that as all is in the hands of God,
who deals undistinguishingly with the righteous and the wicked
(see 7 : 14), so no man can tell whether favor or disfavor is to
be shown him in future. The next verse fully confirms this view,
for he goes on to say that "all have one common lot." I have
translated by *neither love nor hatred* on account of the אֵין *(not)*
that follows. A direct literal translation would be: *both love as
well as hatred no man knoweth,* which sounds rather awkwardly
in our idiom. The true sense is given in the version. *The
whole is before them,* הַכֹּל, *the whole* matter, viz., that which he
is discussing, or rather all that pertains to their future lot in regard to favor or disfavor. *Before them* means that the matter in
question, viz., the showing of these, is yet future, or that the exhibition of these is to be during the period that *is before them,*
i. e., which is yet to come. In other words: No man can tell
whether good or ill fortune is to betide him, because he cannot
know the future.

(2) All are like to all; there is one destiny to the righteous and to the
wicked; to the good and pure and to the impure; to him who sacrificeth
and to him who doth not sacrifice; as is the good so is the sinner; he that
sweareth is like to him that feareth an oath.

The הַכֹּל in this verse becomes *personal,* viz., *the whole* or *every
man is like to every man,* or rather (as in the version): *all are
like to all.* Doubtless it is a kind of apothegm here, applied to
the writer's purpose. Some have supposed that it might be translated, *everything is alike to every person; i. e.,* the same things
happen to all, as the context goes on to show. But the *article*
prevents this rendering by a specific *individual* sense; for הַכֹּל
means the *totality,* like τὸ πᾶν. *Each one* must be כֹּל. *The
whole* are the parties mentioned in 8 : 14—17; for a totality of
things cannot here be made out. The first version is more con-

formable to the original, and seems more easy and natural. *All are like to all* (הַכֹּל generic), gives us the sentiment that every one is like to his fellow in regard to the events or evils of life. Like most proverbial sayings, this will not bear minute scanning. We ask : If *all* is *one totality*, then who are the others whom the first resembles ? " Qui haeret in literâ, haeret in cortice," a maxim of jurisprudence says ; and it applies well here. The simple meaning is : ' Every one is like to all the rest.' Literally the phrase would run thus : *The whole* [is] *according to that which* [is] *to the whole; i. e.*, all share the same destiny, each one is subjected to that which happens to all others. — לַצַּדִּיק, with the article ; and so of all the names of whole classes that follow. — לַטּוֹב, *good*, in the moral sense here, although it seldom has such a meaning in this book. — לַטָּמֵא is opposed both to *good* and *pure*, and was selected as being the opposite of the immediate antecedent, טָהוֹר. In הַנִּשְׁבָּע the construction is changed. If it followed suit, it would be כַּנִּשְׁבָּע. The change of construction is doubtless for the sake of variety. — שְׁבוּעָה is placed before the Part. יָרֵא which governs it, in order to give it emphasis. The *oath* in question may be a civil one (see 8 : 2) ; or more probably it is here a religious one. *To swear by Jehovah* is to appeal to him as the Supreme God, and is an express acknowledgment that he is such. The characteristics of the classes are such here in general as designate moral and immoral, religious and irreligious. The next verse presents to us fully the design of the writer in bringing these discrepant classes together, and placing them side by side.

(3) There is an evil in everything which is done under the sun, that there is one destiny to all ; and moreover the heart of the sons of men is full of evil, and madness is in their hearts while they live, and after that — to the dead.

רָע, *an evil*, not with Rosenm. *the most grievous evil*. The evil in question is described in the next clause. — כִּי, *that*, conj.

מִקְרֶה, *occurrence, lot, luck, destiny.* — וְגַם introduces an additional evil, discrepant from that just described. *Full of evil* is in 8 : 11 expressed by *full to do evil.* In the latter passage this fulness of evil is consequent on the delay of punishment; but in our text it seems to be consequent on the common destiny of all, as to suffering and sorrow. *Madness,* in this book, sometimes denotes unreasonable and obstinate folly in refusing to obey or submit to God. *While they live, i. e.,* during the whole of their lifetime, this madness continues. And then what? — אֶל-הַמֵּתִים, *to the dead,* plainly elliptical, הֹלְכִים *(they will go)* being implied. The brevity adds to the energy of the representation. — אַחֲרָיו, *after that, viz.,* after suffering and doing evil all his days; or it may be simply adverbial, *afterwards.*

(4) Truly, whoever is joined to all the living — there is hope [for him]; for as to a living dog, it is better than a dead lion.

The כִּי at the beginning of the verse seems to be *causal.* But the preceding clause, *they go to the dead,* appears hardly to be so connected with this verse as to call for or admit here a cause or reason of going thither. The critics who call it *causal* (Knobel, Hitzig), do not show how or why it is so. It seems preferable, therefore, since this cannot be readily shown, to take כִּי in its occasional affirmative sense, viz., *profecto* (Germ. *ya* or *aber ya*), *truly;* Lex. כִּי, No. 6, *c.* See on 4 : 16 for כִּי. Then the connection of thought would stand thus : 'They go to the dead ... truly a great evil, since there is hope only for the living,' etc. מִי, although generally interrogative and meaning *who?* is also at times used indefinitely to designate *whoever,* or *he who;* see Lex. s. v. No. 2. If we could join אֲשֶׁר with it, and take both as meaning *whoever,* it would make a facile sense. But I know of no example to support and justify this. We seem compelled, then, to regard the Heb. as running thus: *whoever* [there is] *that shall be joined,* etc. If מִי be made an interrogative = *who is there that is joined?* etc., then no tolerable sense can be made out of the passage. — יִבְחַר has vowels that belong to the Qeri יְחֻבַּר. If the Kethibh be retained, then it must be pointed יִבְחַר. But the clause *who shall choose* (for this is the meaning of יִבְחַר), will make no sense here. We feel obliged, therefore, to adopt the Qeri, as the ancient translators and most of the modern ones have done. A further reason for preferring the Qeri is, that בָּחַר does not take אֶל after it, as here ; while this particle appropriately follows יְחֻבַּר. The latter means : *joined to* or *associated with*. *All the living* designates multitudinous living beings. The whole expression wears a somewhat singular air — *joined to the mass of living beings*, instead of saying simply אֲשֶׁר חַי. The phrase has, I believe, no parallel in the Heb. Scriptures. *There is hope, i. e.*, amidst the vicissitudes of things, the *bright* side may sometimes present itself as well as the dark one. There is hope, then, of some enjoyment. Such a living man is much better than a dead man ; for even a *living* animal, although contemptible, is better than the king of beasts when *dead*. The כִּי here is *causal*. The clause that follows is no doubt a proverbial maxim. Knobel produces one from the Arabic (in Golius's Adag. Cent.) of just the same tenor as our text : " A living hound is better than a dead lion." In the East the *dog* is accounted as a contemptible, unclean, detestable animal. The opposite to the dog is here the king of beasts. The antithesis is striking. If what the proverb says of the dog be conceded, then how much better of course is a *living man* than a dead one ! — לְכֶלֶב, with ל prefix, and yet it is the *subject* of the sentence. Cases of ל prefixed to the Nom. have been generally recognized ; *e. g.*, such cases as in Ps. 16 : 3 ; Is. 31 : 1 ; 2 Chron. 7 : 21. Without appealing, however, to this somewhat doubtful principle, we may solve the difficulty in another way. It is plain that ל not unfrequently means *in respect to, quod attinet ad ;* see Lex. No. 5. We may, however, translate so as to preserve here the usual sense of ל when standing before a Dative : *To a living dog there is good, compared with a dead lion.* Then all runs smoothly, and the same sense comes out as before.　In אֶרְיֵה, the הֵ‍ is a parag. formation, the simple word being אֲרִי.

(5) For the living know that they must die, but the dead know not anything, nor is there any more a reward for them, for their memory is forgotten.

But what comfort is there in knowing that we are to die; specially where there is no definite hope of future happiness? If death is so fearful as the writer (personating, however, the objector) has just told us, it must be only a matter that harasses the mind, and causes dejection of spirit whenever it is thought of. What, then, is this *advantage* or *reward* of the living? And has not the writer said (7 : 1) that " the day of one's death is better than the day of his birth"? Has he not " praised the dead which are already dead, more than the living which are yet alive"? Has he not said that " better than both of those is he that hath not been"? 4 : 2, 3. Yes, all this has been said; but then it was in a despairing moment, and in a dejected and gloomy state of mind. And even now the speaker claims small meed for the living — merely the consciousness that they must die. Is it better, then, to have such a painful consciousness continually, than, like the dead, to have none, or, as he says, " to know not anything"? I cannot, amid such embarrassments, do otherwise than suppose his mind to be intent on what he has said in 7 : 2, viz., that " the living who go to the house of mourning, will lay it to heart." The consciousness that they must die may produce two important effects upon them; the one, that in prospect of death they will soberly and gravely and equitably demean themselves, so as to be prepared for death; the other, that, knowing the shortness of life, they will make the best of it in a sober use of the good things they may possess or acquire; see v. 7 seq. below. If this, or something like it, be not the design of the writer, I know not what it is. Hitzig has shunned the difficulty, and Knobel and Herzfeld have merely " nibbled

at the bait." One must at least have a very gloomy view of
death, if he is willing to deem the mere consciousness that he
must die an important advantage over a state of death. Yet
this would seem to be the literal and obvious meaning of our
text. Then, again, that the dead know nothing, and will not have
even the reward of being remembered (one of the least of all
rewards, because they cannot participate in it), is spoken of as
the consummation of human misery. Must not language like
this come from a worldling who indulges gloomy reveries, and
doubts of any future existence? What Christian can speak so
now? I must believe, then, that Coheleth has given us here
some of the most violent cases of doubt which once passed
through his own mind, or else was suggested to him by some
objector. Chap. 8 : 12, 13 discloses definitely his own views;
and they shine out again in 11 : 9 and 12 : 7, 13, 14, and at least
gleam in 3 : 17 ; 5 : 8. It is impossible to harmonize both classes
of texts, except by filing away until all the strength and substance of the language is gone. Why may we not, therefore,
consent that the objector should speak his full mind, as Paul
often makes him to do? With this position for our basis, we
need be under no serious embarrassment in our interpretation.
Only a dissatisfied, doubting, gloomy mind engenders and broods
over such conceptions as these. — שְׂכָרָם, שֶׁ = אֲשֶׁר, and the verb
is Imperf. Kal, 3d plur. with ו medial omitted, and ־ vicarious
put for ו, i. e., in the room of it; § 8, III. Class b.; the root is
מוּת. *No reward*, i. e., no means of after-enjoyment. Even the
least of all comforts, that of being remembered, is denied to
them.

(6) Moreover, their love as well as their hatred, and also their jealousy,
has already perished ; they have no more part forever in all that is done
beneath the sun.

The deep tone of gloomy and despairing sensitiveness here
speaks out in respect to the supposed condition after death.

Neither *love* of friends, or *hatred* of enemies, or *jealousy* of the more fortunate, agitates them any more. No more can they engage in any worldly pursuit. This probably alludes to the common popular notions about the shadowy רְפָאִים in the under world, the *umbrae* of departed persons, deprived of all substantial life, and enjoyment, and action. *Love* of holiness, *hatred* of sin, and *jealousy* (as we render קִנְאָה) for the honor of God, do all exist in a future state. "The pleasures forevermore," which David anticipated (Ps. 16 : 11) ; "the being satisfied with awaking in the likeness of God" (Ps. 17 : 15) ; "the awaking from the dust to everlasting life" (Dan. 12 : 2), must surely have been out of the mind of him who uttered such complaints as our text and context exhibit, at least for the time being ; and, like holy (but not always consistent and submissive) Job, he was doubtless ready to curse the day of his birth, Job 3 : 1. It seems to me impossible to give any other account of this matter, if the language be fully and fairly investigated, and left to speak for itself.

But what reply does Coheleth make to all this? We shall immediately see in the sequel.

(7) Go, eat with gladness thy bread, and drink with a joyful heart thy wine, for God has long since favorably regarded thy work.

Once more, then, in this extremity, when it is urged that virtue and vice both meet with the same reward, and that all have one and the same inevitable doom, Coheleth betakes himself to the advice so often before repeated (2 : 24; 3 : 12, 22 ; 5 : 18), viz., that one should enjoy the fruit of his labor, and accept what he can enjoy with gladness of heart. But in the present case he goes more fully into this subject, and brings more particulars of enjoyment to view; as the following verses will show. — לֵךְ, Imper. of יָלַךְ. — לַחְמֶךָ, suff. form of לֶחֶם (reg.), with הָ in pause. — טוֹב, *glad* rather than *merry*. The latter, as Coheleth thinks, belongs only to fools. — מַעֲשֶׂיךָ, prob. sing. here, although it has the form of the plural ; see § 91, 9, where it is shown that the suffix state of nouns from roots לֹּה, is often the same in both the sing. and plural. *Thy work* or *thy doing* is the thing done, or to be done, in obeying the command as given above. God has permitted and given his approbation to such doing, is what the writer means to say.

(8) At all times let thy garments be white, and let not oil upon thy head be lacking.

The Hebrews often employ עֵת (sing. number) in the same way as we do the plural. I have translated in accordance with our usual idiom. *Garments be white*, because such were the garments worn by those who were rejoicing, while *sackcloth* was the usual costume of mourners, and of such as fasted. See 2 Sam. 12 : 20 ; 19 : 24, and the opposite of these in Ps. 35 : 14 ; Mal. 3 : 14 ; 2 Sam. 14 : 2. The anointing of the head with oil was another custom observed by those who were rejoicing ; comp. Matt. 6 : 17 ; Ruth 3 : 3 ; Dan. 10 : 3.

(9) Enjoy life with the wife whom thou lovest, all the days of thy vain life which he hath given to thee under the sun, all the days of thy vanity : for this is thy portion in life, and in the toil which thou hast performed under the sun.

רְאֵה, see in 2 : 1, *enjoy.* — כָּל־יְמֵי, Acc. of time. — נָתַן, *he hath given;* who? *God* of course is implied, as it has often been already expressed ; see 5 : 17. — הוּא, masc., but here used for the neuter, *it is* or *this is*, viz., that which had been before 'enjoyed. Ewald says "that this is a 'schlechtes *Kethibh*' (a sorry orthography) of the Babylonian Jews!" But see the same in 3 : 22 ; 5 : 17. It is hardly correct to say that only the fem. הִיא is employed elsewhere as the neuter, although this is the most frequent usage. In the Pent. both are usually written הוּא, but when fem., pointed הִוא, in reference to a supplied Qeri in the margin, הִיא. And besides this, הוּא is fem., or used as fem. in 1 K. 17 : 15 ; Job 31 : 11 ; Is. 30 : 33, see Lex. The position of Hitzig, then, does not seem to be quite firm.

25*

In all this there is nothing Epicurean. It is plainly the sober
enjoyment of life which he commends, and nothing is mentioned
which is unlawful or forbidden. Such is the course to which
Coheleth advises, rather than to indulge in the gloomy views
and feelings that had just been expressed. Here again we,
under the meridian sun of the gospel, are at a loss to see why
he did not point the disconsolate complainer to a brighter and
better world. It would be spontaneous in us to do so. But
this subject has already been discussed above, and the discussion
need not be repeated here. Beyond a doubt, the course advised
is better than gloom and murmuring; and so far as this world
merely is concerned, to pursue this course would make us more
contented and happy than to turn from it or forsake it.

(10) All which thy hand findeth to do with thy might, do [it]; for there
is no work, nor planning, nor knowledge, nor wisdom in the world beneath
whither thou art going.

Thy hand findeth, i. e., whatever thou canst grasp, or whatever
is at thy disposal; comp. Lev. 12 : 8; 25 : 28. — בְּכֹחֲךָ, *by thy
power, i. e.,* with thy might or ability. — עֲשֵׂה, *do* [it], the pronoun being implied after the verb. Do it forthwith and energet-
ically. Why? Because *there is no work,* etc. The ו prefix I
have rendered *nor,* because of the אֵין at the head of the clause.
The advice here given is adapted to increase the enjoyment of a
rational man, one of whose instincts is to be active and engaged
in something. To be and to do this renders him more contented and happy. *There is no work nor planning,* etc., comp.
v. 5 above, where is the same sentiment. Does Coheleth say
this for himself, or does he merely recapitulate what the objector
had said? I prefer the latter view. Then the matter would
stand thus: 'Enjoy thyself all that thou canst; be ever busy
and engaged with something; for this will help thee to forget
thy gloomy forebodings. And this is sound advice, provided
that all you say is true, viz., that *there is no work,* etc. All this

need not hinder the enjoyment that you may reasonably have.' בִּשְׁאוֹל, *in Sheol, i. e.,* the under-world, the world of the dead. The connection in which v. 10 stands does not well admit of the language being ascribed directly to the objector. But his objection seems to be indirectly introduced ; for, as we have seen, the settled opinion of Coheleth himself (8 : 12, 13) was something quite different from this. It would be difficult to make out consistency on any other ground than that here taken. Neological commentary points to this chapter with special confidence, as showing that Coheleth neither knew nor believed anything of a future state. But what if it mistakes an *objector's* words, and ascribes them to Coheleth himself? The positive passages which show his views of a judgment and of a retribution, are too strong to justify us in yielding to suggestions of this nature, prompted and quickened by a spirit of scepticism.

§ 14. *Wisdom profits sometimes, and at other times not; Folly will be sure to meet with due Reward.*

CHAPS. IX. 11—X. 20.

[Vs. 11, 12, bring before us again, on the part of the objector, the subject of an overruling destiny, against which wisdom is of no avail. Men are caught as in a net in spite of wisdom, when evil suddenly befalls them. To this Coheleth replies that he has known some signal cases where wisdom protected from danger; these he produces in vs. 13—15. He therefore eulogizes wisdom more than strength, v. 16. The quiet words of the wise have much more that commands attention in them than the outcry of fools ; wisdom is better than warlike instruments, and the want of it may do great mischief, vs. 17, 18. CHAP. X. Folly spoils everything, v. 1. A fool will disclose his folly in all his actions, vs. 2, 3. Wisdom directs to act prudently, and not foolishly, when rulers are angry, v. 4. Fools, when promoted to honor, show their folly, vs. 5—7. There are various ways in which folly and imprudence may be developed, vs. 8—15. Woe to the land that has foolish rulers, vs. 16, 17. Gluttonous and slothful rulers occasion many evils, vs. 18, 19. Take good care how you utter anything against rulers, for they will be sure to find it out, v. 20.]

(11) I turned and saw under the sun that the race is not to the swift, nor
the battle to the strong; and moreover, that bread is not to the wise, and
also that riches are not to the discerning, and likewise that favor is not to
the knowing, but time and chance happen to all of them.

רָאֹה, Inf. abs. as a definite verb; see cases under לָבוּר in v. 1.
מִלְחָמָה, *victorious contest* here. — וְגַם stands before three particulars in succession.   They are coördinate in Heb. ;ʻ but it is difficult with a negative, as here, to render them into English so as
to give the exact shape of the Hebrew. — גַם denotes *accession*,
and is in its own nature climactic.   But here, as all the particulars are *coördinate*, we can hardly make out any climactic shape
or design of the clauses.   There is no *gradation* in the importance of them. — נְבוֹנִים, Niph. Part. adj. sing. נָבוֹן, from בִּין.
חֵן, *favor.* — עֵת, *time*, viz., seasons when this or that will occur.
פֶּגַע, *chance, i. e.,* whatever happens to or befalls one. — יִקְרֶה,
occur, meet, come upon.   In other words : All are subject to the
sports of fortune, and neither strength, nor wisdom, nor intelligence can prevent it.   This is the old complaint against wisdom,
viz., that it is of no avail.   An irresistible power orders all these
things as it pleases.   All this is aggravated by the fact that men
can have no previous knowledge of disasters so as to shun them.
So the next verse :

(12) For no man knoweth his time; like fishes that are caught in a de-
structive net, or like sparrows which are caught in a snare, so they, the sons
of men, are ensnared in an evil time when it comes suddenly upon them.

עֵת Hitzig explains by *time of death.*   But the last part of the
verse shows that it is the time of misfortune.   The כִּי at the
beginning is *causal.*   The preceding verse declares that *time and
chance come upon all.*   One reason here given for this is, that
no man can do any thing to escape the evils of life, because he
knows not *when* they are coming, and therefore cannot do anything effectual to prevent them.   They come upon men as unexpectedly as upon the fishes and the birds, who cannot anticipate

them. — בְּנֵי הָאָדָם is added to explain הֵם, and is put in apposition with it. — יוּקָשִׁים, Part. Pual of יָקַשׁ, dropping its מ pre-
formative; see § 51, 2, n. 4 and 5. The Dagh. forte which
would regularly be in ק is dropped because of the preceding
long vowel ו — "solvitur ob vocalem longam." — הִפּוֹל=כְּשֶׁהִפּוֹל
and כַּאֲשֶׁר, when. The verb is fem. Imperf. of נָפַל, and agrees
with עֵת, which is fem. Such is the unhappy lot of man, in the
view of the objector. Let us hear the reply, which shows that
wisdom ought not to be so underrated.

(13) I too have seen this [namely], wisdom under the sun, and it was
great to me.

The זוֹ is fem. and refers to the subsequent חָכְמָה. The Hebrew construction is involved. We should naturally expect
חָכְמָה זוֹ. On this account Hitzig writes it זֶה, and translates:
That have I seen: Wisdom, etc. This seems too hard. I should
prefer to repeat the verb רָאִיתִי mentally, and place it before
חָכְמָה. I take זוֹ as anticipative, and have so translated. — הִיא,
was it. — אֵלַי, *to me, i. e.,* in my view, or to my mind or apprehension; comp. Jon. 3 : 3. What the wisdom in question is, he
is going to explain by example.

(14) There was a little city, and the men in it were few; and there came
unto it a great king, and he surrounded it, and built over against it large
towers.

There was is the necessary implication of the text, but is not
written. — קְטַנָּה, fem. of קָטָן, a Pilel form with Dagh. implied
in the final נ, which makes its appearance in the fem.; see
§ 91, 8. — מְעָט, in pause, lit. *fewness. A great king*, here so
called probably from his leading on many troops. — עָלֶיהָ, *against
it*, but this preposition involves something more, viz., *over against*
which means that the towers corresponded to the walls, and probably (of course) overtopped or overlooked them. Such towers
were movable, and could be advanced to the walls, or drawn

back from them, and so gave much advantage to besiegers.
גְּדֹלִים, both *capacious* and *lofty*.

(15) And there was found in it a wise poor man, and he rescued the city
by his wisdom; and yet no one remembered that poor man.

The verb מָצָא is without any Nom. expressed; and of course
we may translate thus: *One found*, etc., or in the Pass. as above.
The two adjectives, חָכָם מִסְכֵּן, are coördinate, and both belong
to אִישׁ. The omission of the conjunctive וְ denotes a close union,
like *poor-wise*, almost a kind of compound word. — הוּא is emphatic, and therefore expressed. *Wisdom* here means *sagacity*,
i. e., in employing the means of defence or aggression. — הַהוּא,
that same, an intensive here.

Hitzig refers this to the besieging of the little town of Dora,
on the sea-shore, by Antiochus the Great of Syria, about 218
B. C. He could not take it with all his troops. So he represents the time of writing the book to be that during the period
of Ptolemy Euergetes's reign. But, in the first place, cases of
this kind are so frequent that there is no necessity of supposing
in the present one that this or that individual fact is before the
writer's eyes, but only a vivid recollection of instances of the
like kind. Secondly, it will by no means follow that we must
come so low down, and insist on finding an appropriate example
that is actually on record? Were there not many such cases at
an earlier period of which we have no existing record, although
they may have once been chronicled? Enough, that the example adduced would be readily admitted as a fact, *i. e.*, acknowledged to be true and in point.

(16) Then I said : Wisdom is better than force; yet the wisdom of the
poor man is despised, and his words are not listened to.

The meaning is not that he then said so and so, but now
says differently, but that he then said and still says. — בְּזוּיָה,
fem. Part. pass., masc. בָּזוּי, from בָּזָה. *And his words*, etc.,

Heb. lit., *and as to his words* (Nom. abs.) *they are not*, etc.
But how then was the city saved if his wisdom was despised,
and his counsel not listened to? The answer is, that the writer
is here characterizing the man in a general way; he is stating
what usually happens, and thus describing the neglect which
such men usually have to suffer; and not telling us merely what
happened in relation to him on the particular occasion now
brought before us. He wishes to show that a poor and wise man,
who commonly is looked down upon, and to whom no one is disposed to listen, because he occupies a low place, may still accomplish important objects, beyond the reach of mere force.

(17) The words of the wise, in a quiet way, are heard rather than the
shouting of a leader among fools.

The meaning clearly is, that the words of the wise are calmly
and modestly uttered, instead of their making a bluster and outcry; for this word, בְּנַחַת, is opposed to the *boisterousness* (זַעֲקַת)
of fools. Even a מוֹשֵׁל, a *leader, prince among fools*, has less
chance of producing any effect by his vociferous addresses than
the wise man quietly giving counsel. This *prince*, by the way,
is himself supposed to be *one of the fools;* for otherwise the point
of the discourse would vanish. A wise man might reign over
fools, and still act wisely. But the *outcry* which this מוֹשֵׁל makes,
shows that he belongs to the fools.

(18) Better is wisdom than instruments of war; and one sinner destroyeth much good.

The meaning of the first clause is evident from vs. 14, 15
above. — חוֹטֶא has final Seghol instead of Tseri, for which see
§ 74, VI. n. 21. The word here evidently points to an offender
against wisdom, *i. e.*, a fool. He who neglects the precepts and
guidance of wisdom can do nothing but harm by his mismanagement; yea, in case he is a מוֹשֵׁל, he will do much
harm, *i. e.*, destroy much good.

Chap. X.

(1) Dead flies make the ointment of the apothecary to stink — to ferment; more weighty than wisdom, and also than what is costly, is a little
folly.

It is difficult, in the first clause, to account for the *sing.* number of the two verbs.   There is a small class of cases where
the verb agrees, in case of a composite subject, with the noun
that follows the const. state, rather than with the const. noun
itself, which is the usual and natural Nom. or subject, § 145, 1.
But most of these cases are such as that a kind of compound
noun may be made of the two nouns; or they are cases in which
the const. noun, *i. e.*, that which comes first, is virtually an adjective, § 104, 1, n. 1.   Here neither of these principles will readily
apply.   We must, then, either suppose this is an unusual extension of the principle above noticed, or that the י in זְבוּבֵי is
merely euphonic, as, *e. g.*, מַלְפִּי־צֶדֶק, and the like.   But these
last forms are mostly compound proper names only.   To render
זְבוּבֵי by the singular, *i. e.*, *fly* (which Ewald has done, and Hitzig seems to approve), is *cutting* the knot, not untying it.   Besides, to talk of *one fly* as corrupting a parcel of unguent, seems
to us very odd, to say the least.   It must be a very small parcel
of ointment, at any rate, and a very large fly.   On the whole, I
see no solution so promising as that *dead flies* are considered *en
masse* here, *i. e.*, as a *totality*, and so the apparently plural subject
may take a verb singular.   The principle of *severalty*, or *individ-
uality*, in the continuance of the sentence after a plural subject
cannot in this case be well admitted, for that again would bring
us virtually to the incredible assertion that *each fly* produces the
effects that are described.   On the whole, however, Hitzig thinks
it most feasible to adopt this solution, and refers us for like examples to v. 15 below and to Hos. 4 : 8.   But both of these
cases are of such a nature, that what is asserted of the many is

specially and plainly true of each individual. But this cannot
be said here; for it is only *the many* which can produce the
effect asserted. On the contrary, he notes a case of the opposite
nature, where the writer goes from the singular over to the
plural (Zech. 14 : 12), בְּפִיהֶם . . . לְשׁוֹנוֹ. But here again the ו is
a pronoun of *multitude*. If the grammar is not in his favor
(and this seems to be the case), the *sense* thus made is still more
against him, because an individual fly could not produce the
effects in question. As to the rendering: *poisonous* or *deadly
flies*, the words might mean this of themselves, but they cannot
do so here. It makes nothing to the writer's purpose to call
them *deadly*, for such would corrupt the mass no more than
others. Moreover, there would then be an implication that
other flies would not corrupt it, which is not true. — רוֹקֵחַ, *of the
unguentarius, i. e.*, of the person who compounds the ointment
for sale. Of course it was a composition which required skill
in order to make it saleable. Both words, רוֹקֵחַ, שֶׁמֶן, indicate
precious ointment, viz., such as was compounded with skill and
care.

יָקָר has here its original sense, viz., *weighty, heavy*. The
imagery is drawn from *scales* in which the greater weight pre-
ponderates. Both clauses here illustrate the latter clause of the
preceding verse, viz., *one sinner destroyeth much good*. The
flies, although small and contemptible animals, may do much
mischief to valuable substance. — יַבְאִישׁ (Hiph.), *makes* or *causes
an ill savor;* יַבִּיעַ (Hiph. of נָבַע), *makes to bubble up, i. e., fer-
ments*. The two verbs are asyndic, *i. e.*, joined without any ו
between them, but we are unable to render either of them adverbially here, or (as usual) to make one qualify the other (§ 139,
3, *b*) as a kind of helping verb. But still there is an intimate
connection between them, for *a rendering fetid* is accomplished
by *causing fermentation*. The *effect* is first named in our text,
and then the *cause* of it is described. This energetic mode of
expression is not unfrequent in Heb., but we can rarely imitate

26

it in English with much success, because the structure of the idioms is so diverse. In the latter clause, the preponderance which only a little of folly has over wisdom and over whatever is precious shows "how great a matter a little fire kindleth," or that "one sinner may destroy much good." Such is the debasing and corrupting influence of folly, that only a little of it will spoil the most valuable and precious qualities or virtues. The object of the verse before us (to confirm what precedes), and the manner of accomplishing this object, seem then to be quite plain; so plain, that the separation of chapters here is incongruous and almost preposterous. It is not improbable that both parts of v. 1 are apothegms, applied here to the writer's special purpose. He might indeed have expressed his present views in plain and direct words; but he has chosen a method of doing it which gives more life and vivacity to the discourse. An ordinary reader mistakes such passages for mere *unconnected* apothegms. But we have seen how little ground there is for this.

(2) The heart of a wise man is on his right, but the heart of a fool on his left.

The *physical* place of the literal heart is out of the question here, for that would reverse the statement, the beating heart being on the left side of the breast. *Right* and *left* are used metaphorically for *dexterous* and *ungained* or *unskilful*. The right hand is the usual one for action; the left is more rarely and awkwardly employed. *Right* and *left*, in the Heb., do not mean merely *right hand* and *left hand*, but the words are more generic, *i. e., right side* or *quarter*, etc. — לְ often marks the *place where*, as לְפֶתַח, *at the door*, etc. — לֵב, as often elsewhere, means *understanding*, because the heart was regarded as the seat of it, not the *brain*, as with us. Sentiment: 'A wise man will use his understanding dexterously, so as often to profit himself; a fool employs his to no purpose, or to a bad one.' Evidently, the same subject as before is in the writer's mind. The

superiority of wisdom to folly is rendered more conspicuous still
by what follows.

(3) And even when a fool walketh by the way his understanding is lacking, and he saith of every one : He is a fool.

Further exhibitions of folly. There is an unusual inversion
of order here in the Hebrew : *Even on the way, when the fool is
walking,* etc. The meaning, however, is the same as that above
given. — בַּדֶּרֶךְ, with the article because it is in such a case
equivalent to the suff. pronoun וֹ, — *his, i. e.,* it is definite. In
כְּשֶׁהַסָּכָל the vowels are adapted to the Qeri, which omits the הַ
(article). But there is no need of this. — סָכָל is the same fool
mentioned in the preceding verse, and therefore, as a renewed
mention, may claim the article. — כְּשֶׁ = כַּאֲשֶׁר, as before. *Walks
by the way;* the meaning is not *while he is on a journey,* but while
going about in the way of intercourse with men is meant. In
such a case, *he leaves his heart (understanding) behind* (הָסֵר).
אָמַר, *says,* but here *says internally* = *thinks* or *supposes.* — לַכֹּל,
with the article, means *each specific individual* in this case.
When generic, or signifying *totality,* it also takes the article ;
just as ὁ ἀετός means a *particular eagle* in distinction from other
eagles, and also the *genus eagle* in distinction from other *genera*
of birds. — סָכָל הוּא are the words which he speaks, or rather
what he thinks respecting every one that he meets. It is a conspicuous proof of his folly that he deems himself to be wise,
and every one else to be a fool. This is another dash of coloring, which makes the picture more glowing.

(4) If the spirit of a ruler riseth up against thee, forsake not thy standing,
for gentlèness appeaseth great offences.

רוּחַ here means *spirit,* in the like sense that we give to the
word when we say : 'He replied with much spirit.' An excited
or indignant state of the mind is really meant. But the *ruler,*
who is he? The answer seems to be : 'The same *ruler* as the

מוֹשֵׁל בַּכְּסִילִים above, in 9 : 17. Meaning: If, then, a foolish ruler gets angry with thee, do not forsake thy steadfastness. *Forsake not thy standing,* מְקוֹמְךָ, lit. *station, place on which one stands.* Here figuratively, *i. e.,* it designates *stability, sober consideration, self-possession.* — מַרְפֵּא means, *what is soothing, i. e., gentleness of demeanor,* in the present case, exhibiting no signs of anger or excitement. — יַנִּיחַ, Hiph. of נוּחַ, see Lex. *to quiet, tranquillize,* or *appease.* *Great offences, i. e.,* such as the angry ruler deems great. Even he, although foolish, may usually be appeased by firmness and gentleness.

(5) There is an evil I have seen under the sun, as an error which proceeds from a prince.

Further confirmation as to what a foolish ruler may do, and often does. Coheleth calls it an *evil,* and with good reason. To designate his special meaning, he goes on to show from what quarter the evil comes. It is such an error as can proceed only from a ruler. After *evil,* the Heb. omits אֲשֶׁר as being of course implied; I have done the same in the version. *As the error,* the כ, says Hitzig, is *Kaph veritatis,* and if so, we may render thus: *verily an error,* etc. But I apprehend that this does not give the exact meaning of the Hebrew. The writer means to say that the evil in question is such an error as rulers only can commit. — שֶׁיֹּצֵא, contracted from the fem. Part. יֹצְאָה, and so agreeing with the fem. שְׁגָגָה. — מִלִּפְנֵי, lit. *from the face of, from the presence of.* But this word is often used in the same way, at least with the same meaning as the simple מִן, which designates the cause or source whence this or that springs: see Lex. E. F. 2. We shall soon see what the error in question is.

(6) Folly is placed in many high stations, and the rich sit in degradation.

Folly is placed, the abstract for concrete, *folly* for *fools.* That the plural is meant is shown by the plur. antithesis, עֲשִׁירִים. By this last word is meant not so much the wealthy merely, as

those in a flourishing and elevated condition. Comp. 1 Sam.
2 ; 7, 8. — בַּשֵּׁפֶל, *in a low place, in a state of degradation.* The
sudden elevation of persons in a low condition to office under an
eastern despot is a transaction that occurs almost every day;
and on the other hand, the degradation of those in office, for the
sake of confiscating their property, is equally frequent in the
eastern world. This oppression, and avarice, and selfishness,
Coheleth deems to be a *grave error*, and the whole affords additional evidence that " one sinner can destroy much good."

(7) I have seen servants upon horses, and princes walking as servants on
the ground.

This is only another method of illustrating what he had just
said. Servants are promoted to office, and ride forth in state;
for horses are used in the East principally by the rich and
nobles. On the other hand, they who once were *princes* are
now cast down, and obliged to take the place and attitude of
servants, who walk on the ground, and hold the bridle of him
who rides. Everything is ὕστερον πρότερον.

(8) He who diggeth a ditch may fall into it; he who breaketh down a
wall, a serpent may bite him.

This looks simply like something merely apothegmatic; and
in fact it is somewhat difficult to discover its connection with the
context. Merely to designate the ordinary business of digging
a ditch or pulling down a wall, we can hardly suppose this to be
intended. The meaning is, that when one digs a ditch or pit-
fall for the annoyance or destruction of others, he may chance to
share himself in their intended fate; not that he certainly will
fall into it, for this cannot be true in such a universal sense.
Accordingly I have translated by *may fall — may bite*, etc. So
the pulling down a wall implies some unlawful destruction of the
hedge or fence. In doing this, the serpents which lodge in the
chinks of the wall may bite him. — גּוֹמֵץ, properly a participial

26*

noun of Pual, so that the doubling of the middle radical (מ) here
is normal. The ו is merely orthographic, being short here by
reason of the Daghesh, and not a proper *Shureq.* — רִשְׁבְּנוּ, Imperf. Kal. of נָשַׁךְ, with suff. נּוּ‑ַ.

(9) He who plucketh up stones shall be annoyed by them; he who cleaveth wood shall be endangered thereby.

I do not find any authority for Gesenius's *excidit lapides*, as
the meaning of מַסִּיעַ אֲבָנִים. The verb נָסַע means to *pluck up,*
e. g., trees, vines, tents, etc., and in connection with the last
meaning, *to move from an encampment,* etc. The action here
which annoys, seems to be the *pulling out* of stones from their
beds in the earth, which often, being rough, and being laid hold
of incautiously in order to pull them out, annoy the persons concerned in the labor. So the *splitting of wood* (עֵצִים, plur. in
Heb.) brings one into danger who does not manage with skill.
יִסָּכֵן is a doubtful word. Its meaning in Kal is *to dwell with.*
It is found in Niphal only in the case before us. It seems best
explained by the Chaldee סַכֵּן, *to expose to danger,* סַכָּנְתָא, *danger.*
Hitzig and Ges. derive it from שַׂכִּין, *coulter,* and so they consider it as a *denominative* verb, meaning *to cut.* Possible; but
hardly probable. The other method is more obvious and satisfactory.

The last two verses seem designed to show how numerous the
dangers and exposures to harm are, even in the common occu-
pations of life, and how important, therefore, that *wisdom* should
be present as a guide in all of them. The cases here stated are
not designed to be statements of things that uniformly and of
necessity occur, but such as need wisdom or dexterity to avoid
all evil consequences that might easily ensue. If so, they help
to elevate *wisdom* at the expense of folly; and this stands in
accordance with the writer's aim.

(10) If one has dulled the iron, and there is no edge, he swings [it] that
he may increase the force; an advantage is the dexterous use of wisdom.

Here the object of the writer comes out fully, *i. e.*, to show
the advantage of making a dexterous use of wisdom. The dexterity here, in case of a tool that is dulled, consists in so swing-
ing it and increasing its force, as still to make it cut. — קָהָה is
to be dull; קֵהָה, Piel, is *to make dull,* or (as we say) *to dull.*
The Nom., then, is the indef. *one,* and הַבַּרְזֶל is in the Acc.
לֹא־פָנִים, *no faces, i. e., no edges,* or *without edge* (see Lex. No. 4) ;
like לֹא־בָנִים, *childless,* 1 Chron. 2 : 30, 32. — פָּנִים means *the
front part* of anything, which, in a cutting instrument, is the
edge. — קִלְקַל, Pilpel of קָלַל, *to move hither and thither;* see
Ezek. 21 : 26, where this is plain. The notion of *polishing* or
sharpening has no etymological ground of support. The other
meaning is supported by the Arabic and Aethiopic. If this be
admitted, the pause-accent should be placed on פָנִים, and not on
קִלְקַל. This last is in the Perf., which may be rendered as
Pres. (§ 124, 3), *he swings* [*it*] *that he may increase the force* or
power. When the Acc. is placed before the verb (as וַחֲיָלִים is
here), then the ו, which belongs to the verb and affects the sense
of it, still has the same power that it would have if the verb
immediately followed it. So here : *that he may increase,* etc., ו,
that, § 152, B. *e.* — הַכְשִׁיר, Inf. abs. *nominascens,* but retaining
its power of governing the Acc. חָכְמָה. By this last clause we
have the key put into our hands which will unlock vs. 8—10.
In all cases of difficulty, embarrassment, or danger in the common business of life, a dexterous use of wisdom is indispensable
to safety and success. To the same purpose Hitzig explains our
text, and, as it seems to me, with satisfactory reasons. Whoever
is curious to see the variety of opinions that have been given,
may consult Knobel in loc.

(11) If the serpent bite without enchantment, then is there no advantage
to him who hath a tongue.

הַנָּחָשׁ, with the article, because it refers to the *serpent* mentioned in v. 8. The idea conveyed by the verse is built on the

universal belief of the East (partly founded on fact) that serpents can be *charmed* so as to render them harmless. It is done every day at Cairo, and has been witnessed by Mr. Lane, a most intelligent and recent English traveller. — יִשֹּׁךְ, Imperf. Kal. from נָשַׁךְ. *Without enchantment; i. e.*, if a serpent bite because he is not enchanted (for if he were enchanted he would not bite) then there is lack of wisdom which might have prevented the bite. The writer has also conveyed this last sentiment in another way. It was only the *wise*, it would seem, who were able to *enchant;* comp. Ps. 58 : 6; Is. 3 : 3. When a man had not *wisdom* to use his tongue so as to render harmless the serpent, then no advantage accrued to him from being בַּעַל הַלָּשׁוֹן, *the possessor of a tongue;* like בַּעַל כָּנָף, Prov. 1 : 17, *possessor of a wing = winged.* In other words, even the most distinguished members of the body are comparatively useless without wisdom to direct their use. This verse, therefore, is of the same tenor as the preceding verses. That the *tongue* was specially employed in *enchantment,* is evident from the fact that this mostly consists of *cantillating* certain forms of exorcism. The Greeks called a man who performed this work ἐπαοιδός, *cantillator.* Although the serpent cannot understand the exorcism, he is, as experience shows, operated on by the power of the music, for he will leave his lurking-place to come out and hear it.

(12) The words of the wise man's mouth are favor : but the lips of the fool destroy him.

Favor, חֵן, *i. e.*, are such as *procure favor;* they are goodly words, such as conciliate *favor. The lips of a fool,* not his literal lips, but what they utter, *i. e.*, the *words.* — שְׂפָתוֹת, the reg. plur. in const. state, instead of the dual שְׂפָתֵי, Ps. 45 : 3, for a like usage. *Destroy him* need not be taken in its full and literal sense, but in that of *doing much injury.*

(13) The beginning of the words of his mouth is folly, and the ending of his mouth is grievous madness.

This gives a reason for what was affirmed in the preceding verse. From beginning to end, he plays the fool in all that he says. What he utters is folly, and oftentimes even a *madness* which is *mischievous* (רָעָה) to himself. Not until this mischief overtakes him will he cease prating; it will be well if he does then. *The ending of his mouth* is an abridged form for *the words of his mouth*, as in the preceding clause, which is in part omitted in order to avoid repetition.

(14) The fool multiplies words, when no man can know what shall be; for what shall be after him, who can tell?

Although much speaking leads to the utterance of many foolish things (5 : 2, 6), yet the fool indulges in it, and this even when neither he nor any one else can tell what mischievous consequences will follow. For *when*, there is no special word in the original; but the connection of לֹא־יֵדַע shows that such a meaning is implied. — וַאֲשֶׁר, *for what*, § 152, B. *c.* *After him*, or *after it*, viz., the utterance of many words. There is no important difference between the two. The first is the most simple and obvious. The reasoning stands thus : He must be a fool who utters things that may have mischievous consequences which none can foretell.

(15) The toil of fools wearies them, because they know not how to go to the city.

But may not *toil* weary others who do know how to go thither? Assuredly it may, if there be much of it; but here the case is supposed of a man who toils much in order to get to the city, and does this because he is so foolish as not to know how to get there in a direct way. — תְּיַגְּעֶנּוּ, in Piel, but *fem.*, whilst עָמָל, the subject, is generally *masc.* Perhaps תִּ here assumes the place of י prefix formative, which would regularly be יְיַגְּעֶנּוּ (see § 69, 2), for the sake of a more euphonic pronunciation. So Hitzig. The true solution doubtless is that a large number of nouns in

Heb. with the masc. form, have a fem. gender; and quite a considerable number are both masc. and fem., *ad libitum scriptoris.* Ewald (Gramm.) has collected a great mass of both these in § 174. Cases of *fem.,* like עָמָל are שֵׁם, רַחַם, צָבָא, פִּתְגָּם, etc. Of course all difficulty vanishes by the aid of this consideration, and תְּיַגְּעֶנּוּ is reg. Piel Imperf. fem. The *sing.* suff. here, ־ֶנּוּ, is either generic, and so can accord *ad sensum,* with כְּסִילִים, or else it *individualizes,* and signifies that each and every fool is wearied in the manner described. The same in respect to יָדַע, which is sing., *i. e., no fool knows,* etc. *Knows not how to go into the city* is doubtless a proverbial saying descriptive of fools. So we may say of a man: 'He has not wit enough to travel on a broad, open highway' (for such are the ways leading to a city). This is only a satirical but covert description of a fool. The labor of a man who has not wit or knowledge enough to keep the broad thoroughfare to a city may well be supposed to *weary* him. *Literally* the thing is not intended to be taken. What is meant is, that when a man is a fool, he does a great many things that weary him and worry him, in consequence of his being so. A little sound wisdom would save such a one much trouble. Here, again, the preference of *wisdom* over *folly* comes into view.

(16) Woe to thee, O land, for thy king is a youth, and thy princes feast in the morning.

The meaning of the word נַעַר is not limited by a particular year. Any one short of some twenty-five to thirty years of age may be so named. However, in the present case the probability is that one who is yet a *child,* a *lad* (as we say) is meant; at any rate, one who, through inexperience and a bad education, is inclined to sensual indulgences. For *thy* in both cases may be substituted *whose.* This would make the meaning less specific: whereas I apprehend from the tenor of the book, and the frequent and loud complaints against oppressive rulers, that the author's design is *specific.* This is bold, then, but not bolder than the Hebrew prophets in general are. *Princes feast in the morning,* therefore at a very untimely and improper season ; see Is. 5 : 11, and comp. Acts 2 : 15. This shows what devotees to sensuality the shameless rulers were.

(17) All hail to thee, O land, when thy king is the son of nobles, and thy' princes feast in proper season, for strength and not for banqueting.

As to אַשְׁרֵיךְ, since the pronoun is *fem.*, the normal form would be אַשְׁרַיִךְ ; but the first form is a mere contraction of the second, which is admissible in a case where the gender of the pronoun cannot be doubtful, and no obscurity can arise from the contraction. However, if *land* be taken for *people* (which in fact it really means here), we might take ךְ as masc. ; in which case, however, we must point it ךָ־. *All hail* gives well the sense of the word. Hitz. : *Heil dir!* — חוֹרִים, *nobles,* from חָרַר, *liber, ingenuus fuit.* So in the Arabic and Syriac. A king of high descent, the writer seems to suppose, will act on a generous and noble scale, and will not feel such temptations to extortion as a poor man does. — בָּעֵת plainly means, *at a proper time* or *season, i. e.,* thy princes are not such debased gluttons or drunkards as to carouse at improper seasons. The *feasting* (lit. *eating*) is temperate ; for first, it is in *proper season;* and secondly, it goes not beyond the measure of obtaining *nutriment* so as to acquire strength. — בִּשְׁתִי, lit. *for drinking, compotation.* The *banquet-drinking,* of course, is meant here; and so I have translated it : *for banqueting.* In the later Hebrew בְּ is sometimes used in the same sense as לְ ; it occurs twice here. See on 2 24. In reality the בְּ stands before the thing obtained by commutation with some other things ; see 2 : 24. The *food* is exchanged to acquire, or is the price of the *strength.* — בִּשְׁתִי, with the article, because it refers to what was included in the יֹאכֵלוּ, which designates both eating and drinking, *i. e.,* feasting. The innumerable evils inflicted on a land by gluttonous and drunken rulers, are too obvious to need specification.

(18) Through idleness the timber decayeth, and through slackness of
hands the house drizzleth.

הַמְּקָרֶה, lit. *beam*, but generic here, and so it means *timber*.
עֲצַלְתַּיִם, lit. *by two idle* [hands]. — יִמַּךְ, Imperf. Niph. of מָכַךְ, *to
dissolve, pine away, decay.* — יִדְלֹף, *drizzles, i. e.*, lets through the
rain, because it is not repaired. Hitz.: *it rains into the house.*
I take *the house* as the Nom. in this case, which makes a sense
nearer to the meaning of the Heb. verb, which is used in speaking of the eye when *distilling* tears. So the house distils rain on
those within it, *i. e.*, drizzles.

(19) For merriment they celebrate the feast, and wine makes life joyful,
and money procures everything.

לִשְׂחוֹק, lit. *for laughter, i. e.*, boisterous merriment; the לְ being
in the place of בְּ, as, *vice versa*, בְּ is in the place of לְ; see 2
Chron. 20 : 21 ; 1 Chron. 4 : 22 ; Ps. 102 : 6 ; Hos. 12 : 9, etc.
עֹשִׂים, Part. used as a verb, does not mean *to make, i. e., to man-
ufacture* bread, but to *keep* or *celebrate a feast* (6 : 12 ; 3 : 12),
of which לֶחֶם, the leading element *(bread)* is taken as a representative. *Life joyful*, viz., their life, *i. e.*, that of the carousing
rulers. *Money procures everything*, lit. *silver makes everything
respond.* The usual coin was *silver.* — יַעֲנֶה is in Hiphil Imperf.,
and so must be rendered *makes everything respond*, viz., respond
to their wishes, will procure everything they wish. In other
words : Their golden key will open all storehouses, and furnish
them with the choicest means of revelling. See on 5 : 19, where
this word (יַעֲנֶה) is particularly explained.

(20) Moreover, in thy thoughts curse not the king, even in thy bed-
chamber curse not the rich, for the birds of the air will convey the report,
and the winged tribe will publish the matter.

That is (after all that has been said in the way of exposing
the debauchery and folly of rulers and rich men) guard well
against indulging bitter feelings of indignation and vengeance

toward them. It is dangerous to do so. In some unforeseen way, what is done in secret will be brought before them ; as if the birds of the air could listen and make report. *The winged tribe*, lit. *the possessor of wings.* Both עוֹף and בַּעַל are *generic*, and so they have the article, which of course must be placed on the following words in the Gen. after a const. state, § 109, 1. Here again *wisdom* or *discretion* is needed in order to restrain a just indignation where the indulgence of it can do no good, and will almost with certainty occasion harm.

It is evident that the rulers of Coheleth's time were very sensual, oppressive, and avaricious men, who made the land to groan under their yoke. But whether they were *foreigners* or *Hebrews* nothing in the text indicates with entire certainty. Nothing is said or even hinted respecting *idolatry* in the whole book. Is not this an indication that the book was written after the exile ? All the bad kings before the captivity were *idolaters ;* and as here there is no reference to this subject, nor any complaint founded upon it, it would seem that the rulers in question were not idolaters.

§ 15. *Counsel in regard to many inevitable Evils of Life; specially in regard to old Age and Death.*

CHAP. XI. 1—XII. 8.

[Many trials and evils must come, and Divine Providence has made them inevitable. One should be prepared for them as well as lies within his power, vs. 1—5. One should be busily engaged in what is useful, and while he is permitted to be joyful he should never forget that the days of sorrow will come, vs. 6—8. The season of youth is specially fitted for enjoyment; which, however, passes speedily away, and while it lasts should be indulged with reference to a future retribution, vs. 9, 10. The Creator should be remembered in *youthful* days, so that when the infirmities and sorrows of old age come, they may be borne with fortitude and cheerfulness, ch xii. 1—8.]

(1) Cast thy bread upon the face of the waters ; for after many days thou shalt find it.

27

Not in the literal sense can this be taken ; for literal bread
cast upon the waters soon disappears, being disintegrated. The
meaning seems to be : Give up the cherishing of definite and
specific expectations of ample *support* (לַחְמְךָ, here the image or
symbol of all needed good) ; leave the future to care for itself,
but still with a hope that in due time, although this time may be
protracted, you will experience what you reasonably desire. He
does not encourage those whom he is admonishing to hope always
for immediate success or relief; but only that *after many days*,
or (lit.) *within much of time*, the expectants may come to have
their wishes satisfied. The amount of all seems to be this : ' It ·
is better to forbear the forming and cherishing of definite and
confident hopes, since this will save us from harassing disappointments. Leave all to Providence. In due time, what we hope
for may come to pass.

(2) Make a portion into seven, and even into eight, for thou knowest not
the evil which shall be on earth.

תֶּן־חֵלֶק לְשִׁבְעָה means *make* or *constitute a portion* into seven
[portions]. See Gen. 32 : 8, 9. — חֵלֶק is not a *part of a whole*,
but a *portion* or *appropriation* more or less. Here the meaning
is, divide what you obtain or possess in such a way as to risk
all in one adventure ; or, as a seaman would say : ' Risk not all
your goods in one ship.' *Into seven* — seven what ? If men or
persons were meant, we should expect them to be named. As
the text now is, we must find a noun to agree with the adj. number *seven;* and what other does the text afford, except חֲלָקִים ?
Therefore תֵּן cannot here mean *give, i. e.,* to another, but *put,*
place, constitute, etc. *Thou knowest not the evil,* etc. The Heb.,
as it stands, seems to read thus : ' Thou knowest not what shall
be [viz.], the evil on earth.' In this way *thou knowest not* must
be mentally supplied before רָעָה. Sentiment : ' I have advised
against definite and confident hopes ; I also advise that you em-
bark not too much on any one pursuit ; for if this fails, then all

is lost.' The addition of *one to the seven*, *i. e.*, the mention of *eight*, is a customary mode of speech among the Hebrews. This idiom is peculiarly and forcibly exhibited in Amos 1 : 3 seq.

(3) When the clouds are filled with rain they empty [it] on the earth; and when a tree falleth toward the south or toward the north, in the place where the tree falleth there it will be.

That is, the great operations and events of nature are controlled by a power above, and cannot be hindered or changed by the efforts of man. It is useless to strive against them. Both parts of the verse wear the air of proverbial sayings, which are here applied by the writer to his particular purpose. *Clouds are filled*, etc. In Job. 38 : 37 it is asked: " Who can stay the bottles of heaven?" This gives the popular idea of the formation, or rather the collection of rain-showers, and on this view is founded the expression before us of *being filled.* — יִמָּלְאוּ, *Imperf.* Niph., rather than Praeter, because what is habitually done is here designated. — גֶּשֶׁם, Acc. after the verb of filling, § 135, 3, *b.* — יָרִיקוּ, Hiph. Imperf. of רוק. The pronoun *it*, corresponding to *rain*, is of course implied here. — אִם יִפּוֹל, *when*, etc., see Lex. s. v. No. 4. — בַּדָּרוֹם, lit. *in the south, i. e.*, in a southern direction. We say *toward* in such a case. — מְקוֹם, Acc. of place, and in reg. before שֶׁ = אֲשֶׁר, § 114, 2. — אֲשֶׁר, *where*, Lex. s. v. No. 6. יְהוּא, apoc. Imperf. of הָיָה = הָיָה. The א is *otiant* and merely orthographical. — יְהוּ corresponds to יְהִי apoc.

(4) He who watcheth the wind will not sow; and he who observeth the clouds will not reap.

That is, what God has arranged we cannot alter, nor can we foretell what he will do. The husbandman, if he wait for the wind to come into what he deems a favorable quarter before he ventures to sow, may not sow in good time. If he depends on the appearance of the clouds, and regards them as ominous of evil, *i. e.*, of bad weather, then, by delaying to sow in due time,

he will not reap a harvest.   One must go straight forward in his
duty, and not make this dependent on slight circumstances and
uncertain omens. — רוּחַ , *wind;* we should expect the article, but
the word is here used in a kind of generic way which would be
shown by striking out *the* in the version, but which corresponds
not with our mode of expression.   In this case the Hebrew has
the advantage, רוּחַ = *any wind.* — בַּעֲצָמִים , with the article, being
the name of a class of specific objects in nature.

(5) As thou knowest not what is the way of the wind, or the bones in the
womb of her who is with child, so thou knowest not the work of God, who
doeth all things.

As thou knowest not what is the way of the wind thou canst
gain nothing by watching it.   The next clause is elliptical, *thou
knowest not* being implied and mentally carried forward from the
preceding clause, and inserted after כְּ .   *The bones in the womb,*
etc. ; *i. e.,* the bones of the *foetus,* which are in a state of formation in the womb. — הַמְּלֵאָה , *the pregnant,* like the Latin *gravida
plena,* and the Greek πληροῦν γυναῖκα. — כָּכָה , *even so, so so,* intensive.   Sentiment : 'As thou art confessedly ignorant of such
matters as these, so thou art in reality ignorant of what God
does, who does everything.'

(6) In the morning sow thy seed, and at evening withhold not thy hand,
for thou knowest not which shall prosper, whether this or that, or whether
they both shall be alike good.

That is, since these things are so, go on in the regular way of
duty and activity, and leave the rest with God.   *Morning* and
evening are mentioned as the times of sowing ; *i. e.,* the former
and latter part of the day, because these are the laboring hours
in Palestine, inasmuch as the heat of the sun obliges laborers to
retreat during four or five hours of the middle of the day. — תַּנַּח ,
Hiph. of נוח , see Lex. — אֵי זֶה , strengthened sign of an interrogative position of the pronoun. — אֵי is const. of אַי before זֶה ,

and both of them merely make out a pronoun equivalent in this place to *which.* — הַזֶּה is זֶה with the interrogative הַ before it, *whether this,* viz., shall prosper ; and so as to the other זֶה, although the interrogative sign is omitted before it, as being unnecessary. — כְּאֶחָד, *as one, i. e., alike, equally* (so to speak), *onely.* וְאִם, in a second disjunctive member of successive interrogative clauses, is the usual interrogative sign after הַ in the first clause. See Lex. B. The Hebrew construction in the last clause, if filled out, would run thus : *Or whether both of them shall be good as one* [*of them is*], *i. e.,* alike good. Sentiment: 'Do your duty, and trust Providence for the issue.'

(7) For the light is sweet, and pleasant is it to the eyes to see the sun.

The וְ at the beginning introduces a species of *causal* clause, and is often employed in like manner, § 152, B. c. This is a reason, then, why one should industriously provide for life as he had just been advised to do With all its evils life intermingles many enjoyments. As only the living can see the *sun*, it may be taken here as "the light of life." *Light* stands connected with *enjoyment.* So Eurip. Iphig. in Aulis, v. 1218 : ἡδὺ γὰρ τὸ φῶς βλέπειν.

(8) But if a man should live many years, let him rejoice in all of them; yet let him remember the days of darkness, for they will be many. All that cometh [into the world] is vanity.

הָאָדָם with the article, to designate an individual particular man and not the genus, although what is said might apply to all. We say *a man,* in such a case, *i. e.,* any or every individual man ; which in Hebrew would be כָּל־אָדָם. — וְיִשְׂמָח, hortative, *let him rejoice,* not *and should rejoice.* The writer, then, is no gloomy, luckless wight, brooding constantly over the evils of life, and never looking except upon the dark side of the picture. He advises to enjoy all that we can rationally enjoy. But still, we must never forget that we have to *suffer,* as well as to act and

27*

enjoy. The days of darkness, *i. e.*, of suffering and sorrow, will come, and will be many. The reason of this is adverted to in the last brief clause. *All that cometh is vanity, i. e.*, all that come into the world; comp. 1 : 4, בָּא דּוֹר, *generation cometh* into the world. Or we may make בָּא a participial noun, *every comer*, which of course means *every one who is born*. Since this is the case, viz., that all who come into the world are destined to a course of trial by suffering and sorrow, there is reason or ground for expecting days of darkness, even many of them.

(9) Rejoice, O young man, in thy youth, and let thy heart cheer thee in the days of thine early life, and walk thou in the way of thy desire, and by the sight of thine eyes; but know thou that respecting all these God will bring thee into judgment.

In v. 8 he had said that *one should rejoice* during all the many years that he may live. Here he specificates that portion of life when enjoyment is most attainable. Therefore the young man (for such a one has special ability to comply with his injunction) is particularly exhorted to do so. *In thy youth, i. e., during* thy youth; not that youth is the object to be rejoiced in, but the season for joy. *Walk in the ways of thy desire,* lit. *of thy heart,* which is the seat of desire. — וּבְמַרְאֵי, as written and pointed, would indicate *things seen;* the Qeri reads בְּמַרְאֵה, *i. e.*, the const. state of the sing., and meaning *sight* or *seeing.* This is doubtless the correct reading; for *the seeing of the eyes* is what excites desire in man, and thus influences his whole conduct. In other words: ' Whatever thou seest and desirest which would increase thy happiness, enjoy it. *But know well, i. e.*, remember in the midst of all thine enjoyment, that God will bring thee into judgment for the manner in which everything of this nature is accomplished.' The purport of the last clause may be stated thus: ' Abuse not his blessings and thy comforts or pleasures. He will surely call thee to an account for all that thou doest.' In this world? or in the next? Hitzig says: In the first; and so he refers to old age as the season of judgment and retribution. The true state of this matter, in the book before us, I have endeavored to investigate in my remarks on 3 : 17 above.

(10) Put away vexation from thy heart, and remove evil from thy flesh, for youth, like the morning-dawn, is vanity.

Put away from thy heart, because the heart is the seat or source of *vexation* or *indignation* at suffering. *Evil from thy flesh*, that is, thy corporeal physical frame. The first precept respects the *mind*, the second, the *body;* both of these make up self, or the *entire man.* The two verbs are in Hiph. Imper. apoc., because they are *hortative.* The paragogic forms in Hiph. belong only to the 1st. pers. sing. and plur. ; the others are *contracted;* see § 48, 4. — הָסֵר from סוּר. This is merely following on in the train of advice given in v. 9. There the command is, to do something positive in the way of enjoyment ; here it is, to shun or avoid evil and suffering. Taking both together, the amount is : 'Enjoy all that a sober, rational man, in view of a day of retribution, can enjoy, and avoid all the evil and suffering that can be properly avoided.' But why is this so strongly urged upon the *young?* Plainly because that even they, although in the best estate of man, hold life by a very frail tenure. "Man in his best estate is altogether vanity." Therefore, as even youth is so frail and evanescent, make the best of it that can be made, keeping a retribution always in sight. It is almost as if he said : Then or never. — וְהַשַּׁחֲרוּת, lit. *and the early dawn;* but the וְ here is one of comparison, and hardly differs in meaning from כְּ. It might be translated *even.* If the sentence were filled out it would run thus : *Youth is vanity, and so early dawn is vanity; i. e.,* one is as vain as the other. Hence the use of וְ in such cases, as the connecting link between the two parts of a comparison. Both the objects named are equal to a *tertium quid,* and therefore one is *like* the other.

If a right view of vs. 8—10 has been presented, it follows of

course that the exegesis is erroneous which assumes that v. 9 is
sarcastic or *ironical.* Certainly this verse is only a comment on
v. 8, where it is said to every one, בְּכָבָּם יִשְׂמַח, *i. e., evermore be
joyful.* No one thinks of irony here. Again, in v. 10 we have
a clear indication that the advice in v. 9 is serious and *bona fide.*
Certainly there can be no objection to Coheleth's advice here,
associated as it is with all his cautions; none except on the part
of mere strenuous ascetics.

Chap. XII.

(1) Remember thy Creator in the days of thy youth, before the days of
evil come, and the years draw nigh when thou shalt say : I have no pleasure
in them.

בּוֹרְאֶיךָ, plur. like other appellations of God, both nouns and
adjectives ; see § 106, 2, *b.* — בְּחוּרֹתֶיךָ, plur. fem., § 106, 2, *a.*
The plur. form comes from the idea of an extended period.
Before the days of evil, etc., lit. *until that the days of evil have
not come,* which would sound harshly in English. The הָרָצָה
with the art. refers to the רָצָה of 11 : 10. Hitzig finds in the
mention of *days* and *years* here evidence that the *time of retribution* is the season of old age, when evil is wont to come; for
as he avers, "the dead have no division of time." But is this
his philosophy, or that of Coheleth? Not of the latter, surely ;
for in the case before us, both *days* and *years* have the same
meaning for substance, *i. e.,* both merely designate *time.* I am
aware that *time* so divided, and philosophically considered, is not
strictly predicable of a future state; but still, the Scriptures
speak everywhere *more humano,* or in the popular way in regard
to the future. *Ages of ages* is a frequent designation of it. That
the writer has *old age* in view in this verse, I should freely admit. But I do not see how this would affect the meaning of
11 : 9 : *God will bring thee into judgment.* According to Hitzig,

this would be merely equivalent to saying : ' God will make thee
to become an old man.' But does not the Old Test. everywhere
reckon *long life* as a *blessing*? What saith the fifth commandment, Ex. 20 : 12 ? And yet this, if Hitzig is in the right, is
held up *in terrorem* here, as an indication of a *penal* period or
process. This will hardly do. Old age has indeed its sorrows,
and they are in some respects aggravated by increasing bodily
weakness, and inability to endure or resist them. But it has its
comforts too ; for "the hoary head is a crown of glory, when
found in the way of righteousness." The *orthodox*, then, are
not the only class of critics (as Hitzig sometimes insinuates)
who practise the *Hineinexegesiren* upon the sacred text. It
needed some resolution, at any rate, to make up and produce
such an argument as that of Hitzig now before us, to show that
Coheleth neither knew nor thought anything of a *future* judgment.

Thus much is true, viz., that *the days of evil* here mentioned
are the days of declining life, the infirmities and sorrows of
which are most vividly painted in the sequel. Accumulated infirmities, with a certain prospect of their increase, are sufficient
to account for the exclamation of the sufferer : *I have no pleasure in them!* — וְהִגִּיעוּ, Hiph. Perf. of נָגַע. — חֵפֶץ . . . אֵין, here
the const. אֵין has two intervening words between itself and the
Gen. following and governing it. But any intervention of this
kind must be of *circumstantial* words only. Otherwise, the const.
and Gen. must be placed in immediate proximity.

(2) Before the sun and the light shall grow dark, and the moon and the
stars, and the clouds return after the rain.

The first part is imagery to portray the joyous season of life.
Light is the symbol of joy. ' Before this light is withdrawn,
do thou remember thy Creator,' is the sentiment. But what is
it to *remember* him ? It is to fear, to love, and to obey him, ever
keeping in mind that he will bring thee to judgment. After

moon and stars, יֶחְשְׁכוּ *(shall grow dark)* is implied from the preceding clause. I have joined *the light* with *the sun,* because the accents do so, and because there is ground to suppose that the writer means to present *two couplets. The clouds return,* etc. ; this happens only in the winter or rainy season in Palestine. The summer showers are short and violent, and are succeeded by a blazing sun. But in winter, day after day the clouds return, and rains are often incessant. This season, then, is the image of old age, the *winter* of life. We of the present time call youth its *spring,* manhood its *summer,* and old age its *winter.* Sentiment: 'Be mindful of God before the days of aggravated sorrow come, before the declining period or winter of life sets in.' The imagery is vivid and beautiful.

(3) In the day when the keepers of the house shall be tremulous, and the strong men bow themselves, and the grinders pause because they are become few, and those that look out of the windows are darkened.

This verse is subordinate to the preceding one, בַּיּוֹם being used instead of repeating עַד אֲשֶׁר. — יָזֻעוּ, from זוּעַ, Imperf. Kal, וּ for וּ. But who are the *keepers of the house?* Evidently the physical frame of the old man is here compared to a *house,* a comparison of the human frame often made in the Old Test. and in the New, Job 4 : 19 ; 2 Cor. 5 : 1 ; 2 Pet. 1 : 13, 14. The *keepers* of this house are the *arms,* specially the *hands* and *forearms,* which often become tremulous in old age. They are called *keepers,* because they are more specially employed in warding off evil or assault. These *keepers* are here regarded as being *out of* the house, not in it ; just as the arms are separate from the body of a man, and extraneous to it. *And the men of strength bow themselves,* seems to mean the *legs,* which are strong in their structure, being formed both to support the body, and to convey it hither and thither. It needs *strength* to bear such a burden and perform such a task. The *bowing* is the usual *crooking at the knees* which takes place in old age, because the mus-

cles are relaxed, and will not support the weight of the body
without bending. In war, to be swift in the race of pursuit or
flight, and persevering in the march, required great strength in
the lower limbs; and he who was ὠκὺς πόδων was accounted
among the best warriors, *i. e.*, among the חַיִל אַנְשֵׁי. To say the
least, if the appellation is not altogether congruous for the *legs*,
it is difficult to find any part of a man to which what is said so
well applies. *And the grinders cease or pause;* the latter is the
better translation, for the *pausing* seems to be in order to take
rest, since they are overtasked in grinding because of their fewness. The *teeth* are doubtless meant by the *grinders;* and we
apply this word in the same way to the teeth. When a few of
these have to do all the work of a full set, some pause in the
labor is occasionally necessary. — מִעֵטוּ, verb denom. from מְעַט,
in Piel and in pause (which occasions the Tseri), meaning *grow
few, become few,* not simply *are few,* which would be *Kal.*
Those which look out, etc., are plainly the *eyes.* The eye-socket
is like to a perforation for the window ; *the eye-lashes* may be
compared to *lattices in the window,* which in oriental windows
are employed instead of glass. *Latticed windows* would be an
exact literal version. But nothing would be gained by such a
translation. It would rather mislead the reader, because it would
seem to point him only to some peculiar kind of a window, when
the idea is in fact generic. The weakening of the sight, or
darkening of the eyes in old age, is too well known to need description ; see in Gen. 27 : 1 ; 1 Sam. 3 : 2 ; 1 K. 14 : 4. *Eyes*
and *teeth* are both fem. in Hebrew, hence the *fem.* participles
agreeing with them.

(4) And closed are the doors on the street, while the noise of the mill is
low, for it rises to the voice of a sparrow, and all the daughters of song are
brought low.

Doors of thy mouth, or *lips,* are expressions in Ps. 141 : 3 ;
Mic. 5 : 7. *The doors of his face* is employed in Job 41 : 14.

There can be no doubt, then, that the *lips* are designated by *the doors on the street; i. e.,* like the outside double or two-valved door of a house, the way of entrance into it, as the lips are the entrance to the mouth. *On the street* serves merely to show that the *entrance* or *outside door* is meant. *Are shut* or *closed,* expresses the position of the lips when the teeth are gone. They are *shut* or *compressed closely together. Noise of the mill is low;* but what is the *mill?* Not the *teeth,* for they are called *grinders* above. There seems to be no tolerable explanation of this, excepting that it is intended to designate the mouth, in which the *grinders* are. The *noise* is that made by the *voice,* as Hitzig and Heiligs. interpret it. In the aged this is weakened and *low.* This too is a trait of old age which is further developed in the sequel. To interpret the clause (which some do) as meaning *the noise made by chewing,* is said to be incongruous. But may it not be said in reply, that old people rarely undertake to eat hard substances, and the chewing of soft ones will make only a low noise? Shall the קוֹל, *noise,* be referred, then, to the *chewing of soft food,* such as the aged must take, because the *noise* in question, in such a case, is יִשַּׁפֵּל, *quite low?* or must it refer to the voice of the aged, as stated above? Neither of the alternatives is very inviting. However, as *eating* seems to be despatched in the third verse, there is some incongruity in supposing it to be again introduced here. But a greater difficulty in the way of this is that the *noise of eating* cannot well be a subject or Nom. to the next clause; it must be the *voice of the mouth.* In a case so doubtful and obscure, this would seem to be a sufficient reason for giving this latter exegesis the preference.

For it rises to the voice of the sparrow, i. e., attains unto the voice of a sparrow; comp. קוּם in Zeph. 3 : 8 ; 1 Sam. 22 : 13 ; Mic. 2 : 8, for a like sense. Translated thus, the last two clauses give the grounds for the assertion in the preceding clause, or at any rate furnish illustrations of it. — וְ, *for,* § 152, B. *c. The voice of a sparrow* is a very slender one; and a voice not louder

than this may well be called *low*. Some interpret this as meaning : ' He (the old man) rises up from his couch very early, as
soon as the voice of the sparrow is heard.' But where is the
proof that the sparrow is an early matin-bird? or that the old
man would be apt to hear his tiny voice? If it were *the crow-
ing of the cock*, the exegesis would seem more probable than it
now does. And last, but not least, where is the proof that aged
and infirm people are wont to be early risers? Early they may
wake, but they are not wont to rise as soon as they wake. Then
again, קוּם is not the word for *such rising;* we should expect
נֵעוֹר.

All the daughters of song is a *locus vexatus*. Still, some things
are plain. *Sons of men* are *men; daughters of men* means *women.* Why may not *daughters of song* mean *songs? Daughters
of Tyre — Babylon — Philistia*, etc., means Tyrians, Babyloni-
ans, Philistines, etc. So in the Talmud : בַּת קוֹל, simply *voice*
(probably = *echo*). All *songs* or *singing*, in old age, usually
becomes *low-toned;* יִשַּׁחוּ, Niph. Imperf. from שָׁחַח, with a Dagh.
in the form. Literally, *are depressed;* but I have translated by
brought low, because there seems to be a kind of *personification*
in the use of בָּנוֹת, which is best carried out by translating *brought
low.* Sentiment : ' All song-singing or music is low-toned, or
with a depressed voice.' When the teeth are gone, and the lips
fall in, as before stated, singing must necessarily be of the sort
here described. If the two last clauses are not properly grounds
or reasons for the preceding one, they at least help to establish it
by illustration.

(5) Moreover, they are afraid of that which is high, and terrors are in the
way, and the almond disgusts, and the locust is burdensome, and the kapper
has no force ; for man is going to his everlasting home, and the mourners
go around the streets.

Afraid of that which is high, because mounting a height makes
the aged pant for breath. The action of the lungs is constringed

28

by age, which contracts the muscles of the breast. To mount a
narrow height, *e. g.*, a tower or precipice, would also create sensations of dizziness. They shun both. In the latter case, the
terror of falling lies in the way, and constantly besets them.
And the almond disgusts, not *the almond-tree blooms*, deriving
יָנֵאץ from נָץַ, and making it = יָנֵץ, and so, as the almond-tree
blooms in the winter, this class of critics say that it represents
the hoary head of the old man. But then the almond-blossom
is not *white*, but pink-colored, or of carnation hue. Besides,
יָנֵאץ for יָנֵץ has no parallel in Hebrew orthography. The root,
then, must be נָאַץ, which means *to despise, contemn, treat with
disgust*. In Hiph., then, it would mean: *causes disgust;* and
there, it seems to me, it should be reckoned, and pointed יַנְאִיץ;
unless, indeed, with Gesenius, we admit a *Syriasm* in the present pointing, viz., "יָנֵאץ *more Syrorum* for יַנְאִיץ." This, however, would not alter the meaning of the word. The *almond*,
once a favorite fruit, now only creates disgust, for want of power
to masticate it. There is no need of an Acc. case after the verb ;
for *to cause disgust*, is in itself intransitive. Still, if ם- suff.
were supplied, then we should translate thus : *makes them to
loathe*. But this is quite superfluous. Hitzig proposes to read
יָנֵאץ, and translates thus : *The almond-tree despises* [them]. Of
course he takes the *tree* as a mere symbol in this case ; like as
the palm-tree (in Cant. 7 : 9) is the symbol of the bride, on
account of its slender tallness and its sweet fruit. In Canticles
the fruit is represented as accessible ; but here the fruit of the
almond-tree is inaccessible to the old man, who cannot ascend
that which is high. This, as he avers, is represented in a kind
of poetic manner, viz., the almond-tree looks down with contempt on the old man, who cannot climb it, and mocks his efforts to obtain its treasures. A *congruous* sense this may well
be called, when we compare it as related to the first part of the
verse — *afraid of heights*. But in this case the verb becomes
so far *active* that it seems to need a complement or object, while

none is supplied. On this account I must incline to the preceding view, *the almond occasions disgust.* I am the more inclined to this on account of the next following clauses, which stand connected with the failure of appetite, so that both are congruous with each other.

חָגָב is a species of the *locust tribe*, winged and edible (see Lev. 11 : 22) ; which passage allows the Hebrews to eat four kinds of the locust. Some species of them are generally eaten in the East, and brought into the markets for sale, even at the present time. The hard-shelled ones resemble a crab-fish in point of taste. Some of them are even regarded as a great delicacy. Hence the sentiment in the text: 'Even the most delicate viands — among which is the eatable locust — become a burden to the aged man, whose appetite fails.' This is perfectly natural. Delicate and rich viands disgust an enfeebled stomach, which cannot digest them. The most simple food is the only food that can be safely taken in these circumstances. Hence the locust, יִסְתַּבֵּל (Hiph. of סָבַל, § 53, 2), *makes itself a burden; i. e.*, becomes burdensome, being difficult of digestion and occasioning *nausea* in the stomach. Hitzig gives the passage quite another turn, referring it, by virtue of a resemblance between חָגָב and עָנָב *(voluptuous delight)*, to sexual intercourse, which becomes forced rather than voluntary. But this seems quite unsatisfactory when a plainer and more facile meaning presents itself. Heiligs. is still more imaginary. "As the locust, when its wings are grown, attempts to fly, but does this at first with great effort, even so the old man, about to 'shift off this mortal coil,' laboriously attempts his flight." Altogether *invitâ Minerva.* The most simple meaning is nearly always the preferable one; and here it is altogether the most congruous. *And the kapper* (in vulgar usage spelled *caper*) *is inert*, or *has no force;* so Van der Palm, De Wette, Gesenius, and others. Hitzig supplies an implied בְּרִית after הֻפַר, and supposes the allusion to be made to an implied agreement that the kapper should aid the עָנָב = חָגָב,

amatory pleasure, which agreement, in this case, is *frustrated* or
annulled; ingenious, indeed, but too forced and far-fetched. The
kopper was used as a *stimulant* for all the natural appetites, inasmuch as it gave life and animation to the system. Specially
was it regarded as a venereal stimulant. In this last sense it
may be taken here. Food disrelishes, even the delicate viands
are a burden. With the appetite for this, the other natural appetites decline, so that venery becomes rather disgusting than
alluring; at any rate, in extreme old age it becomes mischievous
in most cases. The meaning of הָאֲבִיּוֹנָה seems to be well settled
(see Buxt. Lex. Chald., and Ges. Thesaurus s. v.). — הֵפֵר comes
from פָּרַר, and is 3d Praet. Hiph., and one of its meanings is,
irritum fecit. It would seem to demand an Acc. of object after
it, at least an implied one. It usually connects with such objects
as *covenant, law, promise, vow*, etc. Gesenius (Lex.) makes it
intransitive in our text; and so it may be (§ 52), for Hiphil is
often so. But if we insist on the active *transitive* here, then
בְּרִית, or some equivalent word, may be supplied, the verb being
taken as a *constructio pregnans*, § 138. So: *the kapper breaketh
promise.* It was expected, from its qualities, to rouse by excitement, and this is what it usually does; but now it frustrates
wishes or expectations. *It becomes inert, i. e.*, produces no effect. This, indeed, is not a literal translation, but it is in effect,
giving the *sense* of the passage, which, like those that precede it,
is elliptical.

The failure of these powers and appetites is indicative of what
must speedily follow. *For man is going to his eternal home*, הֹלֵךְ,
abiturus, about to depart. Not *has gone*, for his death is afterwards described in vs. 6, 7. As yet it is a *future* occurrence.
Eternal home occurs nowhere else in the Scriptures, but the
Targum on Is. 42 : 11 mentions *eternal houses* or *homes, i. e.,*
sepulchres; the Book of Tobit (3 : 6) calls the *grave* τόπος αἰώ-
νιος; and the Egyptians called their catacombs ἀΐδιους οἴκους.
Compare the sentiment in 3 : 20, 21, and 9 : 3—6. Such a

name for the *grave* does not necessarily imply a disbelief of a future resurrection (Dan. 12 : 2), but only that those who are laid in the sepulchre have a habitation that will never be exchanged, as houses among the living are. *A final home* is a familiar expression even with us. We cannot defend it philosophically or theologically, but it is still in popular use. Just that is meant here by the Hebrew. *And the mourners go around the streets*, Hitzig refers to mourning in *anticipation* of evil; as, *e. g.*, 2 Sam. 12 : 16; Ps. 35 : 13; Esth. 4 : 3; Jer. 48 : 38. But why not render וְסָבְבוּ ג׳, *the mourners will surround*, or *go around*, etc? Then the one occurrence is as much future as the other. This is certainly the more natural. The only difficulty is, that וְ *conversive* before a verb is seldom indeed to be seen in the book before us. *The marching around in the street* looks much like the funeral procession, accompanied by artificial or hired mourners, as is usual in the East. In all the cases of anticipated mourning referred to above, there is nothing that indicates any *procession*. On this ground I must refer סָבְבוּ to the Pres., as to sense (§ 124, 3. *b.*), in the same manner as if a Pres. verb preceded it. The dead man *going to an endless home, i. e.*, the grave, is accompanied by a procession winding through the streets. For such processions see 2 Sam. 3 : 31; Jer. 9 : 16—20, where is a full account; also 2 Chron. 35 : 25; Matt. 9 : 23; 11 : 17; Mark 5 : 38; Luke 7 : 32. The same custom of hired mourners in procession is kept up in the East at the present time. For בַּשּׂוּק, see Is. 15 : 3.

(6) While the silver cord is not broken, nor the cup of golden [oil] crushed, nor the pitcher dashed in pieces at the fountain, nor the wheel crushed at the cistern.

At the beginning of the verse is a resumption of the particles in v. 2, showing that the same subject is still continued. — יֵרָחֵק has a substitute proposed in the Qeri (יֵרָתֵק), probably because the meaning of the first verb *(to remove to a distance)* seems

incongruous. But רָתַק means *to bind*, and it has no Niphal unless this in our text be one. There is no evidence, however,
even if a Niph. form be admitted, that it would be *privative* in
its meaning, viz., *to unbind, to sever* (the sense here demanded),
nor can this be deemed probable in respect to a Niph. conjugation. The probability, then, is, that here (as in the case of יִרְבָּחֻר,
9 : 4), the ח is transposed, and therefore that the word should be
written יֵחָרֵק. In Arabic חרק means *laceravit*, an appropriate
meaning as applied to the *silver cord* or *chain* in the present
case, and so appropriate that we need not hesitate to adopt it.
Silver cord must mean the *silver chain* by which the lamp is
suspended. — תָּרִץ, Imperf. Kal. of רָצַץ (see § 66, n. 9, for the
רֵ instead of רֹ), and is intransitive with a passive meaning.
גֻּלַּת, const., usually translated as meaning the *knob* or *bowl* of
the lamp which holds the oil. But הַזָּהָב can hardly mean *gold*
here. In Zech. 4 : 12 it means *oil*, and tropically so in Job
37 : 22 ; *i. e.*, something of *golden color*. Here, if *silver cord*
represents the thread of life, then the bowl would seem to sym-
bolize the *body*, and the oil (a liquid) the liquid air which fills
the lungs. But to make the life-principle *silver*, and the body
gold, would seem to be incongruous. We may rather acquiesce
in the more general symbol, viz., *the lamp of life* may have the
cord by which it hangs broken, and the lamp be dashed in pieces,
which holds the oil that supplies the flame of life. — כַּד, the
pitcher let down to draw up the water. This may be easily
dashed in pieces (תִּשָּׁבֵר = our English word *shiver*) at the *fountain* or source of the water. *Wheel crushed*, viz., the wheel
which raises the water by the winding up of the draw-rope upon
it. When such things befall the water-apparatus, water ceases
to be had. So, to compare the air we breathe with the water
which we drink, when the apparatus for breathing is broken and
disabled, the breath of course must cease. Beyond this general
comparison we cannot well go ; and this is sufficient, and is also
striking.

(7) Then shall the dust return to the earth as it was, and the spirit to God who gave it.

That man is made of *dust* is often recognized in the Old Test., and the representation takes its source from Gen. 3 : 19. See Ps. 104 : 29 ; Job 34 : 15. *As it was*, viz., before it was made into man. On the subject of the *spirit* and its *return to God*, I must refer the reader to the discussion connected with 3 : 21. What God gave he takes back. But he gave the body as well as the spirit. The body, however, he does *not take back to himself;* nor can he any more be supposed to take back the mere *breath of life,* in such a sense as that it *returns* to him. If this meaning be given to רוּחַ, we must acquiesce in the more general meaning of merely giving and taking away, without attaching to this any idea respecting how that is disposed of which is taken away ; which can hardly be reconciled with the idea of תָּשׁוּב, *shall return*. Is there any *emanation-philosophy* to be discovered here ? Does the *spirit* (רוּחַ) *emanate* from God as a particle (so to speak) of his being; and when man dies, does this particle become absorbed again in his immensity ? for this the philosophy in question teaches. If there were any evidence at all in the Hebrew Scriptures of the emanation-philosophy, we might explain the passage before us by the aid of it. But the whole tenor of these Scriptures is against this view. God and man are beings widely and essentially diverse in their nature. The Hebrews brought God down, in his great condescension, to watch over and to aid and bless man; but they never dreamed of elevating man into the place of God. A *moral* resemblance man might have, and had, to his Maker ; but his ontological nature admitted of no comparison ; for how can *created* compare with *uncreated*, finite with infinite ? *To see his face, to awake* in the resurrection and *put on his likeness*, are the utmost to which the thoughts of the Hebrew extended or aspired. Then what is *returning to God?* Returning to *dust*, we understand. The body becomes united to it, or absorbed in it. But in what

sense does *vital breath* (רוּחַ) *return* to God? This question still
remains, after all that has been said about רוּחַ, and is more difficult to be answered than Knobel and Hitzig seem to imagine.
If *return* has the like meaning in both clauses (the verb in both
is the same in the Hebrew), then must the emanation-doctrine be
recognized here. But we have seen that there is no ground for
supposing this to have been held by the Hebrews. What is it,
then, we ask again — what is it that *returns?* And what becomes of it after its return? In case רוּחַ here means *spirit*, in
our usual English sense of the word, then we have a tangible
meaning. The soul returns to the peculiar and immediate presence of God, there to be judged (according to v. 14). In what
other way can we make out a consistent Hebrew sentiment from
this passage? That God gave the *spirit* of man, is a sentiment
often repeated; *e. g., the God of the spirits of all flesh; the Father
of our spirits,* etc.

(8) Vanity of vanities, saith the preacher, all is vanity

Thus end the discussions of the book, with the same sentiment
which was made its thesis at the beginning. The writer has
gone through the whole round of human employment and enjoyment, and he comes out at last fully with the sentiment which
he announced at the beginning as the thing to be examined.
*Solid, lasting, and unchanging happiness is not to be found in
any worldly occupation, or in any worldly circumstances.* God
has impressed this truth on everything, and made it visible
everywhere.

But the other side of the picture, which presents man's future
condition and destiny, he has only glanced at. It was not his
then present purpose to aim at developing this. We feel it indeed to be strange that he stops where he does. We should not
do so, with our present views. But before we condemn him, we
should at least become well acquainted with his special design
and purposes. We should know what questions of the time

were pressing upon him ; what Epicureanism he was called to encounter on its own ground, and what sensuality needed a powerful check, by reasoning within its own circle. The book is an *argumentum ad hominem*, a refutation from the worldling's own stand-point. The writer certainly accomplishes one thing, and he does this effectually. Christianity would lead us to go farther ; but this, when Coheleth wrote, was yet to "bring life and immortality to light." He stops where Moses stopped in the Pentateuch ; and if we censure him, must we not also censure Moses ? God did not reveal everything, not even every important thing, under an imperfect and preparatory dispensation. The world has had its childhood, is having its youth, and is yet to arrive at complete manhood, and then, perhaps, have its old age. Why need we confound all these stages of human progress with each other ; or why think it strange that the author, living under the first stage, has not written and spoken as if he lived under the second or third ? *Cuique suum;* a maxim as true in respect to revelation, as it is in regard to the business and concerns of life. Many a striking view has Coheleth given of the vanity of mere worldly pursuits ; many a sound precaution has he uttered in respect to incurring dangers and temptations. Above all, he has throughout maintained and inculcated the most profound submission as to the mysterious and afflictive dispensations of a holy Providence. With him, God is all in all ; and there is no way of obtaining safety or comfort left for man, excepting that of absolute and unqualified submission to God. Whatever he does is right ; and therefore it should be acquiesced in by all the creatures of his power. With all the doubtings and struggles of mind which he develops, it is quite evident that at the bottom of his heart lay a deep substratum of pious, submissive, obedient, holy feeling. In the midst even of a paroxysm of despair, when he is gazing intently on some gloomy aspect of the destiny of man until life becomes a burden, he never utters one disrespectful or murmuring word toward God. Indeed, he everywhere

appeals to his rightful sovereignty, in order to hush every tendency to complaint. So firm, so solid was his persuasion that
God is wise and good, that it is enough in his view to hush every
complaint and silence every murmur to call to mind that this
affliction or that was dispensed by his hand. What, now, shall
we say to all this? We must feel ourselves humbled by such an
exhibition. We often murmur or are discontented when we are
called to suffering and sorrow, notwithstanding all the light and
love which the gospel has diffused around us, and in spite of all
our cheering hopes as to the future. What then should we have
done, if placed in Coheleth's condition — bowed down, and in
darkness, and merely catching some glances of the twilight that
was beginning to gleam? The comparison would operate
strongly to humiliate us, even in our own view. If those men
of God who lived many centuries before the gospel was revealed, could think and act as they did, — could bow before God
with the deepest reverence amid the deepest gloom, and never
utter one murmuring word, or indulge one repining thought, —
could believe with unshaken faith in his justice, and goodness,
and wisdom, when the dealings of his Providence were utterly
inexplicable, — then may we not well say: Shame! shame on us,
for all our doubts, and repining, and coldness, and wavering?
If they could feel and act as they did in circumstances such as
theirs were, they might indeed have had far less knowledge than
we have, — in fact, they had far less, — but must they not have
had a more stable and ardent piety, and a more firm and enduring faith than we can justly attribute to ourselves? "He that
doeth righteousness is righteous."

We do indeed possess far more advantages than they had; but
if with all these we indulge in sin, our guilt and condemnation
are highly aggravated. Instead of indulging in self-gratulation
when we look at them in their struggles, we ought to be penetrated with the deepest humility. Little to a good purpose has
he read the Old Test., who, like Schleiermacher, believes that it

is very little in advance of the Greek philosophy, and who casts it aside as among the things which belonged to the merest childhood of mankind. All the philosophy of Greece, and of the whole heathen world, never made one such man as Coheleth; nay more, it never inspired any individual with such views of the Godhead as he exhibits. Where philosophy doubts and despairs, and has recourse to inexorable destiny, and to fate which is superior to the gods, Coheleth may doubt indeed for a time, and for the moment even despair; but he never fails to find a refuge at last in the supremacy and wisdom and goodness of God. He philosophizes in a very different way from the heathen, and comes to very different results.

Many other interesting topics stand connected with the subject before us; but they belong more properly to an *Introduction* to the book, and will be found there. We proceed to the EPILOGUE or CONCLUSION of the book.

§ 16. *Conclusion of the Book.   Summary of Results.*

CHAP. XII. 9—14.

[Since Coheleth was a *Hākām, i. e.,* a man devoted to study and writing, or a σόφος, he occupied himself with practical views of human life. He has come to many results, which he commits to writing as truths to be depended on, vs. 9, 10. His words may help to stimulate others to do their duty, for he has brought together what may be regarded as firm and established, v. 11. What he has written is sufficient for admonition; to make many books with labor and weariness would be to little purpose, v. 12. The conclusion of all is, that *we should fear God, and obey him;* and this admonition extends to all men, v. 13. Men should do thus, because all that they do, and say, and think, and feel, will at some future period be brought into judgment, v. 14.

Döderlein, Bertholdt, Knobel, and others, have assailed the genuineness of this epilogue; but, as Ewald and Hitzig well declare, without any good reason. The language and style is the same as elsewhere in the book; the conclusion is natural, and is naturally looked for by the reader. Their main reasons are altogether on *a priori* ground. "The epilogue is not genuine," they say, "because the author did not know or believe what it contains." But what is the evidence of this? Has he not repeatedly urged elsewhere to the fear of God, and to obedience? This cannot be denied. Has he not repeatedly brought to view the truth that there is a time appointed for the judgment of what men do? He who examines 3 : 17 ; 8 : 11, 12 ; 11 : 9, with care, and then compares with these passages the many which speak in concurrence with them, will be slow to say that there is anything specially new in v. 14 here. "But the particularity of the assertion, viz., that *every work and every secret thing* shall be brought into judgment, makes it certain," says Knobel, "that a *future* judgment is meant, and of this Coheleth knew nothing, and therefore could not have written the passage." But the assumption that he knew nothing of all this is without proof, and, as we have seen, without any good foundation. If we concede all that Knobel asserts in his premises, we might follow him in his conclusion. I say *might* follow, not *must*; for even if the other parts of the book develop nothing of such a knowledge, this would not decide that there can be no *new* truth in the epilogue. At all events, the objections to the genuineness rest on grounds which are too slender to support them; and the great body of critics have failed to concede that they have any force. This question may be regarded, on the whole, as a settled one, and one that will soon cease to be seriously debated any more.]

(9) And further, [I say] that Coheleth was a wise man; moreover, he taught the people knowledge, and he weighed and searched out — he set in order many parables.

וְיֹתֵר, *and further*, with an implication of אָמַר, *I say*. This is indicated by the שֶׁ = אֲשֶׁר, *that*, which follows. So: *And further* [I say], *that*, etc. So Ewald, Hitzig, and others; and rightly. *Coheleth was a wise man*, חָכָם, not *the wise man*, but one belonging to that class, a *Hakim*, as such a one is still called in Arabia. It was the business of such to make investigations. He speaks of himself in the *third* person here, as often elsewhere. — עוֹד, *further*, introducing a clause which stands as coördinate with *was a wise man*, giving an account of what such a man's employment was. *He taught the people knowledge*, two Accusatives after a verb of *teaching*, viz., the one describes those who were taught, the other the thing that was taught. *Weighed and sought out*, he weighed מְשָׁלִים already known, and sought out new ones. The Acc. is not supplied here, viz., that which he weighed and sought out; but the next clause supplies it, which is subordinate to the present one. It is of course מְשָׁלִים. The verb תִּקֵּן means *to arrange, to set right* or *in order*. It has no ו before it, which shows that it is subordinate and epexegetical; see the like in 1 K. 13 : 18 ; Gen. 48 : 14; Jer. 7 : 26, al. The *seeking out* and *weighing* are first in time ; then *putting the result in order* is the next subsequent process. For this sense of תִּקֵּן, see also 1 : 15 ; 7 : 13. — מְשָׁלִים, *similitudes, resemblances,* a kind of composition in which *comparison,* by reason of resemblances or of contrast, frequently takes place. Hence *parables* in the sense of the Greek παραβολαί, which denotes that things are brought together and compared. Whether similitude or contrast be the result, both are called *parables.* So the Book of Proverbs, מְשָׁלִים, where this species of composition so much abounds. But our word *proverb* is not coextensive with the meaning of מְשָׁלִים, which the Hebrews applied to any species of composition where comparisons or similitudes abound. So the book before us is filled with cases of contrast and of resemblance. That Coheleth *set these in order* was a subordinate work ; and so our text makes it, when the grammatical construction is well understood. It is worthy of note that all the three verbs are here in *Piel,* in order to denote continued and repeated effort.

(10) Coheleth sought to find agreeable words, and correctly to write down words of truth.

חֵפֶץ, *of agreeableness, of pleasantness.* Altogether appropriate ; for a book like Coheleth's needs pains-taking with the diction, in order to render it spirited and attractive.— כָּתוּב, pointed as a Part. pass. here, but erroneously. It should plainly be כָּתוֹב, Inf. abs., for it is, as it were, in apposition with the preceding לִמְצֹא, Inf. const. This is nothing strange. See in 1 Sam. 22 : 13;

25 : 26, 33, comp. 31 ; Ex. 32 : 6, al., examples of the same nature, where the Inf. abs. continues the discourse after the Inf.
const. — יֹשֶׁר, lit. *correctness,* but it is *adverbial* Acc. of manner
= *correctly.* The second clause is rather *coördinate* with the
first than subordinate. The writer does not mean merely that
he first sought for proper words, and then proceeded to write the
same down, but he means to convey the additional idea that *he
wrote words of truth* as well as acceptable words.

(11) The words of the wise are as goads, and as nails driven in are those
who make collections, which are communicated by one shepherd.

דָּרְבֹון (read *dŏr-bōn,* although Dagh. *lene* is not inserted in the
ב, as we might expect) is the ground-form of דָּרְבֹנֹות. But we
have other examples of the like kind; *e. g.,* קָרְבָּן in Ezek. 40 :
43, and אָבְדָן in Esth. 8 : 6. The Methegh after (ָ) in two of
these three cases, would seem to indicate a long *ā* sound for
Qamets ; but etymology is against it in these forms (they being
Pual derivates, and so with the first vowel *short*), and Methegh
is not put here for the sake of the (ָ), but in accordance with a
principle which frequently admits it on a *penult* syllable when it
is short and closed, § 16, 2, n. *c.* In the plural form in our text,
the (ָ) supplies the place of the Methegh in the ground-form.
The meaning of the word is *goad,* but not exclusively *ox-goad,*
as Ges. (Lex.) seems to imply. The goad may, indeed, be used
for oxen, but so it may also for any other beast that needs to be
urged on. Of course the sense is *figurative* here. *Stimulant* is
the meaning, or that which excites, or which pricks so as to make
a vivid impression. The reference here is not to all the words
which the wise may utter, but to those which have a *sententious
form,* to the מְשָׁלִים of v. 9, adapted to seize the attention and
impress the memory ; in a word, the reference is to such sayings
and precepts as this book contains. — מַשְׂמְרֹות is formed from סָמַר,
to bristle, but it is here written with *Sin* (שׂ = ס), *nails* or *spikes.*
The image is essentially of the like nature with that of *goads;*

i. e., both are *sharp-pointed* instruments, and therefore make a lively impression. But in this second case there is another circumstance added, viz., the nails are *driven in*, as it were *fast planted*, they are נְטוּעִים, *i. e.*, made fast and sure. This either marks the impression as both deep and abiding, or (so Hitzig) designates the stable and permanent nature of the *writings* (v.. 10) in question. But what is it which is like to the *nails* thus *driven in?* The answer is, בַּעֲלֵי אֲסֻפּוֹת ; *i. e.*, the *collections of the* חֲכָמִים. For בַּעֲלֵי see first the use of בַּעַל in Lex., and compare Ecc. 10 : 11, 20 (comp. 7 : 12 ; 8 : 8). It is manifest, from a comparison of all the peculiar uses of בַּעַל, that the idea of *possessor* (which of course follows in the train of *lord, master*, etc.) enters into all the cases where it occurs in the const. state. Thus בַּעֲלֵי הָעִיר, lit. *possessors of the city*, means its inhabitants, Judg. 9 : 51 ; בַּעַל כְּנָפַיִם, *possessors of wings, i. e.*, *winged*, Ecc. 10 : 20; Abraham and his neighbors were בַּעֲלֵי בְרִית, *possessors of a covenant; i. e.*, leagued together, Gen. 14 : 13 ; בַּעַל נֶפֶשׁ, *possessors of desire ; i. e.*, greedy, Prov. 23 : 2 ; even in בַּעַל פְּרָצִים, the name of a town (2 Sam. 5 : 20), the meaning of בַּעַל is still retained, viz., *possessor of breaches, i. e.*, a town on which breaches have been made. In this last case we see it applied to *things* as well as to *persons;* the latter, however, is the most common usage. So in Is. 41 : 15, בַּעַל פִּיפִיּוֹת, *possessor of edges, i. e.*, sharp, is applied to a new threshing-drag. Any person or thing, having any quality, or marked by any attribute or peculiarity, is (or may be) named בַּעַל in respect to that *quality*, etc. This seems to render plain the meaning of בַּעֲלֵי אֲסֻפּוֹת. The word אֲסֻפּוֹת (plur. of אֲסֻפָּה) is a Pilel formation from אָסַף, and means simply *collections, collectanea*. Hitzig has rendered the two connected words merely by *Gesammelten, i. e., collectanea*. But then what becomes of the modification made by בַּעֲלֵי ? Clearly *persons* are here concerned ; for what says the previous parallel clause ? It says that *the words of the wise* (חֲכָמִים) are like goads. A class of *persons*, who utter the

words in question, are hereby designated. So in the next clause
(now before us), the בַּעֲלֵי אֲסֻפּוֹת designates such of the wise
men as made *collectanea* of wise and prudential sayings. The
first class utter these; the second *collect writings* (כָּתוּב in v. 10)
which contain them. Both are *goads* and *nails* to the careless
and indifferent. The first *quicken* and *stimulate* by their addresses; the second do the same thing, but also *fasten* the im-
pressions made more lastingly, because they are not only *nails*,
but *nails driven in, firmly planted* or *fixed*, since, in consequence
of the maxims being reduced to writing, they take an enduring
or permanent form. It seems plain, then, that the nature of the
parallelism here demands *persons* as agents in both its parts·
The explanation now given meets that demand. If, with some
critics of note, we translate here: *masters of assemblies, i. e.*, of
literary consessus, then we must incur the difficulty, not to say
absurdity, of these masters *being given by one shepherd*. It is
things which this רֹעֶה, *shepherd, i. e.*, teacher, gives, and not persons.

They are given by one shepherd. What are *given?* Clearly
the things just mentioned. So plainly is this the case, that even
אֲשֶׁר before נִתְּנוּ is dispensed with as unnecessary. Nor is there
any serious difficulty here. *The words of the wise* are given,
and the *collectanea* of one class of them, *i. e.*, maxims and monitions already reduced to writing and collected by them, are
both given by Coheleth. For what says he in the context? He
says that 'he sought out, and weighed, and arranged מְשָׁלִים, and
that he reduced to writing what he found to be true.' He is the
man, then, the רֹעֶה, whose object it is to feed others with knowledge. As to the first two clauses of v. 11, where the plural
number is used, a mere general fact or truth is here stated. The
writer says that the wise (the *Hakams*) speak words that are as
goads, and that their associates, who collect writings of this sort,
are as *nails*. He takes it for granted that this will be conceded
in the general form in which he states it. If so, then he, who

has sought out, and weighed, and duly arranged all of these
matters, and now brings them forward, is entitled to a hearing.
Nay, he boldly intimates in the next verse that his book contains
the essence of all, and moreover that it comprises all which is
needed. The whole of vs. 9—12 is one consistent and connected
view of what he had done, and of the credit which he thinks is
due to it.

We can now easily dispose of the last clause. — נִתְּנוּ is plural
Perf. of Niph; its Nom. is אֲשֶׁר implied; and אֲשֶׁר refers of
course to the words and writings just mentioned. Coheleth has
searched thoroughly, and written down whatever he judged to be
true and important to his purpose. And now in his book *are
given* to the world the results of his labors. — מֵרֹעֶה אֶחָד, *by one
shepherd.* This word Hitzig points מִרְעֶה, and renders it *pasture;*
that is, as he avers, the writer has collected all the scattered particulars, and thrown them into *one pasture,* where his readers
may feed. But נִתְּנוּ (as plur. Niph.) said of the writer would be
abnormal; for the sing. active Kal, נָתַן, would in such a case be
required. In the *passive,* then, the verb must be made. He
renders thus : *which are presented as a united pasture;* which
at least wears the air of something far-fetched and *outré.* It has
no like in all the Scriptures. His objection to rendering מֵרֹעֶה
אֶחָד, *by one shepherd,* is that מִן does nowhere else stand before
the efficient cause, when connected with the passive. But in
this he is mistaken; see Gen. 9 : 11; Ps. 76 : 7; and *instru-
mentalities* are not unfrequently preceded by מִן (מְ), as in Is.
28 : 7; Ps. 28 : 7; Ezek. 28 : 18, al. There is no difference
between these two classes of cases, in regard to the *principle*
concerned in the grammatical construction. Then, again, he suggests that "the *one* (אֶחָד) makes an insuperable difficulty here.
Why one shepherd? And what difference is there, whether the
gift is from *one,* or from *many?*" Yet to my mind this difficulty
does not seem weighty. Of whom had the writer just been
speaking? Of *wise men,* and of the *possessors of collectanea.*

These are *many*, and what they have given lies in many scattered portions. Coheleth has made a selection and a summary from them, and instead of being obliged to consult the *many* חֲכָמִים and בַּעֲלֵי אֲסֻפּוֹת, learners find in *one* teacher all that they need. The *one* רֹעֶה is plainly in contrast with the *many* רֹעִים. The next verse fully confirms this view of the subject. But why does the writer call himself רֹעֶה? This word literally means *feeder, e. g.*, of cattle, sheep, etc. *Tropically* it is very significant, and designates *rector, curator, governor, king, prince* (like Homer's ποιμὴν λαῶν) ; and in Prov. 10 : 21 the verb רָעָה means *feeding with knowledge*. Of course רֹעֶה (the Part.) tropically designates a *teacher*, an *instructor*. He tells us expressly (v. 9) that *he taught the people knowledge;* and also that he searched out and arranged and wrote down words of truth, such as the wise utter, vs. 9, 10. He, then, is the רֹעֶה. He feeds the flock with knowledge. In this view of the subject all the difficulties seem to vanish.

I do not deem it necessary or expedient to recount and refute the almost endless varieties of opinion that have been given concerning this *unique* and hitherto difficult verse. It would be time spent to little purpose. Where conjecture takes the place of grammatical investigation, and random guessing of sober exegetical examination, opinions may be endless and discrepant ; but the history of them is not always worth preserving. But I am not disposed to be over-confident, in such a case, in my own opinion. I have aimed to get out the meaning by a simple grammatical and philological process. If I have not succeeded, I hope that others will be more fortunate.

(12) And further : by these, my son, be thou admonished ; to make books abundant — without end, and much eagerness of study, are a weariness of the flesh.

To translate, with Herzfeld, *To make many books would admit no end;* or with Knobel and Ewald, *Admits no end — has no end,* gives an irrelative and incongruous sense; or at least one that cannot be true without much allowance for hyperbole. — אֵין קֵץ seems to be added merely for the sake of intensity to הַרְבֵּה. Hitzig, *to make endlessly many books;* and this, no doubt, gives substantially the true idea. — אֵין קֵץ here == מְאֹד, which last, by the way, is never employed in this book. Doubtless there is hyperbole in the expression, even thus considered; but still, only such as is very common in animated discourse. *To make very many books* gives the real meaning; while the form of expression in Hebrew is thus: *To make books, many, without end.* The last two words are merely a circumstantial addition, qualifying what was before said. Thus far we have only one subject or Nom. of the sentence. But a second subject follows: *and much eagerness of study.* For לַהַג, found in Hebrew only here, see Lex. But the word is found in Arabic, and corresponds there with the meaning given in the version. Both of these *subjects* are now followed by the *predicate;* viz., *is a weariness of the flesh* or *body.* Much study would be requisite to make very many books, at least if they were worth reading. And such books as are worth it, Coheleth has in view, for they are such as are *goads* and *nails,* not *trecentos versus in hora, stans pede in uno.* Verse 9 shows that he had made strenuous exertion to write one book. The character of this, as it stood in his view, we have yet to consider.

For the rest, my son, be thou admonished, or *get for thyself admonition from them,* or *by them,* viz., *from the things that are communicated* by the one shepherd. — מֵהֵמָּה refers to those things, and we may render מ either *from* or *by,* as the particle is capable of either sense, and either will fit the passage. — בְּנִי, *my son,* is the familiar address of a teacher to his pupil; Prov. 1 : 8, 10, 15; 2 : 1; 3 : 1, 11, 21; 4 : 1, 10, 20; 5 : 1, 20, etc. — הִזָּהֵר may be interpreted either by the simple passive, or the *reflexive,* as Niph. is often employed in the latter sense, and in accordance with this I have translated above.

Sentiment: 'Reader, be diligent to learn, from the things that I have communicated, all needful admonition. Many books are unnecessary for such a purpose, and the labor which they would cost is severe, and would now be little more than useless.'

(13) The conclusion of the whole matter let us hear: Fear God and keep his commandments; yea, this every man [should do].

סוֹף is not *summary, sum,* nor even *final result* here. It means the *concluding part* of the whole discussion, and so that which the writer has most of all at heart. "Finis coronat opus." *The whole matter,* where הַכֹּל has the article, but דָּבָר, in apposition, is without it. — כֹּל is not an adjective, but a noun, denoting *the whole, the totality.* Literally, *a conclusion of the matter, of the whole* [of the matter]. The article in this case, where there is a speciality of emphasis on the second word, is designedly added; see § 109, 2, *a.* The accents give the following sense: *Conclusion of the whole; all is heard; Fear God,* etc. The punctators were misled by not comprehending the true design of the article in הַכֹּל. — *Yea, this should every man* [*do*]. With Hitzig, I have rendered כִּי as an *intensive* here, as it often is in this book, and in the contemporary (?) Book of Job; *e. g.,* 11 : 6; 30 : 11; 31 : 18, 23; 39 : 19. But it may be causal, *for, i. e., fear — keep,* etc., *because it is every man's duty to do so.* Our translation runs thus: *The whole of man,* and is against the Hebrew idiom, and without any tangible sense, for כָּל־אָדָם cannot mean *the whole of man,* but *every man.* All that is lacking here is the verb, which, however, the context supplies, viz., יִשְׁמֹר; and then the clauses run thus: *Keep his commandments; yea, for this every man* [*should keep*]. If filled out entirely it would run thus: *For this* [last commandment] *every man* [*should keep*]. *This* (זֶה) refers to the commandment, or to each commandment just given. In other words: 'When I command you to keep the commandments of God, obey this my command.' As to supplying a verb in such obvious cases, there are examples enough; see in

2 : 12, comp. Deut. 20 : 19. Such ellipses are nothing strange, where the verb is so easily supplied.

(14) For every work will God bring into the judgment concerning every secret thing, whether it be good or whether it be evil.

With every secret thing (so our version), the Hebrew does not say. The word עַל does not mean *with.* The simple fact is that עַל כֹּל defines and qualifies the word *judgment,* without making (as our version does) *every work* one thing, and *every secret thing* another. — מִשְׁפָּט should plainly be written with the article, בַּמִּשְׁפָּט, as it is in 11 : 9. I have followed the accents, in my pointing of the first clause. So we have, by this well-authorized change of the vowels, *the judgment,* viz., the one which God has appointed, 11 : 9; 3 : 17. But what kind of judgment will that be, or to what extent will it go? It will extend *over* (עַל) or *unto* even every concealed thing, *i. e.,* concealed from men; it will take cognizance of all actions whether good or evil. The word מִשְׁפָּט is mentally repeated or implied, before עַל — [the judgment] *concerning,* or *having respect to,* every concealed thing, etc.

No wonder that Knobel here finds a *future* judgment. "If," says he, "one considers this passage without prejudice, he must acknowledge the idea of a formal judgment, occurring, as men suppose, after death." He then states two reasons for this conclusion: (1) "*Every work* is brought into judgment; (2) The expression *every secret thing* is always employed with reference to a judgment after death;" for which he refers to Rom. 2 : 16; 1 Cor. 4 : 5; 1 Tim. 5 : 24, 25. Other passages might be added. He considers this so plain and certain as a result of the language, that he denies the genuineness of the verse, because, as he says, Coheleth had no knowledge of such a judgment, or belief in it. How much there is of sound argument in this last conclusion, has already been examined, in the remarks above made on the closing part of the book. That his *philological* conclusions are sound, it would not be difficult to prove. The writer plainly believes in a future judgment. Hitzig (on 11 : 9) endeavors to show that all the judgment which is spoken of there is the evils which attend old age, or which come upon it. He tacitly extends this same view to the verse now before us; but he is silent in regard to the matter in his commentary upon it. I have (in remarks on 11 : 9) already examined his views, and found good reason, as it seems to me, to differ from them.